THE GUN DIGEST BOOK OF
TRAP & SKEET
SHOOTING

By Art Blatt

DBI BOOKS INC.

Staff

Editor
Harold A. Murtz

COVER PHOTOGRAPHY
John Hanusin

PRODUCTION MANAGER
Pamela J. Johnson

PUBLISHER
Sheldon L. Factor

Our Covers

Trap and Skeet can be shot with "Plain-Jane" equipment or that which has all the "bells and whistles" hung on it.

Our cover shows one of each type—a stock factory gun and a custom job.

Remington's 1100 Skeet gun (top) may look fancy, but that's factory wood! It's a 12-gauge gun with 26-inch vent rib barrel.

The Perazzi Mirage trap gun has 32-inch barrels and custom wood by Anton. The gun was elaborately engraved and gold inlaid by George B. Spring III of Old Lyme, Connecticut.

The guns and gear are owned by Jim Schroeder of Fox Lake, Illinois, a successful, highly competent shooter of both trap and Skeet.

ACKNOWLEDGEMENTS

I'M DEEPLY INDEBTED to Dr. Ralph C. Glaze who prepared the historical background information for this book. Ralph's research was bountiful and well-supported. As any writer knows, every hour spent at the keyboard requires 5 hours of diligent and intelligent gathering of facts. Thanks again, good Doctor, for a job well done.

There are also those who provided valuable insight and information on their own time and at their own expense with one common goal in mind—that this book proves to be timely, informative and most important, make Skeet and trap shooting a little more fun for you.

My personal thanks go to: David Bopp, A.T.A. Manager; Dave Bishop; Dick Dietz, Remington Arms; Chuck Elton, Golden State Traps; John Falk, Winchester; Betty Ann Foxworthy, *Trap & Field*; Howard French, *Guns and Ammo*; Bob Gioia; Myles Johnson; Frank Kodl, Shooting Sports; Larry Mesch, Eclipse Target; Phil Murray; *Skeet Shooting Review*; Kay Ohye; Robert Paxton, Paxton Arms; Chuck Poindexter; Jim Poindexter; John Satterwhite; Bill Siems, Federal Cartridge Co.; and Walt Weaver.

The views and opinions of the author expressed herein are not necessarily those of the publisher, and no responsibility for such views will be assumed.

Arms and Armour Press, London, G.B., exclusive licencees and distributors in Britain and Europe; Australasia; Nigeria, South Africa and Zimbabwe; India and Pakistan; Singapore, Hong Kong and Japan.
ISBN 0-910676-66-6   Library of Congress Catalog Card #83-070143

Contents

Foreword

IN THIS BOOK, the author has presented a comprehensive view of the shotgun sports of trap and Skeet. The book is much more than a mere instruction manual of shooting techniques, although a vast quantity of valuable information concerning practical applications of shooting methodolgy is included. Primarily, this is a compendium of information that is essential to a complete understanding of aerial target shooting.

Beginning with a brief history of the sport of shooting flying targets as practiced in days long gone by, the development of trap and Skeet as formal competitive shooting events is traced from humble origins to contemporary World Championship Tournaments. A thorough knowledge of the background of any sport enhances enjoyment of that sport by both participants and spectators alike. Since trap and Skeet are spectator sports, especially for families of competitors, reading of many parts of this book will be most helpful in making trap and Skeet more interesting to those who only watch and wait.

For novices, or those who are only contemplating entry into the world of trap and Skeet, there is a wealth of information to be found in this book that will serve as a much needed confidence booster. Not only is the tyro told what to do when first starting out, but also why things should be done in a certain way. Such subjects as safe gun handling, range etiquette, gun mounting, swing and lead, foot and body position, as well as basic rules are covered in great detail.

It is hoped that even advanced or expert trap and Skeet shooters will benefit from many of the small but important points that are brought to light. Perhaps much of the information contained in this book will be "old stuff" to experienced shooters, but there is bound to be much that is new—or at least represents a slightly different viewpoint. Even the most knowledgeable among us can frequently learn more by simply being exposed to ideas that act as a reinforcement to concepts that have perhaps been submerged by time.

It would be highly (and improperly) presumptuous to claim that this book contains all there is to know about these fascinating shooting games. No one knows it all, not even the greatest of champions—a fact that most top shooters will freely admit. However, this book does offer to dedicated shotgunners a source of information gleaned from interviews with experts, extensive research into the literature of the sports, and many years of personal experience in competitive shooting.

For the first time, as far as is known, the complete rules of trap and Skeet are here included in a book about these shooting sports. The importance of a thorough understanding of rules and regulations cannot be over-emphasized. A competitor who has a solid background in the proper conduct of an event will exhibit an air of confidence that can only be beneficial to his scores. Not only will a knowledgeable shooter avoid costly or embarrassing mistakes, but he will also be able to stand up for his rights with authority on those occasions when a question arises during the course of a competitive event. Knowing the rules will also enable a competitor to realize some of the problems and responsibilities that confront the organizers of tournaments.

There is one thing this book is guaranteed not to do. Reading a book cannot make a shooter a champion overnight. Only one thing can do that—practice. Constant, consistent practice is the secret of successful shotgunning. Though there is no substitute for years of experience, knowledge gained through reading, if conscientiously applied, can speed up a shooter's progress toward a hard-won championship. And that is the purpose of this book—to help clay bird enthusiasts achieve their goals in the world of trap and Skeet.

Early History **1**

THE ORIGIN of man's desire to hurl projectiles at flying targets is lost in prehistoric antiquity. There can be little doubt that cavemen threw rocks at airborne birds, but we can only speculate on the degree of success attained by the ancient hunters. It's probable that most of us, at one time or another, have cast a stone toward a bird in flight. It is equally probable our percentage of hits closely approximated that of our cave-dwelling ancestors—near to zero!

From the beginning of man's existence on earth and until comparatively recent times, hunters have had to

(Right) Light, shoulder-fired flintlocks of the French pattern encouraged 17th century sportsmen to pit their skill against flying birds. Shooting from horseback enjoyed a brief vogue among the nobility in France and England.

be content with catching birds on the ground. Traps, nets, stones, and patient stalking were the means used to take grounded fowl. Skills essential to bagging grounded birds ultimately became extemely sophisticated, and the quality of game harvested for food grew to enormous proportions. But the air, a bird's natural habitat, remained inviolate. Hunters had to wait for the development of far better tools than rocks and spears to drop birds from the sky with any acceptable consistency.

Bows and arrows greatly increased our progenitors' hunting capabilities, but flying game still eluded all but the finest bowmen. Slings added to the range of pebble projectiles, but did little to improve a hunter's aim. There are many tales in folklore and literature of archers who were proficient enough to put an arrow into a flying bird, but these are the bowmen of legend, not average hunters whose lives depended on their ability to bring game to the cooking pot.

One might naturally assume that the advent of hand-held firearms in the 14th century would have marked a turning point in the development of hunting arms. In fact, such is not the case. Early firearms were clumsy,

difficult to aim, slow to fire, and totally unsuited for use in the pursuit of game of any sort, much less *flying* game. Centuries would pass before firearms technology advanced to a level that would make aerial shooting a feasible proposition.

The first shoulder-mounted firearms were matchlock muzzle-loaders. To fire a matchlock, one must first pour a proper charge of black powder down the muzzle, followed by a ball tamped firmly against the powder. Additional powder is placed in a pan located above a small hole leading into the breech section of the barrel.

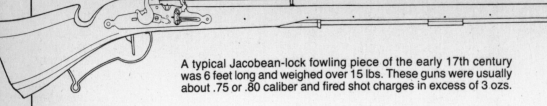

A typical Jacobean-lock fowling piece of the early 17th century was 6 feet long and weighed over 15 lbs. These guns were usually about .75 or .80 caliber and fired shot charges in excess of 3 ozs.

(Left) This 1740 German print shows that wing shooting had at last become practical—at least for those who could afford a proper fowling-piece. Judgment of correct lead on fast-flying ducks was no simple matter.

produce a widely scattered pattern of small projectiles. All early fowling pieces were smooth bored, of course; bores were mostly cylindrical, although bell-mouthed blunderbusses enjoyed a brief vogue in certain parts of the world. It was thought that "belling" the muzzle would spread the shot into a wider pattern, but such is not the case—as later experiments proved. The belled mouth only facilitated loading, although its foreboding appearance proved to enhance its "scare" value.

In spite of improvements in ignition systems, most birds taken by flintlock-wielding hunters were shot while on ground or water. Wing shooting was impractical in those days when game was abundant. An almost certain miss at a bird on the wing had to be weighed against the high probability of hitting a number of grounded birds with a single shot aimed into a huddled flock. Reloading a fowling piece took so long that immediate second shots were virtually impossible.

It was not until the late 18th century—when light and properly stocked flintlocks were developed—that wing shooting became an accepted practice. Double-barreled guns were coming into common use at this time, thus enabling hunters a second chance at flying targets.

Even though flintlock guns had been vastly improved, wing shooting did not emerge as a distinct form of sport until the arrival of reliable percussion cap ignition in the 1830s. Percussion guns were lighter than flintlocks, lock time was much faster and, as a bonus, they were virtually weatherproof. The days of percussion muzzle-loading shotguns were numbered, however, for breech-loading guns appeared within a few years.

The first truly successful breech-loading shotshell was a brass-cased pinfire. Origins of the pinfire are somewhat obscure, since French gunsmiths Houiller, Lepage, and Lefaucheux all contributed to its evolution during the 1840s. The pinfire gave hunters a self-contained shotshell that could be reloaded quickly in newly invented break-action guns. Practical, efficient wing shooting had at last arrived—some 500 years after invention of the gun.

A smoldering string, or "match," is touched to the powder in the pan. Flames from the pan enter the touchhole and ignite the powder in the barrel. Rapidly expanding gases, generated by the burning powder, force the projectile out of the muzzle. This entire operation takes time. By the time a loaded matchlock could be shouldered, aimed, and the necessary firing sequence completed, a high-flying target would be well into the next county. So much for the matchlock as a bird-getter.

When wheellocks and, later, flintlocks became common replacements for the earlier matchlocks, bird hunters had a far more useful and reliable firearm to carry into the field. Special guns were developed for the sport. Known as "fowling pieces," they had shorter barrels than contemporary muskets. They were loaded with lead shot, cut pieces of lead, small scraps or iron and other metals—in fact, almost anything that could

Pigeon shooting in the late 18th century was strictly a gentleman's sport. Top hats and tail coats were the prescribed dress of the era, even for "casual" shooting events.

Pinfire ignition quickly gave way to the centerfire system which emerged as an aftermath of experiments carried out during the American Civil War. By 1870, centerfire cases were the standard and, with minor improvements, remain so to this day. In a brief half-century, from the 1830s to the 1880s, firearms and ammunition enjoyed far greater advancement than had been achieved in the preceding half-millennium.

This abbreviated historical resume has no positive connection with trap or Skeet shooting, but is presented as an explanation of why these shooting games could not have existed until proper guns and ammunition had been produced for these types of activities.

Competition among marksmen is as old as shooting itself. Indeed, the urge to vie with one's peers in all fields of endeavor would seem to be an inborn human trait. Archers of ancient times improved their skill and competed with each other on target ranges.

All sorts of targets were used, including live animals and birds. In various places around the world, including ancient Greece and China, birds were tied to the tops of poles to act as targets for competing bowmen. This form of marksmanship later was known as "popinjay" shooting. Popinjay is an Old English word for parrot, so these birds may have been used as targets in times gone by; certainly any available species would have served as well, however.

Along with live birds, stuffed birds or bird-like effigies were known to be used. To add spice to popinjay shooting, a live bird frequently was tethered to a pole by a string attached to one leg. With this arrangement, a bird could attempt to fly, but the restraining tether would limit it to a frantic flapping about the pole, which presented a much more difficult target. Naturally, as suitable firearms were introduced, popinjay was taken over by musketeers and wild-fowlers as a competitive sport.

Live birds, usually pigeons, were thrown into the air to become winged targets. This sport is still practiced in some countries, particularly in Latin America where it

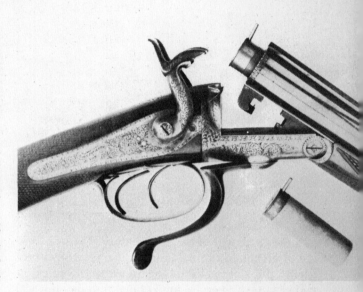

The development of pin-fire, breech-loading, double-barreled shotguns did much to promote trap shooting as a popular sport. The ability to load and fire rapidly is a key factor in successfully shooting at flying targets.

is known as *columbare*. In this sport, a shooter stands at the edge of a large circle drawn on the ground and at his signal, a thrower, like a baseball pitcher, launches a pigeon into the air. When a bird is suddenly tossed into the air, it takes off in extremely erratic flight. Rules of the game require the bird be dropped within the scribed circle. *Columbare* presents a difficult challenge to a shotgunner. Come to think of it, the pigeon has a pretty rough time as well.

In times past, various targets ranging from bottles to bricks, and most everything in between, were hurled into the air to give a shotgunner a chance to practice his art. It can logically be assumed that such shooting was done in some competitive format at one time or another. Therefore, it is curious, even considering the shortcomings of their firearms, that shotgunners apparently did not shoot in any type of regulated competition

Hornsey Wood House Pigeon Club, founded in 1810, was the first facility designed exclusively for the new sport of trap shooting. Dogs were used to recover birds downed within boundary fences.

England's Notting Hill Gun Club, opened soon after the club at Hornsey Wood, was for many years the world's finest trap shooting establishment. Lavish bar and dining areas were provided for members and guests.

until the latter half of the 18th century. The first mention of organized trapshooting is to be found in an old English publication called the *Sporting Magazine,* issued in 1793. The article implies that trap shooting was a well established form of recreation at that time, so we can only assume trapshooting originated some time before the 1790s, perhaps as early as 1750.

The term "trap shooting" was added to the English vocabulary because live birds were released from wooden boxes in which the birds were "trapped." At a signal from the shooter, a trap man, usually a servant, would give a sharp tug on a rope attached to the lid covering the trap, allowing the bird to take flight. The shooter would then shoulder his gun and fire at the flying target. Many varieties of traps were employed, including holes in the ground covered with boards, and old top hats under which birds were placed.

The first trap shooting club of which we have any recorded history was founded in 1810 at the Hornsey Wood House Pigeon Club in England. A day of shooting at the club was a social event for members. They brought their servants, set up tents, and spent the whole day eating, drinking, talking with friends, and, once in a while, shooting. Trap operators sat behind the shooters, and pulled cords to release birds from the traps, either at a signal from the shooter or from a referee. Guns

could not be mounted until birds took flight, and any bird dropped beyond 100 yards was considered a miss.

A much finer shooting ground was established at Notting Hill, also in England. The Notting Hill club drew a large membership from the hunting oriented gentry. Notting Hill had an elaborate clubhouse with a superb dining room and bar. Members were allowed to bring their wives and lady friends several times a year to enjoy the social life that surrounded their shooting activities.

In 1832, an English shooting club called the "High Hats" was founded. The name derived from the special trapshooting rules of the club. Shooters placed live birds under their stove-pipe hats on the ground near their feet. Hats were lifted on a signal from a referee, freeing the trapped bird. Shooters were required to replace the hats on their heads before shooting at a released bird. The time it took to do this gave the bird a head start toward freedom, and made the shoot a more sporting proposition.

Trapshooting at live pigeons and other birds was quickly taken up as a sport throughout the British Empire. By the middle of the 19th century, trapshooting clubs had sprung up wherever the Union Jack flew.

It was only natural that such a popular sport would find its way to America, where shooting and hunting

Old top hats, of the type commonly worn in the early 18th century, were often used as traps for live pigeons. The hats were tipped over by a sharp tug on a rope, allowing birds to fly free.

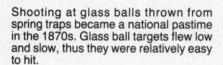

Shooting at glass balls thrown from spring traps became a national pastime in the 1870s. Glass ball targets flew low and slow, thus they were relatively easy to hit.

were a vital part of everyday life. It is likely trapshooting was practiced in this country as early as 1825, but the first official records of such events are found in the journals of the Sportsmen's Club of Cincinnati, Ohio, written in 1831. This date is generally selected to mark the beginning of organized trapshooting in America. In 1840, the Long Island Gun Club was established. At the same time, the New York Sportsmen's Club in New York City held their first trapshooting meets. These three organizations formed the foundations of formal trapshooting in the New World for many years.

In the 1850s, live pigeon shooting had reached such a high degree of popularity that non-hunters began to complain. They decried the shooting of live birds for sport. Bleeding hearts were rampant even in those unenlightened days. Legislation was introduced in state after state to outlaw live bird shooting competitions.

The numbers of wild birds, notably passenger pigeons, were rapidly diminishing in more populated areas of the United States. This fact, combined with preservationist's outcries, drove shooters to seek some other form of airborne target as a substitute for live birds. Another factor in favor of inanimate targets is real birds do not fly consistently, giving unfair advantages to some shooters over others in serious competition where considerable sums of money might be in-

volved as prizes. In England, similar problems existed, so the search for suitable targets took on international scope.

Charles Portlock, of Boston, Massachusetts, introduced glass balls as targets in 1866. Soon, these balls, usually about 2½ inches in diameter, were in widespread use. The balls were placed in a launching device consisting of a cup containing a compressed spring. When the spring was released, a ball would be thrown into the air. To simulate live birds, feathers were attached to the balls or contained within them — when a ball was hit, feathers flew. Often, black powder was added to the balls which gave off a flash or a cloud of smoke when hit squarely. Glass balls had their shortcomings, however. Hardness was inconsistent; some would break in flight, while others were too strong to break at all. One of the more serious problems was a matter of housekeeping. Heavy shooting left the range littered with tons of broken glass that presented a bit of a disposal dilemma. Nonetheless, glass ball shooting remained a major sport for over 20 years, and exhibition shooters used them well into the 20th century.

Various types of targets made of baked clay were introduced around 1870. As with glass balls, hardness and brittleness were difficult to control, and consistent shooting was well-nigh impossible. Targets made of

9

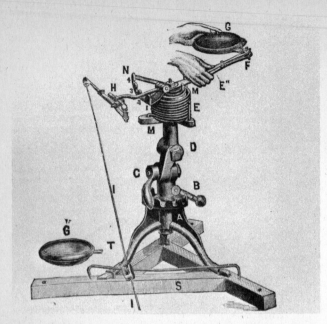

Clay pigeons, invented by George Ligowsky in 1880, quickly supplanted glass balls as the standard inanimate target of trap shooters. Ligowski also developed and marketed the first trap machine for launching the new targets.

(Right) *Hunting & Fishing*, and *National Sportsman* magazines announced a contest in February, 1926, to select a name for a new shooting game. Mrs. Gertrude Hurlbutt, of Dayton, Montana, won $100 by suggesting the name "Skeet."

wood, rubber and cardboard were also tried, all with indifferent success.

George Ligowsky, of Cincinnati, perfected a clay target in 1880 that overcame some of the previous difficulties experienced with other targets, and this marked the beginning of modern trapshooting. In the same year, an Englishman named McCaskey invented a target made of pitch and river silt that gave the desired qualities of durability and brittleness. With some changes in ingredients, this is the target in use today. Trapshooters at last had a target that equalized competition.

During the 1870s and early 1880s, trap shooting spread all across this country, so it followed that a national meeting should be held to determine who was the best at the game. In February, 1885, the first national trapshooting tournament was held in New Orleans, Louisiana, under the sponsorship of the National Gun Association. In 1890, the Interstate Association of Trapshooters was formed, with headquarters on Long Island in New York. They conducted both live bird and clay target events, and held what many regard as the first Grand American Handicap Tournament.

In 1900, the American Trapshooting Association was created to act as the governing body for the entire nation. The Association was controlled by the makers of sporting arms and ammunition, a situation that led to many misunderstandings and abuses. As a result of some of the ill will, the *Amateur* Trapshooting Associ-

ation took over as the prime organization in 1924 and remains as the official arbiter of trap competition in the United States and Canada. With headquarters in Vandalia, Ohio, the A.T.A. sponsors the annual Grand American Handicap, the world's premier trapshooting event, and promulgates the rules that are followed by trapshooters all over North America.

Trap shooting was a long time arriving at its present state of development, but progress has not ceased by any means. Minor rules changes are made almost annually as the evolution of the sport continues, but the basic game has remained the same for over 50 years. As we have seen, this shooting game called trap has developed ever so slowly over a long, long period of time.

Skeet shooting is a slightly more sophisticated derivative of trapshooting that presents targets thrown at various angles to simulate flight paths of birds as they might be encountered in actual hunting situations.

Skeet is a game devised by C. E. Davies, his son Henry W. Davies, and Henry's friend William H. Foster. The elder Davies owned Glen Rock Kennels in Andover, Massachusetts, and it was on the kennel grounds that Skeet was developed between 1910 and 1915. In 1915, together with a group of friends, these three men organized a program that gave each shooter a prescribed series of shots making up a competitive course of fire that was radically different from straight trapshooting, although using the same equipment.

In its beginning form, and for a number of years, Skeet was called "shooting around the clock." A circle having a radius of 25 yards was laid out on the ground with 12 shooting stations marked like the face of a clock. A trap was placed at 12 o'clock that threw targets over the 6 o'clock position. Two shots were fired from each station, with the last shot from a box of 25 shells being taken from the center of the circle.

In 1920, when a neighbor started a chicken farm on land adjoining the kennel property, Davies' shooting layout had to be altered to keep shot from peppering the chickens. William H. Foster decided to position a second trap at the 6 o'clock station on the clock face, throwing a target over the original trap located at 12 o'clock. The full circle was cut down to a semicircle oriented so firing did not endanger their neighbor's livestock. By placing traps at both ends of the semicircle, shooting angles remained the same as with the full circle arrangement, but with a danger zone only half as large.

Foster, newly appointed assistant editor of *National Sportsman* magazine, wrote an article on "shooting around the clock" that appeared in the November, 1920, issue. Other articles followed and, by 1924, large numbers of readers had taken up "shooting the clock," and were writing to the *National Sportsman* for assistance in setting up shooting programs in their own communities. In answer to these requests, Foster drew up a set of uniform rules for the game which were presented to the public in both the *National Sportsman* and *Hunting and Fishing* magazines in February 1926. Modern Skeet shooting can be said to have had its beginning at this time.

Realizing that a new, shorter name was needed to replace "shooting around the clock," a contest was announced by the magazines offering a prize of $100 for the best name submitted. From over 10,000 entries, the winner was Mrs. Gertrude Hurlbutt, of Dayton, Montana. Mrs. Hurlbutt's suggestion was "Skeet," taken from an old Scandinavian word meaning "shoot." The name stuck, and is now a permanent part of our language.

The National Skeet Shooting Association, controlled by the publishers of *National Sportsman* magazine, became the governing body of competitive Skeet. The first national Skeet championship under NSSA auspices took place in 1935 in Cleveland, Ohio. In 1946, the Association severed all relations with the publishing firm, and emerged as an independent organization.

Trap and Skeet were conceived primarily to afford hunters an opportunity to practice shooting skills in off-season periods and in areas closed to hunting. Over the years, however, both sports have drawn adherents who shoot for the sheer fun of it, not merely to develop hunting prowess. In fact, many of the competitors don't hunt at all, but simply enjoy the challenges and sportsmanship that can be found on trap and Skeet fields.

The first "high house" on C.E. Davies' original Skeet field was a cut-off tree trunk. Skeet was developed by Davies, his son Henry, and William H. Foster in Andover, Massachusetts, between 1910 and 1925.

2 Targets and Traps

MASTERY of the shotgun, as any scattergunner knows, comes only after countless sessions of patient practice. Literally thousands of rounds must be fired before skills essential for consistent downing of flying targets are developed to the highest level. Though it is true that some people may have more natural ability than others, no one is born with the level of proficiency that is required to be a competent, assured shotgunner. There is no substitute for practice, not only to gain the necessary skills, but also to maintain them.

In the era of muzzle-loaders, it was well nigh impossible to do enough field shooting to become a first class wing shot. It simply took too long to load and fire the guns for the average shooter to achieve anything near mastery of the basic techniques of shotgunning. When breech-loading, double-barreled shotguns appeared on the scene near the middle of the 19th century, wing shooters had, at last, equipment that allowed them to engage in the intensified practice so essential to the development of field shooting skills.

With modern, quick-firing guns finally at hand, it soon became evident that hunting birds in the wild didn't provide sufficient opportunities for shotgunners to take full advantage of the shooting potential inherent in their newly developed hunting arms. Even though flying game was still more than plentiful in those days,

birds had begun to disappear near burgeoning population centers. City-dwelling hunters had to range farther afield to find the increasingly elusive wildfowl. With transportation as slow and uncertain as it was in the mid-1800s, a day's shooting could easily take on some of the qualities of an expedition. It was becoming apparent that some form of organized target practice must be devised to allow shooters to satisfy their desires for practice without having to resort to a full blown hunting trip.

Shooting at trapped live birds was a common sport of the era, of course, but this sort of target practice had many limitations. Birds to be used as targets, generally pigeons, had either to be trapped in the wild or raised in captivity for the purpose. While labor was relatively cheap, live birds delivered to a shooting range were expensive. Even though the cost of target birds might easily be affordable to more affluent shooters of the period, collecting and housing the hundreds, or even thousands, of birds required for a day's shooting by a large club could pose serious logistical problems. For scattergunners of modest means, live bird shooting was simply too costly even to be considered as a regular activity.

In addition to the cost and inconvenience of live bird shooting, erratic and unpredictable flight patterns of pigeons released from a trap made competitive shooting

This early English sheet metal pigeon trap flipped open when a locking pin was removed by pulling a long cord leading to the shooting line. Birds were given a boost skyward by a spring-loaded plate on the floor of the trap.

In the beginning, glass balls were made with a smooth outer surface and were quite thin and easy to break. Often they were filled with feathers or leaves which would float to earth when a ball was broken by shotgun pellets.

America's first glass ball trap was imported from England in 1866. Reportedly made by the famous English gunmaker, it was not very powerful, and threw targets almost straight into the air.

on an equitable basis an unfair proposition at best. Some birds might fly slowly and straightaway, giving an easy shot, while others might take off quickly into irregular and fitful flight paths that could defy the best efforts of expert gunners to bring them down.

Ever increasing numbers of affordable, reliable, quick-firing, breech-loading shotguns were in the hands of American hunters in the years immediately following the Civil War. Wild bird populations had begun to decrease dramatically in the eastern part of the country, and cities and farms were voraciously encroaching on wildlife habitats. Shotgunners were beginning to find it difficult to practice their art in the field.

Since organized live bird shooting as a means of practice was too expensive for most shotgun enthusiasts, the stage was set for the introduction of some sort of inanimate target that would satisfy requirements of both practice and competition.

European shooters faced even more serious difficulties than their American counterparts. Not only were wildlife numbers diminishing, but most of the prime hunting regions in England and on the continent were in the hands of the nobility or landed gentry. Hunting on these lands was strictly off-limits to shooters of modest means. With the low standards of living then prevailing in Europe, live bird shooting for practice was far too costly for average shooters to afford. Old World shotgun devotees were searching for some solution to their dilemma with perhaps greater zeal than were American shooters of the time.

The earliest known targets specifically designed to be thrown by a mechanical device were hollow glass balls. Available evidence indicates that artificial glass "birds" first saw limited use in England in the early 1860s. It was the introduction of glass ball targets to American shooters by Charles Portlock of Boston, Massachusetts, in 1866, however, that established "breakable birds" as standard aerial targets for many years thereafter.

Where the idea came from is unknown, but Portlock and others may have been influenced by the glass balls used as floats for fishing nets, principally in Japan. It has also been suggested that glass ball targets were the outgrowth of a medieval superstition that prevailed even into Portlock's time.

It was rather widely believed that keeping hollow glass balls filled with feathers, dried flowers or other colorful objects on display in a house would keep witches away from the premises. These glass spheres, ranging in diameter from 1 to 6 inches or more were called "witch balls," and were given places of prominence in many households. Since Boston, Portlock's home, was in the heart of America's "witch country," this may be a valid explanation of the origin of glass ball aerial targets.

It would seem at first glance that glass balls might make the best possible targets for shotgunners, since glass is quite breakable under normal conditions. But there were numerous problems connected with the use of glass ball targets. Each ball had to be blown, either freehand or in a mould, from a blob of molten glass into a hollow sphere. Manufacturing methods available in the 19th century could not assure uniform wall thickness or consistency of glass composition. While one glass target ball might be readily shattered by the impact of a single pellet, another could conceivably withstand the concentrated force of a full charge of lead shot

The Bogardus trap of 1877 was a great improvement over the original Purdy trap. It threw targets more straightaway to distances up to 35 yards. Captain Bogardus also marketed his own brand of roughened glass balls.

(Below) Later glass balls had patterned surfaces to promote breakage and resist ricochets. Balls were made in a variety of colors to increase visibility.

Improved models of the Bogardus trap threw targets farther and faster, and could be turned to change the direction of flight. Card's rotating trap of 1889 could also throw doubles.

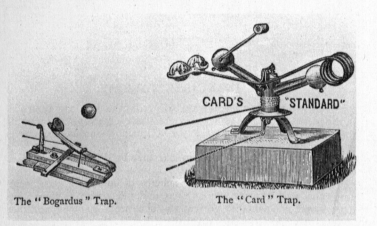

The "Bogardus" Trap.   The "Card" Trap.

without breaking. Other problems encountered with glass ball shooting were their high, arching trajectory and their susceptibility to wind deflection—especially when the air was turbulent or gusty.

As glass ball shooting gained in popularity, it soon became apparent that the disposal of tons of broken targets accumulating on ranges could pose a serious problem in itself. The only practical method of ridding the landscape of this unsightly and hazardous waste was to bury it in some out-of-the-way place. Although this was a perfectly feasible means of disposal, it added to the burdens of range operators as well as increasing the cost of shooting.

In the beginning, glass balls were not thrown very far or very fast. The first target thrower in general use in this country was said to have been made by, or licensed from Purdey, the famous English gunmaker, although advertisements in American periodicals spelled the name "Purdy," without an "e." It consisted of a single wooden bar, hinged near the middle to a vertical stand. A cup on one end held a glass target ball, while the other end was restrained by a rubber cord. In operation, the cup end of the bar was pulled down against tension

of the rubber band. When released, a glass target would be tossed only about 10 yards at quite low velocity. Obviously, this type of target presented no real challenge to an experienced shotgunner.

The substitution of a steel coil spring for the original rubber band improved matters somewhat, but the results were still far from ideal. Velocity remained low and distances thrown were not very long. Even so, sport shooters were quick to try their hands at the new game. The first American Glass Ball shoot was held in Boston's Beacon Park in 1867, using the Purdy trap.

Notwithstanding its shortcomings, Purdy's trap was in use for over 10 years before someone produced a better one. In 1877, Captain Adam H. Bogardus perfected a trap that could hurl glass targets, both singles and doubles, as far as 35 yards at a speed that was challenging to all shooters regardless of their abilities. The Bogardus trap used a steel single-leaf spring fastened to a base at one end, arching concavely upward to a cup on the other end that held a glass ball. When the cup end of the spring was pulled downward, it was held or caught by a notch in a vertical lever. With a glass ball, or two for doubles, placed in the cup, or cups, a tug on a rope attached to the lever released the spring and threw one or two balls a considerable distance at a speed approaching that of a game bird in flight.

Traps designed by Bogardus were almost universally used by leading shotgunners, despite the fact that some three dozen patents for other glass ball traps were issued between 1876, when Ira A. Paine received the first U.S. patent, and 1883, the year in which glass ball shooting reached its peak in this country.

Bogardus traps and glass balls achieved their wide ranging popularity almost solely through the efforts of Captain Bogardus himself. He was a former market hunter who turned to exhibition shooting when declining wildlife populations reduced his income to an unacceptable level. An exceptional wing shot, Bogardus toured the country, giving exhibitions and taking on all comers in glass target shooting for wagers that sometimes ran to thousands of dollars. Since he almost invariably won all bets, his fame—and income—soared.

An entrepreneur of the first water, Bogardus not only sold thousands of his patented traps, but also made a handsome profit from the sale of his own patented brand of glass balls. Bogardus' "rough glass balls" were manufactured by Palmer O'Neil and Co. in Pittsburgh, Pennsylvania. They were packed in sawdust in barrels containing over 300 balls, and sold at the factory for about $11 per thousand. Traps were simple to manufacture, and could be retailed at a profit for the low price of only $6 each.

Glass balls were usually made of clear glass, although various colors were also tried at times. Red, green and blue were the favorite alternative colors. Glass targets were about 2½ inches in diameter, usually with some sort of pattern on the outer surface that was thought to make them easier to break and less likely to produce ricochets. Innumerable designs for the ball targets appeared during the 20 or so years of the sport's peak popularity. Most of these have been long forgotten, and are unknown today even to collectors of such memorabilia, but a few of them have survived to become prized mementos of a bygone era.

One of the more widely accepted variations of regular glass ball targets was conceived by Ira A. Paine. His *Champion Filled Glass Balls* were stuffed with chicken and guinea feathers. When one of these balls was broken, upwards of 300 feathers floated slowly down to earth. It was the nearest thing to live bird shooting that could be provided by a non-living target, and proved to be particularly esteemed by shotgunners accustomed to firing at pigeons released from traps. Although they were more expensive than plain ball targets, Paine's feather filled balls enjoyed a brief period of general acceptance prior to the adoption of standard clay targets.

A variation of Paine's feather-stuffed ball had feathers attached to the outside of the ball. Though this gave visual indication of a hit in the absence of total breakage, the feathers slowed the target's flight so much as to make it virtually useless.

Powell's Patent Puff Balls, made by Henry Sears, seemed for a while to be an efficient replacement for glass balls. A puff ball was made of paper and was filled with dust. A perforating tool was used to punch holes

One of the most popular glass ball targets was developed in 1876 by Ira A. Paine, a renowned exhibition shooter of the period. Paine's balls were filled with chicken and guinea feathers that scattered spectacularly when a ball was shattered. They were widely advertised in sporting journals.

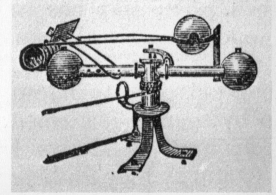

The revolving trap invented by W. F. Carver was a successful competitor of Card's trap, but it couldn't throw double targets. Doc Carver's fame as a shooter greatly aided sales.

The "Steel Passenger Pigeon" was an attempt to emulate a bird's flight by rapidly pulling a metal "pigeon" along wires stretched between two chain-driven reels. Needless to say, it enjoyed only limited acceptance.

Ligowsky's clay pigeon and trap were the basis for all subsequent developments in inanimate target equipment. The trap shown, an improved version of the original, was without peer in the 1880s.

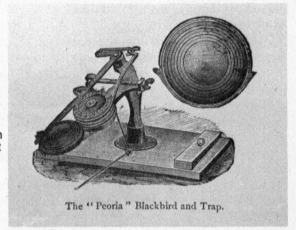

The "Peoria" Blackbird and Trap.

The "Peoria Blackbird" target and trap was first sold by Fred Kimble of Peoria, Illinois, in 1884. "Blackbird" targets had two ears that were clasped by the trap to insure consistent flight.

around the surface of the ball so that dust could escape when the ball was hit. Widely advertised as being completely safe to handle, Powell's balls contained no explosives or hazardous material and left no undesirable waste on shooting grounds. They were reusable up to ten times, and could be launched by any glass ball trap. Nonetheless, Puff Balls faded from view after a few short years.

One of many targets devised as a glass ball substitute was a hollow sphere made from a composition substance that today would be termed bio-degradable. This was intended to do away with the mountains of broken glass that were building up rapidly on shooting ranges across the country. Advertisements for the composition ball claimed that remaining fragments dissolved into fertilizer when rained upon. In spite of its ecological desirability, it never caught on with America's shotgunners.

Another suggested successor to the glass ball was a brass target called *Colonel Fletcher's Bell-Metal Ball*, that rang when struck. Unfortunately these were much

too heavy and could not be thrown as far or as fast as a glass ball. Other enterprising inventors made targets from pottery clay that were generally too hard to break easily. Several makers devised targets that gave off a large puff of smoke when fairly hit. Perhaps the most spectacular of all proposed target alternatives was one that exploded with a loud bang and a brilliant flash of light, followed by a cloud of smoke. Impressive as this must have been, somehow it, too, never caught on. Cardboard discs with rubber balloon centers were also tried without success.

Glass ball shooting attracted scattergunners for many reasons, not the least of which was the noise that accompanied the smashing of a target and the subsequent tinkling of broken shards as they fell to earth. The combination of visual and auditory stimuli was quite satisfying. No doubt the major factor contributing to the widespread acceptance of glass ball shooting, however, was the ease with which they could be hit. Glass balls traveled slowly, perhaps not over 30 feet per second or thereabouts, and the trajectory of their flight was a high looping arc. Even novice shooters stood a fair chance of scoring a hit the first time they tried the game.

Top shooters of the day, such as Bogardus, Paine and Carver, often broke tremendous numbers of targets in a short period of time. Captain Bogardus once broke 5,000 glass balls in less than 500 minutes—and loaded his own guns to boot! Exhibitions in which 1,000 targets were smashed in less than 90 minutes were not uncommon during the glass ball era.

As experience with glass ball targets mounted, along with piles of shattered glass, scattergunners came to the inescapable conclusion that something better would have to be developed. A faster-flying target that more nearly emulated a bird's flight path most certainly would improve the sport. A target that had predictable flight characteristics and resistance to breakage was definitely long overdue.

Two target systems that were seen near the end of the glass ball heyday deserve mentioning. The first was the "steel passenger pigeon," a metal "bird" that was pulled along cables stretched between two poles. Painted with a chalky blue substance, puffs of blue powder were given off when the steel bird was struck by a pellet. Although this was an ingenious solution to a real problem, steel pigeons did not move fast enough, and their trajectory along cables was entirely predictable. After a fair trial, they were abandoned as unworkable. A better device was the "gyro pigeon," which looked very much like the blades of a modern electric fan. It was powered by a coil spring, and was launched from a spiraling center post that gave it a strong spin. Acting as a propeller, it rose upward and outward upon release. It had to be painted each time it was used, as scoring depended on counting the number of hits on its surface. This type of target is still used in England, where it is known as the ZZ target.

An English invention, the *Jones Snipe Throwing Trap* made use of a powerful catapult to fling a large metal bird in irregular, undulating flight to a distance of 50 to 60 yards. When hit, a puff of blue powder was given off. An inflated rubber balloon could also be attached if desired. Since Jones's "bird" had to be recovered and repaired after each launching, the Snipe Thrower didn't prove to be the ideal target envisioned by its creator.

Thinking on this side of the Atlantic seemingly followed similar lines, for in 1884 the G. F. Kolb Co., of Philadelphia, marketed *Belcher's Patent Paper Bird*. This one used a wire ball to which a stiff paper cutout of a bird could be attached. The ball could be thrown from any glass ball trap. Paper birds were reusable after shot holes were marked, but, as with Jones's Snipe, it was quite bothersome to have to rebuild targets after every round of shooting, so Belcher's Bird also had a very short life.

Dissatisfaction with the performance of glass balls led to the invention or development of literally hundreds of possible substitutes during the 1870s and 1880s. Most of them were some variation of a spherical shape, since thinking was oriented on that direction by habitual use of the glass ball. Numerous materials were tried, including clay, pitch, paper, rubber, celluloid, metal, and wood—all with little or no success. However, a new approach to the problem was under consideration in the late 1870s that would eventually replace glass ball targets on shooting ranges the world over.

The Clay Pigeon

The first practical improvement over glass balls was developed by two men almost simultaneously and completely independently of each other. George Ligowsky, of Cincinnati, Ohio, supposedly got the idea for his saucer shaped, spinning clay target while watching small boys skipping clam shells across the surface of a lake. Whether the Englishman McCaskey had a similar inspiration isn't known, but it is a fact that what we know today as a "clay pigeon" appeared on both sides of the Atlantic in the same year—1880. History records that Ligowsky experimented with about 40 variations in disk design before perfecting the dome-shaped saucer that he finally patented.

The first recorded appearance of a clay bird in organized competition in America was at a live bird shoot on Coney Island, sponsored by the New York State Game Association in 1880. Listed as the final event of a lengthy shooting session, the official program states, "The last contest is a shoot at flying clay pigeons. The pigeon consists of a clay disk and on being thrown from the trap sails a long distance with considerable speed. Only a small surface is presented to the shooter and it requires more quickness and skill than shooting at glass balls. There are to be shot ten birds at eighteen and fifteen yards rise."

It would seem that clay birds made something of an instant hit with shooters at that historic meeting, for it wasn't long until clay pigeons all but replaced glass balls in inanimate shooting contests countrywide. It was to take many years, however, before the exact shape and composition of clay pigeons would become entirely satisfactory for all shooting conditions.

The first clay pigeons, oddly enough, were made of clay. Ligowsky's birds were baked in cast iron moulds heated in a long, narrow furnace where they were moved along in assembly line fashion. After baking, the red clay targets were removed to a brick kiln to be fired again. However, temperatures of both kiln and baking furnace were impossible to control with sufficient accuracy to produce a consistently hard target. Some were quite soft, while others resisted breakage to the point where they rang like a bell when hit by pellets. Most shooters of the time agreed that clay pigeons were just about impossible to break. Obviously some material other than clay would have to be developed if "clay" pigeons were to be universally accepted as replacements for glass balls.

The problem, of course, was to produce a target that was not easily broken in transit from factory to range, and that could withstand the initial thrust of the trap. Even with these conditions satisfied, targets had to be brittle enough to break readily when struck by a just a single pellet. Time has proved that these are, indeed, tough criteria to meet, but hundreds of hunters, shooters, inventors, gunsmiths and tinkerers devoted a lot of time and energy to the perfection of the clay pigeon during the 1880s.

Formulas for target material included such substances as coal tar (asphalt), plaster of paris, sand, cinders, gypsum, various pottery clays, sawdust, celluloid (a then newly-discovered plastic), common dirt, and silt from river bottoms.

It is claimed that the first composition saucer-shaped target was introduced by Fred Kimble, of Peoria, Illinois, in 1884. Called the *Peoria Blackbird,* it was made of river silt and plaster of paris and, according to reports of the period, seemed to work reasonably well. Kimble's formula was strikingly similar to the Kimber composition ball target developed in 1881. Note the coincidental similarity of names of these two men. They knew each other, so it is quite likely that Kimber gave his formula to Kimble for use in making disk targets.

A Kentuckian named Al Bandel promoted a target made principally of tar. This bird, called the *Lark,* performed fairly well when the weather was cold, but on a warm day it sagged into a useless blob that could neither be set in motion properly nor broken in flight.

Various metal target disks were devised, basically with the idea of re-use in mind. One, the Parkersburg tin target was supposed to release a wire ring when hit that would cause the target to fall quickly to the ground.

It must not have worked as advertised, for it was only on the market for a year or so. A similar target was invented by W. T. Best, and distributed by the Champion Tin Target Co. of Chicago. The Best bird had a large flange that dropped down when struck by a shot stream. Interfering with its aerodynamics, the flange caused the disk to flop to the ground like a wounded bird. Many flanges refused to behave in the proper manner, however, and these targets sailed on their way with no evidence being given of a fair hit. Needless to say, shooters didn't take kindly to this sort of reaction from a target, and Mr. Best was soon out of the Tin Bird business.

Some inventors couldn't seem to get away from the idea of stuffing targets full of feathers. The Lafayette Target Co., of Lafayette, Indiana, made a clay bird chock full of feathers that showered down when hit. One can only wonder how the bird flew with its extra payload. Not too well, apparently, since it was only made for a short time in the late 1880s.

One of the most awesome targets offered during that long ago era of experimentation was the *Blue Rock Paper Pigeon,* invented by Charles Franzmann. Made of pasteboard, it was covered with a layer of fulminate of mercury, then given an outer coating of sand and glue to add necessary weight. When struck by shot it exploded, releasing a cloud of smoke. The inventor claimed that it wasn't dangerous to handle or transport. Either shooters of the time didn't believe the advertising or the paper pigeon did not perform as promised, because this brilliant design died an almost instant death. The mere thought of hauling a barrel containing 500 of these explosive devices over a bumpy road is not only chilling, but it's enough to ruin your whole day.

After a multitude of designs had been tried, and most found wanting, the solution to the problem of "clay" bird material turned out to be a combination of asphalt

The Blue Rock Pigeon.

The "Blue Rock" clay pigeon was the first successful target without any projections for the trap to grip. Thin in the center with a sturdy rim, it was the forerunner to today's clay birds.

(Right) "Blue Rock" brand clay pigeons as made today by Remington are considerably different in shape from Fred Kimble's original 1887 model. Design principles remain the same, however.

REMINGTON TRAP & SKEET EQUIPMENT

Ice targets were an interesting alternative to conventional clay pigeons. Frozen on the spot, the targets left no debris on the range, and involved no transportation problems. Sadly, costs were too high for widespread acceptance.

(Below) Today's modern clay targets are made of usually secret ingredients known only to manufacturers. The diameter of the target is 4¼ inches with a profile of 1¹⁄₁₆ inches and it weighs 3½ ounces.

and silt, or asphalt and gypsum. When mixed in the correct proportions, these ingredients will give a flying target the desired properties of transportability and fragility. Curiously, the first disk-shaped targets marketed in England by McCaskey were made from tar and river silt.

Near the end of the 19th century, two brands of clay targets had emerged as leaders in popularity, the *Blue Rock,* and the *White Flyer.* The White Flyer was made by the Western Trap and Target Co., of St. Louis, Missouri, while the Blue Rock was produced by both the Chamberlin Cartridge and Target Co. and the Cleveland Target Co., in Cleveland, Ohio.

It's interesting to note the variety of names given to flying disk targets during the years of their development. The English, for some inexplicable reason, called them "spheres." In America, they were referred to as inanimate targets, asphalts, flying disks, traps, blackbirds, baked birds, muds, soil disks, river bottoms, clay birds, and clay pigeons. The last two names stuck and, even though not made of clay for almost 100 years, we still call them by these anachronistic names.

As the beginning of the 20th century rolled around, clay targets had evolved into roughly the same size, shape and composition that is in use today. Modern clay birds are made of pitch (asphalt tar) and ground limestone or gypsum, and size and weight have been standardized. Today's bird is 4¼ inches in diameter, 1¹⁄₁₆ inches in height, and weighs 3½ ounces. It's a far cry from glass balls, but isn't too far removed from designs that were first introduced 100 years ago.

Even though modern clay pigeons are entirely satisfactory as aerial targets, efforts are still being made to find a way to improve them. A novel method of producing targets was developed some 20 years ago that, for a

time, appeared to be a most practical idea. The system relied on a quick-freezing machine to make ice targets. The freezer, containing a mould in the shape of a regulation clay pigeon, was installed next to the trap. Water injected into the mould was almost instantly frozen into a target that could be placed immediately into the trap. A continuous freezing process produced targets as fast as a commercial freezer makes ice cubes. Colored targets were easily made by putting dye of the desired hue into the water before molding. Ice would seem to be an ideal material for targets, because there is no debris left on the range, and there are no problems of transportation or storage. Unfortunately, the cost of ice targets delivered to the trap is higher than the cost of clay pigeons. Someday, perhaps, ice targets will be revived in a system that will be competitive with present practices. The concept is basically quite sound.

Trap Improvements

Along with the development of better targets, vastly improved traps were also being produced. Though a more or less simple catapult is adequate for launching a

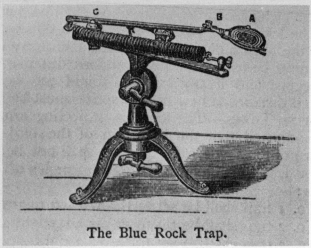

The Blue Rock Trap.

"Blue Rock" traps had a simple clip, attached to the trap arm by a pivot, to control the target as it was being launched. Introduced in 1887, this trap, with improvements, lasted well into the 20th century.

(Right) Odd-looking though it was, the Magau trap was the first successful automatic target launcher. An extremely complicated machine, it was difficult to operate and maintain.

glass ball down range, a disk target requires a different sort of trap. A clay pigeon must be given a certain amount of spin as it is thrown to give it the stability necessary for consistent flight.

Early clay birds had a small "tongue" on the rim that fitted into a clamp on the trap arm to hold the target in place and to aid in imparting a spin as it left the trap. This tongue was either moulded into the lip of the clay bird or was made of cardboard and glued to the target. Later developments in both birds and traps showed that the tongue was an unnecessary appendage, and perfectly round targets were used thenceforth.

The first, and for years the most widely used, clay pigeon trap was one patented by George Ligowsky and manufactured by the Ligowsky Clay Pigeon Co. Although it was similar in principle to later traps, it differed in one major respect. As in more modern versions, it consisted of an arm that was drawn back against the tension of a coil spring and held by a notch on the main frame. A tug on a rope activated a releasing mechanism that allowed the arm to fly forward, sending a target spinning on its path down range. The clay bird, however, was held in place by a clamp on the end of the arm that clipped onto the aforementioned tongue. There was no other support for the target. Since the clamp was subject to slippage, especially in wet weather, performance of Ligowsky's trap could sometimes be unpredictable. As with the proverbial mousetrap, so it is with target traps, and thus it wasn't long until a better one was built, and everyone began to use it.

Kimble's *Blackbird* trap was designed to throw his *Blackbird* clay pigeon, which had two projections on its rim, diametrically opposed to each other. Targets were held on the end of the trap's throwing arm by a clip that partially encircled the rim of the bird, holding it tightly enough to keep it in place as the arm flew forward. Kimble's system was a distinct improvement over Ligowsky's. Patented in 1884, the Blackbird enjoyed a very short life, as it was rendered obsolete by the 1887 introduction of the *Blue Rock* trap and clay pigeon.

The Blue Rock pigeon was perfectly round, with no projections on its rim. In shape it was quite similar to modern clay targets. The Blue Rock trap held a clay bird in a clip that was pivoted on the end of the throwing arm. Action of the pivot reduced initial shock, and thus lessened the chance of a bird being broken as it was launched from the trap. An improved version of the Blue Rock trap, first sold in 1889, had a more positive method of holding the target—much the same system that is used in many modern traps today.

An English trap, the *Highflyer,* had a tray mounted on the end of the throwing arm that was only a bit wider than the target bird. As the trap arm moved forward under force from a heavy coil spring, the bird slid forward along the edge of the tray giving the target a spinning motion. A variation of this principle has been used on many traps and is still to be found on traps in use at the present time.

Traps had been produced in the glass ball era that could throw doubles and at various angles, so it didn't

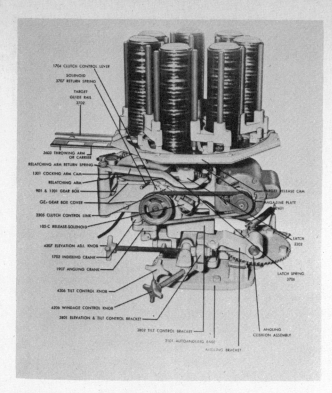

Remington Model 4100 is adaptable for either U.S. trap shooting or Modified Clay Pigeon. Auto-angling feature prevents "reading" of targets by shooters. The 4100 is fully automatic.

(Above left) Remington Model A100T for trap shooting offers automatic loading from a magazine for completely remote operation. Angles are changed at random to prevent memorizing target path sequences.

(Below left) Skeet traps must be reliable and throw targets with consistent accuracy. Remington Model M200S meets both requirements. Remotely controlled, it needs attention only for reloading the magazine.

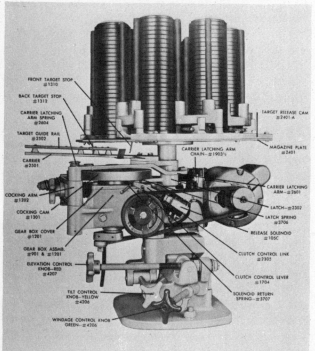

delivery were controlled by an operator who powered the machine by pedaling a bicycle sprocket that was connected by a chain to the operating mechanism. Clever as this device was, it had many obvious faults and was soon supplanted by an electric powered trap that could be remotely controlled.

The *Dickey Bird Automatic Trap* was first marketed in 1905 by W. S. Dickey, of Kansas City, Missouri. It was simple and positive in operation, and could throw singles or doubles at the will of the operator at precisely prescribed angles. It was in general use for many years, and ranks as one of the more successful traps of its era.

A. M. McCrae, of Lamar, Missouri, sold the patent rights to his automatic trap to the Western Cartridge Company, of East Alton, Illinois, in 1909. Marketed under the *Western* name, McCrae's trap was the ancestor of a long line of Winchester-Western traps that have proven to be so popular over the years.

The Champion Trap, devised by H. W. Vietmeyer of Indianapolis, Indiana, in 1914, had foot rests for the operator to use in changing angles. It was not fully automatic, being loaded by the trap boy for each delivery of a target, but it was exceedingly simple in construction and easy to operate. It could be pulled mechanically or by remote electric control. After 1916, an improved model, called the *Black Diamond,* was made by the Black Products Company in Chicago. An off-shoot of the Black Diamond is still being used worldwide.

take very long for someone to make a workable multiple trap for clay birds. The first one capable of this feat to meet with any degree of success was the *Davenport Revolving Clay Pigeon Trap* introduced by A. F. Martin of Davenport, New York, in 1884. It could throw both singles and doubles, but had to be hand loaded.

The *Magau Trap,* made by the Chamberlin Company, of Cleveland, Ohio, in 1897, was the first practical automatic trap to see widespread use. It was a highly complicated apparatus, whose speed and direction of

Electric regulation trap from Western holds targets in a rotary magazine. Angles are changed at random by an interruptor gearbox powered by a separate electric motor.

(Right) Western's self-loading electric Skeet trap Model V1574A holds a single stack of targets, enough for one round of Skeet.

Skeet, then a new shotgun game, exhibited a marked increase in popularity during the 1930s, but financial conditons associated with the great depression kept many people from actively participating in the sport. After World War II, in an era of economic prosperity, interest in Skeet again took an upturn, spurred by thousands of ex-GIs who had been introduced to it as a wartime marksmanship training program.

With the building of many new trapshooting facilities after the war, manufacturers of trap equipment were able to modernize many of their products. Much of today's sophisticated trap machinery originated during this post-war period.

Typical of present day automated traps is the *Remington Model 4100,* designed for both U.S. and simulated International-style trap shooting. Its magazine holds 154 targets and is readily refillable. Non-readable angle selection is offered in eight angle spreads. The magazine is easily detachable to allow loading of doubles. Target release is by remote electronic control.

Remington's *Model A100T* also is in use on many trap fields. It is similar in operation to the Model 4100, but has a larger magazine capacity, holding 203 targets in seven columns. A companion machine, adapted for Skeet shooting, is the Model M200S. Remote electronic release is provided in both models.

Western's Model V1577A for trap shooting, and Model V1574A for Skeet are found in many clay-bird shooting installations. Like the Remington traps, these are fully automatic in operation, requiring only periodic manual loading of their magazines.

For International Trap, Western offers their Model V1583A, which is a modification of Model V1582A, a regulation trap for U.S. trap shooting. Model V1583A has provision for interrupted vertical motion, plus increased power for throwing 75-yard targets as required in I.S.U. regulations. Larger diameter International targets are easily accommodated in the 190-target magazine. The trap is also adaptable for shooting A.T.A. Modified Clay Pigeon.

A less expensive machine for both trap and Skeet is *Remington's Wonder Trap.* A manual unit, it requires the services of an attendant for both cocking and loading. Wonder traps are in use by many smaller clubs all over the country. Target release may be either mechanical or electric.

For private use, a trap such as Remington's *Expert* is ideal. A simple single-loading trap, it may be installed permanently or is handily portable for informal shooting sessions. A slightly more sophisticated trap, designed for permanent installation, is Remington's *Blue Rock* model, especially suited for small clubs and private shooting areas. It may be used for both Skeet and straight trap, and is manually loaded and released. The Blue Rock has a tray-type carrier that allows throwing of double targets. Both units are ideal for moving games such as Quail Walk that use several traps placed in various locations along a trail.

Lightweight, inexpensive, portable traps are available from *Hoppes, Outers* and *Trius.* Basically, all these units are similar in appearance and operation. They may be simply placed on the ground or installed on a semi-permanent base. They are easy to cock and load, and are perfectly suited for informal practice or impromptu clay target games. All are capable of throwing doubles.

Western®

AUTOLOADING REGULATION TRAP V1582A
(MODEL "U")

AUTOLOADING INTERNATIONAL TRAP V1583A
(MODEL "US" – ILLUSTRATED)

REMINGTON WONDER TRAP

For Skeet or Trap Shooting

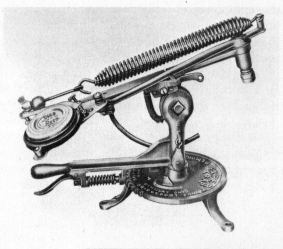

Wonder Skeet Outfit with Singlever Pull

The Remington "Wonder Trap" may be used for both trap and Skeet shooting. Completely manual in operation, it requires the services of a trap attendant for cocking and loading.

(Left) Western's Autoloading Model V1583A is intended for use in International Trap. It throws targets farther and faster than traps designed for U.S. trap shooting.

Remington's "Expert" trap is light enough for portable use, although it also may be permanently mounted if so desired. It is adjustable for both elevation and lateral angle.

The hand target thrower, this one by Remington, is ideal for informal practice. Easily portable, hand traps are quite inexpensive, yet capable of excellent performance. There are a number of brands and styles on the market.

Outer's "Mini Grand" trap features an adjustable throwing arm for a variety of patterns at different speeds. It may be used anywhere, and is perfect for casual clay bird shooting.

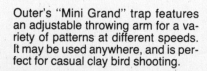

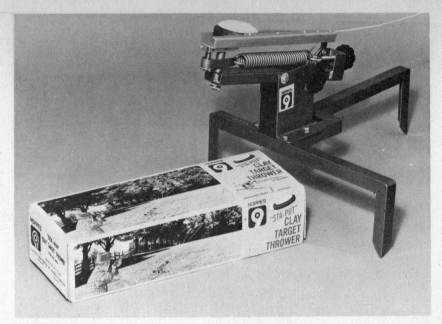

Hoppe's "Sta-Put" portable clay target thrower is perfect for private practice or informal shoots among friends. The cost is low enough to make traps of this type affordable for many who otherwise would not be able to participate in clay target sports.

Simplest of all traps—and the least expensive—is the hand trap. Many makes are carried in stock by most sporting goods stores and gun shops. Hand target throwers are perfect for teaching beginners the fundamentals of Skeet and trap shooting, as well as providing excellent practice for hunters honing their preseason skills.

A full catalog and description of all available clay target throwing machines is beyond the scope of this book, but this brief summary is indicative of the variety of such units from which a shotgunner may choose. There is also a large selection of clay targets, all of standard size and weight, but with differing forms and colors. Manufacturers of clay pigeons all have their own ideas as to construction, and it's up to the individual shooter to pick the one that seems to perform best for him.

Present day clay pigeons of whatever manufacture are as nearly as impeccable in design, materials and consistency as one could wish, but that level of perfec-

tion was not achieved over night. It is the result of nearly a century of refinement and developemnt, and represents the combined efforts of innumerable people, most of whom are not mentioned in written records. Trap and Skeet shooters owe them all a big "thank you," because without their pioneering work our sport would not be as enjoyable as it is today.

Trap machines available to scattergun aficionados today range all the way from simple hand throwers to those marvels of sophistication and mechanical ingenuity that are used for International trap shooting. We've come a long way from Purdy's glass ball throwing machine. It would seem that perfection has been achieved in the development of trapshooting equipment, but who knows what the future might bring? Every time we seem to have gone as far as we can go in any given field, someone invariably pops up with an improved model. Unbelievable as it might be, better trapshooting equipment is probably even now on the way.

Clay Target Games **3**

SHOTGUNNING clay targets is a sport with almost limitless variations. When clay pigeons are mentioned, we generally think of trap or Skeet, but there are countless other games that can be played with shotguns and clays. All that one needs to enjoy these activities is a safe place to shoot, a shotgun, a simple trap, a box of targets—and a good supply of shells. One can even shoot alone for practice by setting up a trap in such a manner that it may be activated by the shooter, although it's usually more fun when two or more can play. Though trap and Skeet are governed by long established rules, even these games may be altered by mutual agreement to provide challenges of varying degrees of difficulty according to the individual abilities of participants.

For shotgunners interested in formal competition, organized trap shooting is the game that has been around longer than any other. Some will argue that of all possible clay target games, trap is the most challenging, although confirmed Skeet fans might be prone to differ with this opinion.

There are currently five prinicpal standard trap games controlled by governing bodies that sanction events, issue rules and keep records. These are: Singles (16-yard), Handicap, Doubles, Modified Clay Pigeon and International Trap.

Singles, Handicap and Doubles are sanctioned by the Amateur Trapshooting Association (ATA). In the United States, The National Rifle Association (NRA) is responsible for Modified Clay Pigeon and International Trap. Outside this country, and for Olympic competition, International Trap is controlled by the Union Internationale de Tir (UIT), headquartered in Wiesbaden, West Germany. In English speaking countries, the UIT is known as the International Shooting Union (ISU).

(Right) Claybirding can be practiced alone if provisions are made for remote release of the target. Experience gained in this way could prove invaluable in formal competition or in hunting fields.

Four squad members wait while the fifth man shoots in this photograph of a simple trap layout of the late 1930s. Mechanical puller may have been used for reasons of economy, or perhaps electric power was not available at this country site.

American Trap

American Trap is the name given to the trap shooting game as practiced in this country, simply to differentiate it from International Trap, which has a different set of rules. In general usage, American Trap is referred to simply as "trap," and everyone understands this to mean the American game. When one speaks of the International version, a qualifying adjective, International, Olympic or "bunker" is added to make the distinction.

In American Trap, the target launching machine is mounted within a "house" about 8 feet square, and 6 feet high. Half of the height, more or less, is below ground level. The front of the house has an opening through which targets emerge. Shooters stand behind the trap house, with no view of the trap itself.

When a gunner calls "pull," the referee or puller presses a button on an electrical cord running to the trap release mechanism. A clay bird is sent down range on a randomly selected course that may lie anywhere within an arc of 44 degrees measured from the trap. A shooter therefore never knows what path a clay bird might take. It could fly anywhere between 22 degrees to the left of the trap and 22 degrees to the right. These angles were chosen, of course, to simulate the flight pattern of a wild bird rising ahead of a hunter and taking to the air away from the source of apparent danger. A clay pigeon leaves the trap at a speed of 41 miles an hour on a low trajectory that keeps it airborne for about 50 yards.

When shooting the Singles trap course, participants stand 16 yards behind the trap house. In Handicap events, however, shooters are moved back from the trap according to their demonstrated abilities, up to a maximum of 27 yards for the most adept scattergunners. Since most birds are broken between 30 and 40 yards from the gun when firing from the 16 yard line, it's obvious that shooting from a 27-yard handicap position requires more than a little skill and quickness.

Trap is shot from five stations, the center one being directly behind the trap house. The other stations are spaced 3 yards apart on either side in an arc so that all five positions are equidistant from the trap. Positions are numbered, One through Five, starting at the left end of the line. Each participant fires five shots from each station, making a total of 25 shots per "round," which is the number of shells in a box.

A shooter may fire a round alone, but it is more common to have enough competitors to form a squad of five, in which case each shooter moves one station to his right after each string of five shots has been fired in rotation by all members of the squad. Each station presents a different view of the target, which can be anywhere from straight ahead to sharply right or left, depending on the position.

A hit is scored when any part of the target, no matter how small, is seen to separate from the main body of the disk. A direct hit at fairly close range will literally pulverize a clay bird. There is no question of a hit or miss in that case, but when a single pellet chips off only a small piece of the target, an occasional argument ensues. That is the time when a referee earns his pay—if any. In all questions on trap or Skeet fields, the official arbiter's decision is final. Only poor sports will dispute the judgment of a referee. As with an umpire in baseball, even if he's wrong, he's right! There is no other way to run a competitive event. Someone must be in charge at all times, not only to interpret rules, but to see that matters are handled fairly and safely.

In essence, trap is an exceedingly simple game. On taking his place at the designated station, a shooter shoulders his gun with cheek tight against the stock comb and his eye sighted straight down the barrel rib. Pointing the muzzle toward the place where the bird will appear as it emerges from the trap house, he calls, "Pull!" The bird, released electrically by the puller, comes out of the house only an instant after the call is made. The shooter must track the target with both gun and body, then, slightly accelerating his swing, pass the target and press the trigger. If track and lead have been correct, with smooth swing and follow-through, the target will break. Sounds easy enough, doesn't it? It really isn't quite that simple, because even experts miss every now and again, and it sometimes takes years of practice to get good enough to break 21 or 22 out of 25 birds. Rank beginners frequently shoot up several boxes of shells before ever scoring on a clay target. But, as in any other sport, the challenge is there and most shooters are hooked once they try the trap game. Otherwise why would they keep coming back for more?

Trap shooting is excellent practice for the upland hunter, but there are some differences between practice and actual shooting that should be noted. In trap, the gunner has his gun shouldered and ready to fire before the bird comes into view. He knows where the target will first appear and when it will pop up. Swing, timing and lead will improve with practice, but conditions in the field are not quite the same. A clay pigeon starts off fast and then slows down, while a game bird takes off slowly and then speeds up. In spite of existing differences, however, a good clay birder will probably be a better wing shot in the field than a shooter who has trouble with traps.

Trap Doubles

Trap Doubles is considered by many to be the most difficult of all trap games. Two clay targets are released at the same time on separate courses. One bird goes to the extreme left, while the other is sent off to the far right. Even though the shooter knows the paths the targets will take, it's no easy matter to break them both before they hit the ground. The usual method is to attempt to break the bird that is most straightaway first, then

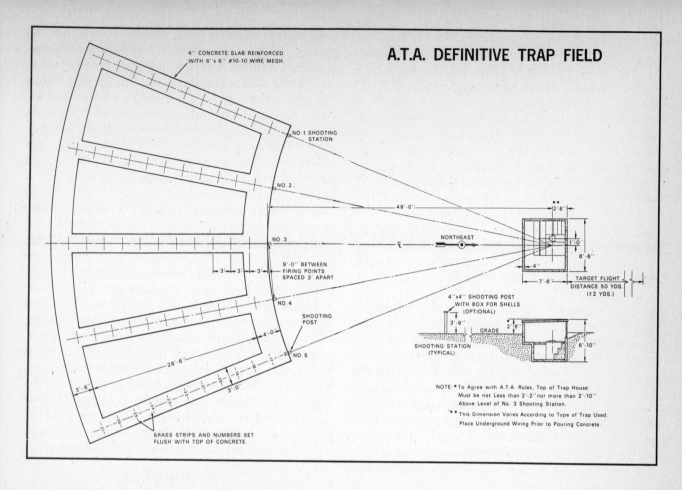

A.T.A. DEFINITIVE TRAP FIELD

4'' CONCRETE SLAB REINFORCED WITH 6''x 6'' #10-10 WIRE MESH.

NO.1 SHOOTING STATION

NO. 2

48'-0''

2'-6''

NORTHEAST

1'-0''

8'-6''

NO. 3

9'-0'' BETWEEN FIRING POINTS SPACED 3' APART

3' 3' 3'

4''

7'-6''

TARGET FLIGHT DISTANCE 50 YDS. (±2 YDS.)

NO. 4

SHOOTING POST

4'-0''

4''x4'' SHOOTING POST WITH BOX FOR SHELLS (OPTIONAL)

3'-6''

2'-6''

GRADE

6'-10''

NO. 5

28'-6''

3'-6''

3'-0''

SHOOTING STATION (TYPICAL)

BRASS STRIPS AND NUMBERS SET FLUSH WITH TOP OF CONCRETE.

NOTE: * To Agree with A.T.A. Rules, Top of Trap House Must be not Less than 2'-2'' nor more than 2'-10'' Above Level of No. 3 Shooting Station.

** This Dimension Varies According to Type of Trap Used. Place Underground Wiring Prior to Pouring Concrete.

A trap shoot in progress, showing spectators displaying various degrees of interest. Both trap and Skeet are good spectator sports because action is fast and results are immediately apparent.

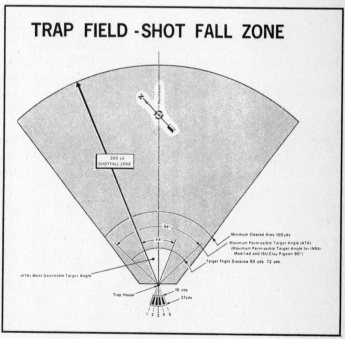

TRAP FIELD - SHOT FALL ZONE

300 yd SHOTFALL ZONE

94°

44°

Minimum Cleared Area 100 yds

Maximum Permissible Target Angle (ATA) (Maximum Permissible Target Angle for (NRA) Modified and ISU Clay Pigeon 90°)

Target Flight Distance 50 yds. ±2 yds.

(ATA) Most Desireable Target Angle

Trap House   16 yds
27 yds

1 2 3 4 5

swing smoothly over to take the second target. The Doubles game is nowhere near as popular as Singles or Handicap trap, because it's much more difficult to master and requires that the shooter own and use a different shotgun. Over 93 percent of Doubles shooters use an over-under gun with the balance made up of autoloaders and very few pump actions. Side-by-sides are extinct on today's trap line.

Those who are reluctant to shoot Doubles are probably of the widely held opinion that bringing down two targets in rapid succession is far too difficult. This argument doesn't quite hold water, however, when one considers that in Skeet two targets are in the air simultaneously and flying in two different directions. Skeet shooters are able to handle this seemingly more awkward situation without questioning its possibility or apparent difficulty.

Trap Doubles is not a new game, as it was introduced into tournament programs in 1911. The avowed purpose ascribed to its inauguration was to allow more practice for field shooting where two or more birds might rise at the same time. The value of such training for taking doubles in the field should be perfectly obvious. Mastering the art of Trap Doubles is not easy, but it is also far from impossible. It is certainly a most exciting and challenging alternative to singles.

Handicap Trap came into being for the same reasons that handicaps are utilized in other sports such as golf

and bowling. By giving a less skillful participant a bit of an edge, competition is more nearly equalized. In trap shooting, distance is used as the basis for making all shooters as equal as possible. Trap handicaps begin at the 18-yard line. Distance is added as skill increases up to the maximum handicap of 27 yards. Handicap yardages are added for good shooters up to the point where their advantage in overall scores disappears. The ATA determines shooter's individual handicaps based on past performance in both registered and unregistered events.

Even though handicaps are issued by the ATA, individual clubs may use a different handicap procedure for their own *unregistered* events. A simple system allows for penalizing a shooter a certain number of birds in accordance with his existing average. A gunner who normally drops 96 birds out of 100 might be assigned a handicap of 2 points. An 80 shooter could draw a handicap of 18 points, while a 70 average would have 28 points added. An average of 60 could be given 38 additional points, etc. If all shot their previous averages, they would end in a tie at 98 out of a hundred. This never happens, of course, but a point handicap system is in some ways more fair to less proficient shooters than a yardage handicap. There are many different methods of figuring point handicaps, and each club must determine which one best suits their particular circumstances.

International Trap

International Trap, also called International Clay Pigeon or Olympic Trap, is almost entirely different from American Trap. The field layout is much more elaborate (and much more expensive), and the traps are housed in a structure whose roof is at ground level—the same height as the shooting stations. A ditch, known the "Olympic Trench," is dug into the ground ahead of the trap line to allow clearance for targets. There are 15 traps—three for each shooting station. Traps for each individual position are spaced 1 meter apart. The center trap is set to throw targets within 15 degrees to the right or left of the straightaway setting. The left trap covers an area from straight forward to 45 degrees to the right. The right trap releases targets from dead ahead to 45 degrees to the left. At a distance of 10 meters from the trap, each machine is set to angle clay birds upward from a minimum of 1 meter to as high as 4 meters above ground level. Shooting stations are located 16 meters to the rear of the centers of the traps, and in a straight line—not an arc as in American Trap.

Each trap is pre-set and locked in place, but when a target is released, it may come from any of three traps and fly within the limits of 45 degrees right or left azimuth and from 1 to 4 meters elevation at a point 10 meters from the trap line. Trap selection is entirely at random, being controlled by an electronic device that is independent of all human input. When the shot is called and the puller presses his control button, a trap that is

In Handicap Trap, better shooters stand farther away from the trap. Shooter at left is at the maximum 27-yard position, while the man to his right is placed 2 yards closer to the bird.

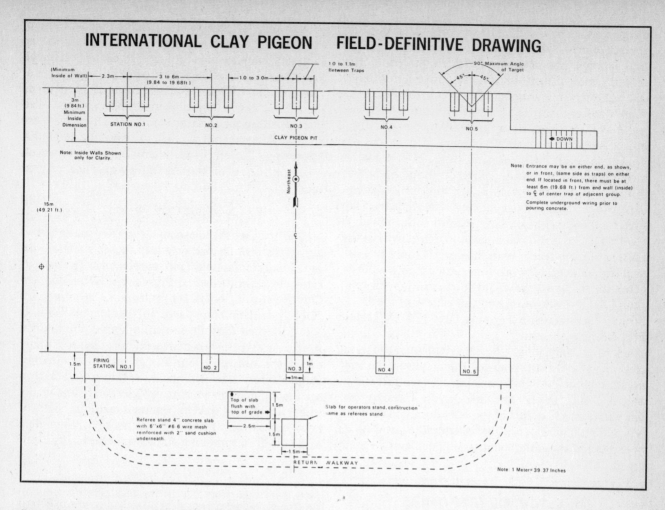

INTERNATIONAL CLAY PIGEON FIELD-DEFINITIVE DRAWING

(Minimum Inside of Wall)
2.3m
3 to 6m (9.84 to 19.68ft)
1.0 to 3.0m
1.0 to 1.1m Between Traps
90° Maximum Angle of Target
45° 45°

3m (9.84 ft.) Minimum Inside Dimension

STATION NO.1   NO.2   NO.3   NO.4   NO.5

CLAY PIGEON PIT

Note: Inside Walls Shown only for Clarity.

Northeast

Note: Entrance may be on either end, as shown, or in front, (same side as traps) on either end. If located in front, there must be at least 6m (19.68 ft.) from end wall (inside) to ₵ of center trap of adjacent group.

Complete underground wiring prior to pouring concrete.

DOWN

15m (49.21 ft.)

1.5m

FIRING STATION NO.1   NO.2   NO.3   NO.4   NO.5
1m
1m

Top of slab flush with top of grade
1.5m
Slab for operators stand, construction same as referees stand.

Referee stand 4" concrete slab with 6"x6" #6-6 wire mesh reinforced with 2" sand cushion underneath.
2.5m
1.5m
1.5m

RETURN WALKWAY

Note: 1 Meter= 39.37 Inches

A squad is on the line for International Trap. Shooter number one is at the ready, while other squad members wait their turns. The trap installation is superimposed on a regulation Skeet field. As can be seen, there is no problem connected with this arrangement.

International trap layout superimposed on a Skeet field. This type of installation conserves space without causing interference, since the two events are never conducted at the same time.

directed solely by the electronic "brain" releases a target in a direction that cannot be known to the shooter. International Trap birds also fly faster and farther than in the American version, and the minimum distance covered by an International bird is 77 meters.

Six shooters comprise a squad. Five are on the line while one is walking from station five back to station one. Stations are changed after each man on the line has fired at one bird. Two shots are allowed at each bird. A bird is counted as "dead," whether hit by the first or second shot. Twenty five birds constitute a single event.

Due to the high cost of building an International Trap field, as well as the increased cost of each individual round, there is not much interest in this activity at the present time. In recent years, however, more and more shooters have become involved in this highly sophisticated sport, thanks mainly to sponsorship by the National Rifle Association and the efforts of the U. S. Army Marksmanship Training Unit (USAMTU) at Fort Benning, Georgia.

There are only about a dozen International Trap facilities in all of North America. The first two to be built are on military bases at Fort Benning, Georgia, and in San Antonio, Texas. The first private International Trap field was installed at the Hamilton Gun Club in Vinemount, Ontario, Canada. A few more installations are scattered about the country, although most of them are too small to conduct a truly International program. The new facility built near Los Angeles, California, for the 1984 Olympic Games promises to be the best on the North American continent.

International Trap is gaining in popularity, but it will almost surely never enjoy the mass appeal of American Trap, solely on economic grounds. This Olympian sport will always remain out of reach to all but the extremely wealthy and those who are heavily sponsored by such organizations as the United States Army and the National Rifle Association.

Modified Clay Pigeon

Modified Clay Pigeon shooting was devised as a practical method of encouraging trap shooters to train for and enter International Trap tournaments. The game is known by several other names such as "NRA Modified Clay Pigeon," "NRA International Clay Pigeon," "UIT Automatic Trap," and "ISU Automatic Trap."

In Modified Clay Pigeon, trap houses suitable for American Trap are acceptable as long as the roof of the trap house is no more than 34 inches above the level of Station Three. A single Winchester trap is used that has been modified to move both vertically and horizontally within limits prescribed for International Trap competition. The trap may be fired either mechanically or electrically, and may be either automatic or loaded by hand.

ISU AUTOMATIC TRAP RANGE

TARGET FALL ZONE

75-82 YDS.

90°

1'

7'6"

8'0"

16½ YD. RADIUS TO FRONT OF TRAP HOUSE

6

9'0"

2

3

4

5

3'

3'

WALKWAY

NOTES:
1. Basic dimensions are those of the standard American trap installation.
2. Trap house roof must be on the same level as shooting stations.
3. Overall house dimensions are minimum requirements.
4. Shooting stations may be 36" to 40" square.

Houses are made from logs on this rustic Skeet range. Station One is marked only by a round slab of concrete. Simple layouts like this one can be made to blend pleasantly into the surrounding environment.

Targets are released at random and, as in International Trap, the shooter has no inkling of where the bird may fly.

Modified Clay Pigeon was developed largely by Michael Tipa of the National Rifle Association, and it was almost entirely through his efforts that the game was recognized as a Championship event by the Amateur Trapshooting Association and the International Shooting Union in 1962. Interest in the game has been steadily increasing ever since.

The rules of Modified Clay Pigeon closely follow those of International Trap, in that six shooters comprise a squad, each shooter moves over one station after each shot, 25 shots make up a round, and two shots may be fired at each bird. In club events, it is not unusual for some of these rules to be altered slightly as local conditions dictate, but as long as the regulation trap is used, these programs are excellent practice for the "big-time" of Internationl Trap.

Skeet

Skeet is similar to trap shooting only in that a shotgun is used to break the same size clay pigeons. The field layout is distinctly different, traps used for throwing the targets are set up in a unique manner, and shooting angles are not at all alike. That is not to say that experience gained in shooting trap is not transferable to the Skeet field. Techniques of gun mounting, swing and lead are much the same, although some differences in shooting methods and equipment have been introduced since Skeet first became popular in the 1920s.

Skeet, sometimes called American Skeet to differentiate it from International Skeet, is shot on a field that is approximately semi-circular, and with eight shooting stations. Two traps are used, one mounted in an elevated position at the left of the field in what is called the "high house." The other trap is at the right side of the layout in the "low house." Trap houses are 40 yards apart. Targets are thrown in a consistent flight path from each house. Target paths from the two houses cross at a point 6 yards outward from shooting Station Eight which is located midway between the two houses. Shooting Stations One through Seven are situated on an arc of 21 yards radius having its center at the target crossing point, 6 yards in front of Station Eight.

A round of Skeet consists of 25 shots. Each competitor fires at two targets from each station, one from the high house and one from the low house. Doubles, in which targets are launched from both houses at the same time, are shot from Stations One, Two, Six, and Seven. Five shooters comprise a full squad for a round of Skeet, although any number from one to five may play in practice sessions.

Shooting rules often seem a bit complicated to begin-

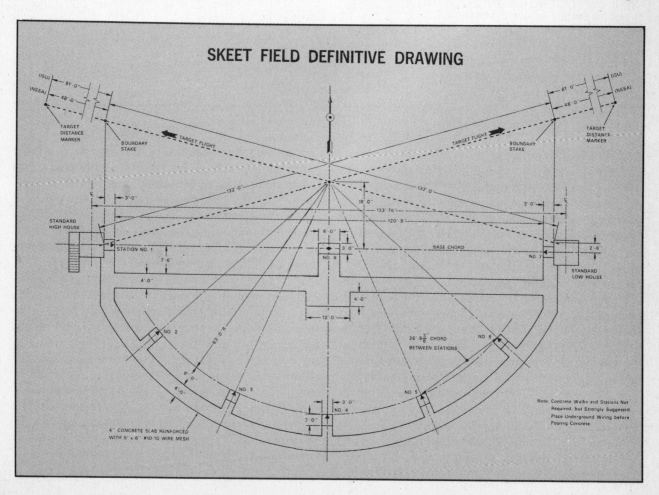

SKEET FIELD DEFINITIVE DRAWING

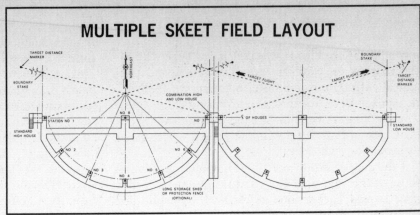

MULTIPLE SKEET FIELD LAYOUT

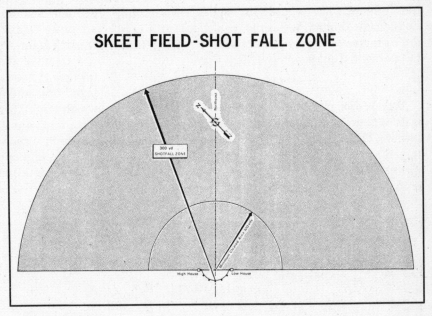

SKEET FIELD-SHOT FALL ZONE

This Skeet shooter is at the ready for a low house bird at Station One. His attitude is one of relaxed concentration, a necessary posture for successful Skeet shooting.

ners, but following through a round of Skeet should clarify procedures. All squard members gather at Station One, and the first shooter steps forward into firing position. He shoots first at a target from the high house, then from the low house—calling "Pull!" for each bird. He stays at Station One and shoots doubles, where targets are released from both houses simultaneously. When all members of the squad have taken their shot at Station One, all move along to Station Two, where the sequence prescribed for Station One is repeated. At Station Three, singles are shot—high house first, then the low house. Singles are shot in turn from Stations Four and Five. At Stations Six and Seven, both singles and doubles are fired, repeating the procedure followed at Stations One and Two. At Stations Six and Seven, targets from the low house are shot first, then from the high house—in opposite order from Stations One and Two. At Station Eight, each member of the squad shoots at the high house target in turn, then each fires at low house targets in the same order. Adding up the shots taken to this point will show a total of 24. The 25th

shot is called "optional," and is fired from station Eight at the low house target if no shots have been missed up to that point. If a shooter scores a miss anywhere along the line, his optional shot must be taken as a repeat of the shot that was missed. This routine may be a bit confusing to a newcomer to the Skeet field, but after shooting a couple of rounds it all begins to make sense and things fall into place quite easily.

Skeet offers a greater variety of shooting angles than trap, and more nearly simulates actual hunting conditions, with both incoming and departing birds being represented. Near overhead shots from Station Eight are similar to those that might be encountered when shooting from a duck blind. The sanctioning body for Skeet is the National Skeet Shooting Association (NSSA), with headquarters in San Antonio, Texas.

Most Skeet shooters use a 12-gauge shotgun, although events are scheduled in major tournaments for .410, 28, and 20 gauges as well. Scoring with smaller bored guns is more difficult because of reduced pattern density. Skeet with a .410 is a true expert's game!

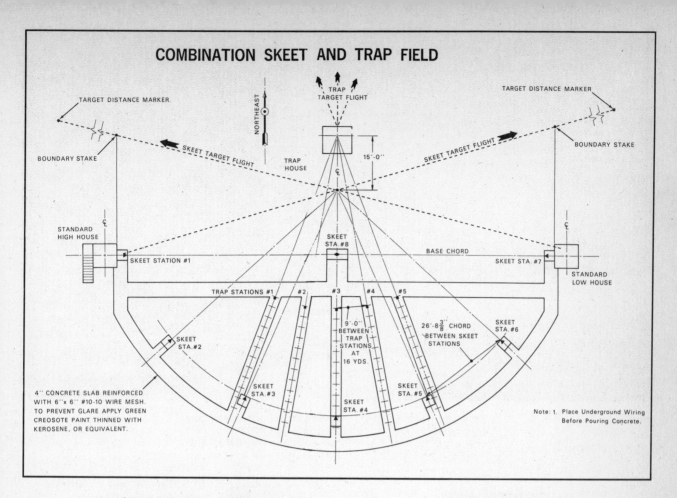

COMBINATION SKEET AND TRAP FIELD

TARGET DISTANCE MARKER

TARGET DISTANCE MARKER

NORTHEAST

TRAP TARGET FLIGHT

SKEET TARGET FLIGHT

SKEET TARGET FLIGHT

TRAP HOUSE

BOUNDARY STAKE

BOUNDARY STAKE

15'-0"

STANDARD HIGH HOUSE

SKEET STA. #8

BASE CHORD

STANDARD LOW HOUSE

SKEET STATION #1

SKEET STA. #7

TRAP STATIONS #1   #2   #3   #4   #5

SKEET STA. #2

9'-0" BETWEEN TRAP STATIONS AT 16 YDS.

26'-8 3/8" CHORD BETWEEN SKEET STATIONS

SKEET STA. #6

SKEET STA. #3

SKEET STA. #4

SKEET STA. #5

4" CONCRETE SLAB REINFORCED WITH 6" x 6" #10-10 WIRE MESH. TO PREVENT GLARE APPLY GREEN CREOSOTE PAINT THINNED WITH KEROSENE, OR EQUIVALENT.

Note: 1. Place Underground Wiring Before Pouring Concrete.

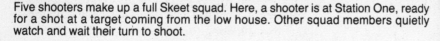

Five shooters make up a full Skeet squad. Here, a shooter is at Station One, ready for a shot at a target coming from the low house. Other squad members quietly watch and wait their turn to shoot.

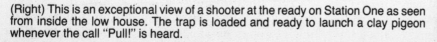

(Right) This is an exceptional view of a shooter at the ready on Station One as seen from inside the low house. The trap is loaded and ready to launch a clay pigeon whenever the call "Pull!" is heard.

Trap and Skeet are not solely daytime sports. Many clay pigeon fields are lighted to allow night shooting. This scene is at the Grand American Handicap in Vandalia, Ohio.

International Skeet

International Skeet, more popular in Europe than in this country, is a more difficult version of the American game. The International field layout is the same, but there are some major differences in rules and procedures. Shooters are required to hold the gun at hip level when calling for a target. After the target appears, the gun must be raised to the shoulder before firing. This rule puts a premium on speed and mounting technique. The targets fly faster from an International Skeet trap, being required to travel 72 yards, as opposed to 60 yards in American Skeet. In order to withstand the added stresses of being launched at a higher velocity, International birds are made from a harder material—and so are a little tougher to break.

In American Skeet, a target is launched immediately after a shooter calls "Pull!" In International Skeet, there may be a delay of up to 3 seconds before a bird emerges from its house. The order of target presentation is different in International Skeet, with the optional shot being eliminated. Shots are as follows:

Station:
One — 1 single (high house) plus one pair of doubles.
Two — 2 singles (1 H, 1 L) plus one pair of doubles.
Three — 2 singles (1 H, 1 L) plus one pair of doubles.
Four — 2 singles (1 H, 1 L) — no doubles.
Five — 2 singles (1 H, 1 L) plus one pair of doubles.
Six — 2 singles (1 H, 1 L) plus one pair of doubles.
Seven — No singles—only one pair of doubles.
Eight — 1 single high plus 1 single low.

There are also several rules concerning loading and gun handling that are not the same as in American Skeet. American Skeet shooters may experience some difficulty in switching over to the International sport, but if one wishes to compete in other countries or in World Championship events, a bit of concentrated effort in making the transition could be highly rewarding.

The ISU is the world-wide governing body for International Skeet, but in the United States the National Rifle Association is the guiding organization.

International Skeet is a scheduled event in the Olympic Games and other World Championship programs, but it has never attracted much of a following in America. Although equipment for International Skeet is not as complex as that needed for International Trap, there is an added expense involved in altering range machinery to produce target velocities essential to International competition. Many gun clubs are reluctant to spend money to equip Skeet field that are usable only for International shooting.

Other Games

As an alternative to regulation competition, there are many games that can be played using equipment already in place on standard trap and Skeet fields. With

A hand trap may be used for many informal shotgun games. Pictured here is what might be called a "poor man's quail walk." The thrower is ready to send a clay bird past the shooter as they walk across an open field.

In a "Buddy Shoot," two-person teams take positions at each trap station. A hit is scored if a target is broken by either team member, but they must shoot in turn.

these novelty games, shooters can obtain needed practice in a more relaxed atmosphere.

Two of the many variations of regular trap shooting are **Rabbit Run,** and **Quail Walk.** For Rabbit Run, the throwing trap is set to cast targets as close to the ground as possible. A shooter stands either on the trap house roof or immediately behind it and fires downward at the target, in much the same manner as one might shoot at a rabbit flushed from under foot. Each round usually consists of 25 shots. Quail Walk (or Grouse Walk) may be played with either one or two shots allowed per target, or it may be arranged for shooting doubles. The shooter starts from Station Three and walks steadily toward the trap house. The puller may release the target anywhere along the route once the shooter calls "Ready!" but he must keep moving until the bird appears. If a trap field is superimposed on a Skeet field, as is the case at many installations, further variety may be added by using all three trap machines. A more realistic Quail Walk requires a special installation of traps, arranged on either side of a trail laid out through brushy country. As the shooter progresses along the trail, birds are released in unannounced and unpredictable patterns, closely simulating the rise of live birds. This type of Quail Walk provides many of the challenges of an actual hunting situation, and it takes a most skilled and alert shooter to break 25 straight.

The **Buddy Shoot,** sometimes called **Protection Trap,** or **Back-up Trap,** is fired with two shooters at a single station. Both assume the ready position and, when the target is launched, the person on the left fires first. If he misses, his partner on the right takes his shot. If the first shooter hits the target, the second teammate does not shoot. If the second partner fires after the first shooter has hit the target, it is scored as a miss. There is a bundle of hot and heavy action in this game, and participants must really keep on their toes. With two gunners on each target, scores are generally high, and it requires more than the usual amount of concentration to win. A Buddy Shoot may be consist of 10, 15 or 25 targets according to prior agreement.

An increasingly popular trap game is the **Annie Oakley.** For this event, as many shooters as can safely line up shoulder to shoulder on the 27-yard line may participate. Each competitor is assigned a number by lot, and they line up in numerical order. Shooter number one calls for a bird. If he hits it, he is credited on his score sheet. If shooter number one misses, number two may take the shot. If number two breaks the target, number one is eliminated, but if number two shoots at a bird that number one has already hit, number two is out of the game. The game progresses in this manner until there is only one shooter left, who is the winner. When as many as 35 or 40 contestants assemble for this one, things get wild and woolly. Obviously not a game for rank beginners, a great deal of discipline is needed for the sake of everyone's safety.

Follow the Leader is a game that produces a lot of

(Right) "Follow the Leader" is a game where the lead shooter sets the rules, and every other participant must make the same shot as the leader. Each shooter has a chance to name his own game when his turn comes to be leader. One of many possibilities is shooting from a sitting position.

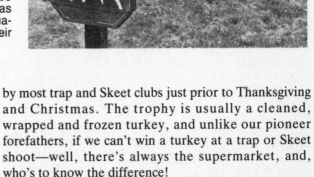

Shooters are at the 27-yard line for an "Annie Oakley." If number one misses, number two may take the shot. If number two breaks the bird, shooter number one is eliminated. The last shooter remaining in the game is the winner.

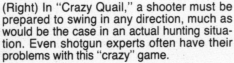

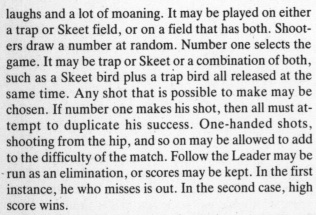

(Right) In "Crazy Quail," a shooter must be prepared to swing in any direction, much as would be the case in an actual hunting situation. Even shotgun experts often have their problems with this "crazy" game.

laughs and a lot of moaning. It may be played on either a trap or Skeet field, or on a field that has both. Shooters draw a number at random. Number one selects the game. It may be trap or Skeet or a combination of both, such as a Skeet bird plus a trap bird all released at the same time. Any shot that is possible to make may be chosen. If number one makes his shot, then all must attempt to duplicate his success. One-handed shots, shooting from the hip, and so on may be allowed to add to the difficulty of the match. Follow the Leader may be run as an elimination, or scores may be kept. In the first instance, he who misses is out. In the second case, high score wins.

One of the oldest shotgun games, but one that is still popular in many parts of the country is the **Turkey Shoot**. Today's shoots are mis-named, as live turkeys are not the target, but often as not the prize for winning. Obviously, these shoots are annually conducted by most trap and Skeet clubs just prior to Thanksgiving and Christmas. The trophy is usually a cleaned, wrapped and frozen turkey, and unlike our pioneer forefathers, if we can't win a turkey at a trap or Skeet shoot—well, there's always the supermarket, and, who's to know the difference!

The Skeet field can provide a variety of games even greater than can be devised from regular trapshooting. Perhaps the most enjoyable and challenging of these is **Doubles At All Stations**. As the name implies, double targets are shot at each of the eight stations adding to the difficulty of the contest. Since only 16 shells are expended, other combinations of shooting postions may be included to make a total of 25 shots. Games such as this are strictly informal, and rules may be made or changed on the spot. It's all for fun, and no records ordinarily are kept. By using a little imagination, innumerable games can be invented for the Skeet field.

"Crazy Quail" targets are thrown from a pit located so that the shooter cannot see the trap. Clay birds may be launched in any direction, even straight at the shooter. In the case of an incoming target, the shooter may not fire once the bird has passed overhead.

A Crazy Quail is smoked into dust as this shooter scores a direct hit on a fast-moving high bird. Crazy Quail is quite popular with hunters who find that it is a good form of pre-season practice for upland game shooting.

(Right) Duck Tower is excellent preparation for hunting high-flying waterfowl. Judgment of correct lead is quite different from that required for trap shooting and Skeet.

Shooters should remember, however, that safety always must be given prime consideration when deviating from a normal established shooting scheme.

For shotgunners who, for one reason or another, may not wish to enter into competitive events at established trap and Skeet fields, there are many alternative clay target games that may be better suited to their needs. Some, such as **Crazy Quail** and **Duck Tower** require at least a semi-permanent installation, but many others need only a portable trap or a hand trap and a place to shoot.

Crazy Quail makes use of a trap located in a pit below ground level, and mounted on a central pedestal fitted with a seat for the trap operator. Trap and seat can rotate through 360 degrees, so that targets may be sent in any direction—even toward the shooter. The target may be delayed for up to 10 seconds after a competitor calls "Pull!," which adds to the element of surprise. On

an incoming target, the shooter may not, for safety reasons, fire at the bird after it has passed him. Gunners may stand anywhere from 16 to 20 yards from the trap, according to agreed handicaps assigned. Rules for Crazy Quail are quite flexible, and are frequently formulated on the spot by the competitors themselves. This is a shoot strictly for fun, and there is no sanctioning organization, nor are records usually kept.

Duck Tower is another game for which there are no rigid rules. A trap is situated at some convenient height above the shooter's stations, usually a man-made tower, but the side of a steeply sloping hill will serve as well. The idea of the game is to present targets flying at angles similar to the flight of a duck over a blind. Shooting procedures follow local rules, and conform to no fixed pattern. The original purpose of the Duck Tower game was to provide practice before the beginning of duck hunting seasons, but it is so enjoyable that many

(Left) This shooter is ready for a high overhead bird from the Duck Tower perched on a hillside. The flight path of the target is not known until the bird is released. Long range and high angle make this a tough game.

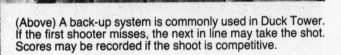

(Above) A back-up system is commonly used in Duck Tower. If the first shooter misses, the next in line may take the shot. Scores may be recorded if the shoot is competitive.

(Left) Shooting stations in Hunter's Clays are best located in areas that simulate actual hunting conditions. The cage prevents a shooter from swinging his gun into a position that could endanger others.

A Hunter's Clays low-tower station offers angles much like those encountered in upland game shooting. Rules specify guns may not be loaded until shooters are at their stations, and then only with two rounds.

who shoot it never go anywhere near a duck blind.

Hunter's Clays, or **Sporting Clays** as they are known in other parts of the world, is a shotgunner's game being promoted in the U. S. by the National Shooting Sports Foundation. Rules are quite flexible, with 12 gauge or smaller guns being allowed. A full squad consists of six shooters who move from one shooting stand to another. Stands are designed to simulate local hunting conditions as closely as possible. On fixed stands, shooters fire from cages, simple wooden structures, that keep participants from turning guns toward the other traps—a necessary safety measure. On "walk-up" stands, of course, there are no cages since all targets will be going away from both trap and shooter. Stands may also be built in the form of duck-blinds or goose pits to add realism to the course. A hillside stand overlooking a pond or stream makes for interesting shooting at low targets, as shots striking the water give vivid indication of mistakes in lead or tracking.

Guns may not be loaded until the shooter is on the stand, and then with no more than two rounds. When the shooter is ready, the toe of his gun stock must touch the waistline. It may not be shouldered until after the target appears, just as in International Skeet.

Targets may be either singles or doubles, thrown from traps that may be located at ground level or as high as a tree top. Hunter's Clays layouts should utilize

Trap shooting is by no means strictly a man's sport. Women have participated almost from the inception of the game, but in recent years the number of women shooters has increased tremendously.

Only basic, simple traps are needed for Hunter's Clays. Several traps may be placed in different locations for each station, so that shooters never know the direction from which the next bird is coming.

natural obstacles, such as trees or hillside outcropings, that one might encounter while actually hunting. The total number of stands is limited only by the imaginations and financial resources of those involved. Anywhere from three to 10 stands is adequate, and the total number of targets thrown may vary from 25 to 100 depending on the size and layout of the course. Until Hunter's Clays becomes a standardized game, which seems unlikely, rules may be made to suit local needs.

Hunter's Clays is excellent training for field shooting. Initially, an experienced upland game hunter will probably do better than Skeet or trap shooters, but with a bit of practice for the claybirders, this advantage should even out. Hunter's Clays might well grow to be one of the leading shotgun games in times to come.

There is no possible way to list all of the games that have been devised for clay target shooting. Given a gun, a trap, a few boxes of shells, and the wide open spaces, shotgunners can think up their own games that will provide endless fun for themselves, family and friends. When trying a new or different clay bird shoot, safety should always be the first thing to be considered. One should be absolutely sure that people, livestock and property are entirely out of harm's way before a shot is ever fired. No matter which of the clay target games is favored, there are very few sports that can offer such a challenge to individual skill.

Hunter's Clays, being promoted by the National Shooting Sports Foundation is gaining interest and popularity all over the country.

This shooter is only an instant away from firing. His concentration is totally centered on his target. The puller and other squad members wait and watch.

Shooting Records 4

KEEPING accurate records is a highly important adjunct of all well established sports. In some activities, such as baseball, the numbers of categories deemed record-worthy have proliferated to the point where ponderous tomes are needed to list them all. Fortunately, shotgun shooting records are not quite so extensive as to require massive volumes to provide a permanent register of individual and team achievements.

In general, when we speak of records, we are referring to outstanding performances—the best of the best. Superior accomplishments by champion shooters are the sort of records that form the basis of this chapter. It should be noted, however, that there are other kinds of records.

Individuals keep records of their own as a testimonial to personal progress as skills are gained through practice. Clubs and sponsoring organizations keep records for purposes of awarding prizes or computing handicaps. National and International groups, as exemplified by the Amateur Trapshooting Association, National Skeet Shooting Association, National Rifle Association, and International Shooting Union keep records of individual and team scores in order to classify shooters according to their proven abilities. A distinction

Both the ATA and NSSA keep accurate records for all registered shooters and they're published annually in these "Average Books."

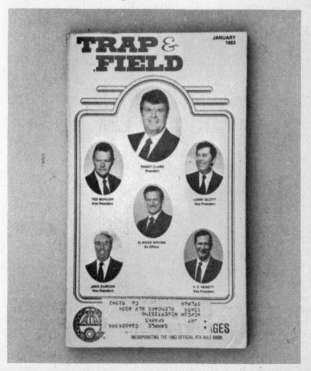

The trophy room at the Grand American. The most coveted prizes are these which are awarded only to the best of the best. Silver and crystal have been the ATA's hallmark for decades.

should be made between records of unique performances and records that are assembled for other purposes.

Except for an occasional article gleaned from contemporary periodicals, there are few written reports of the doings of shotgunners in the early days of live bird trap shooting. Consistent rules had not been established, and there were no sanctioning organizations to regulate competition. Only a mere handful of shooting clubs existed, and most contests were friendly matches hosted by owners of large estates. These gatherings were primarily social events, with shooting being only one of many diversions presented for the entertainment of guests. Pigeon traps often were located alongside or near country inns where local residents of lesser social

(Above) Here's a tough pair to beat, in their day—D. Lee Braun (left) and Grant Ilseng. Between these two men, they've shot over 1,000,000 registered trap and Skeet targets and with a combined average envied by any of today's most dedicated shooters.

In the 19th century, contests were often held by using driven game birds as targets and scores were kept to determine "winners." Usually large sums of money were wagered to make shooting a bit more interesting.

The Coast Pigeon (Blue Rock).

(Left) The Blue Rock Pigeon started it all. Bred mainly in England for tournament use, this tough target often bested the finest wing shots. Small in body and quick starting, these birds proved to be an honest challenge.

Early 19th century pigeon shoots were largely social occasions. Records of these events were not kept as a rule, and there was no national governing body for this sport.

status could also do a bit of shooting while enjoying the pleasures of food and drink offered by the establishment. Innkeepers usually presented winners of such informal matches with prizes of medals, cups, or merchandise.

Sometimes pigeon shooting matches took on international overtones, with individuals and teams from Britain pitted against shooters from other countries—notably France. In addition to shooting trapped birds, it was quite common for contests to be held wherein participants fired from fixed stations at game driven toward them by beaters. Winners in driven game matches were determined by the total number of birds bagged in a given time. Rules for these events were extremely variable. Alternate shots were taken when it was desirable to attempt to give each contestant an equal opportunity, but more often than not the shooting turned into a free-for-all with every man for himself.

Penned some years after the event, which took place in the early 19th century, a written account describes a driven game match between six-man teams from France and England that encompassed three days of shooting in southern France. Total bag at the end of the contest was 2,200 birds. The winning French team also bagged a wager of 10,000 pounds sterling—a veritable fortune in those times.

Fundamental characteristics of flintlock and percussion fowling pieces of the period precluded high percentage scores. Downing merely half of the birds released from traps was considered to be a major accomplishment. As a means of improving scores, larger guns came into use at pigeon clubs everywhere. Specialized guns for trap shooting only were devised. "Pigeon guns" were shorter than field guns, and frequently carried no ramrod or other extraneous furniture in the interest of lighter weight.

Single-barreled shotguns as large as 4-bore were regularly in use at the traps in the early days of the percussion era. The diameter of a 4 gauge barrel is just under an inch, while a 12 gauge tube measures slightly less than ¾-inch. Shot strings from a 4-bore contain about twice the number of pellets propelled from a "normal" 12 gauge. Despite the advantage of enormous shot loads, the winner of the Crinden Medal at the "Old Hats" club in July, 1821, killed only 32 out of 60 birds. Though this score is not terribly impressive by today's standards, it was obviously better than typical scores of the time.

As more and more big-bore shotguns were in evidence on pigeon fields, many sportsmen felt that rules should be made to ban them, in the interest of fairness to all concerned. Ultimately the 12 gauge was accepted as the standard pigeon gun, and shot charges were generally limited to 1¼ ounces. These criteria have remained more or less in effect to the present time, although 10 gauge guns were used for a time in the United States toward the end of the 1800s. Elimination of big-bore shotguns from pigeon fields caused an immediate drop in match scores, but improvements were rapidly adapted to standard 12 gauge guns that caused a steady rise in "dead bird" counts.

With the advent of light, well-balanced breech-loading shotguns, live pigeon shooting scores improved dramatically. In the 1830s, downing 50 birds out of 100 was thought to be a prodigious feat of marksmanship, but by 1870, scores of 75 to 80 were becoming rather commonplace. At the end of that decade, top shooters were often scoring 100 percent.

The name of the first man ever to kill 100 healthy, well-launched pigeons in a straight run will probably never be known. Most written accounts of shooting events that took place over a century ago are no longer

available to us. Moreover, it is quite likely that even such a momentous achievement as 100 straight was not reported in any contemporary journal. The first man known to have accomplished this feat for sure was Captain Adam H. Bogardus. On October 21, 1869, only a year after taking up the sport, Captain Bogardus killed 100 birds straight in a well documented shoot at St. Louis, Missouri. In the same year, he downed 500 pigeons in 528 minutes to win a $1,000 purse.

In a match at New York on November 12, 1891, E. D. Fulford scored 100 to his opponent's 99. On October 12, 1894, J. A. R. Elliott duplicated Fulford's effort in a match in which he defeated the world-renowned marksman, "Doc" Carver who chalked up a losing 99.

There are so many variables in live pigeon shooting that a comparative listing of scores is very nearly an exercise in futility. Flight patterns of birds may be affected by weather conditions, the length of time they remained in close captivity, the type of trap used, their level of ex-

citement due to noise and other factors, their age and general health, and so on. Distance from shooter to trap was inconsistent, particularly in the earlier matches, varying from as little as 10 to as much as 35 yards—or in some cases even more. Differences in ammunition also had a greater influence on scores in those times than it does today.

It is not to be implied that live pigeon shooting records on a given day might be more difficult than 100 straight on another day in another locale. Only after the invention of reliable inanimate targets would comparative scores become more nearly relevent.

Glass ball shooting, which largely replaced live pigeon contests in the years between 1866 and 1885, inspired shooters to set some records that may never be broken. Glass balls flew neither very far nor very fast. Their trajectory was a high, looping arc, with the ball slowing appreciably near the apex of its path. In comparison with live birds, glass balls were so much easier to hit that scores took a giant leap upward—especially for expert scattergunners. Shooters of the order of Bogardus, Carver, Paine, Mitchell, Kimble and Stubbs—to mention a few—were able to break glass bubbles with monotonous regularity. For this reason, shooting matches tended to turn into endurance contests, with strings of over 100 targets being commonplace.

In exhibitions of shooting skill, Captain Bogardus, Ira Paine and Doc Carver would regularly astound their spectators by breaking 1,000 balls in less than 90 minutes.

At Lincoln, Illinois, on a hot, sultry Fourth of July in 1879, Bogardus set an all-time record by breaking 5,000 balls in 500 minutes. In this grueling marathon, he had to average one shot every 6 seconds for 8 hours and 20 minutes. Actually, his shooting pace was slightly faster than this, because he missed 156 targets, so that in breaking 5,000, he fired 5,156 shots in 20 minutes less than the allotted time. Stress and strain on the vocal cords alone, shouting "Pull!" that many times is more than most men could survive. That he could even move, much less lift a gun to his shoulder after such an ordeal, is mute testimony to his great physical strength and mental control.

By way of illustration of the inaccuracies that exist in early trapshooting records, some authorities assert that Bogardus shot his 5,000 birds in New York City in 1877. In the absence of contemporary newspaper reports to definitely establish the site, we have a choice of what to believe.

Not satisfied with this achievement, a year later Captain Bogardus announced his intention of breaking 6,000 targets in two consecutive days of shooting. Two sets of barrels were used on his W.&C. Scott gun, of 10 and 12 gauge. Shells were loaded with 4 drams of Dittmar powder in 10 gauge, and 3½ drams in the 12 gauge, each getting 1½ ounces of LeRoy tin-coated shot. Barrels were frequently cooled in water during the course of the event.

At the end of the first day's shooting, 3,000 targets had been broken without a miss. On the second day, shooting continued apace, although the Captain now sported bandages on his blistered left hand and right thumb, made sore by cocking the exposed hammers of his gun. His first miss came on the 5,681st ball. From this point on, Bogardus missed 12 more targets, so to complete the announced total of 6,000 he fired a total of 6,013 shots.

It would seem highly unlikely that the Captain's run of 5,680 consecutive hits will ever be duplicated. Shooting events of this nature no longer arouse the interest they created 100 years ago, and such a phenomenal run against modern clay targets appears to be an impossibility. However, when a challenge is presented, someone always steps up to accept it. For anyone aspiring to shotgunning immortality, the record is there to be broken—step right up!

Not many women were shooting trap in the 1880s, but it was beginning to be recognized that trap shooting was not solely a man's province. The first woman trapshooter of note, and certainly the most famous, was Annie Oakley. Her shooting and riding exploits with Buf-

(Left) Captain A.H. Bogardus was deemed "The Father of Shotshell Target Shooting" because of his success and dedication to promoting this shooting sport.

The Bogardus glass ball was designed by Captain Adam Bogardus and was very popular in the 1880s. Most of the Captain's remarkable shooting exploits were achieved using his own brand of glass ball targets.

falo Bill's Wild West Show won the hearts of spectators all over the world. Much of her shooting was pure showmanship, and did not require any extraordinary skill to perform. The same must be said, incidentally, of most of the men shooters in Wild West shows of the time. Audiences were notably naive, and were easily dazzled by show-business flummery into believing that rather easy trick-shooting was exceptionally marvelous shooting.

If theatrical gimmicks are ignored, however, there can be no doubt that Annie Oakley was indeed an exceptional shooter. Perhaps her greatest performance with a shotgun came in 1885, when she broke 4,772 glass balls out of 5,000 thrown from a trap at 15 yards rise. Not many present day scattergunners of either sex could guarantee to equal her accomplishment.

Glass ball shooting as a popular pastime declined rapidly after the mid-1880s. Newly developed "clay" targets and better traps to throw them doomed "glass birds" to extinction. Exhibition shooters continued to use them for some years longer, but glass-ball tournaments were largely a thing of the past by the end of the 19th century. Clay targets flew farther and faster than

glass balls, and as a result, scores plummeted as shooters grappled with changes in technique required by the new game. It would be many years before the long runs common to glass ball shooting would be equaled.

The first national trap shooting tournament in which clay targets were used exclusively was held in Chicago in May, 1884. Sponsored by the Ligowsky Clay Pigeon Company, it was billed as The First National Inanimate Clay Target Tourney. It was a team shoot, with five men to a team. Each entrant shot 10 single birds at 18 yards rise and five doubles at 15 yards. A prize of $750 was offered to the winning team, with a $250 diamond badge to the high scorer. For some unknown reason, despite widespread publicity, only a mere handful of shooters attended the meet. Since the country's top shooters were not present, the tournament was a failure as a true national championship event. It is unfortunate that names of the winners, and winning scores of this historic shoot are not mentioned in any reference the author has been able to locate, since this was, without question, the first clay target tournament of nationwide significance.

On February 11-16, 1885, the first national clay pi-

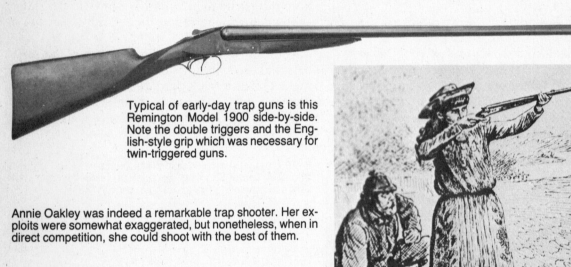

Typical of early-day trap guns is this Remington Model 1900 side-by-side. Note the double triggers and the English-style grip which was necessary for twin-triggered guns.

Annie Oakley was indeed a remarkable trap shooter. Her exploits were somewhat exaggerated, but nonetheless, when in direct competition, she could shoot with the best of them.

Found in the pages of history is this ancient photo of two of trap shooting's most famous adversaries — Doc Carver (left) and Adam Bogardus (right), here at an exhibition clay target match in the late 1890s.

geon championship meeting under the auspices of the National Gun Association was held in New Orleans. Unlike the Chicago tournament of the previous year, the New Orleans competition was well attended by many of the nation's top shooters, including such big names as Captain Bogardus, Doc Carver, J. A. R. Elliott, Al Bandle, Frank Chamberlin and Captain Stubbs. This meet was quite successful. Doc Carver took top honors with no misses. The New Orleans tournament, because of the class of competition, is generally considered to have been the first true national clay bird championship meeting.

Shooting exhibitions of sheer endurance had not entirely gone out of fashion in 1885, when Doc Carver announced that he would break 60,000 clay targets in six days. At his hometown of New Haven, Connecticut, he started his shooting marathon on a Monday, and by Thursday evening, he fired at 64,880 targets, breaking 60,616. This record has never been broken, nor is it likely to be. Except for the fact that it is so well documented, Carver's feat would be almost totally unbelievable.

In the late 1880s, trap shooting zoomed in popularity.

the first time. R. A. Welch topped 20 other entrants to capture the 1893 title with a score of 23. By 1900, the Grand's entry list had grown to 224, and scores had improved significantly. The winner in the live bird event was H. D. Bates who went 25 straight, and then added 34 more to his string in a shoot-off. The first Grand American Clay Target Champion was Rolla O. (Pop) Heikes, who broke 94 targets out of 100 at 16 yards.

In 1903, the Grand became the world's first all clay target tournament, and live birds were seen no more in championship contests. Martin Diefenderfer was the first Grand American All-Clay Champion, with a score of 94x100.

The first man to win the Handicap with 100 straight was Riley Thompson who did it in 1910, and that was a feat that wasn't to be repeated until 16 years later, when C. A. Young took the title. The first shoot-off for the championship did not come about until 1949, when Pete Donat and William Sonderman tied at 100 each. Donat won all the marbles with 23x25 in the decider.

Numerous events are scheduled during the annual Grand American meeting, but the two most prestigious are the Grand Handicap, fired from 18 to 27 yards, and

C. W. FLOYD 1902   M. DIEFENDORFER 1903   R. D. GUPTILL 1904   R. R. BARBER 1905

This quartet of early 20th-century trap shooters were pioneers in the clay target era. C.W. Floyd was the last live champion in 1902. Diefenderfer, Guptill and Barber were the Grand American all-clay target champions in 1903, 1904 and 1905, respectively.

"Championship Tournaments" sprang up all over the country but, with no central governing body, most of these were not productive of true "National Champions." Meets sponsored by the National Gun Association came closest to being legitimate contests to determine the best shooters of the year, and it was the Association's successor, the Interstate Manufacturers' and Dealers' Association, that promoted the first Grand American Handicap in March, 1893, at Dexter Park, New York. This organization underwent several name changes, finally evolving into the Amateur Trapshooting Association, today's sponsor of the Grand American.

The Grand American Handicap of 1893 was a live pigeon shoot, as were all succeeding annual events until 1900, when clay targets were added to the program for

the North American Clay Target Championship, fired from 16 yards only. Though the Handicap has generally been won outright, the 200-bird Clay Target shoot has more often than not involved a shoot-off to determine the eventual winner. The first to break 200 straight for the North American Championship was Steve Crothers, and that was in 1925. In only one year since that time has a score of less than 199x200 been good enough to win, and it has taken a 200x200 or better to do the job in 44 of the other years.

Competition at the Grand is considered by many shooters to be the world's finest. The tournament has grown so large that today over 20,000 individual entries are received from aspiring champions for all events on the Vandalia, Ohio, program.

Skeet, of course, has a much shorter history than trap

Ammunition makers took great pride in touting the use of their products with shooter's testimonials. This advertising practice continued up to the late 1940s when more "institutional"-type advertising prevailed.

This sleek Parker Skeet gun could be found in the hands of affluent shooters from coast to coast. The beavertail fore-end and long, graceful stock design set the Parker above most other Skeet guns in the 1930s.

shooting. Even though Skeet had been introduced to the American public in 1926, it wasn't until August 16, 1935, that the first national championship tournament was held in Cleveland, Ohio. There were 113 entries in the 12-gauge event, which was not a bad turnout for such a comparatively new sport. Trap shooting was still king of shotgun clay target games, as indicated by a total registration of over 600 hundred competitors for the 1935 Grand American Handicap.

In the late 1930s, Skeet steadily increased in popularity until the onset of World War II. Wartime shortages of guns, ammunition and other equipment virtually put an end to Skeet for civilians. The armed forces, however, used Skeet as a valuable training aid, and thousands of young GIs were introduced to the sport in this manner.

The Army Air Force included Skeet as part of a broad gunnery program for all aircrew members. Then, when all those ex-servicemen came home after the war, many wanted to continue Skeet shooting in civilian life. As result, there was a tremendous nationwide resurgence of interest in Skeet shooting activities. The National Skeet Shooting Association, dormant during the war, was re-organized in 1946.

Modern Skeet shooting may be said to have begun in 1947, under the aegis of the rejuvenated NSSA. Rules and procedures were changed slightly from those of pre-war days, so that there was not a common basis for pre- and post-war records. In 1954, rules again underwent modification to such an extent that records from that date to the present occupy a special niche in Skeet history. For record purposes, there are three separate periods to consider: 1933-1947, 1947-1954, 1954-present.

Records have been kept for all gauges, for both individuals and teams, but the records that are of greatest interest to most of us are the High Overall achievements and long runs during registered competition. High Overall perfect score is 550/550, including 250 targets for 12-gauge, and 100 targets each for 20, 28, and .410 gauges. The difficulty of this event may be judged by a look at the records: Only seven people have scored perfect 550s since 1935—and all of them accomplished this in the years after 1975. Either shooters are getting better, or Skeet has become an easier game. Since there is little or no evidence that clay birds break any more readily than they did 40 years ago, we can only conclude

The famous Lordship Gun club in Connecticut was built by Remington Arms and today continues to draw large numbers of shooters. Lordship has been the scene of many record-breaking performances.

(Right) Skeet shooting boomed after World War II because many ex-servicemen were exposed to this fascinating shooting sport while in the service.

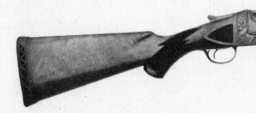

The fabled Parker Single Barrel trap gun was "King of the Hill" on the trap fields up to World War II, when this old war-horse was discontinued by Remington Arms, who purchased the Parker tooling in 1940.

that both shooters and equipment have improved with time. HOA record holders with perfect 550/550 scores to date are: Charles Parks, Ohio—1976; Walter Badorek, Oregon—1977; Wayne Mayes, Tennessee—1979; Richard Boss, New York—1982; William Rogers, Canada—1983; Phil Murray, Texas—1983.

At the 1983 Grand American Tournament, a new High All-Around trap shooting record was established by Roger Smith of Kansas. Not satisfied with shattering 200x200 and 75x75 in the shoot-off to win the coveted North American Clay Target Championship, Smith came back the next day to break a perfect 100x100 from the 27-yard line and, via shoot-offs, won the Grand American Handicap event to boot. This tremendously difficult accomplishment has never been done before by a single individual. And, on the last day of competition, Smith cranked out a 99x100 in the Doubles Championship to record a near-perfect 399x400. Indeed, a remarkable trap shooting feat and one that will stand for years.

All shotgunners can relate to long run records, simply because they are seemingly so far beyond the realm of reasonable expectation. Wayne Mayes, of Tennessee,

A Skeet shooting legend of the 1960s was Pete Candy of Los Angeles, California. The owner of many long-run Skeet records, Candy was one of the most consistent and stalwart performers ever to shoulder a Skeet gun. A believer in Winchester Model 12s and 42s, Candy was lightning-smooth in stroking these pump guns in doubles.

Here's a trap squad with longevity. In 1979, the combined ages of these veterans was 393 years! The marvelous aspect of trap and Skeet shooting is that it's a game for all ages and sexes.

The long and the short—Dan Orlich (left) and a 13-year old Jim Poindexter tied at a handicap event at Reno, Nevada. Both broke 99x100 and guess who won the shoot-off? Yep, young Jim!

Three of trap shooting's greats. Left to right, Col. Bill Everhardt, Dan Orlich, Joe Devers.

The broad grin belongs to Ricky Pope, who in 1977 shattered 399x400 targets at the Baton Rouge Gun Club in the four-gun event.

ATA President, Tom Dillon of Idaho, presents the keys to a brand new Jeep Cherokee to Junior Shooter Dean Shanahan, the 1979 Grand American Handicap winner.

Dan Orlich, the "King of trap shooting" accepts his award for being admitted to the ATA's Hall of Fame. Dan's accomplishments are legend, and shot in an era when guns and ammunition weren't up to today's exceptional quality and consistency.

The Dean of Skeet and trap shooting's writers, Jimmy Robinson has been a proponent and enthusiastic booster of trap and Skeet shooting for over a half-century.

Every shooter, either trap or Skeet, should attend the "Nationals" once in his shooting career to join in the festivities of these popular events.

set the 12-gauge record in 1979-80 with a total of 1711 straight broken birds in registered competition. The 20 Gauge honors go to Chip Youngblood, of Florida, who shattered 1620 consecutively in 1981-82. Michael Schmidt, of Minnesota, broke 900 straight in 1983 for a new 28-gauge mark. Longest run with a .410 was also upped in 1983 by Morton Benson, of Virginia, who pulverized 401 clay birds without a miss. Gary Lowe, of Indiana, holds long run honors for doubles at 277, accomplished in 1981-82. These records valid at this writing.

Records are meant to be broken, to be sure, but some shotgun records may stand forever. Long runs such as those of Bogardus and Carver are not likely to be eclipsed, if only for the reason that no one today would be motivated to attempt a feat of this sort. Some other records, like Adolph Nelson's lifetime achievement of firing at a total of over 412,000 registered trap targets, may not ever be bettered by virtue of time limitations

alone. One would practically have to live at a trap field to do that much shooting.

Records set in regular tournaments probably will continue to be shattered. Today's long run trap shooting records are over 2,000 straight at 16-yards, over 250 straight at handicap and over 400 straight at doubles. Improved training methods, better equipment, and tougher competition all work together to push scores ever upward. There are some who say that both trap and Skeet are too easy today, and that something should be done to make the sports more difficult. Perhaps this is true for the top guns of the world, but the rest of us mere motals find the game hard enough. If trap and Skeet were made much tougher, it could discourage a lot of folks who are just beginners. Let's leave it the way it is, then we can all go after one of those elusive records with the same conditions prevailing as were met by those who have gone before.

5 The Competition Shotgun

THE SHOTGUN is the most important piece of equipment the competition shooter owns. The manipulation and handling of it must be purely a reflex action to be taken care of by the subconscious mind, in order that the real effort and attention of the shooter be concentrated on the problem at hand—hitting the target.

In order to accomplish this and to eliminate mechanical hindrances and distractions, the shotgun must come as near as possible to being perfectly fitted, balanced and suitable to the shooter. In other words, the shotgun must work *with* the shooter—not against him. And while it isn't usually possible for a shooter, particularly a beginner, to get the proper gun the first time he tries one, he should conscientiously study and experiment with several guns. In a comparatively short time, he'll find one that suits both his pocketbook and shooting needs.

Once that determination has been made, let me say forcefully that when you find this gun and shoot it with comfort and satisfaction, keep it, guard it and *don't*—if you get into a mild shooting slump—alter it! If you don't stick with any suitable gun for at least 10,000 shots, then you can't possibly learn the gun's idiosyncrasies. This familiarization process requires a great deal of shooting and time. But, suddenly you'll develop a rapport with that particular gun that blossoms into a relationship that will withstand the sands of time.

It isn't good practice for a newcomer to clay target shooting to blindly purchase a trap or Skeet gun without some investigation—and preferably, test firing. How can you try a shotgun before buying one? Borrow or rent one. Many gun clubs have gun rental privileges and for a couple of bucks, a new devotee can shoot quite a few different makes and models for a minimum of cost. There's still another way. Introduce yourself to shooters at a local gun club and tell them that you want to "rent" their gun to ascertain if that particular make and model is just what you're looking for. Most of the time, these shooters will let you borrow their gun, providing you only use factory ammunition. Never shoot reloads in a borrowed shotgun!

On any given Sunday at a fairly active gun club you'll find at least 20 to 30 different makes and models of either trap or Skeet guns in the gun racks. Another "no-no"—never pick up a gun from a rack without first receiving the owner's permission. Simple courtesy goes a long way to kindling new friendships.

Although there are seven basic types of shotguns—the autoloader, pump, over-under, single barrel, side-by-side, lever action and bolt action—only the first four types are generally found on today's competition fields. The latter three are either too slow to manipulate or are

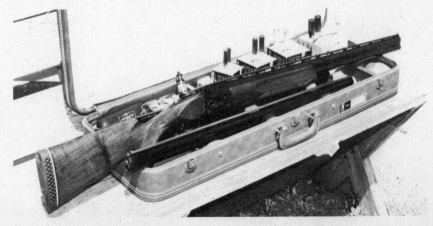

Browning's four-barrel Skeet gun set is an excellent buy on today's market. Each barrel assembly is precisely scaled to the exact weight of each other. Thus, the gun weighs and handles the same regardless of which barrels are installed.

Although the Ljutic Space Gun bears absolutely no resemblance to a classic shotgun, those trap shooters using this new concept in gun design are quick to praise Ljutic's innovations.

obsolete as is the case of the lever action. The particular type of shotgun one chooses is strictly a personal preference. Each has its weaknesses and strengths and it will require some study of each action type plus intelligent advice for you to make the right decision. We'll go into greater detail later in this chapter and fully describe each of the proven and popular types of shotgun actions.

It is not necessary to own an expensive gun in order to shoot well, but it is necessary to own a gun of good quality and workmanship. A poorly-made shotgun cannot withstand the vigorous use demanded in trap and Skeet shooting. Consider that the average American hunter could conceivably—during an active and productive bird-hunting season—shoot up a case of ammunition (500 shotshells). Extending this higher-than-average use to a 20-year span, the hunter could fire 10,000 rounds from his gun in a normal hunting lifetime. An active trap or Skeet shooter will consume a like quantity of ammunition in 4 to 6 months! Get the point? Competition guns, at least the better ones, can withstand this rugged use and still come back for more.

The weight of the shotgun is extremely important. I believe that the average male shooter should be able to handle a trap gun in the 8- to 8½-pound range. I believe in weight, especially *muzzle* weight. The additional for-

ward weight helps the shotgun "stick" on the target when pointed and tends to eliminate muzzle flip or whip which is the cause of many misses—especially when shooting at doubles targets. A lightweight gun that handles too fast is apt to overrun the target and promotes "herky-jerky" movements by the shooter. Like most competitive events, smoothness of style brings about better results. Skeet guns, too, should be heavier than their field-model counterparts, for the same reasons as described for trap guns.

One of the most used words describing a competition shotgun is "balance." Writers will describe a gun's balance as the mid-way point. On most over-under-type shotguns, this reference is usually at or near the hinge pin or where the barrels and receiver join; for single barrel repeaters—pumps and autoloaders—where the barrel couples to the receiver. Why, then, can five different shooters pick up the same gun and all emphatically state that the gun's balance is different for each of them? The reason is hand placement. A shotgun is only "balanced" *if* the shooter places both hands an equal distance from the physical balance point of the shotgun. As a rule, the "master" hand—the one which the grasps the grip—is fairly inflexible in its position because the index finger must be able to reach the trigger while the rest of the hand is wrapped around the grip. So, there-

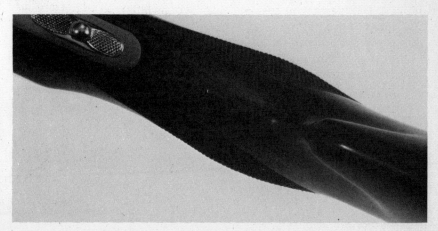

Palm swells are becoming more popular because this innovation fills the void in the shooter's master hand and greatly contributes to better control of the shotgun.

53

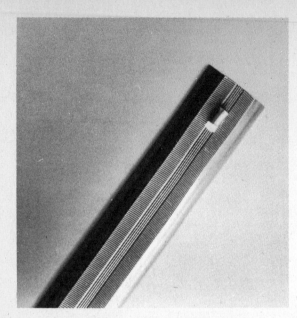

Some shooters prefer a narrow ventilated rib, some wide, like this ½-inch wide variation with a "sighting track" down the center which is claimed to guide the shooter's eye to the target. The white Bradley-type front bead is one of the best front sights installed on a shotgun, both for trap and Skeet shooting.

(Right) The line-up of guns available from Shotguns of Ulm is impressive and ranges from trap and Skeet models through "live-bird" versions. Hand-fitted, old-World craftsmanship is hallmarked by these West German imports and they boast several features not found on any other marques.

front bead is located near the muzzle, the rear is situated about half-way between the muzzle and the rear of the barrel. The relative position between these two sighting beads determines the shotgun's vertical point of impact. If the barrel is true and straight—meaning that the shot swarm (charge) impacts at 40 yards downrange to the corresponding line of sight—then the two beads should appear to be superimposed. The rear bead, the smaller of the two, should appear to be perfectly placed within the diameter of the larger front bead. If there is a gap between the two, the shot charge will be above the line of sight in proportion to the amount of space seen between the two beads.

The shooter's master eye is actually the shotgun's rear sight. Therefore, as in pistol or rifle shooting, if the sights are not properly lined up on the mark, the target will be missed. But, unlike pistols and rifles, the shotgun has three sights—two beads mounted on the barrel and the shooter's master eye. To the beginning shooter, it might appear more difficult to align and control three sights over the customary two, but that isn't so. This three-sight theorem is not used to sight on the target, but rather to determine and establish proper shotgun stock fit. I must digress for a moment and clarify the use

fore, the "off" hand—the one supporting the front of the shotgun—must be slid forward or rearward to bring the gun into proper "balance." We shall go into greater detail fully describing shotgun balance techniques in another chapter, but it is important, at this time, that you know something about it.

The word "fit" is a three-letter word that is ambiguous. How does the shotgun "fit" the shooter, or is it the other way around and the shooter must "fit" himself to the shotgun? There are two theories and both are extremes. The majority of custom stockmakers will emphatically state that the factory-manufactured gunstocks will not properly fit *anybody!* On the other side of the coin are those preceptors who blindly oppose any alterations or modifications to a factory-installed gunstock for fear of diminishing a gun's value. To both of these hypotheses I say hogwash!

To better understand "fit," we first have to understand how one "sights" a scattergun. Unlike rifles or handguns that are equipped with either mechanical or optical sights that are used to line up on the target, the shotgun must be "pointed" instead of "sighted." Virtually all competition shotguns are equipped with two metal or plastic sights which are called "beads." The

of shotgun sights. To become a proficient trap, Skeet, or field shooter, one must look *past* the sights at the ultimate target while tooking *down* the barrel. The sighting beads are used *only* to align the shooter's eye and head in the correct shooting position—no more, no less!

The manner in which a shooter—novice or veteran—mounts a shotgun greatly influences stock design. There's only one proper method to mount a shotgun and it cannot be stressed strongly enough: *Always bring the shotgun up with both hands to the face and cheek.* Never, never, bring the shotgun to the shoulder and then tilt the head down to the top of the stock. So, in order to determine how a shotgun "fits," the shooter must first learn how to "mount" a shotgun. I have been witness to hundreds of complaints by both trap and Skeet shooters about their *improperly* fitted stocks. When these distressed shooters were asked to mount their guns, no less than 50 percent mounted them incorrectly. After a few minutes of instructing them how to bring the gun up to their face, and replacing their previous faulty gun mounting method with this proven technique, suddenly the gun fitted perfectly. And as a result, there were fewer missed targets and these enlightened shooter's scores zoomed appreciably higher.

The point to be made is, in order to evaluate a product, one must first understand how to properly use it. And, therefore, to establish if a factory-made gun stock, or even a custom gun stock properly fits a shooter, he or she must first learn how to mount it in the correct manner for proper determination.

There are two general models of trap stocks found on today's trap guns—the Monte Carlo and straight stock. Some shotgun makers offer their wares in either configuration. So that you can better understand what your choices are, and how either may benefit you, let's go into greater detail.

The overwhelming majority of trap guns are equipped with a Monte Carlo stock. By simple definition, the Monte Carlo stock has a higher comb height than a straight stock because the butt is stepped down. For all intents, a straight stock may have the same comb height but the relative position of the butt is approximately on the same line as the comb or top of the stock. Which is best for you? It depends primarily on your physical dimensions. Those shooters who have "long" necks are usually more comfortable with a Monte Carlo stock. Those of us who are "bull-necked" get along just fine with straight stocks. The dimension factor is measured from the shooter's "formed" pocket in his shoulder to the cheekbone. The greater this distance, the more drop is required in the Monte Carlo stock at the rear. There is a wealth of information regarding stock fit to be found in a later chapter of this book.

The following sub-chapters are devoted to an in-depth look at the various types of trap and Skeet guns currently available and point out their strengths and weaknesses. From the "fashionable" standpoint, the single barrel trap gun is the "in" gun. As in any sport, the participant secretly desires to own and use a specialized piece of equipment. Trapshooters are no different, but for either economic or traditional reasons, there are other types of actions still seen on the trap fields.

The single barrel trap gun was developed before the turn of this century and was immediately seen as a "status symbol." They were then, as today, considerably more expensive than pump guns or autoloaders. They were a single-purpose tool designed expressly for competitive clay-target trap shooting and those who used them were considered "rich" by other people's standards. Even today, single-barreled trap guns, for the most part, are "hand-made" with limited sales, and they demand a higher price than pumps and autoloaders made on a production line. Great names in shotgun manufacturing produced thousands of single

Today's autoloading shotguns bear the label reliable if they are properly cleaned and lubricated. The Remington Model 1100 is also available in a left-hand version which southpaw's will appreciate.

barrel trapguns . . .Parker, Ithaca, LeFever, and Baker were some of the more popular American products. The English custom gun makers also produced quite a few single barreled trap guns for the affluent "colonists" with Greener, Purdey and Woodward the major contributors.

The single barrel trap gun is unquestionably the most dependable and strongest shotgun action ever built. It has changed little in design and concept from guns of yore. Typically, they are all based on a simple break-open action, although various types of locking systems are employed. Because the single barrel trap gun has only one objective, to fire a single shot without bothersome magazines to facilitate follow-up shots, it is the epitome of rugged simplicity.

Unquestionably, today's hot set-up is the Italian-made Perazzi shotgun. First imported into the United States in the early 1970s, it was—pardon the pun—an instant "hit." During that time, there was only one American-made single barrel trap gun still in produc-

Skeet guns have made a remarkable change in the past double-decade. The venerable Winchester Model 12 with a Cutts Compensator on the muzzle was the hot set-up until the mid-1960s. Remington Models 870 and 11-48 were favored arms of some Skeeters. The most popular stack-barrel gun was the Belgian-made Browning—preferably in Lightning grade. The Krieghoff Model 32 didn't hit the fields until the late 1950s, although a cherished few Remington Model 32s were available at exorbitant prices.

In 1963, when Remington introduced their fabulous Model 1100 (as this tome was being written, the 3,000,000th Model 1100 rolled off the assembly line) this sweet-shooting, light-recoiling, gas-operated autoloader put thousands of pseudo "Skeet" guns into shooter's storage closets. The 1100 took over Skeet fields and made a pretty large dent in trap fields to boot. It wasn't long before Remington realized that they had a highly acceptable competition shotgun (and at a reasonable price) and the same holds true today.

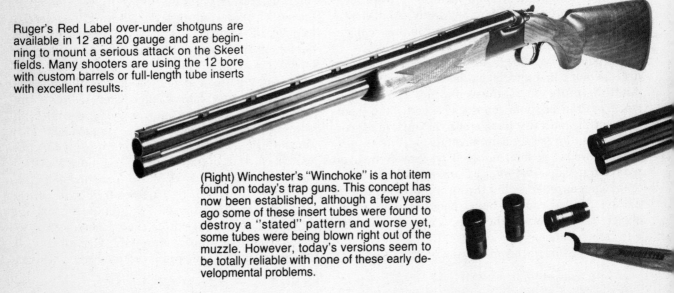

Ruger's Red Label over-under shotguns are available in 12 and 20 gauge and are beginning to mount a serious attack on the Skeet fields. Many shooters are using the 12 bore with custom barrels or full-length tube inserts with excellent results.

(Right) Winchester's "Winchoke" is a hot item found on today's trap guns. This concept has now been established, although a few years ago some of these insert tubes were found to destroy a "stated" pattern and worse yet, some tubes were being blown right out of the muzzle. However, today's versions seem to be totally reliable with none of these early developmental problems.

tion—the Ithaca Single Barrel. The Ithaca was expensive, well over $1500 for a plain-Jane model. The Model 5E then carried a price tag about the same as a new, low-end Ford or Chevrolet. Therefore, when the Perazzi Comp I infiltrated the American trap fields with a retail price tag of $800—and often discounted to $600 to stimulate sales—American shooters went head over heels for this "spaghetti-gun."

Another popular import, at about this same time, was Browning's BT-99. Made in Japan, and blessed with a retail price of about $275, the BT-99 became the chosen favorite for new trap shooters who were on the fence, undecided if they should buy a Winchester Model 12 or a Remington Model 1100. These three guns were priced fairly close to each other, and though the BT-99 didn't penetrate the Perazzi market, it greatly diluted competitive sales of pump or autoloading trap guns.

Over-unders are the "in" guns for the Skeet shooters, and like trap shooting's single barrel gun, the stack-barrel scattergun is a prestige shooting tool. Browning, Perazzi, Rottweil, Krieghoff and K-80s are in wide use despite their higher initial cost over pumps and autoloaders. There always seems to be a buyer for quality firearms as none of the aforementioned firms are begging for business and each year the prices go up.

The over-under combines many important features into a single gun. The stack-barrel configuration enables the shooter to utilize the advantages of twin tubes while peering down a single, and narrower sighting plane, than as presented with side-by-side shotguns. Nearly all of today's o-u's offer a single selective trigger mechanism, either mechanical or inertia operated. Interestingly, some of the Russian shooters have shied away from single triggers in favor of the older style double trigger abomination with reliability being the excuse. Perhaps Big Red can't make a competition shotgun with a reliable single trigger mechanism—funny, the rest of the Free World can!

Also, the major makers of over-unders equip their guns with selective automatic ejectors that propel fired shells out of the chamber when the gun is scissored open. Some shooters disable this feature, claiming it's easier to pull the empty hulls from the gun's chamber than to pick them up off the ground. If you have found this to be a problem, here's a little tip. Instead of operating the opening tang lever with your thumb and forefinger, slide your hand up on the back of the receiver and set the opening lever inside the palm of your hand. Swing the lever to the right and extend your fingers over the top of the receiver and you'll form a "cage" to catch the empties. Try it, it works!

Another reason for the stack-barrel's popularity is the advent of insert barrel tubes which quickly convert a 12 gauge shotgun into a four-gauge Skeet gun ensemble. This is a practical and most economical way to

Tube systems offer unique advantages over the four-gauge autoloading Skeet gun sets and over-under shotguns with four sets of barrels. Consistency, which is the name of the game in Skeet, is one of the direct results by using a tube set. The shooter becomes familiar with one stock, one trigger, one "feel" because he can shoot all four gauges with the same gun. He doesn't have to adapt to different conditions when switching gauges.

Of course the same holds true with the four-barrel over-under ensemble. What then does the tube concept hold over the four-barrel set? Economics for one, because tubes are much less expensive than barrels. Second, there is the weight factor. Over the past decade, shooters have taken a serious look at the theory and mechanics of Skeet shooting. Most agree that a heavier gun can help produce higher scores than the lighter autos, pumps and four-barrel sets highly popular in the 1950s and 1960s. Tubes will add an average of 14 ounces to a gun and this has created a new "standard" for the weight of Skeet guns. Today, barrel and gun weights of every type are very popular

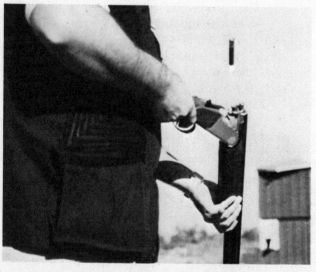

Briley tubes are custom fitted to the Rottweil and are available through Paxton Arms. During the past decade, both Skeet champions and novices have switched over to this shooting system in the search for consistent gun handling characteristics when switching gauges.

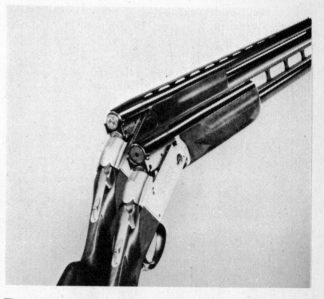

The combo concept is both beneficial to shoot and expensive to own. Most all major trap gun manufacturers offer these two-barrel, one-receiver ensembles.

shoot all "four guns" during a Skeet program.

Over the past 10 years, insert tube systems for Skeet guns have transformed from a novelty item into the most popular multi-gauge Skeet shooting set-up today. The tubes are full-length barrel inserts which enable one to shoot the three smaller gauges—20, 28, and .410 bore—in one common 12 gauge over-under shotgun.

The inserts are actually barrels which fit inside, and are supported by, the existing 12 gauge barrel. Some of the tubes on the market today are made entirely of anodized aluminum, where other makers make the barrel portion of the tubes with anodized aluminum and the chamber area out of either stainless steel or titanium.

items, as Skeeters are adding weight to their lighter guns to get that "tube set feel."

What are the reasons behind the trend of heavier Skeet guns? One is "automatic" follow through. A heavier gun is harder to stop after the trigger has been pulled, giving the shooter a slight hedge against stopping his swing; the added weight also creates a smoother, more consistent follow through.

As Skeet is now shot with the gun already mounted, it is only natural that heavier guns have evolved since the 1950s when the gun had to be off the shoulder on the call. Back then, the style of shooting called for quick gun movement and snap shooting techniques. Today, the game requires more deliberate methodical actions for one to be consistent. Third, recoil has been recognized as a "killer of consistency," and new recoil reduction devices are hot items on the Skeet aftermarket. Since overall weight and recoil have a direct relationship, the built-in weight of a tube set tames much of the recoil of an over-under. Barrel weight, especially near the muzzle, helps to reduce muzzle rise during recoil which is critical while shooting doubles.

Other pros and cons exist regarding tubes sets, but it is my firm belief that a tubed gun can improve the consistency of most shooters. One thing is for sure—because of the benefits that are built into the tube system, it is no longer a novelty and it's here to stay.

What separates a "competition" gun from a standard field or hunting model? Actually, very little in outward appearance, but the emphasis is on the best quality materials, precise fitting of parts (both metal-to-metal and wood-to-metal), along with nuances that transform a run-of-the-mill shotgun into a skillfully prepared shooting tool.

Both trap and Skeet shooters are the shotgun manufacturer's "proving grounds." If a shotgun has an inherent weakness, a poorly designed part, you can be sure that competition shooters will soon find the gun's inbred faults. If a shotgun that is hawked by a manufacturer has either Trap or Skeet model in its name, it had better be able to withstand the vigorous use and punishment demanded by competition shooters or else word will quickly get around about its faults and it'll soon be off the market. The most important criteria in a competition-grade shotgun is a ten-letter word entitled "dependable."

Webster defines dependable as "to trust or rely." If a shotgun breaks down during its early life, say within a couple thousands shots, it will have a stigma attached that is virtually impossible to overcome. Shooters will tolerate small inconveniences as part of the game, but repeated "annoyances" will not be tolerated. These same shooters are usually meticulous about keeping their equipment in top-notch condition. They have learned from experience that cleanliness contributes greatly to dependability. If they don't keep their equipment in prime operating condition, they will shoulder most of the blame in the event of equipment failure. But should a certain problem occur with regularity that costs a shooter even a single target, then that shotgun, ammunition, etc. will be abandoned. And, for good reasons. The competition shooter should only have to be concerned with the flight of the target—never the equipment in his hands.

Let's now take a closer look at today's trap and Skeet guns and "flesh them out" to see what may be the perfect shotgun for you.

Trap guns, like trap shooters, come in all styles and configurations. This quartet is armed with (left to right) Winchester Model 12, Ljutic Mono Gun, Browning BT-99 (old style), Ljutic DynaTrap and a Comp I Perazzi.

ARMSPORT

After 2 years of design and tooling, Armsport's new Competition Trap shotgun is available in mono-trap under barrel and over-under models as well as in multi-barrel sets. Coupled with new technological advances, the gun is delivered with a complete extra interchangeable trigger mechanism. All moving parts of the fire control system are housed within the trigger group, which can be quickly and easily removed and replaced for cleaning and service. The receiver is carved from a solid block of special gun steel and reinforced for additional strength by precision heat treating. Coil springs are used throughout the entire gun. Both individual trap guns and multi-barrel sets are delivered in a handsome, handcrafted fitted leather case.

The Model 4046 is a 34-inch mono-barrel, but a shorter 32-inch version is available as the Model 4047. Model 4048 is a set, with 34-inch single barrel and a 32-inch over-under barrel group. Model 4049 is a shorter variation, having a 32-inch single tube combined with 30-inch over-under barrels.

Models 4032, 4033, 4034 and 4035 have the same barrel dimensions listed above, but they are fitted to a simpler boxlock action without the removable trigger feature. Receivers are fully hand engraved, and auto ejectors are standard.

ASTRA

Makers of fine Spanish shotguns for many years, Astra trap guns are now imported into this country by L. Joseph Rahn, Inc. Astra's trap gun has 30-inch over-under barrels choked Modified & Full. Of boxlock design, the Model 750 Trap has a broad vent rib with front and middle bead sights. A single selective trigger is used, along with automatic ejectors. Receivers are scroll engraved, and the stocks are select European walnut with a Monte Carlo comb; fore-end and pistol grip are hand checkered. The Model 750 Trap is a nicely finished, modestly priced shotgun that should do very well in competition.

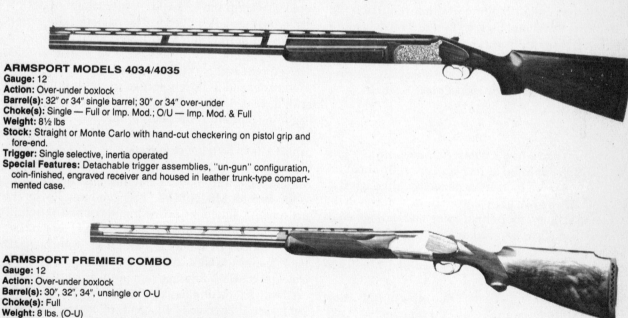

ARMSPORT MODELS 4034/4035
Gauge: 12
Action: Over-under boxlock
Barrel(s): 32″ or 34″ single barrel; 30″ or 34″ over-under
Choke(s): Single — Full or Imp. Mod.; O/U — Imp. Mod. & Full
Weight: 8½ lbs
Stock: Straight or Monte Carlo with hand-cut checkering on pistol grip and fore-end.
Trigger: Single selective, inertia operated
Special Features: Detachable trigger assemblies, "un-gun" configuration, coin-finished, engraved receiver and housed in leather trunk-type compartmented case.

ARMSPORT PREMIER COMBO
Gauge: 12
Action: Over-under boxlock
Barrel(s): 30″, 32″, 34″, unsingle or O-U
Choke(s): Full
Weight: 8 lbs. (O-U)
Stock: European walnut with checkered pistol grip and fore-end
Trigger: Single selective
Special Features: Available as Unsingle or over-under or as a set; removeable trigger mechanism.

ASTRA MODEL 750
Gauge: 12
Action: Over-under boxlock
Barrel(s): 30″, ventilated rib
Choke(s): Full & Mod.
Weight: 6½ lbs.
Stock: European walnut with hand checkered pistol grip and fore-end
Trigger: Single selective
Special Features: Scroll engraved receiver, selective automatic ejectors.

BENELLI

A new dimension has been added to the field of auto-loading shotguns by Benelli. Heretofore, semi-automatic shotguns have been operated either by barrel recoil or gas action. Benelli guns have fixed barrels and rely on the recoil of the entire gun to initiate the "blow-back," and not by harnessing the gas. Unlocking of the action is accomplished by a small inertia block, then residual gas in the barrel forces the breechblock to the rear to complete the ejection-cocking-loading cycle. Feed time is exceptionally short, and the system is highly adaptable to different shot loads. Takedown and reassembly are extremely simple, facilitating cleaning and maintenance. Recoil is markedly lower than in other auto-loaders because of the force absorbed by the rather heavy breechblock. Five shots may be fired from the Benelli in less than 1 second, so that there is absolutely no waiting for a second shot on trap doubles. A full-length magazine is supplied with Benelli's Model 123V trap gun, but plugs are available to cut the capacity to two shots for the trap field. The lower receiver is made of high-strength aluminum alloy, and may be had in natural finish or black matte. The barrel is 28 inches long, choked Full or Modified, with a ventilated rib. The stock is the Monte Carlo style of fine walnut, with a double-vented recoil pad. The broad fore-end is hand checkered, as is the pistol grip. Weight is approximately 7 lbs., 10 ozs. Benelli shotguns, made in Italy, are imported into this country by Heckler and Koch, Inc.

BERETTA

Beretta is the world's oldest manufacturer of firearms. Over 4 centuries of fine craftsmanship stand behind every Beretta shotgun made today. Although Bartolomeo Beretta had been a noted cannon maker in the early 16th century, the present company bearing that illustrious name was founded in 1680 by Pietro Beretta for the purpose of making all types of firearms. The company has been under continuous family management ever since.

From Gardone Val Trompia in Northern Italy, Beretta has expanded overseas to a second home in Accokeek, Maryland, headquarters for Beretta U.S.A. The American market is serviced by the Maryland facility, but traditional old-world standards of excellence have remained unchanged.

Competition shotguns by Beretta have won more gold, silver and bronze medals than any other make. Berettas are the first choice of a host of trap shooters all over the world. The current Beretta catalog lists three models specifically designed for trap shooting.

The Model A302 Competition Trap Gun is a gas-operated shotgun. Gas-action autoloaders are preferred by many shooters because the gas system absorbs a good share of the shock of recoil. The A302 has a wide, grooved fore-end, and a handsome walnut stock fitted with a thick, recoil-absorbing butt pad. The barrel is topped by a wide, floating ventilated rib. Two fluorescent bead sights are provided, one at the front, and the second at mid-rib. Monte Carlo stocks on A302 models are adjustable for drop by means of a cleverly designed stock bolt that allows for changes to fit individual requirements. The fore-end and pistol grip are hand checkered in a handsome yet utilitarian pattern. Barrels are available in 32-, 30- and 28-inch lengths. The two longer tubes are Full choked, while the 28-incher boasts Multichoke interchangeable choke tubes. Tubes are made in Full, Improved Modified, Modified and Improved Cylinder constrictions to suit all competition needs. Receivers are forged alloy to help hold overall weight down to a tad over 7 pounds.

The Beretta Model 680 Competition Trap Gun is a boxlock over-under with interchangeable 30- or 32-inch barrels that are choked Improved Modified & Full. An alternate barrel, the Mono Trap, has a high ventilated rib in place of the top barrel. The Mono Trap barrel is made in 32- and 34-inch lengths in Full choke only for maximum effective range in Handicap Trap shooting. The 680 has premium grade walnut with hand checkered pistol grip and fore-end. A wide choice of stock dimensions may be supplied to discriminating claybirders, assuring a perfect stock fit. Beretta 680 receivers are hand engraved, and triggers are gold plated. A thick, curved butt pad is standard equipment. Ejectors are automatic, and a single selective trigger is fitted, along with a manual safety. Rebounding hammers and floating firing pins are at the heart of the 680's action. Pride of ownership is enhanced by the beautiful fitted case in which Model 680s are delivered.

A superlative shotgun combining all the best of traditional design with modern materials and workmanship is the Beretta Model SO-4. This gun has a low-profile action with sidelocks providing maximum reliability with minimum lock time for long life and fast shooting. The finest quality walnut is used for the wide hand-filling fore-end and high-combed stock—sans Monte Carlo cheekpiece. Both fore-end and pistol grip are well covered with hand-cut, fine-line checkering. The receiver is lightly scroll engraved—by hand, of course. The SO-4 has automatic ejectors, single selective trigger and manual safety. Barrels are either 28-inch Modified & Full, or 30-inch in both Improved Modified & Full or Modified & Full. Receivers are made of forged steel, heat treated for long, reliable service. A fitted case is supplied with this superb top-of-the-line trap gun.

No matter whether one prefers an auto-loader, over-under or mono gun, Beretta has a model for all.

BROWNING

Shotguns have been synonymous with the Browning name for longer than most of us can remember. Brownings are always well represented on trap and Skeet fields everywhere. Current models made especially for

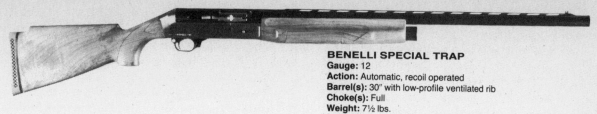

BENELLI SPECIAL TRAP
Gauge: 12
Action: Automatic, recoil operated
Barrel(s): 30″ with low-profile ventilated rib
Choke(s): Full
Weight: 7½ lbs.
Stock: Monte Carlo with tight-curl pistol grip and extended fore-end
Trigger: Standard pull
Special Features: Fitted with curved trap-type recoil pad and the fastest cyclic-rate of any autoloading shotgun on today's market.

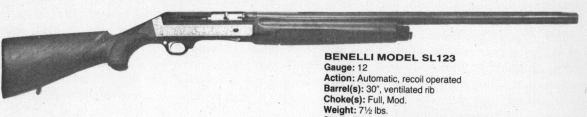

BENELLI MODEL SL123
Gauge: 12
Action: Automatic, recoil operated
Barrel(s): 30″, ventilated rib
Choke(s): Full, Mod.
Weight: 7½ lbs.
Stock: European walnut with hand checkered pistol grip and fore-end
Trigger: Standard with cross-bolt safety in the rear of the trigger guard.
Special Features: Easily interchangeable barrels; silver and black engraved receiver.

BERETTA SO-4 OVER-UNDER
Gauge: 12
Action: Sidelock
Barrel(s): 30″ with ventilated rib
Choke(s): Imp. Mod. & Full or Mod. & Full
Weight: 7¾ lbs.
Stock: European walnut with Monte Carlo
Trigger: Single selective
Special Features: Fine line hand-cut checkering, delicate scroll engraving and gold inlay "TRAP" in trigger guard.

BERETTA MODEL 680 COMBO
Gauge: 12
Action: Boxlock, Mono-barrel combo
Barrel(s): 32″-34″ single barrel, 30″ or 32″ over-under
Choke(s): Single—Full or Imp. Mod. O/U—Mod. & Full
Weight: 8 lbs.
Stock: European walnut with Monte Carlo
Trigger: Single selective
Special Features: Low-profile boxlock action. Fitted with special recoil pad and fitted case.

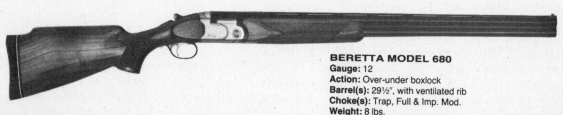

BERETTA MODEL 680
Gauge: 12
Action: Over-under boxlock
Barrel(s): 29½″, with ventilated rib
Choke(s): Trap, Full & Imp. Mod.
Weight: 8 lbs.
Stock: European walnut with hand checkered pistol grip and fore-end, trap dimensions
Trigger: Single selective
Special Features: Silvered, engraved receiver; luminous front and middle bead sights

trap shooting are the BT-99, BPS, Citori and Superposed.

The BT-99 single-barrel has a wide beavertail fore-end that tapers to the rear, along with either a straight stock or Monte Carlo. The receiver is machined from a solid block of steel, and all internal parts are hand fitted. Barrels are available in 32- and 34-inch lengths, choked Full, Improved Modified or Modified. Extra barrels are easily interchangeable if a different length or choke should be desired for any reason.

The BPS (*Browning Pump Shotgun*) is made in special trap configuration with a 30-inch ribbed barrel choked Full, Improved Modified or Modified. The action is operated by twin action bars for smoothness and to prevent binding. Ejection and loading are from a bottom port. A magazine cut-off allows loading without disturbing shells in the chamber, or to convert the gun from repeater to single-shot operation. The stock has a Monte Carlo comb, the fore-end a semi-beavertail style with wide finger grooves. The pistol grip and fore-end are checkered 18 lines to the inch. A deluxe recoil pad is standard equipment.

Browning's Citori model is an over-under gun that has become almost standard equipment on many American trap fields. The Standard 12 is supplied with either 30- or 32-inch barrels, choked Improved Modified & Full or Modified & Full. The Citori Standard 12 Combo Trap gun has over-under 32-inch barrels choked Full & Full, Improved Modified & Full or Modified & Full, together with a single 34-inch interchangeable barrel choked Full, Improved Modified or Modified. The single barrel unit occupies the same position as the top barrel of the over-under set, while the lower barrel is replaced with a weight designed to vary the gun's balance point to suit a particular shooter's preference. A high-post, floating target rib tops all Citori trap gun barrels, raising the sighting plane to keep recoil low and away from the shooter's face.

A single selective trigger may be set to fire either barrel by a mechanism incorporated in the tang-mounted safety lever. Pushing the safety to the right means the under barrel fires first; a shift to the left allows the over barrel to lead off the sequence. A second shot follows from the other barrel when the trigger is pulled again. All Citori guns are fitted with automatic ejectors, stocks are all Monte Carlo style, finely checkered in the grip area, and capped with a thick, curved, recoil-absorbing butt pad. The fore-ends are of the broad, beavertail variety with finger grooves and checkering on the lower surfaces. Weight of the 32-inch version is 8 lbs., 3 ozs., while the 30-incher is 2 ounces lighter. The single barrel weighs a nominal 7 lbs., 12 ozs., which may be increased by use of the optional balance weight when installed in place of the missing lower barrel. Five grades of finish are offered, varying in quality of wood and engraving.

Browning's Superposed model is their top of the line shotgun. It is available with a long list of options that allows a buyer to have a truly custom built gun. Because of the many variables that may be specified by a purchaser, it's virtually impossible to adequately describe all the features of this superb shotgun. Suffice it to say that the Superposed, in whatever configuration, is one of the world's finest firearms. Additional information may be had from Browning.

Browning BT-99, BPS and Citori model trap guns are now available with Invector interchangeable choke tubes. These tubes screw completely into specially threaded muzzles so that they are invisible when viewed from the side. A special wrench needed for their insertion and removal is supplied with the units. Tubes choked Full, Improved Modified and Modified are normally supplied with trap guns, although other chokes are available on request. The Invector system allows a shooter to alter his gun's pattern without the expense of extra barrels.

CAPRINUS SWEDEN

Shotguns by Caprinus are made in Varberg, Sweden, and are imported and distributed in this country by Caprinus U.S.A. The frames and all working parts of Caprinus guns are made of stainless steel, but the barrels are conventional gun steel, deeply blued to a fine finish. The action opener is a standard top lever that works around a circular receiver segment, as opposed to a conventional bolt. The Caprinus system results in a smaller vertical dimension at the breech than is found on regular break-action shotguns, which places the center of gravity a bit lower than normal for improved recoil characteristics. The firing pins are cocked by movement of the opening lever, and a single selective trigger is standard. Barrel selection is by means of a projection located immediately ahead of the trigger. Automatic ejectors, offered as an option, are activated by gas pressure. Interchangeable choke tubes are available in six standard styles, with others as optional alternatives. As the optional choke tubes are eccentric, they can be positioned to raise, lower, or make left or right adjustments to shot patterns. Either Monte Carlo or straight stocks may be had, all with fine checkering. The fore-end is a modified beavertail style with finger grooves. Overall weight of the Caprinus trap gun with 30-inch barrels is 7¾ lbs. Caprinus Sweden trap guns are delivered in an elegant fitted case covered with Indian water buffalo hide.

ITHACA

Shotguns from Ithaca have been held in high esteem since 1880. Ithaca guns are "built," rather than "mass produced." Parts are precision machined, but final assembly is accomplished by hand fitting and finishing.

Ithaca's pump gun for trap is the Model 37 Supreme Trap, with a 30-inch Full choke barrel. A wide ventilated rib provides a continuous line of sight with the top of

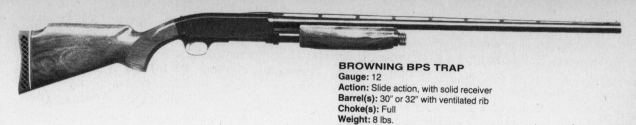

BROWNING BPS TRAP
Gauge: 12
Action: Slide action, with solid receiver
Barrel(s): 30″ or 32″ with ventilated rib
Choke(s): Full
Weight: 8 lbs.
Stock: French walnut with Monte Carlo comb
Trigger: Specially tuned for trap shooting with let-off set at 4 lbs. Gold-plated.
Special Features: Ejection/loading port in bottom of receiver; cut-off switch for single-shot action. Trap pad and twin beads. Invector screw-in chokes available.

BROWNING CITORI COMBO
Gauge: 12
Action: Boxlock with 2 sets of high-profile ventilated rib barrels
Barrel(s): 34″ single barrel 32″ over-under barrels
Choke(s): Single—Full; O/U—Imp. Mod. & Full
Weight: 8½ lbs.
Stock: French walnut with Monte Carlo comb
Trigger: Single selective
Special Features: Invector screw-in chokes available. Trap pad installed and 16 line-per-inch checkering on pistol grip and fore-end.

BROWNING BT-99
Gauge: 12
Action: Boxlock, single barrel
Barrel(s): 32″ or 34″ with high-profile ventilated rib
Choke(s): Full, Imp. Mod. or Mod.
Weight: 8 lbs.
Stock: French walnut with Monte Carlo
Trigger: Single, with crisp 3½ lb. pull
Special Features: Automatic ejector, deluxe curved face recoil pad. Hand checkering on pistol grip and fluted fore-end. Available in Pigeon Grade with fancier wood and heavily engraved receiver.

BROWNING SUPERPOSED
Gauge: 12
Action: Over-under boxlock
Barrel(s): 30″, ventilated rib
Choke(s): Full & Full, Full & Imp. Mod., or Full & Mod.
Weight: 8 lbs.
Stock: European walnut with special trap dimensions
Trigger: Single selective
Special Features: Basically a custom-made gun with many options available; silvered, engraved receiver.

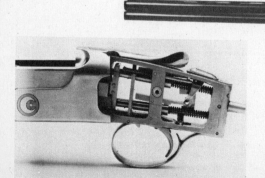

CAPRINUS SWEDEN
Gauge: 12
Action: Boxlock over-under
Barrel(s): 30″ with low-profile ventilated rib
Choke(s): Screw-in, Full, Imp. Mod. and Mod.
Weight: 7¾ lbs
Stock: Straight or Monte Carlo comb
Trigger: Single selective
Special Features: Stainless steel construction with optional screw-in chokes to alter point of impact. Fine European walnut with hand-cut checkering. Deep pistol grip.

the receiver. The wood is select, figured walnut, with hand checkering on pistol grip and fore-end. A thick recoil pad is standard. The gun has a short stroke action and ejection is from the bottom. Weight of the Model 37 Supreme is only 7 lbs.

The Model 51A Supreme Trap is a gas operated, semi-automatic, take-down type that has a reduced number of parts for increased reliability. It can be fully stripped for cleaning without the use of tools. It has a recoil pad, vent rib, and hand checkered wood. Stock design is either regular or Monte Carlo, with special finishes, dimensions, etc. available if desired.

Ithaca's Single Barrel Trap gun is hand built to special order only. Fit and finish of both wood and metal are carefully done by master craftsmen to the highest standards of workmanship. Wood is specially selected figured walnut, and the receiver is highly engraved and inlaid. Either 32- or 34-inch barrels are supplied in Full choke. The "regular" Single Barrel Trap gun is known as the 5E Grade. An even finer version, with more elaborate engraving and inlays of precious metals is the Dollar Grade. Other specifications of the two guns are identical.

K.F.C.

La Paloma Marketing, Inc., is the importer and distributor of Japanese-made K.F.C. (Kawaguchiya Firearms Co.) shotguns. Three models are of interest to trapshooters: Model 250 autoloader, and Model OT-Trap E1 and E3.

When equipped with a 30-inch vent rib barrel and suitable high-comb stock, the M-250 becomes a viable trap gun. Interchangeable choke tubes are optional, allowing for a complete range of pattern adjustments. The gun is gas operated through an action rod that is

not directly connected to the breech block. Initial impact of the action rod unlocks the breech block with sufficient energy remaining to force the block rearward on its own. No gas is vented at the rear of the gas cylinder. Much of the residual gas is returned to the barrel through the gas port, providing a self-cleaning effect. Take down for maintenance is quick and simple and no tools are needed. The entire operating system is contained within the trigger group. K.F.C's Model 250 is safe and simple and recoil is minimal. Engraved receivers and select wood are options.

K.F.C.'s over-under, Model OT-Trap E1, is made with either a straight stock or Monte Carlo of high grade French walnut. The pistol grip and fore-end are hand checkered in a practical pattern. The 30-inch vent-rib barrels are chrome lined and choked Improved Modified & Full. The action is a boxlock with single selective trigger, automatic ejectors, and manual safety. A fancier version with chromed receiver, more extensive engraving and deluxe walnut is known as Model OT-Trap E3. Weight is about 8 lbs. Interchangeable choke tubes are available as an option on both E1 and E3.

LANBER

Recently introduced to this country, Lanber shotguns are imported from Spain by Lanber Arms of America. The trap gun, Model LCH-E:Rival I, has 29½-inch barrels topped by a ventilated rib. They are joined only at the breech and muzzle, leaving space between for cooling. The compact action design results in a low profile gun with excellent weight distribution. A single trigger and selective automatic ejectors are standard. Stock and fore-end are plain walnut, hand checkered in a large pattern on the pistol grip and underside of the

ITHACA MODEL 37 SUPREME TRAP
Gauge: 12
Action: Slide-action
Barrel(s): 30″ with medium- profile ventilated rib
Choke(s): Full
Weight: 7½ lbs.
Stock: American walnut with straight comb
Trigger: Standard, with cross-bolt safety located at rear of trigger guard
Special Features: Solid steel receiver; hand-cut checkering on pistol grip and fore-end; bottom loading/ejection port.

ITHACA MODEL 5E SINGLE BARREL
Gauge: 12
Action: Single shot, boxlock action
Barrel(s): 32″ or 34″ ventilated rib
Choke(s): Full
Weight: 8 lbs.
Stock: AAA-grade American walnut with straight comb or optional Monte Carlo
Trigger: Hand-honed and tuned to 3½-lb. pull
Special Features: Special order to customer's specifications. Engraved receiver, carved and hand-checkered pistol grip and fore-end.

ITHACA MODEL 51A DELUXE TRAP
Gauge: 12 only
Action: Gas-operated, semi-automatic
Barrel(s): 30″ with medium-profile ventilated rib
Choke(s): Full
Weight: 7¾ lbs.
Stock: American walnut with Monte Carlo or straight comb
Trigger: Special competition type with fast lock-time and pull set at 3½ lbs.
Special Features: Hand-cut checkering on pistol grip and beavertail fore-end. Steel receiver has matte finish.

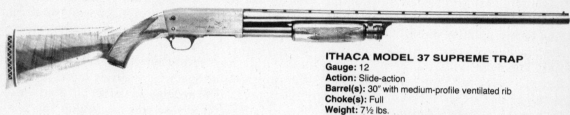

ITHACA MODEL 37 SUPREME TRAP
Gauge: 12
Action: Slide-action
Barrel(s): 30″ with medium-profile ventilated rib
Choke(s): Full
Weight: 7½ lbs.
Stock: American walnut with straight comb
Trigger: Standard with cross-bolt safety at rear of trigger guard
Special Features: Solid steel receiver. Hand-cut checkering on pistol grip and fore-end. Bottom loading/ejection port.

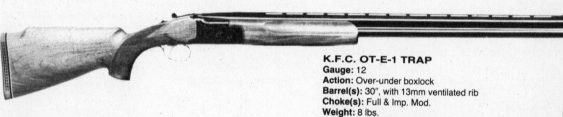

K.F.C. OT-E-1 TRAP
Gauge: 12
Action: Over-under boxlock
Barrel(s): 30″, with 13mm ventilated rib
Choke(s): Full & Imp. Mod.
Weight: 8 lbs.
Stock: French walnut with hand checkered pistol grip and fore-end, oil finish
Trigger: Single selective
Special Features: Engraved, blued receiver; wide gold-colored trigger; rubber recoil pad

K.F.C. OT-TRAP-E3
Gauge: 12
Action: Boxlock, over-under
Barrel(s): 30″ with low-profile ventilated rib
Choke(s): Imp. Mod. & Full
Weight: 7¾ lbs.
Stock: Straight-grained walnut with Monte Carlo comb
Trigger: Single selective
Special Features: Scroll-engraved, silvered receiver. Dual sighting beads. Recoil pad and gold-plated trigger blade.

LANBER MODEL 2009
Gauge: 12
Action: Boxlock, over-under
Barrel(s): 30″ with medium-profile ventilated rib
Choke(s): Screw-in on bottom barrel, fixed Full choke on top barrel
Weight: 7¾ lbs.
Stock: European walnut, straight comb with deep pistol grip and fluted fore-end
Trigger: Single selective, inertia operated
Special Features: Smooth face recoil pad and hand-checkered pistol grip and fore-end.

fore-end. The fore-end not only has finger grooves, but the grooves are serrated to give better control of gun position. Interchangeable choke tubes, called the LanberChoke system, are supplied in Full, Improved Modified and Modified constrictions. Overall weight is 7¾ lbs. Lanber's trap gun is competitively priced and represents an excellent value.

LJUTIC

Ljutic Industries is known throughout the world as innovators in shotgun design. Ljutic guns are engineered for target shooters, with models for both trap and Skeet. Functional simplicity is the cornerstone of their design philosophy, resulting in guns of outstanding accuracy and reliability. All Ljutics are custom made to the buyer's specifications.

The Bi-Matic model is a two-shot, gas-action, semi-automatic. Both pull and release triggers are offered. Stocks are made to the customer's dimensions from select high grade walnut. Barrels may be from 26 to 32 inches in length, although 30 inches is standard. Choke is at the option of the buyer. Weight of the Bi-Matic is a little greater than some more conventional shotguns, running about 10 lbs.

The Ljutic Mono-Gun, a single shot for trap shooting, is a break-action with the action opener in the form of a button on the front of the trigger guard. The removable trigger assembly contains both trigger and hammer mechanisms. A 34-inch barrel is standard, with either a regular vent rib or a high Olympic rib giving a 35½-inch sighting plane. Once again, choke is optional with the customer. Stocks are made strictly to customer specifications, but typically feature a high Monte Carlo cheek-piece with a rather slim wrist, cut low for easy hand hold.

The Ljutic Bi-Gun over-under model is based on an action similar to the Mono-Gun except it's modified to fire two barrels instead of one. Over-under barrels are 32 inches long, and are joined only at the breech and muzzle to provide maximum cooling. Other barrel lengths and choke selections are available. A Bi-Gun Combo is also made, and is supplied with two trigger units, one for single-shot, and one for double-barreled use.

By far the most revolutionary gun in Ljutic's "armamentarium" is the Space Gun, a truly futuristic design that might feel right at home on the set of "Star Wars." Incorporating a recoil absorbing mechanism, the Space Gun is said to be nearly recoilless. The Space Gun has no stock in the conventional sense, but rather a straight backward extension of the barrel and action unit, culminating in a simple shoulder pad. The standard barrel is 30 inches long, Full choked. Both a plain front sight and a raised rib sight are available. Either regular pull or release triggers are also offered. The weight runs about 8½ lbs. As with other Ljutic guns, there are numerous options that may be selected to provide the buyer a truly custom-built shotgun.

LANBER MODEL 2009 LCH
Gauge: 12
Action: Over-under boxlock
Barrel(s): 30" with ventilated rib
Choke(s): Full & Full LanberChoke tube system
Weight: 7 lbs.
Stock: European walnut with checkered pistol grip and fore-end
Trigger: Single selective
Special Features: Blued, lightly engraved receiver; selective ejectors; no middle rib for extra cooling.

LJUTIC SPACE GUN
Gauge: 12
Action: Single shot, recoilless design
Barrel(s): 30" with optional sight or short-ramp ventilated rib
Choke(s): Screw-in
Weight: 8½ lbs.
Stock: Integral with barrel and action
Trigger: Button-type with choice of release or pull setup
Special Features: Revolutionary design which incorporates special recoil pad and pistol grip.

(Left) The shortened rib on the Ljutic Space gun is another interesting concept as it provides the shooter with a "mini-ramp" for sighting. It's well above the barrel to prevent heat waves from distorting the shooter's sight picture.

Scopes are no longer "oddities" on shotguns, especially trap guns. This Ljutic Space Gun is equipped with an older Weaver 1X scope. Once the shooter becomes accustomed to using this optical device, it is difficult to return to the "traditional" method of looking down the barrel.

LJUTIC MONO GUN
Gauge: 12
Action: Single shot, boxlock
Barrel(s): 34″ with high-profile ventilated rib
Choke(s): Special to customer's specifications
Weight: 9 lbs.
Stock: High-grade American walnut with Monte Carlo comb and tight pistol grip
Trigger: Removable assembly, release or pull
Special Features: Totally custom made; push button opener on front of trigger guard.

LJUTIC OLYMPIC MONO GUN
Gauge: 12
Action: Single shot, boxlock
Barrel(s): 32″, 33″ or 34″ with special Olympic high-post rib
Choke(s): Screw-in choke tubes
Weight: 9¼ lbs.
Stock: Monte Carlo with tight pistol grip. Choice of woods and finishes
Trigger: Removable assembly, pull or release
Special Features: Only made to customer's specifications and with various options.

LJUTIC BI-GUN
Gauge: 12
Action: Over-under, boxlock
Barrel(s): 28″ to 34″ with high-profile ventilated rib
Choke(s): To customer's specifications
Weight: 9½ lbs.
Stock: Monte Carlo comb with tight pistol grip and made to customer's dimensions
Trigger: Removable trigger/hammer assembly. Choice of pull or release triggers
Special Features: Push button opener on front of trigger guard. Custom-made to customer's desires.

LJUTIC BI-MATIC
Gauge: 12
Action: Gas-operated, semi-autoloading, two-shot capacity
Barrel(s): 30″ with medium-profile ventilated rib
Choke(s): Full, Imp. Mod., Mod. or choked to customer's specifications
Weight: 10 lbs.
Stock: Modified Monte Carlo with deep pistol grip, choice of select grade hardwoods
Trigger: Pull or release mechanism
Special Features: Left or right-hand models available.

MAROCCHI

Another new entry in the shotgun field is Marocchi. The guns are made in Italy and imported by Marocchi U.S.A. Designed specifically for American trap, the Model America is a boxlock over-under with 27- to 30-inch barrels. A 32-inch trap mono barrel is available either as a high rib under or top barrel single. The stock is hand checkered select walnut with right or left-hand palm swell and high Monte Carlo cheekpiece. The fore-end may be either beavertail or Schnabel type. The frame has medium engraving coverage with three grades of finish. Weight is about 8 lbs. Stock dimensions and a few small detail changes are optional at no extra charge. The gun is delivered in a fitted hard-shell case. A slightly less expensive, though similar, version is the Model Contrast. A deluxe model, the SM28, is entirely custom made to a customer's specifications, using the same frame and action as the America, but with superior finish and all options, including extra barrels.

MOSSBERG

Based on their time-tested Model 500 frame and action, Mossberg is offering the Model 500AHT pump-action trap gun. Fitted with a high-comb trap stock, the 500AHT has either a 30-inch Full-choked barrel or a choice of 28- or 30-inch barrel with ACCU-CHOKE interchangeable choke tubes. Three tubes are supplied, Full, Improved Modified and Modified. A high, Simmons Olympic rib rides atop the 500AHT barrel for improved sighting. The Mossberg 500AHT is low in price when compared with many other trap guns, but performance is quite adequate for successful trap competition.

PERAZZI

Ten plus years ago, most American trap shooters thought that Perazzi was a misspelling for a tasty Italian pie. Danielle Perazzi, a dynamic promoter of the shotguns that bear his name, figuratively speaking, "owns" the trap gun market. A few years ago, at the 1981 Grand American Tournament, a survey was taken of all the gun marques used by the shooters, and nearly 40 percent of the shooters were using Perazzis! That is truly incredible when one considers that over 5,000 shooters participate in this annual event.

Like any successful entrepreneur, Daneille Perazzi keeps close tabs on the market and like automobile manufacturers announces annual models. The original Comp I is long gone, along with the MT-6 in its original stripped receiver version. Today's lineup of Perazzi's is staggering—along with the suggested retail prices.

The old standby MX-8 combo is still with us as are the DB-81 combo and the Mirage. A recent entrant is the TMX series along with the MX-3 models. Virtually every type of stock configuration, rib height, and barrel arrangement are available from Perazzi in plain-Jane grades to near-museum quality engraving and gold embellishments. Some models have fixed trigger assemblies, whereas most competition-grade guns boast removable trigger groups. This is a feature that Perazzi helped initiate and is a most desirable characteristic on a trap gun. First, should a trigger spring or hammer break at an inopportune time, a replacement trigger assembly can be quickly exchanged for the broken one. With input from Dan Bonillas, the Perazzi Model DB-81 shotgun (so named for this great California-based trapshooter) has all the features and design qualities of a truly great trap gun. First, it is a combo and uses a common receiver with two sets of barrels. Twin trigger assemblies are part of the set and all are housed in a well designed compartmented hard case.

The newest MX-3 series of trap guns are of a different receiver design than that found on the MX-8 models and should become very popular. Screw-in chokes are available on some versions. The laundry list of Perazzi options is absolutely staggering. The newest Perazzi brochure is a wealth of information and worth having. Perazzi U.S.A. is the importer.

REMINGTON

As might be expected, this old and revered company has a full line-up of shotguns for the target shooter. A pair of pump guns, a semi-auto, and an over-under cover the field.

The Model 870 pump action is made in two versions for trap shooting: the standard 870TA, and the 870 Competition. The TA has a special sear, trigger and hammer assembly designed specifically with the trap shooter in mind to improve lock time and smooth out the trigger pull. A ventilated rib lies along the top of a

MAROCCHI MODEL AMERICA
Gauge: 12
Action: Over-under, boxlock
Barrel(s): 28½″, 29¼″, 30″, with ventilated rib
Choke(s): Full & Imp. Mod.
Weight: 8 lbs.
Stock: Fancy European walnut with checkered pistol grip and fore-end
Trigger: Single selective
Special Features: Blue or silvered, engraved receiver; stock dimension to customer specs.

MOSSBERG MODEL 500 AHT/AHTD
Gauge: 12
Action: Slide-action repeater
Barrel(s): 30″ with Olympic Rib and fixed choke; 28″ with Olympic Rib and Accu-Choke
Choke(s): 30″ Full; 28″ Accu-Choke with three insert tubes, Full, Imp. Mod. and Mod.
Weight: 7¾ lbs.
Stock: Special high-comb trap stock with deep pistol grip
Trigger: Standard single
Special Features: Select grade American walnut with machine-cut checkering. Sliding type, top-tang safety.

PERAZZI MX-8 COMBO
Gauge: 12
Action: Over-under combo
Barrel(s): 34″ single barrel; 32″ over-under
Choke(s): 34″ single — Full; 32″ O/U — Imp. Mod. & Full
Weight: 8 lbs.
Stock: European walnut with choice of straight or Monte Carlo comb designs
Trigger: Non-selective, removable assembly
Special Features: Various stock designs and comb heights; other models based on MX,-series: DB-81, MX-3 series; engraved models available.

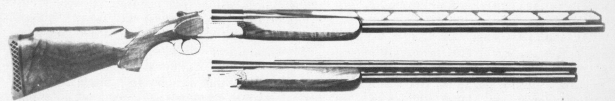

The overwhelming favorite "combo-gun" is the Italian-made Perazzi. The advantage of a single frame, buttstock and trigger "feel" combined with a brace of barrel assemblies — one for singles and handicap shooting and the other for doubles work — is the logical way to go if you can afford the big bucks necessary for this high class outfit.

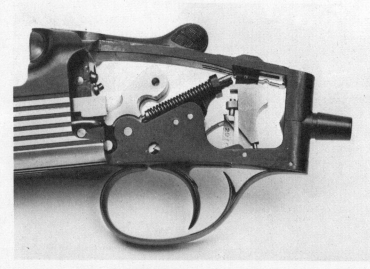

The boiler room of a Perazzi MX-6 is both simplistic in design and finely finished. Often, trap and Skeet shooters shake their heads at the retail prices of shotguns, but after close inspection of the working mechanisms, you can better understand the high price tags these guns carry.

(Right) Perazzi's newest offering, the MX-3 combo. If there were such an award, it should be voted the "Import Gun of the Year." Excellent balance and various stock designs should appeal to many shooters, both veterans and beginners.

30-inch Full-choked barrel in the standard configuration, although other lengths and chokes may be had on special order. Model 870 receivers are machined from solid bars of ordnance steel for maximum strength and durability. Twin action bars eliminate binding and twisting, so that second shots come as fast as a shooter can pump and pull the trigger. A cross-bolt safety is located at the rear of the trigger guard. High-comb stocks for the 870TA are solid American walnut with impressed checkering, and a 1-inch thick, recoil-absorbing butt pad. Weight is about 7¾ lbs.

The Model 870 Competition is a single-shot adaptation of the regular model. Placed inside the magazine tube is a gas-operated recoil reducing mechanism. Felt recoil is lowered to about the same level as the Model 1100 semi-auto, while functioning and reliability of a pump action are retained. Barrel and stock options are the same as for the Model 870TA. The Competition 870 is a mite heavier than the 870TA, tipping the scale at around 8½ lbs.

Remington's Model 1100 has become a veritable legend in the world of shotgunning. More Model 1100s have been made than any other shotgun model. Two versions of the Model 1100 are made for trap shooting, the 1100TA, and 1100 Competition Trap. The Model 1100 is a gas-operated, semi-automatic that self-adjusts to the load being fired. Because of the energy absorbed in the gas action, recoil of the Model 1100 is more of a soft push than a jarring jolt. Model 1100 trap guns are supplied with a broad vent rib and high-combed stock in either straight or Monte Carlo style with trap-style recoil pad. The standard barrel is 30 inches long, choked Full, but optional barrels are available in 28- and 30-inch Modified, plus 28- and 34-inch Full. A left-handed model is made for southpaw shooters. Weight of Rem-

ington Model 1100 trap guns is a tad under 8 lbs. in most configurations.

Remington's Model 3200 Trap is an over-under with separated barrels, topped by a wide ventilated rib. The high-comb stock (choice of straight or Monte Carlo) is of fancy walnut, checkered 20 lines to the inch on pistol grip and fore-end. Barrel options are 30- or 32-inch choked Improved Modified & Full, or 30-inch choked Full & Full. A single selective trigger mechanism, which boasts a super-fast lock time, is one of the Model 3200's outstanding traits. A combination barrel selector and safety is located on the top tang, easily accessible to the shooter's thumb. The Model 3200 is not made as a mono-gun, but some gunsmiths have made single-barrel conversions of the gun. One of the most famous of these was the Simmons "UN-GUN" that had a high, Olympic-type rib in place of the top barrel. A pioneering innovation, Simmons' conversion aroused considerable interest among trap shooters in the early 1970s.

ROTTWEIL

Shotguns from Rottweil, made in West Germany and imported by Dynamit Nobel of America, are the first choice of many leading trapshooters. Rottweil's standard trap gun is the Montreal model. The receiver of this gun is milled from a solid block of special gun steel, insuring rigidity and long life. All action parts are contained within the quickly removable trigger group. Coil springs, used throughout, are guided by telescoping sleeves that keep the springs in line and dirt out. Firing pins are of the rebounding type that retract automatically after firing, so that there is no possibility of their interfering with opening of the gun. They are also identical in dimension and are fully interchangeable. The ejectors are selective and automatic. A sliding safety,

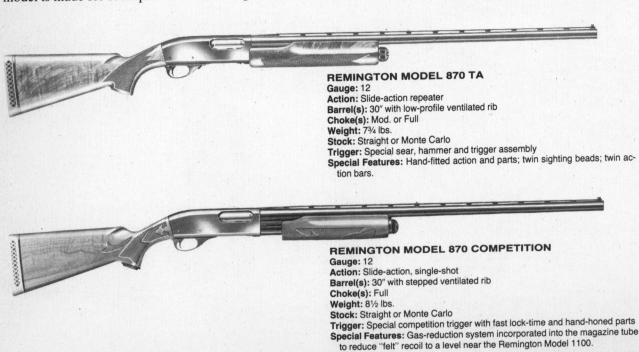

REMINGTON MODEL 870 TA
Gauge: 12
Action: Slide-action repeater
Barrel(s): 30″ with low-profile ventilated rib
Choke(s): Mod. or Full
Weight: 7¾ lbs.
Stock: Straight or Monte Carlo
Trigger: Special sear, hammer and trigger assembly
Special Features: Hand-fitted action and parts; twin sighting beads; twin action bars.

REMINGTON MODEL 870 COMPETITION
Gauge: 12
Action: Slide-action, single-shot
Barrel(s): 30″ with stepped ventilated rib
Choke(s): Full
Weight: 8½ lbs.
Stock: Straight or Monte Carlo
Trigger: Special competition trigger with fast lock-time and hand-honed parts
Special Features: Gas-reduction system incorporated into the magazine tube to reduce "felt" recoil to a level near the Remington Model 1100.

Remington's Model 1100 is a pleasant gun to shoot due to its greatly reduced "felt" recoil, which helps to prevent shooter's fatigue over a 300-target day.

(Left) Remington's Model 870 Competition shotgun is starting to pick up steam on the trap fields. Combining the recoil-reducing feature of the built-in gas-port and piston along with the dependability of a pump-gun action, this single-shot "repeater" is an outstanding gun for its reasonable retail price.

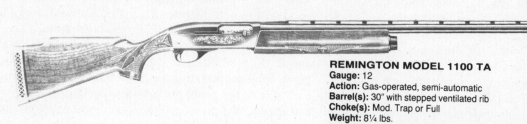

REMINGTON MODEL 1100 TA
Gauge: 12
Action: Gas-operated, semi-automatic
Barrel(s): 30" with stepped ventilated rib
Choke(s): Mod. Trap or Full
Weight: 8¼ lbs.
Stock: Select walnut with straight or Monte Carlo comb
Trigger: Standard single with cross-bolt safety located at rear of trigger guard
Special Features: High-gloss finish, impressed checkering pattern and ventilated recoil pad.

REMINGTON MODEL 3200 COMPETITION TRAP
Gauge: 12
Action: Over-under, boxlock
Barrel(s): 30" and 32" with stepped ventilated rib
Choke(s): 30" Imp. Mod. & Full or Mod. & Full; 32" Mod. & Full
Weight: 8½ lbs.
Stock: Straight or Monte Carlo stock with full pistol grip
Trigger: Single selective
Special Features: Super-fast lock time; hand-cut, 20 lines-per-inch checkering on pistol grip and fore-end; separated barrels; engraved receiver.

In 1970, Simmon's Gun Company made the first commercially-available "Un-Gun." Sawing off the top barrel and replacing it with a high-post ventilated rib converted this Remington Model 3200 into a revolutionary trap gun concept. Within a few months a host of shotgun making firms such as, I.A.B., Beretta, Perazzi, Zoli, K-80, SKB, Winchester, Armsport, and others jumped on the Un-Gun bandwagon and produced their own versions.

positioned on the top tang, deactivates the trigger. Selected fine-grain walnut is used for the high combed stock and fore-end, both of which are hand checkered. The fore-end is a broad beavertail with fluted grooves for better grip. A satin oil wood finish is applied that lends an elegant appearance. Barrels are 30 inches in length and are choked Improved Modified & Full. Cross-hatch machining of the vent rib assures minimum reflection from the top surface. The white plastic front sight is encased in a metal sleeve, while a central metal bead is found midway along the rib. Average weight of the Rottweil Montreal is about 8 lbs., 2 ozs.

Rottweil's Model 72 AAT is designed specifically for American trap shooting. The AAT name stands for Adjustable American Trap, because of the unique point of impact adjustment that is the principal feature of the gun. Infinitely variable changes in point of impact may be made by use of a collar surrounding the barrel at the muzzle. A wedge machined into the top of the collar rides against an opposing wedge on the lower front end of an extremely heavy and rigid top rib. When loosened with a special wrench, the barrel collar may be slid back and forth on the barrel, creating more, or less, pressure against the rib which actually bends the barrel, changing the point of impact. Two single-barrels are available: a 32-inch, choked Improved Modified, and a 34-inch choked Full. Double-barreled units are 32 inches long, choked Improved Modified & Full. Three different fully interchangeable trigger groups are made for the AAT: Regular Pull/Pull, Release/Release, and Release/Pull which should satisfy any trapshooter, regardless of his trigger preference. AAT Monte Carlo stocks are of select French walnut, satin oil finished, with fine hand engraving at the pistol grip and on the fluted beavertail fore-end. A thick, double ventilated recoil pad is fitted. Unfinished stocks and fore-ends are also available for those who wish to create a truly custom fitted gun. Weight of the Rottweil AAT, in both single and double configurations is about 8½ lbs.

SHOTGUNS OF ULM

Distributed in the United States by Dieter Krieghoff of Shotguns of Ulm, the Model K-80 Trap gun is made in the ancient arms making city of Ulm, West Germany. The K-80 is a boxlock with a machined steel frame.

Locking of barrels to frame is by means of a massive top lock plate that slides over the rear of the barrels. Frames are finished in hard satin nickel, but blued models may be had on special order. Single selective triggers are used, the selector button located ahead of the trigger and within the trigger guard. The trigger is adjustable fore and aft to allow a shooter to alter length of pull to suit varying conditions. Standard double barrels are made in both 30 and 32-inch lengths, choked Improved Modified & Full. Single trap barrels may be ordered as conventional top units or as an Unsingle with a sturdy high-post rib in place of the top barrel.

Single barrels are made in 32 or 34-inch lengths, and are Full choked. Bottom barrels of the double units are free floating, being solidly joined only at the breech end. A ring spacer is fitted between barrels at the muzzle. Spacers of six different thicknesses are provided to allow easy changing of the point of impact spread between the two barrels. Point of impact may be altered on the Unsingle barrel also by means of a screw adjustment located at the muzzle between the barrel and the rib. A wide adjustment is afforded, ranging from 7 inches low to 35 inches high at 40 yards. The locking screws for adjustment of the Unsingle are easily loosened with a coin. Stocks are either straight trap or Monte Carlo of select grade European walnut. Fore-ends are offered in several shapes to suit individual taste and needs, and both fore-end and pistol grip are meticulously hand checkered. A palm swell is incorporated on each side of the pistol grip to accommodate both right and left-handed shooters. Stocks are fitted with a Pachmayr Pigeon recoil pad. Interestingly, stocks may be detached from the K-80 without removing the butt plate by using a special long screwdriver supplied with the gun. The K-80, fitted with 30-inch tubes weighs about 8½ lbs. For the complete trapshooter, Shotguns of Ulm offers a trap combo, consisting of the K-80 over-under with 30 or 32-inch barrels, together with a conventional single or Unsingle barrel in 32 or 34-inch length, delivered in a handsome fitted case. Since there are so many small variations from standard that may be built into a K-80, it is impossible to list them all. An inquiry directed to the importer should provide an answer to any questions one might have concerning optional equipment or alterations.

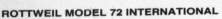

ROTTWEIL MODEL 72 INTERNATIONAL
Gauge: 12
Action: Over-under, boxlock
Barrel(s): 30" with low-profile ventilated rib
Choke(s): Imp. Mod. & Full
Weight: 7½ lbs.
Stock: Straight comb, select European Walnut
Trigger: Removable trigger group, single selective, inertia operated
Special Features: Ventilated recoil pad; oversize fore-end with hand-cut checkering on fore-end and pistol grip.

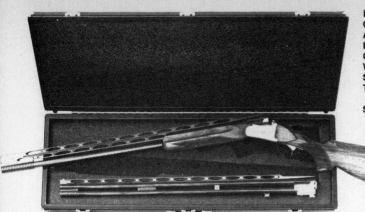

ROTTWEIL AAT
Gauge: 12
Action: Over-under, boxlock, combo
Barrel(s): 32″ and 34″ single barrel; 32″ over-under
Choke(s): 32″ single — Imp. Mod.; 34″ single — Full
Weight: 8 lbs.
Stock: Selected French walnut with Monte Carlo comb and oil finish
Trigger: Removable assembly with choice of pull/pull, release/pull or release/release
Special Features: Special point-of-impact adjustment wedge on single barrel from 5″ low to 34″ high from line of sight.

SHOTGUNS OF ULM MODEL K-80
Gauge: 12
Action: Over-under combo, boxlock
Barrel(s): 32″ and 34″ single barrel (under barrel); 30″ and 32″ over-under
Choke(s): 32″ and 34″ single — Full; 30″ and 32″ O/U — Imp. Mod. & Full
Weight: 8 lbs.
Stock: European walnut with Monte Carlo comb and Wundhammer-swell pistol grip
Trigger: Single selective, adjustable for fore and aft positioning
Special Features: Dial adjustable rib to change point of impact; quick-detachable buttstock; satin nickel receiver; oil-finished stock and fore-end.

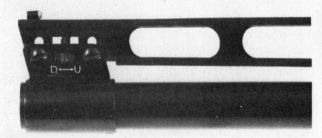

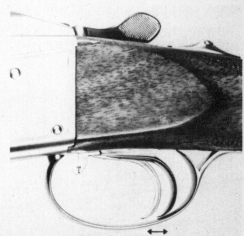

The key to the K-80's versatility is the adjustable rib design. By loosening the twin locking screws, the front of the rib can be raised or lowered by rotating the adjustment wheel which in turn, will influence the point of impact nearly 40 inches, measured vertically at 40 yards.

(Above right) Shotguns of Ulm's Model K-80 is a modern-day Remington Model 32 with a blending of classic styling and modern-day features. The K-80 is one of a handful of today's "best" trap gun combos.

The trigger blade on the K-80 is adjustable for fore and aft movement which enables the shooter to slide the trigger blade to the exact comfortable location in contact with the trigger finger.

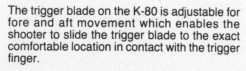

SMITH & WESSON

A new line of target shotguns, based on their Model 1000 autoloader, is now being offered by Smith & Wesson. The Model 1000 Trap has a scroll engraved steel receiver, providing maximum strength and durability to withstand the rigors of the trap fields. A 30-inch barrel with Multi-choke interchangeable tubes supplied in Full, Improved Modified and Modified variations, is standard. A stepped, medium-width rib tops the barrel, with a Bradley front and white mid-point bead. The stock is a Monte Carlo, combined with a broad, hand-filling fore-end. Both stock and fore-end, of American walnut, are extensively hand checkered. The trigger of the Model 1000 has been hand tuned to meet the special requirements of trap shooting. A minor feature, but a convenient one, is a built-in wire shell catcher that holds empties when shooting singles, yet may be quickly removed for doubles. A cross-bolt safety is provided that is usable by either right- or left-handed shooters. The Model 1000 is a nicely finished and efficient trap gun at a surprisingly affordable price.

VALMET

Built in Finland, Valmet shotguns are distributed in the United States by Valmet Sporting Arms. Their trap gun, known as Model 412KE Trap, is based on a time proven all-steel frame with double locking lugs for barrel attachment. The 30-inch over-under barrels are topped by a wide rib with a centerline groove, and are choked Improved Modified & Full. Chrome alloy steel is used in forging barrels by the cold hammering process. A single selective trigger is used, with a barrel selector button built into the upper part of the mechanical trigger mechanism. This allows the second barrel to fire even if the first chamber is empty. Indicator buttons located to the rear of the top-mounted tang safety give both visual and tactile evidence as to which barrel has been fired. Two-piece firing pins are an exclusive Valmet feature that greatly reduce chances of breakage. The safety is automatic, being set by opening the action. Ejectors are automatic, giving smooth, positive extraction. All external metal is finished in a high gloss deep blue. Overall weight of the 412KE Trap is about 8 lbs. Valmet's Model 412KE is a well made, sturdy trap gun with many exclusive features at a modest price.

WEATHERBY

Four trap guns bear the Weatherby name, a pump, an auto-loader, and two over-unders. Weatherby guns have a long established reputation for fine fit and finish, as well as outstanding performance. Their trap guns are no exception, being both handsome and functional.

Gas operation was chosen to power the Model 82 automatic because of the superior realiability of a gas system. A unique Weatherby floating gas piston eliminates alignment problems often associated with gas actions. A trigger disconnect system is incorporated that prevents accidental firing of a shell unless the bolt is fully closed and locked. Two barrel options are offered: a fixed-choke 30-inch (choked Full) and a 30-inch Multi-Choke barrel. Modified and Full insert tubes are supplied with the Multi-Choke barrel.

Weatherby's Model 92 is a short-stroke pump action that operates on precision double rails to eliminate twisting and binding. Barrel options are the same as for the Model 82 automatic. Barrels on both models have ventilated ribs fitted with front and mid-rib bead sights. Both models have high comb trap stocks of Claro walnut, fine line hand checking, and are finished in a high gloss. Rosewood pistol grip caps are an added touch to an already handsome appearance. Receivers are etched in a scroll pattern, and all metal surfaces are deeply blued.

Weatherby's Orion over-under is offered with 30-inch barrels choked Full & Modified or Full & Improved Modified, or 32-inch tubes choked Full & Improved Modified. The hand fitted monobloc and receiver are machined from high strength steel and finely polished for smooth functioning. The strong boxlock design uses a modified Kersten-type cross-bolt locking system, and special sears maintain hammer engagement to prevent doubling and avoid accidental discharge. Selective automatic ejectors kick out only fired shells, and simply raise unfired shells for easy extraction. The safety is a slide-type located conveniently on the upper tang. A single selective trigger allows instant barrel choice for the first shot by pressing the marked selector button found on the trigger body. A mechanical switch-over automatically allows the second barrel to be fired in the vent of a misfire, since recoil is not required to set the trigger. An adjustment may be made, however, that

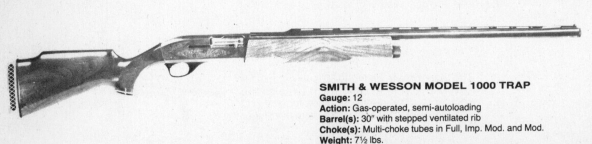

SMITH & WESSON MODEL 1000 TRAP
Gauge: 12
Action: Gas-operated, semi-autoloading
Barrel(s): 30" with stepped ventilated rib
Choke(s): Multi-choke tubes in Full, Imp. Mod. and Mod.
Weight: 7½ lbs.
Stock: American walnut with Monte Carlo comb
Trigger: Specially tuned
Special Features: Built-in shell catcher; ventilated recoil pad; hand-cut checkering and extended fore-end.

VALMET MODEL 412KE
Gauge: 12
Action: Over-under, boxlock
Barrel(s): 30″ with low-profile ventilated rib
Choke(s): Imp. Mod. & Full
Weight: 7¾ lbs.
Stock: French walnut with Monte Carlo comb and full pistol grip
Trigger: Single selective, mechanically operated
Special Features: Automatic selective ejectors; top tang-mounted sliding safety and sliding breech cover.

Valmet is making inroads in both trap and Skeet shooting. Many newer shooters are buying the Model 412KE for its quality and proven features at a price well below their competition.

WEATHERBY ORION
Gauge: 12
Action: Over-under boxlock with Kersten-type cross-bolt
Barrel(s): 28″, 30″ ventilated rib
Choke(s): Full & Mod.
Weight: 7½ lbs.
Stock: American walnut with checkered pistol grip and fore-end
Trigger: Single selective, mechanical or inertial
Special Features: Selective automatic ejectors; top tang safety; barrel selector in trigger.

WEATHERBY ATHENA
Gauge: 12
Action: Over-under boxlock with Kersten-type cross-bolt
Barrel(s): 28″, ventilated top and middle ribs
Choke(s): Full & Mod.
Weight: 7⅜ lbs. (12 ga.)
Stock: American walnut with hand checkered pistol grip and fore-end
Trigger: Single selective, mechanical or inertial
Special Features: Fully engraved, silvered action with false sideplates; selective automatic ejectors; barrel selector on trigger.

WEATHERBY MODEL EIGHTY-TWO AUTO
Gauge: 12
Action: Gas-operated autoloader
Barrel(s): 28″, 30″ ventilated rib
Choke(s): Fixed Full, Mod., Full Trap or Multi-choke tubes
Weight: 7½ lbs.
Stock: Walnut with hand checkered pistol grip and fore-end
Trigger: Standard, with cross-bolt safety in the rear of the trigger guard
Special Features: Engraved receiver; gold trigger; fluted bolt

will permit recoil induced switchover if desired. The Orion's stock and fore-end are of Claro walnut, hand checkered, and with a thick recoil pad and rosewood pistol grip cap. Orion owners have a choice of a high-combed straight stock or a Monte Carlo. All external metal is deeply blued. A wide ventilated rib with both front and center bead sights provides a perfect sighting plane. The ribs between barrels are also ventilated for extra cooling. The Orion weighs in at about 8 lbs.

Weatherby's Athena is essentially the same as the Orion, but with a few extra touches for the sake of beauty rather than utility. Specially selected, highly figured Claro walnut is used for the stock and fore-end. Sideplates are appended to the frame to provide more graceful lines, and both frame and plates are engraved in a graceful scroll pattern. Receiver, sideplates, trigger guard and locking lever are bright coin-finished; the barrels are blued. A gold trigger completes the panoply of color. Both the Orion and Athena are made by SKB especially for Weatherby. This highly respected firm pulled out of the American shotgun market a few years ago, but now it is back under the Weatherby banner.

WINCHESTER

The Winchester Group of the Olin Corp. presents a variety of trap guns based on their Model 101 shotgun. The Diamond Grade over-under is available with 30- or 32-inch barrels, choked Full or with Winchoke inserts as desired. Stocks are of high grade walnut with either straight trap or Monte Carlo design. A single barrel version is 34 inches long with four Winchoke tubes supplied in Extra Full, Full, Improved Modified or Modified constrictions. The single utilizes the lower barrel position, with a high vent rib occupying the top spot. A combo set is also offered, with one set of double barrels plus a single in lengths of the buyer's choice. Frames are deeply engraved in a diamond pattern. A vent rib is fitted to the double set with front and middle white sight beads. The ribs joining the barrels are also vented. The frame is gray steel, the barrels are blue.

Winchester's Model 501 Grand European is the finest of the line. Available in over-under configuration only, it is more lavishly engraved than the Diamond Grade, and has fancier wood. Barrels are either 30- or 32-inch, choked Improved Modified & Full. The average weight of Winchester trap guns is between 8¾ and 9 lbs.

That concludes the line up of trap guns available today. There may be a few we've missed due to publication deadlines, and to those manufacturers, we offer our apologies. We couldn't include suggested retail prices due to the constant fluctuation, but all the aforementioned manufacturers and importers will be pleased to send you complete literature and current list prices for all their products.

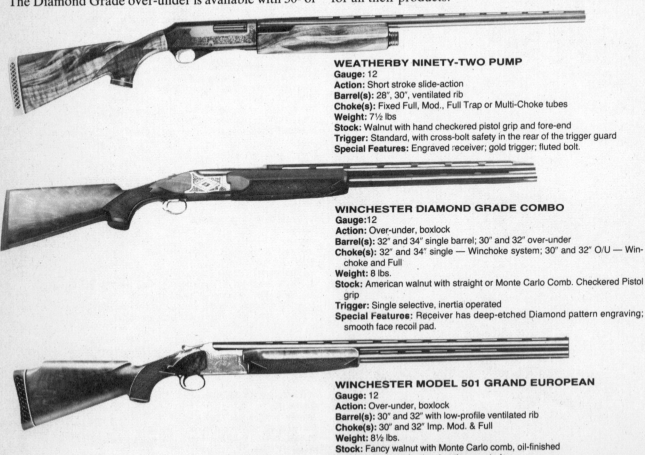

WEATHERBY NINETY-TWO PUMP
Gauge: 12
Action: Short stroke slide-action
Barrel(s): 28″, 30″, ventilated rib
Choke(s): Fixed Full, Mod., Full Trap or Multi-Choke tubes
Weight: 7½ lbs
Stock: Walnut with hand checkered pistol grip and fore-end
Trigger: Standard, with cross-bolt safety in the rear of the trigger guard
Special Features: Engraved receiver; gold trigger; fluted bolt.

WINCHESTER DIAMOND GRADE COMBO
Gauge: 12
Action: Over-under, boxlock
Barrel(s): 32″ and 34″ single barrel; 30″ and 32″ over-under
Choke(s): 32″ and 34″ single — Winchoke system; 30″ and 32″ O/U — Winchoke and Full
Weight: 8 lbs.
Stock: American walnut with straight or Monte Carlo Comb. Checkered Pistol grip
Trigger: Single selective, inertia operated
Special Features: Receiver has deep-etched Diamond pattern engraving; smooth face recoil pad.

WINCHESTER MODEL 501 GRAND EUROPEAN
Gauge: 12
Action: Over-under, boxlock
Barrel(s): 30″ and 32″ with low-profile ventilated rib
Choke(s): 30″ and 32″ Imp. Mod. & Full
Weight: 8½ lbs.
Stock: Fancy walnut with Monte Carlo comb, oil-finished
Trigger: Single selective, inertia operated
Special Features: Coin-finished and engraved receiver; engine turned breech; fine-line cut checkering.

What is a Skeet gun? Is it different from a field grade shotgun? In actual performance, probably not. Due to the nature of the game, Skeet guns have stock dimensions virtually identical to field guns. Then what are the special ingredients that separate a Skeet gun from a field gun? This can basically be summed up in two words—dependability and price.

For a manufacturer to assure long-term dependability, he must take extra measures to guarantee that his product will withstand the vigorous use of shooting competitive Skeet. Skeet guns are not subjected to the heat build up problem incurred by trap guns, yet they do digest the same number of rounds fired year after year. Because there is more time between shots, Skeet guns are less susceptible to heat-related problems than their trap gun counterparts.

A newcomer to the game of Skeet can start nicely with any field grade shotgun equipped with an open-choked barrel—Cylinder bore, Improved Cylinder or Skeet. If the novice already owns a shotgun—pump or autoloader—and optional barrels are available, he would be wise to buy one of those three chokes mentioned to be fairly well equipped to begin learning how to shoot the game. Then if the "bug" bites him, as it has done to thousands of field shooters, he can then go ahead and choose a pure "Skeet" gun to satisfy his wants and wallet.

ARMSPORT

The "Armsport-Zoli" Model Premier Competition Skeet Gun is made to meet the demand for a rugged, strong and reliable shotgun at an affordable price. Its exceptional balance, sighting plane, and ease of pointing give this Italian over-under all the performance necessary for the rigid requirements of Skeet shooting. A nicely grained European walnut stock with palm swell pistol grip is combined with an attractively engraved action to make this a gun to own and shoot with pride. Model 4055 has 26-inch barrels, and the Model 4056 sports 28-inch tubes. A broad ventilated rib is fitted, with front and mid-rib bead sights. The Armsport Premier Skeet Gun is made in 12 gauge only, and is imported by Armsport.

ASTRA

Astra's Model 750 over-under Skeet gun is imported from Spain by L. Joseph Rahn, Inc. Barrels are 28 inches long, choked Skeet & Skeet, and the stock is European walnut with checkered pistol grip and fore-end. The receiver is scroll engraved, and all metal is a deep lustrous blue. A single selective trigger and automatic ejectors are standard, although extractors only may be specified if desired. In 12 gauge only, the Model 750 Skeet weighs in at about 6½ lbs.

BENELLI

Although not specifically designed as a Skeet gun, the Model SL 121V with a 26-inch barrel and choked Improved Cylinder does a pretty fair job of powdering clay birds. Excellent balance, combined with exceptionally short feed time makes the Benelli a good gun for the game, especially when shooting doubles. The gun's inertia unlocking system greatly reduces felt recoil. All-up weight of the Model SL 121V is a shade under 7 lbs. The Benelli might be an excellent choice for the occasional Skeet shooter who has need of a fine field gun as

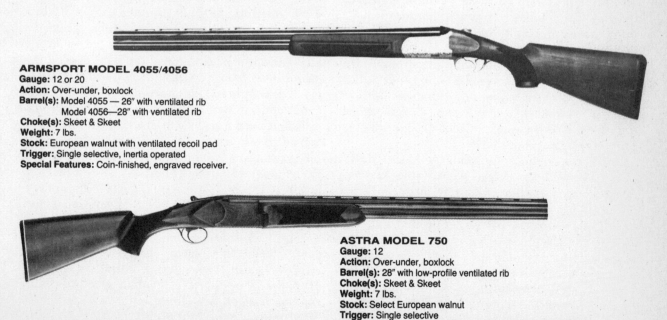

ARMSPORT MODEL 4055/4056
Gauge: 12 or 20
Action: Over-under, boxlock
Barrel(s): Model 4055 — 26" with ventilated rib
Model 4056—28" with ventilated rib
Choke(s): Skeet & Skeet
Weight: 7 lbs.
Stock: European walnut with ventilated recoil pad
Trigger: Single selective, inertia operated
Special Features: Coin-finished, engraved receiver.

ASTRA MODEL 750
Gauge: 12
Action: Over-under, boxlock
Barrel(s): 28" with low-profile ventilated rib
Choke(s): Skeet & Skeet
Weight: 7 lbs.
Stock: Select European walnut
Trigger: Single selective
Special Features: Scroll-engraved receiver, automatic ejectors.

well. An interchangeable barrel with a tighter choke makes the gun a winner against both clay birds and wildfowl.

Benelli's true Skeet gun, the Model Special 80 Skeet is made in 12 gauge only, and has a white (natural alloy) engraved lower receiver, plus a vent rib and finely tuned trigger. Wood is select European walnut with hand checkering on pistol grip and fore-end, and rubber butt pad. The 28-inch barrel is choked especially for Skeet. A plain version, *sans* engraving, may be had on request. Benelli shotguns are imported by Heckler & Koch.

BERETTA

As the world's oldest established firearms manufacturer, Beretta has an enduring reputation for fine craftsmanship. Nowhere is this more evident than in their Skeet guns. An autoloader and two over-unders comprise their product line for Skeet shooters.

The Beretta Model A302 Competition Skeet, made in both 12 and 20 gauge, is a gas-action autoloader with excellent balance, "swing" and pointability. Barrels have a high ventilated rib with fluorescent front and mid-rib sights. Either a 26-inch barrel choked Skeet, or a 28-incher with interchangeable Multichoke tubes is offered. The receiver is forged high-strength alloy engraved with simple floral motifs. The stock is of select walnut, with hand checkering on pistol grip and fore-end. The stock has Beretta's unique adjustable stock drop system that is controlled by an eccentric washer under the head of the stock bolt. All external metal is deeply blued, and a gold trigger adds a decorative touch to this handsome gun.

For the Skeet fields of America or the International circuit, there is a delicate balance in the Model 680 over-under Competition Skeet gun that makes it swing and track targets with astonishing ease. It is perfectly suited for Skeet tubes, allowing a shooter to change gauges quickly and easily. Stock and fore-end are hand checkered premium grade walnut; the receiver is all steel, forged and hardened for lasting strength, with light hand engraving. The action is a low profile boxlock with single selective trigger and automatic ejectors. Barrels may be either 26 or 28 inches in length, choked Skeet & Skeet with a wide ventilated rib. Weight of the Model 680 Skeet is about 7½ lbs.

Beretta's premium Skeet gun is the Model SO-4, a back-action sidelock with readily removable sideplates. The receiver is an all-steel forging, beautifully machined and polished, with extensive engraving on both receiver and sideplates. Barrels are furnished in either 26- or 28-inch lengths, and choked Skeet & Skeet. Barrel tube inserts may be used, of course, to change gauges. Single selective trigger, automatic ejectors and manual safety are standard. The stock and fore-end are of presentation grade walnut, with fine-line hand checkering on pistol grip and fore-end, which is a wide, fluted

beavertail-type. The Model SO-4 Skeet weighs a bit under 8 lbs. There are many more fine details that make this a truly outstanding shotgun, one of which is the beautiful fitted case in which the gun is delivered.

BROWNING

The senior citizen of Browning's lineup of Skeet guns is the doughty Auto-5. This recoil-operated autoloader, invented by the legendary John M. Browning, has been in production far longer than any other current design. Over two million Auto-5s are in the hands of sportsmen all over the world. Primarily a field gun, there is also a Skeet version that still holds its own in competition. With either a 26- or 28-inch barrel, choked for Skeet, the gun is a reliable clay bird buster. One of the keys to the Auto-5's success on the Skeet field is its long sighting plane. Beginning at the squared-off rear of the receiver and continuing along a low vent rib, the shooter's eye follows naturally to the target. Recoil is minimized in the gun since much of the force is taken up in moving a rather large mass to the rear during the operating cycle. Appearance of the Auto-5 is enhanced by tasteful hand engraving on the receiver, plus a highly polished and deeply blued finish on all external metal parts. A most desirable feature of the Auto-5 is that the breech remains open after the last shot is fired, making reloading quick and easy. More "modern" Skeet guns may come along, but the old Auto-5 seems destined to go on forever.

The B-80 is a gas operated shotgun built with the old fashioned Browning attention to detail. In appearance, the B-80 bears a family resemblance to the Auto-5 with its squared-off receiver. The rear of the B-80 is not perfectly square, but it does have a contour that attracts the shooter's eye and speeds up the sighting process. With a rib fitted atop a 26-inch Skeet barrel, lining up on a flying clay bird is fast and sure. Recoil of the B-80 is much softer than might be expected because of the energy absorbed in operating the gas action system. Trigger action is crisp and positive. A cross-bolt safety is immediately at hand, located in the front of the trigger guard. B-80 wood is of select walnut, with cut checkering on pistol grip and the underside of the fore-end. The gun is made in both 12 and 20 gauge. The receiver is cold forged and machined from high grade steel, or aluminum alloy in the case of the Superlight version. Barrels are drilled and bored from Nickel-Chromium-Molybdenum steel bars and internally chrome plated for long life. The B-80 weighs a bit under 7 lbs. in the 12-gauge Superlight, and about 8 lbs. in the standard model.

The Citori over-under is Browning's premier Skeet gun. Available in all gauges, 12, 20, 28 and .410 bore, the Citori meets the needs of all Skeet shooters. Both 26- and 28-inch barrels, choked Skeet & Skeet, are available in all gauges. Overall weights vary from 6 lbs., 9 ozs., in the 26-inch .410 to 8 lbs., 2 ozs. in the 28-inch

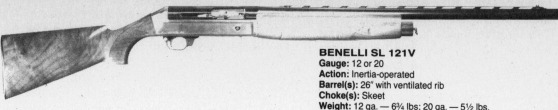

BENELLI SL 121V
Gauge: 12 or 20
Action: Inertia-operated
Barrel(s): 26″ with ventilated rib
Choke(s): Skeet
Weight: 12 ga. — 6¾ lbs; 20 ga. — 5½ lbs.
Stock: European walnut with hand-checkered pistol grip and fore-end
Trigger: Standard
Special Features: Quick interchangeable barrels; cross-bolt safety; engraved versions available.

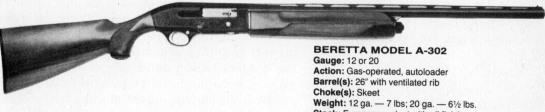

BERETTA MODEL A-302
Gauge: 12 or 20
Action: Gas-operated, autoloader
Barrel(s): 26″ with ventilated rib
Choke(s): Skeet
Weight: 12 ga. — 7 lbs; 20 ga. — 6½ lbs.
Stock: European walnut with oil finish
Trigger: Standard single
Special Features: Alloy receiver with scroll engraving; magazine cutoff; cross-bolt safety.

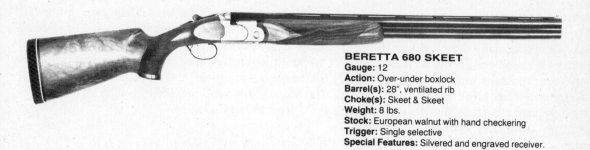

BERETTA 680 SKEET
Gauge: 12
Action: Over-under boxlock
Barrel(s): 28″, ventilated rib
Choke(s): Skeet & Skeet
Weight: 8 lbs.
Stock: European walnut with hand checkering
Trigger: Single selective
Special Features: Silvered and engraved receiver.

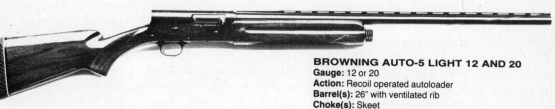

BROWNING AUTO-5 LIGHT 12 AND 20
Gauge: 12 or 20
Action: Recoil operated autoloader
Barrel(s): 26″ with ventilated rib
Choke(s): Skeet
Weight: 12 ga. — 7¼ lbs.; 20 ga. — 6⅜ lbs.
Stock: American walnut with epoxy finish
Trigger: Standard single
Special Features: Receiver hand engraved with scroll designs and border; double extractors; cross-bolt safety; magazine cut-off.

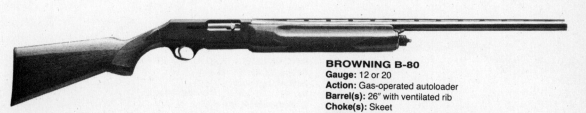

BROWNING B-80
Gauge: 12 or 20
Action: Gas-operated autoloader
Barrel(s): 26″ with ventilated rib
Choke(s): Skeet
Weight: 6½ lbs.
Stock: American walnut with high-gloss finish
Trigger: Standard single, gold plated
Special Features: Non-reflective, matte finished, ventilated rib; steel receiver; cross-bolt safety.

12 gauge. A high post target rib is standard on all barrels. Skeet Citoris have all-steel receivers, single selective triggers, and automatic ejectors. A sliding safety is located on the top tang, conveniently positioned for quick and easy operation. At least four grades of finish are offered, with other details available on request. Each Citori is delivered in a fitted luggage case.

For more affluent Skeet shooters, Browning offers the Superposed series of over-unders. The Superposed is available in all gauges and a wide variety of finishes. This is truly a custom gun, with more options than can possibly be listed here. Anyone interested in this superb shotgun should contact Browning for complete information. Prices are high, running from about $5,000 to over $18,000 for complete sets, but the quality is outstanding.

CAPRINUS

Caprinus Sweden guns use nothing but stainless steel for all working parts, and only the barrels are the conventional ordnance steel. The Caprinus action opens around a circular receiver segment rather than the usual bolt. The hinge serves both as a bolt and a recoil-absorbing surface. Using this system allows the Caprinus to have an exceptionally thin breech, measuring only 2.2 inches from top to bottom, less than any other over-under, and even less than many side-by-sides. The Caprinus hinge places the center of gravity a bit lower than usual, giving better balance and recoil absorption. Choke tube inserts are fitted to all barrels, allowing the shooter to not only change patterns, but also to alter the point of impact up, down, left, or right. A crisp single selective trigger is fitted, with a barrel selector located inside the trigger guard and just ahead of the trigger. Skeet barrels are 28 inches long, and have a wide, low vent rib. A rubber recoil pad accompanies a fancy figured European walnut stock, which may be either straight or Monte Carlo. An automatic safety is located on the top tang for maximum convenience. Firing pins are set by the top opening lever. The Caprinus is a rugged, beautiful shotgun, made to assure long life. It upholds the fine attention to detail that we have come to expect from Swedish craftsmen. Balance and feel are superb, with its overall weight of 7½ lbs. perfectly distributed. Imported by Caprinus U.S.A.

ITHACA

Ithaca's Model 37 Supreme pump action shotgun is a versatile, lightweight gun that has performed well on Skeet fields for nearly a half-century. Weighing only 6½ lbs., the Model 37 Supreme Skeet is supplied with a vent-ribbed, 26-inch barrel choked Improved Cylinder. Pump action is quick and virtually effortless, thanks to an action system that eliminates binding during operation. The stock is select, figured walnut, with checkering on pistol grip and fore-end. Ejection is from the bottom, allowing easy recovery of empty shells. Trigger action is crisp and clean, making the Model 37 a fast shooting, easy handling gun that should satisfy most claybirders who are addicted to pump-action shotguns.

The Model 51A Supreme Skeet autoloader, available in either 12 or 20 gauge, is often seen on Skeet fields. The Model 51A is a simple, dependable gas-action semi-automatic that has fewer parts than most other autoloaders. Field stripping for cleaning can be accomplished in less than half a minute without the use of tools. Model 51A receivers are precision machined from solid forged steel bars. The bolt is chrome plated, the action link is stainless steel, and action bars are shot peened to assure long and trouble-free life. Trigger pull is crisp and consistent. The Model 51A's vent rib barrel is 26 inches long, choked Skeet. The stock is of selected nicely figured wood with hand checkering on the pistol grip and fore-end. A Skeet recoil pad is fitted. Special finishes and dimensions may be had on special order. The Model 51A Supreme Skeet weighs about 7½ lbs. From Ithaca Gun Co.

K.F.C.

The K.F.C. M-250 autoloader has an exceedingly simple operating system that reduces the gun's total number of parts to only 79. There is no direct connection between the gas cylinder and the breech bolt. Initial unlocking is accomplished by the impinging of an action rod, driven by expanding gas, against the locking mechanism on the head of the bolt. Residual gas pressure in the chamber, plus inertia imparted by the gas-powered action rod, drives the bolt to the rear. A spring located in the buttstock returns the bolt to battery. Extraction, ejection, cocking and reloading are accomplished during this cycle. Standard barrel length for the

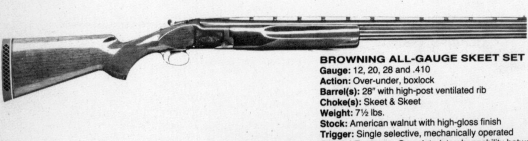

BROWNING ALL-GAUGE SKEET SET
Gauge: 12, 20, 28 and .410
Action: Over-under, boxlock
Barrel(s): 28″ with high-post ventilated rib
Choke(s): Skeet & Skeet
Weight: 7½ lbs.
Stock: American walnut with high-gloss finish
Trigger: Single selective, mechanically operated
Special Features: Complete interchangability between all four barrels. Fitted Skeet-type recoil pad; deluxe fitted case.

The flat, wide-bottomed, fore-end helps the Skeet shooter to hold the Citori in a proper shooting position and prevents "canting" the gun.

(Left) Like any quality Skeet gun, the Citori's ejectors are regulated and empty hulls hit the ground "side-by-each," the mark of a finely-tuned shotgun.

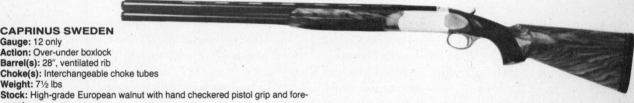

CAPRINUS SWEDEN
Gauge: 12 only
Action: Over-under boxlock
Barrel(s): 28", ventilated rib
Choke(s): Interchangeable choke tubes
Weight: 7½ lbs
Stock: High-grade European walnut with hand checkered pistol grip and fore-end
Trigger: Single selective
Special Features: Stainless steel action and parts; barrel selector in front of the trigger; gas pressure activated automatic ejectors.

ITHACA MODEL 51A SUPREME
Gauge: 12 or 20
Action: Gas-operated autoloader
Barrel(s): 26" with ventilated rib
Choke(s): Skeet
Weight: 12 ga. — 7½ lbs.; 20 ga. — 7¼ lbs.
Stock: Fancy American walnut with hand-checkered pistol grip and fore-end
Trigger: Specially tuned for competition
Special Features: Hand fitted and engraved receiver; reversible safety; Ray-bar front sight.

K.F.C. MODEL 250 AUTO
Gauge: 12
Action: Gas-operated autoloader
Barrel(s): 24½", 26"
Choke(s): Fixed in standard constrictions or interchangeable choke tubes
Weight: 7½ lbs.
Stock: American walnut with hand-checkered pistol grip and fore-end
Trigger: Standard with reversible cross-bolt safety at rear of trigger guard
Special Features: Gun has only 79 parts. Ventilated rib barrel, alloy receiver

Skeet model is 26 inches, although a 24½-inch barrel is used when interchangeable choke tubes are supplied. Weight of the M-250 is about 7½ lbs.

K.F.C. also makes an over-under specifically designed for Skeet, known as the Model OT-Skeet E-1. In 12 gauge only, it has either 26- or 28-inch barrels choked Skeet & Skeet, with a 13mm vent rib fitted with bone white front and metal bead sights. Bores are hard chrome lined for smoothness and long life. Receivers are of solid steel, and are lightly scroll engraved. The wood is high grade French walnut with hand checkering on pistol grip and fore-end. A single selective trigger and automatic ejectors are standard. The safety is top tang mounted and is of the non-automatic type. A fancier version, the E-3, has super deluxe wood and more extensive engraving. K. F. C. (Kawaguchiya Firearms Company) shotguns are imported from Japan by La Paloma Marketing, Inc.

LANBER

Lanber shotguns are made in Spain and imported by Lanber Arms of America. The Skeet guns, known as the Model LCH EST: Rival II, or more simply catalog number 2.008, are over-unders with 28-inch barrels in 12 gauge only. Interchangeable choke tubes (Lanberchoke) are supplied in Full, Improved Modified, Modified, Improved Cylinder and Cylinder. Ventilated ribbed barrels are separated to allow better cooling. The competition-grade Lanbers are equipped with single selective triggers and automatic ejectors. Stocks are of fine grained walnut, checkered on pistol grip and fore-end with serrated finger grooves on the wide fore-end. Lanber receivers are lightly engraved in a simple, tasteful pattern. Weight is about 7½ lbs. The Skeet guns are sturdy, well-made, and handsome guns that any shooter would be proud to own.

LJUTIC

Known as an innovator in shotgun design, Ljutic makes two guns specifically for Skeet shooting. The Bi-Matic is a two-shot autoloader with a high vent rib that extends backward almost to the rear of the receiver. Recoil is minimized by the design of the gas action system. These are custom-made guns with many options available to the purchaser. Barrel lengths, chokes and stock dimensions are manufactured to order. The gun is made in 12 gauge only, and weight is variable from under 8 to about 10 lbs.

Ljutic's Bi-Gun Skeet is an over-under with separated barrels, milled vent rib and a host of options. Their patented "Paternator" chokes are made integral with the barrel. Sets are offered with matched barrels in 12, 20, 28 and .410 gauges. The Bi-Gun has a unique opening button located just ahead of the trigger guard. As with the Bi-Matic, the Bi-Gun is strictly custom made. Buyers may choose from a long list of options that satisfy the most discriminating shooter.

MAROCCHI

The Marocchi is a high-ribbed over-under that boasts a wide selection of options to make it almost a custom gun. Barrel lengths from 26 to 29 inches are supplied and topped with a wide and high vent rib. Ventilation is also provided between the barrels. Stocks are hand checkered select walnut with a choice of either a beavertail or Schnabel fore-end. Receivers are all steel, lightly engraved, although more extensive engraving is available on order. Two models are offered, the America and the Contrast. Both models are similar, with the Contrast being the least expensive of the two. These fine shotguns are imported from Italy by Marocchi USA.

PERAZZI

The Perazzi lineup of shotguns has been primarily aimed toward the trap shooter, but in the past few years, these magnificent shotguns have slowly, but surely, infiltrated the American Skeet fields. The MS-80, along with the MT-6 are both Skeet guns built to satisfy the most demanding needs of competition shooters. The MS-80 is available only in 12 bore and is a cut above the MT-6 in finish and wood selection. It also has a longer list of options.

A few of the more important features found on both of the aforementioned models are: a non-detachable trigger assembly with coil springs; a single selective trigger which is inertia operated; the action-opening top lever has a positive opening stop; easily removable stock; and the fore-end has built-in adjustment for wood-to-metal and metal-to-metal play. The last feature is worth some elaboration and exemplifies this great gunmaking firm's foresight. All of the new Perazzi shotguns are equipped with a means to compensate and adjust for wear in the critical area between the fore-end iron and the fore-end. As a result of the shock of firing tens of thousands of shells, the fore-end wood separates from the iron, which can seriously distract the shooter and cause annoyance due to the loosened grip.

This aggravation has been eliminated by fitting two rods through the back of the fore-end iron, which screw into the locking bolts inside the fore-end. At the first sign of any looseness between the fore-end and fore-end iron, any gap can be taken up by tightening these screws. To further prevent any loosening problems, a special flat spring, which rests against the catch bolt in the fore-end iron, takes up any metal-to-metal play which might develop.

The newest Model MX-3 over-under is being hawked as Perazzi's workhorse paragon and is available in various grades and finishes, yet it's confined to 12 gauge only and 27⅝-inch barrels. A specially-designed four-barrel set (12, 20, 28 and .410 bore) is now available. I have seen this magnificent ensemble and if you can afford the relatively steep price tag, it's worth a closer look. It's pure unadulterated quality!

LANBER MODEL 2008
Gauge: 12
Action: Over-under, boxlock
Barrel(s): 28″ with ventilated rib
Choke(s): Skeet & Skeet or LanberChoke
Weight: 7¼ lbs.
Stock: European walnut with oil finish
Trigger: Single selective, inertia operated
Special Features: Screw-in LanberChoke system; wide ventilated rib; hand-cut checkering on pistol grip and fluted fore-end: top-tang sliding safety.

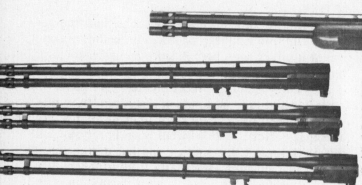

LJUTIC BI-GUN SKEET SET
Gauge: 12, 20, 28 and .410
Action: Over-under boxlock
Barrel(s): 28″ with hollow-milled, ventilated rib
Choke(s): Skeet & Skeet
Weight: To customer's specifications
Stock: French or American walnut with oil finish
Trigger: Single, non-selective
Special Features: A custom Skeet gun set made only to special order with choice of checkering and carved panel patterns.

LJUTIC BI-MATIC AUTO
Gauge: 12
Action: Gas-operated autoloader
Barrel(s): 26″ to 32″
Choke(s): To customer specs.
Weight: About 10 lbs.
Stock: To customer specs.
Trigger: Single, pull or release
Special Features: Two-shot low recoil auto with one-piece actuating rod; available with right or left-hand ejection.

MAROCCHI CONTRAST CAP
Gauge: 12 or 20
Action: Over-under boxlock
Barrel(s): 26″ to 29″, ventilated top and middle ribs
Choke(s): Skeet
Weight: 7¼ lbs.
Stock: Select walnut with right or left palm swell; optional different stock available
Trigger: Single selective
Special Features: Beavertail or Schnabel fore-end; custom finishes, engraving inlays available

PERAZZI SCO
Gauge: 12 or 20
Action: Over-under, sidelock
Barrel(s): 27½″
Choke(s): Skeet & Skeet
Weight: 7 lbs.
Stock: AAA-quality European walnut with oil finish
Trigger: Single, non-selective
Special Features: Delicate engraving and gold inlays; automatic selective ejectors; fitted leather-edged case.

REMINGTON

For over 30 years, Remington's Model 870 has been a leader in the field of pump-action shotguns. It is the most popular pump gun in history, with over three million sold. Rugged dependability is the keystone of Model 870 design. The receiver is machined from a solid billet of ordnance steel and vibra-honed for smoothness. Double action slide bars eliminate binding and twisting that could interfere with consistent feeding. Barrels have a wide ventilated top rib with both front and mid sights. Model 870 Skeet guns are made in all four gauges, 12, 20, 28 and .410. The 12 and 20 gauge are available with 26-inch, Skeet-choked barrels, the 28 gauge and .410 barrels are 1 inch shorter.

Remington's Model 1100 is America's most popular shotgun. Its fine handling qualities and low recoil have endeared it to shooters everywhere, but it is especially appreciated on the Skeet field. The 1100 is built to last, having a receiver and barrel cut from single blocks of ordnance steel. The Skeet model is made in all four gauges, with 25- and 26-inch barrels choked for Skeet. Multi-event Skeet shooters will appreciate the weight equalizer kits, as they give 20 and 28 gauge and .410 guns the same weight and feel as the larger 12 gauge. Model 1100 stocks are made of American walnut, with impressed checkering on pistol grip and fore-end. The standard Model 1100 Skeet is known as the SA grade. A better finished version, the Tournament grade, has select American walnut with hand-cut checkering, and is available at a slightly higher price.

An over-under, the Model 3200 completes the roster of Remington Skeet guns. It has an all-steel engraved receiver, meticulously machined and polished. Barrels are 28 inches in length, topped by a vent rib fitted with ivory front and white metal middle sights. Barrels are separated for maximum cooling. The 3200 boasts a super-fast lock time, for which it has become world-famous. A sliding manual safety, located on the top tang, does double duty as a barrel selector, and a single selective trigger is used. Though the basic Model 3200 is made only in 12 gauge, barrel sets are available in 20 and 28 gauge and .410, but only when purchased as a set with the basic gun. Each set is hand fitted to the frame for perfect matching of all parts. The Model 3200 is a fine, time-tested and proven Skeet gun.

ROTTWEIL

The Rottweil American Skeet was designed from the ground up with emphasis on strength, endurance and simplicity. With its superb balance and elegant classic appearance, the Rottweil AS provides all the qualities demanded by American Skeet shooters. The gun is especially designed to make use of American barrel tube sets for conversion of the 12 gauge to smaller bores. The 12-gauge barrels are 26¾ inches long, bored Skeet & Skeet. The barrel rib is specially machined to eliminate glare, and it mounts a white plastic front sight housed in a durable metal sleeve, along with a metal mid-rib bead. The stock is select French walnut with satin oil finish, and hand checkering on both pistol grip and fore-end. A double ventilated recoil pad is also fitted. The action has rebounding locks, automatic ejectors, and the firing pins are spring mounted to retract after firing, thereby preventing damage to firing pin noses and possible interference with the loading cycle. Readily removable trigger groups contain the hammers, and coil springs are used throughout. Light engraving is used on the receiver, which is sandblasted to avoid reflectons. Weight of the Rottweil American Skeet gun is about 7½ lbs. Rottweils are imported by Dynamit Nobel of America.

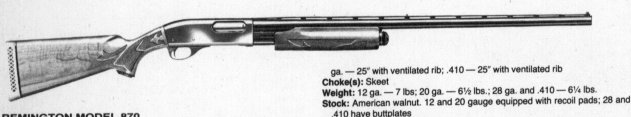

REMINGTON MODEL 870
Gauge: 12, 20, 28 and .410
Action: Slide-action repeater
Barrel(s): 12-ga. — 26" with ventilated rib; 20 ga. — 26" with ventilated rib; 28 ga. — 25" with ventilated rib; .410 — 25" with ventilated rib
Choke(s): Skeet
Weight: 12 ga. — 7 lbs; 20 ga. — 6½ lbs.; 28 ga. and .410 — 6¼ lbs.
Stock: American walnut. 12 and 20 gauge equipped with recoil pads; 28 and .410 have buttplates
Trigger: Standard single
Special Features: Double sighting beads; chrome-plated bolt; DuPont RK-W hard finish on stock and fore-end. Over 3,000,000 guns sold

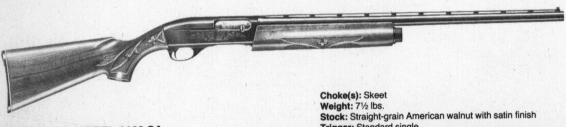

REMINGTON MODEL 1100 SA
Gauge: 12, 20, 28 and .410
Action: Gas-operated autoloader
Barrel(s): 26" with ventilated rib
Choke(s): Skeet
Weight: 7½ lbs.
Stock: Straight-grain American walnut with satin finish
Trigger: Standard single
Special Features: Available in various grades and finishes. Left-hand version available in 12 gauge; Tournament Skeet versions with removable barrel weights

REMINGTON MODEL 3200 SKEET GUN
Gauge: 12
Action: Over-under, boxlock
Barrel(s): 26" or 28" with ventilated rib
Choke(s): Skeet & Skeet
Weight: 7¾ lbs.
Stock: Fancy American walnut with fitted recoil pad
Trigger: Single selective
Special Features: Upgrade of pre-war Remington Model 32, finely balanced for Skeet shooting. A proven competition shotgun

ROTTWEIL 72 AMERICAN SKEET
Gauge: 12
Action: Over-under, boxlock
Barrel(s): 26¾" with low profile ventilated rib
Choke(s): Skeet & Skeet
Weight: 7½ lbs.
Stock: European walnut with fine-line checkering and oil finish
Trigger: Detachable and interchangeable trigger groups, single selective
Special Features: Interchangeable buttstocks; hard-chrome, satin finished receiver with light engraving.

The barrels on the Rottweil American skeet gun are chrome lined to help prevent rust and corrosion in the event the shooter doesn't clean the bores with regularity. Now, you're not guilty of this, are you?

Rottweil's American Skeet gun is a fine performer on the competitive fields. This Italian-made shotgun bears a West German label and is quality through and through. It has a host of innovative features that Skeet shooters have demanded and now have in one tidy package.

Full-length tubes are designed for a snug fit and are "set" in place with a small plastic drift and mallet. They are removed by tapping them out, muzzle back, with the same "stepped" drift which properly fits all six diameters — three for chambering and three for removing.

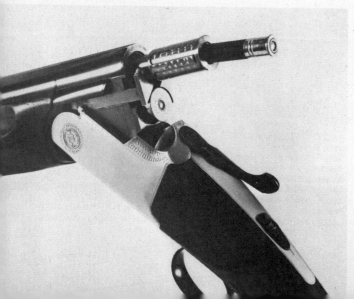

(Left) The Rottweil Skeet gun has massive ejectors and super-strong springs to kick empty cases well clear of the gun's action. These parameters are necessary when insert tubes are employed, as the shotgun's main ejectors must operate the "slave" ejectors on the insert tubes.

RUGER

A relative newcomer to the shotgun scene is the Ruger Red Label, now available in both 12 and 20 gauge versions. A light over-under, the Red Label offers Skeet barrels in both 26- and 28-inch lengths in 20 gauge, and 26 inches in 12 gauge. The Red Label has a combination automatic safety and barrel selector, and the stock is of American walnut with cut checkering on pistol grip and fore-end. The Red Label is a strong, well-made shotgun, crafted in the finest Ruger tradition.

SHOTGUNS OF ULM

K-80 Skeet guns from Shotguns of Ulm have lightweight receivers, hard nickel plated, with a satin gray finish. The locking mechanism consists of a massive top locking plate that moves over the rear of the high-pivoted barrels. The mechanically activated single trigger has the barrel selector located just ahead of it within the trigger guard. The position of the trigger is adjustable fore and aft, making it possible to make small changes in the effective length of pull. Standard vent rib barrels are 28 inches long, choked Skeet & Skeet. The K-80 stock is select European walnut with hand checkering on the palm swell pistol grip and on the fore-end. The stock may be removed without taking off the buttplate through use of a special long screwdriver that is supplied with the gun. The K-80 is specifically designed for the use of barrel insert tubes, and tube sets are available in 20 and 28 gauge and .410. The K-80, with its rugged dependability and excellent shooting characteristics, is rapidly becoming one of the world's leading Skeet guns.

SMITH & WESSON

Smith & Wesson's Model 1000 is a gas operated low-recoil autoloader that is made in three variations: Alloy Skeet, Steel Skeet and Super Skeet. The Alloy Skeet has a light aluminum alloy receiver that reduces overall weight by several ounces. The Steel Skeet is identical except that the receiver is machined from solid steel. Both guns have scroll engraving on both sides of the receiver, and come with 26-inch barrels choked Skeet. Double sighting beads are mounted on the matte finished cross-hatched vent rib. Barrels are premium quality molybdenum steel, cold hammer forged to length and shape, then precisely reamed to gauge and polished to near perfect smoothness. The gas system has a unique pressure compensator that moves forward in the gas cylinder to release excess pressure. Only enough gas pressure is retained to move the piston to the rear and function the action. An internal gas metering system compensates for pressure differences in ammunition to control bolt velocity and minimize stresses on the receiver and action parts. Both the bolt and bolt carrier are hard chromed to resist wear and corrosion. Stock and fore-end on all Model 1000s are made of select American walnut, with extensive hand cut checkering. All Model 1000s are fitted with a cross-bolt safety that is interchangeable for either right- or left-handed shooters. Smith & Wesson's Alloy Skeet gun weighs about 7½ lbs. The Steel Skeet model is about 8 ozs. heavier.

Smith & Wesson's Model 1000 Super Skeet uses the steel receiver, and internal workings are the same as in the lesser models. The trigger of the Super Skeet, however, is hand fitted and finely tuned to provide a near perfect let-off. It is also asymmetrically contoured for added comfort and control. Stock is cast-off, precisely angled to the right, for fast, positive eye alignment. The pistol grip has a right-hand palm swell to position the hand and trigger finger. The Super Skeet in 12 gauge weighs 8 lbs., 4 ozs., while the 20 gauge comes in at 7 lbs., 14 ozs. The unique feature of the Super Skeet is its barrel, which has a special recessed Skeet choke with 15 muzzle vents to reduce muzzle jump and soften recoil.

VALMET

Built in Finland, Valmet's Skeet gun, the Model 412KE, is an over-under available in both 12 and 20 gauge. The 12 gauge barrels can be had in 26- and 28-inch lengths. The 26-inch tube is choked Cylinder & Improved Cylinder, while the 28-inch barrel is choked Skeet & Skeet. All Valmet barrels are made from pre-drilled blanks with final dimensioning on the cold hammering machine taking place in one single operation. The chamber and the bore are simultaneously forged for dimensional accuracy. Barrels are chrome alloy steel, while receivers are chrome-molybdenum steel alloy. A single selective trigger also houses the barrel selector. The second barrel will fire even if the first barrel is empty. An automatic tang safety is provided, along with two indicator buttons located immediately behind the safety that give both visual and tactile indication of

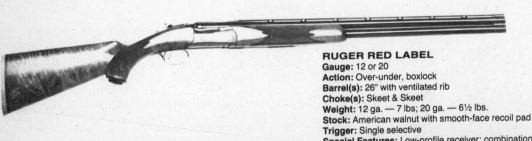

RUGER RED LABEL
Gauge: 12 or 20
Action: Over-under, boxlock
Barrel(s): 26″ with ventilated rib
Choke(s): Skeet & Skeet
Weight: 12 ga. — 7 lbs; 20 ga. — 6½ lbs.
Stock: American walnut with smooth-face recoil pad
Trigger: Single selective
Special Features: Low-profile receiver; combination barrel selector and safety; automatic ejectors; checkered pistol grip and fore-end.

SHOTGUNS OF ULM FOUR-BARREL SKEET SET
Gauge: 12, 20, 28 and .410
Action: Over-under, boxlock
Barrel(s): 26″ or 28″ with ventilated rib
Choke(s): Skeet & Skeet
Weight: 8½ lbs.
Stock: European walnut with hand-cut checkering
Trigger: Single selective, mechanical, and adjustable for fore and aft location
Special Features: Quickly removable buttstock; adjustable point of impact by changing barrel hanger; palm swell; twin sighting beads. Outstanding workmanship.

The K-80 has optional barrel hangers which alter the point of impact and regulation between the two barrels. Changing them is a simple procedure and may be quickly accomplished by the shooter — no gunsmithing knowledge is required.

SMITH & WESSON MODEL 1000S
Gauge: 12
Action: Gas-operated autoloader
Barrel(s): 25″ with ventilated rib
Choke(s): Special Skeet with Tula-design and built-in compensator system
Weight: 8¼ lbs.
Stock: Select American walnut with hand-cut checkering
Trigger: Standard single
Special Features: Recessed-type Skeet choke; right-hand palm swell (Wundhammer); Fluorescent red front bead; interchangeable fore-end cap weights.

The deeply recessed choke on Smith & Wesson's Super Skeet Model 1000 is an adaptation of the famous Tula choke. The muzzle has 15 gas-relieving slots milled into it — five on each side and five along the bottom. A brilliant, light-gathering red fluorescent front sight catches the shooter's eye quickly and helps guide the shot to the target.

SMITH & WESSON MODEL 1000
Gauge: 12 or 20
Action: Gas-operated autoloader
Barrel(s): 26″, ventilated rib
Choke(s): Skeet
Weight: 7½ lbs
Stock: American walnut
Trigger: Standard single
Special Features: Alloy receiver with scroll engraving; reversible cross-bolt safety; front and middle bead sights.

VALMET MODEL 412KE SKEET
Gauge: 12 or 20
Action: Over-under, boxlock
Barrel(s): 26″ with ventilated rib barrel
Choke(s): Skeet & Skeet
Weight: 7½ lbs.
Stock: European walnut with low-profile Monte Carlo
Trigger: Single selective, mechanically operated
Special Features: Automatic ejectors; sliding breech cover; bright blued finish; barrel cocking indicators

which barrel has been fired. The center screw of the safety may be tightened to change the safety to manual operation if desired. Weight of the Model 412KE is about 7½ lbs.

WEATHERBY

Weatherby offers four shotguns expressly designed for Skeet shooting. The Athena and Orion over-unders, the Model 82 semi-automatic and the Model 92 pump gun. The Model 92 has an exceptionally short stroke for fast reloading when the shooting gets hot and heavy. Its slide action operates on double rails to prevent twisting and binding. The bolt is fluted to allow functioning under adverse conditions of dirt build-up in the action. The Model 92 Skeet has a 26-inch barrel, choked for Skeet, of course, with a vented top rib fitted with both front and middle sights. Weight of the Model 92 is 7½ lbs.

The Model 82 autoloader shares many features of the Model 92 in barrel length and finish, and weights are about the same. Gas operation of the Model 82 absorbs much of the recoil, giving a softer shooting action. Weatherby has devised a floating gas piston that eliminates alignment, drag and friction wear problems found on some other autoloaders. A disconnect system is incorporated that prevents accidental firing of a shell unless the bolt is fully closed. Stocks of the 82 and 92 are select claro walnut protected with a durable high gloss finish. Rosewood pistol grip caps add a touch of elegance. Ample fine-line hand checkering is provided on pistol grip and fore-end. Receivers of both models are scroll engraved and finished in a lustre blue.

The Orion over-under is a strong boxlock design using time-proven Kersten cross-bolt locks. The monobloc and receiver are machined from high strength steel and jewelled to a highly polished finish for smooth functioning. Selective automatic ejectors kick out only fired hulls, while slightly raising unfired shells for easy removal. Its safety is a traditional slide-type conveniently located on the top tang. The single selective trigger also allows instant barrel selection for the first shot by just pressing the selector button located on the trigger. A mechanical switchover automatically allows the second barrel to be fired in case of a misfire, since recoil is not required to set the trigger. However, an adjustment will permit changeover to a recoil switchover if desired. The claro walnut stock and fore-end are meticulously fitted to the action and the barrels, and then protected with a durable high gloss finish. Distinctive hand checkering, recoil pad and rosewood pistol grip cap are accents to an elegant firearm. The chrome moly barrels and receiver are deep blued in a lustrous finish. Available in both 12 and 20 gauge, the Orion is fitted with 26-inch barrels in both gauges. Barrels are topped by a broad ventilated rib, and vents are also machined into the interbarrel ribs for added cooling. The Orion weighs 7½ lbs. in 12 gauge, a pound less in the 20 gauge version.

The Athena model shares all the features of the Orion, except that it has ornamental sideplates added along with extensive engraving and better quality wood in the stock and fore-end. Receiver, sideplates, locking lever and trigger guard are finished in a rich silver gray color that complements the deep blue of the barrels. Both of these quality stackbarrel shotguns are made by the respected Japanese firm of SKB expressly for Weatherby.

WINCHESTER

The Winchester Group of the Olin Corporation offers two Skeet guns based on the Model 101 over-under action. There are four gauges offered in the Diamond Grade: 12, 20, 28 and .410 bore. All barrels are 27½ inches long, Skeet choked, and the muzzles are ventilated to reduce recoil and control muzzle jump. All have a tapered and elevated rib with both front and middle sights. The receiver is deeply etched in a diamond pattern. Straight or Monte Carlo stocks are optional; wood is select walnut with fine-line checkering on pistol grip and fore-end. Diamond Grade Skeet guns weigh from 6½ to 7¼ lbs. The Grand European model, based on the same action, is the top of the line, with superior wood and copious engraving. The wood is oil finished in the traditional manner. The Grand European Skeet is made in both 12 and 20 gauge, both with 27-inch barrels especially choked for Skeet. The 12 gauge weighs 7½ lbs., while the 20 gauge weighs at just 6½ lbs.

All of the guns mentioned so far are called "Skeet" guns by the manufacturer, and yet, there are many models of field grade shotguns made by Mossberg, Marlin, New Haven Brand, Savage, Stevens, Winchester (U.S.R.A), Tradewinds, Franchi and others that qualify nicely as Skeet guns on an interim basis. All of them should be seriously considered by tyros.

Skeet shooting's golden era was the 1930s, and during this decade, it was considered as elegant as playing polo. It was a shooting game for well-known personalities and unlike many of today's big-name "closet" shooters, movie stars like Clark Gable, Roy Rogers, Gary Cooper and others made it publicly known they "liked guns" and liked to shoot them. It's a pity that our shooting sports don't receive favorable publicity like that anymore.

Great American gun makers during this same time period made special Skeet guns. Winchester's Model 21 side-by-side was a favorite arm for many "name" Skeet shooters. The Model 21 Skeet guns were specially bored and the barrels were marked "Skeet 1, Skeet 2" or "Skeet In, Skeet Out." The 21 was available in any gauge from 12 through .410 bore and even the 16 gauge Skeet model was very popular though there were no 16 gauge events.

Iver Johnson, a popular handgun maker, joined the Skeet bandwagon in the 1930s and introduced a sleek,

WEATHERBY ATHENA
Gauge: 12 or 20
Action: Over-under, boxlock
Barrel(s): 12 ga. — 28" with ventilated rib; 20 ga. — 26" with ventilated rib
Choke(s): Skeet & Skeet
Weight: 12 ga. — 7½ lbs; 20 ga. — 7 lbs
Stock: AAA Claro walnut with epoxy finish
Trigger: Single selective, mechanical or inertia
Special Features: Modified Kersten-type locking system; false hand-engraved sideplates; fine-line checkering on pistol grip and fore-end.

WEATHERBY ORION
Gauge: 12 or 20
Action: Over-under, boxlock
Barrel(s): 12 ga. — 28" with ventilated rib; 20 ga. — 26" with ventilated rib
Choke(s): Skeet & Skeet
Weight: 12 ga. — 7½ lbs.; 20 ga. — 7 lbs.
Stock: Claro walnut
Trigger: Single selective
Special Features: Barrel selector button located in trigger blade; automatic and selective ejectors; light scroll engraving; rubber recoil pad.

WEATHERBY MODEL 92
Gauge: 12
Action: Slide-action repeater
Barrel(s): 26" with ventilated rib
Choke(s): Skeet
Weight: 7½ lbs.
Stock: Claro walnut with fitted recoil pad
Trigger: Standard single
Special Features: Short stroke action, cross-bolt safety; action release lever located on lower right side of receiver; hand-checkered pistol grip and fore-end; white line spacers

WEATHERBY MODEL 82
Gauge: 12
Action: Gas-operated autoloader
Barrel(s): 26" with ventilated rib
Choke(s): Skeet
Weight: 7½ lbs.
Stock: Claro walnut with recoil pad
Trigger: Standard single
Special Features: New gas-operating system to reduce felt recoil; fluted bolt; gold plated trigger; hand-cut checkering on pistol grip and fore-end; white line spacers.

WINCHESTER DIAMOND GRADE
Gauge: 12, 20, 28 or .410
Action: Over-under, boxlock
Barrel(s): 27" with stepped ventilated rib
Choke(s): Skeet & Skeet
Weight: 7¼ lbs.
Stock: Select grade walnut with recoil pad
Trigger: Single selective, inertia operated
Special Features: Combination barrel selector/safety; hand-cut checkering on pistol grip and fluted fore-end; engraved receiver in Diamond motif.

WINCHESTER 501 GRAND EUROPEAN
Gauge: 12 or 20
Action: Over-under boxlock
Barrel(s): 27″, tapered ventilated rib
Choke(s): Skeet & Skeet
Weight: 7½ lbs.
Stock: Full fancy walnut with hand rubbed oil finish and checkered pistol grip and fore-end.
Trigger: Single selective
Special Features: Silvered and engraved receiver, engine-turned breech interior; selective automatic ejectors; chrome bores.

(Left and above) Claude Purbaugh, a pioneer and expert in the manufacturing of full-length Skeet tube inserts, has both promoted and shot his products for many years with outstanding success. Other prominent tube makers are Briley and Kolar.

straight-grip, short-barreled side-by-side and appropriately named it the "Skeeter." Not many of these guns were produced and few are seen today outside the hands of gun collectors.

Marlin's Model 90 over-under came on the scene a few years later and was chambered in 12 and 20 gauge plus .410 bore. It was one of the first American-made over-under shotguns which used spring-loaded strikers instead of the traditional internal hammers.

Possibly the most popular Skeet gun of its short-lived career was Remington's Model 32. In production for less than a decade, it was big, heavy, clumsy, had poor triggers, and would often "double." Yet in spite of all

these "features," it was the preferred gun of Skeet shooting champions. Alex Kerr shot one for many, many years as did a host of other champions.

At the start of World War II, Remington was forced to discontinue all "sporting" gun production and concentrated their entire output to the war effort. After the war, they sold all their tooling for the Model 32 to the old-time German gun-making firm of Krieghoff. By the late 1950s, Krieghoff got their guns into production and started to ship these "new" Remington over-unders to the United States and called them the Krieghoff Model 32. The rest is history.

ANY BOOK written about shotguns must have a special section devoted to the venerable Winchester Model 12. This revered veteran has probably gathered more trap and Skeet shooting honors than any other single model shotgun ever produced. There's no way to tell for certain, but I doubt that I'll get many disagreements. It's doubtful there's a trap shooter today who at one time or another hasn't either owned or tried to shoot the winningest Winchester of all time. There's a certain ingredient, call it style, balance or feel, that sets the old "pumper" apart from today's sophisticated trap and Skeet guns.

Truly one of the all-time great classic-style shotguns, the Winchester Model 12's appearance was often emulated by other manufacturers. Even Winchester themselves, after discontinuing production of the Model 12 in the early 1970s, hyped their new autoloader—the Super X-1—as having Model 12-like handling characteristics. In fact, the Super X-1's receiver profile closely followed the smooth, flowing lines of the Model 12.

trap shooter after spending nearly 3 years of floundering and getting bloody on Southern California Skeet fields. I, like many fellow shooters, "paid my dues" and watched some of the greatest Skeet and trap shooters routinely pocket my entry and option money.

Some of the greatest champions have used, and are still using, the Winchester Model 12. Arnold Riegger from Washington shot one for many years and it was a used gun when he bought it. Anyone who had the privilege of watching Riegger take his old Model 12 out for a doubles event will recall how smoothly he and that old Model 12 would grind up targets. It was like watching Toscanini handle a baton while conducting a Philharmonic orchestra.

The brothers Poindexter, Chuck, Tom and Jim, all have shot Model 12s throughout their illustrious careers. Another West Coast trap shooter, Phil Ross can still be seen today using his Model 12 with a plastic Hydro-Coil stock that is only a decade or so younger than he. Ross's phenomenal scores and yearly averages at-

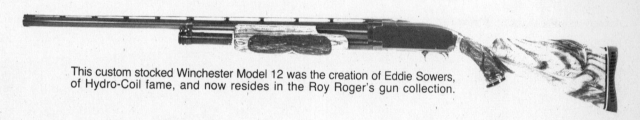

This custom stocked Winchester Model 12 was the creation of Eddie Sowers, of Hydro-Coil fame, and now resides in the Roy Roger's gun collection.

Although the Model 12 has been out of production for over 5 years, with over 2,000,000 guns produced, there is still an overwhelming number of them found on today's trap and Skeet fields. Yes, there are still a few "die-hards" who fondly shuck their doubles on the Skeet range.

Not long after I decided to become a registered trap shooter in 1960, my search for a trap gun was then limited to relatively few choices. There was only one single barrel trap gun in production, the Ithaca, but that was well out of my financial reach. The Browning Broadway and discontinued Remington Model 32 were just not my cup of tea. Of the other two acceptable pump guns—Remington's Model 870 and the ancient Model 31—neither at that time suited my fancy. Therefore, by process of elimination, the Winchester Model 12 was the logical choice—and it was a good one.

In 1960 a trap grade Model 12 had a list price of $203.50. There were no "deals" in those days as the consumer was protected by the Fair Trade Act and retail prices were rigidly enforced. The Model 12 had a 30-inch ventilated rib barrel, nicely figured walnut stock and fore-end with hand-cut checkering. Now I was a

test to the gun's ability to break targets in the hands of a competent shooter.

Thinking back to the 1960s, the names Peter Candy and William Hay Rogers come to mind, and both of these Skeet shooting whiz-bangs used the old "corn-sheller." Rummaging through old-time Skeet and trap magazines, it was graphically proved that the Winchester Model 12 was the "fair-haired boy" of the trap and Skeet fields up to the early 1970s. There are numerous stories about Joe Devers, perhaps the greatest all-around shotgun shooter of all time, who took his Model 12 to Europe and made a mockery out of the super-difficult game of Live Pigeon shooting.

During the mid-1970s the European imports made their lasting impression and infiltrated both the pocketbooks and hands of the American shooters. The heydays of the Winchester Model 12 were obviously numbered and Winchester retired the venerable veteran twice—first in 1964 and again in 1979. Once "King of the Hill," the King is now dead. Long Live The King!

For those who would like to know the actual production numbers and years of manufacture of the Winchester Model 12, we've included the following list.

Winchester Model 12 Production

Year	Serial Number Range	Year	Serial Number Range
1912	1-5308	1938	754251-779455
1913	5309-32418	1939	779456-814121
1914	32419-79765	1940	814122-856499
1915	79766-109515	1941	856500-907431
1916	109516-136412	1942	907432-958303
1917	136413-159391	1943	958304-975640
1918	159392-183461	1944	975641-975727
1919	183462-219457	1945	975728-990004
1920	219458-247458	1946	990005-1029152
1921	247459-267253	1947	1029153-1102371
1922	267254-304314	1948	1102372-1176055
1923	304315-346319	1949	1176056-1214041
1924	346320-385196	1950	1214042-1252028
1925	385197-423056	1951	1252029-1290015
1926	423057-464564	1952	1290016-1328002
1927	464565-510693	1953	1328003-1399996
1928	510694-557850	1954	1399997-1471990
1929	557851-600834	1955	1471991-1541929
1930	600835-626996	1956	1541930-1611868
1931	626997-651255	1957	1611869-1651435
1932	651256-660110	1958	1651436-1690999
1933	660111-664544	1959	1691000-1795500
1934	664545-673994	1960	1795501-1800000
1935	673995-686978	1961	1800001-1854794
1936	686979-720316	1962	1854795-1909588
1937	720317-754250	1963	1909589-1964384

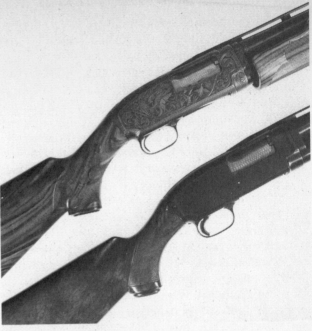

A standard trap-grade Model 12 (bottom) was beautifully converted to a museum-quality work of art by Pachmayr Gun Works (top). The stock is hand-carved with exquisite 32 line-per-inch checkering. High contrast English walnut was used on the buttstock and fore-end.

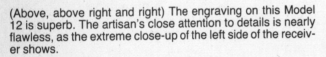

(Above, above right and right) The engraving on this Model 12 is superb. The artisan's close attention to details is nearly flawless, as the extreme close-up of the left side of the receiver shows.

Winchester Model 12 Historical Notes

1912 The first Model 12 was introduced. Available only in 20 gauge with a 25-inch plain barrel.

1914 The Model 12 was first offered in 12 gauge. Two different versions were available, a Tournament Grade and Trap grade. Both were discontinued in 1931.

1919 The ventilated rib barrel was first offered as an option on 12 gauge guns.

1931 The Improved Modified choke was first offered.

1938 A Cartridge Guide was attached to the ejection side of the shell carrier. The specific purpose was to eliminate the possibility of a loaded shell dropping out of the ejection port.

1938 The New Style Trap Gun was introduced and later discontinued in 1964. These guns, in serial number range 754,251 through 1,964,384, represent the much-sought "pre-64" trap guns.

1939 A ladies and junior Trap Gun in 20 gauge in the style and configuration of the larger 12 gauge

model. Discontinued in 1941.

1940 The first year the Monte Carlo stock design was offered.

1943 Winchester presented the 1,000,000th Model 12 to Lt. General Henry (Hap) Arnold, Chief of the Army Air Forces. Interestingly, the gun was equipped with a 30-inch Full choke, ventilated rib barrel and a Skeet stock and fore-end.

1960 An all-new ventilated rib design, replaced the older "round-post" version on 12 gauge Skeet, Trap and Pigeon Grade guns.

1963 In December, Winchester announced that regular production Model 12s with a retail price of $205.00 would be discontinued. However, the gun could be specially ordered in Super Pigeon Grade 12 at a retail price of $825.00

1972 The Winchester Model 12 "Y"-series guns were introduced as a result of tremendous pressure from the shooting public.

1979 This was the final year the Model 12 was offered in any configuration.

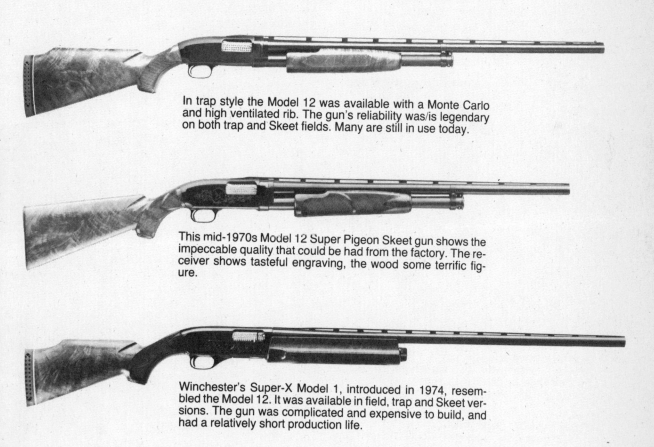

In trap style the Model 12 was available with a Monte Carlo and high ventilated rib. The gun's reliability was/is legendary on both trap and Skeet fields. Many are still in use today.

This mid-1970s Model 12 Super Pigeon Skeet gun shows the impeccable quality that could be had from the factory. The receiver shows tasteful engraving, the wood some terrific figure.

Winchester's Super-X Model 1, introduced in 1974, resembled the Model 12. It was available in field, trap and Skeet versions. The gun was complicated and expensive to build, and had a relatively short production life.

OLDIES BUT GOODIES

AS A professional gun writer, I'm often asked the question, "Is it a good idea to buy a used shotgun for Skeet and trap competition?" I usually answer by stating, "Buying a used shotgun is similar to buying a used car. Buyer beware!"

True, shooters as a rule are honest and straightforward in their evaluation of guns they are trying to sell for various reasons. But over the years of swapping, buying and selling personal guns, I've never been "taken" by a reputable gun dealer. What makes a dealer "reputable?" If he has been in business for a long period of time, you can bet your last shotgun shell that he's honest and doesn't misrepresent a gun to his buying public; otherwise, he wouldn't still be in business today.

Who are these honest folks? Well, take a look at the back of special periodicals like *Shotgun Sports, American Shotgunner, Skeet Shooting Review,* and *Trap and Field* to name just a few. If you recognize dealers' names year after year, you can book that they're okay. If you're still not sure, write or call one of them nearest you and ask for references. The "up-to-snuff" fellows will be happy to rattle off a few names and then you can carry the ball from there.

There is a myriad of used trap and Skeet guns floating about, not only from gun dealers, but private parties as well. The aforementioned magazines usually have a list of "Classified Ads" that contain private party offerings. Dealing with individuals is a bit more difficult to sort fact from fiction and all too often, a certain individual will attempt to sell a pet shotgun for more than it's really worth. But, "worth" is an arbitrary statement. Perhaps, the owner has "customized" the gun with a new stock or special gunsmithing. In some cases, this may increase the gun's value, but only if the new stock properly fits the potential buyer. If you need a trap gun with a 14-inch pull and the one offered measures 15¼ inches, it will cost you a few hard-earned dollars to alter the stock to your dimensions. Therefore, the owner of the used shotgun should take this factor into consideration and price his ware accordingly.

These Skeet shooters are checking out "ice targets" during a Skeet shoot in 1965. The shooter on the left is armed with a Browning Pigeon grade Superposed while the one in the fur cap is cradling the then-popular Remington Model 58 gas-operated autoloader.

William Hay Rogers, super Skeet shooter in the 1960s, won countless trophies and events using his Remington Model 31 pump gun.

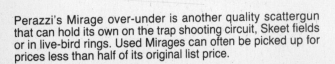

Perazzi's Mirage over-under is another quality scattergun that can hold its own on the trap shooting circuit, Skeet fields or in live-bird rings. Used Mirages can often be picked up for prices less than half of its original list price.

Some competition trap and Skeet guns are no longer in a manufacturer's lineup for a variety of reasons. Some may only be out of production for a year or two, others for a quarter-century. Others of the "classic" category are marvelous to shoot and own, but when it comes time to have them repaired, you'll have to dig deep into your wallet to cover the expenses as most parts will have to be made from scratch.

Personally, I'm a fanatical fan of classic shotguns. Just a few years ago I was able to put together the ultimate—in my opinion—trap shooting combo: a pair of Remingtons—a Model 31 TC pump and a Model 32 TC over-under. Over the years of shooting, I had previously owned similar guns, but never at the same time due to a lack of funds (does anyone else have this same problem?). The Model 31 is like lead crystal, beautiful to look at and own, but very fragile. I expect there will be a hue and cry from dyed-in-the-wool Model 31 owners who challenge this statement, but none of them own *my* 31! Through shooting the Model 31 in dozens of events over the years, I've been able to build up a fairly good-sized heap of junk and broken parts—firing pins, ejectors, extractors, and action bars to name a few. I've had the gun fail me at the most inopportune time, like on

the first day of the Grand, and no replacements parts could be found. Yet, if I can choose my belongings, I'll take the cherished Model 31 to my grave. Similar experiences have occurred with my Model 32, although I don't shoot it as much as the old pump gun.

The point is, if you want to shoot these classics, then be prepared for the consequences. It's not that these guns were fragile when first made, but time has simply taken its toll and the metal is fatigued through use and age. Single barrel Parkers and early Ithacas were heralded as super-tough guns in their day. After 30 to 50 years of hard use, they will probably break down at critical times. I'm sure today's Ljutics, Berettas, Winchesters and Perazzis will give their owners fits in 2020 A.D.

Therefore, to be on the safe side, newer "classics" are the logical choice in the used gun marketplace. Guns that have been out of production for only 10 years or so are still considered to be excellent buys if in good operating condition. Even should a critical part fail, most gun makers still carry a decent inventory of spare parts. If the manufacturer no longer carries parts, then one of the many surplus parts houses like Numrich Arms, Sherwood Distributors, etc. often run full page

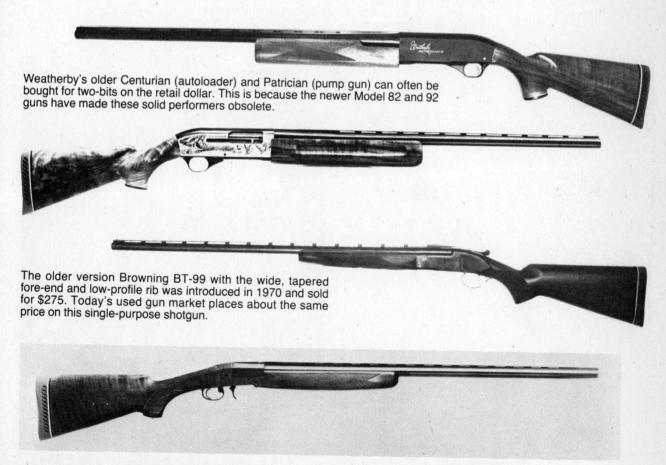

Weatherby's older Centurian (autoloader) and Patrician (pump gun) can often be bought for two-bits on the retail dollar. This is because the newer Model 82 and 92 guns have made these solid performers obsolete.

The older version Browning BT-99 with the wide, tapered fore-end and low-profile rib was introduced in 1970 and sold for $275. Today's used gun market places about the same price on this single-purpose shotgun.

Beretta's (Galef) Model TR-2 trapgun didn't sell well for a number of reasons. Originally priced at about $100, the main reason for the gun's disappearance was its lack of "snob appeal" as it was nothing more than a converted single-shot "Companion," changed by adding a trap stock and beavertail fore-end.

ads in *Shotgun News* for spare parts ranging from trigger screws through firing pins.

Like used cars, pre-owned shotguns may be bought relatively inexpensively when compared to today's retail prices. True, most of the asking prices are near or more than what the gun may have originally cost, but based on today's dollar value, they are considered to be excellent buys.

How can a used-gun buyer ascertain if a particular shotgun is a good buy? Price-wise, probably the best guide is DBI's book, *The Gun Digest Book Of Modern Gun Values*, which clearly and accurately states used gun values along with original production dates and specifications. The other factor to be considered is the gun's condition. Obviously a well-worn shotgun cannot command the same price as a near-mint model. I heartily recommend that before purchasing any used firearm, the potential buyer know what the gun is worth before making a deal, and browsing through a current copy of *Modern Gun Values* is an excellent starting point.

What are some of these guns? Well, for starters, the older Krieghoffs are excellent guns and stated prices I've seen in ads are well below today's retail prices. On the other hand, used Winchester Model 12s are commanding prices well above what they sold for new—and only a few years ago. Ditto for Belgian-made Browning Superposed models, especially the Broadway and Lightning models. Browning's short-lived Double Automatics are rare finds as most of them are in gun collectors' hands—especially the low-production numbered "Twentyweight." The Browning ST-100 led a short and unsuccessful life due to its high retail price tag. This over-under did all it claimed to do, yet trap

Winchester's Model 101 combo, which included a fitted trunk-type gun case, listed for $469.95 in 1966. How many would you like to buy today at that same price.?

Marlin's Model 120 made a valiant attempt to emulate the Winchester Model 12, combining similar styling features and excellent workmanship at a price well beneath the Model 12. Unfortunately, this trap version never fared well.

(Right) The brothers Poindexter, Chuck (left), and Jim (circa 1963) cut their teeth on Winchester Model 12s. Both "kids" are still using them and still winning, too.

Early model Krieghoffs, like this cased set complete with a full-complement of insert tubes, are still available at affordable prices. For some inexplicable reason, Krieghoff guns haven't held their values as well as other marques.

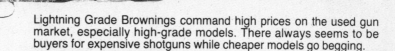

Used Belgian-made Browning Broadways are eagerly sought over-unders. Introduced in the late 1950s, the broad rib concept was quickly accepted by shooters and other shotgun manufacturers emulated this design on many of their shotguns.

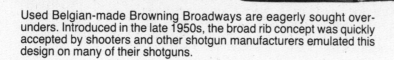

Lightning Grade Brownings command high prices on the used gun market, especially high-grade models. There always seems to be buyers for expensive shotguns while cheaper models go begging.

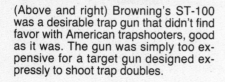

(Above and right) Browning's ST-100 was a desirable trap gun that didn't find favor with American trapshooters, good as it was. The gun was simply too expensive for a target gun designed expressly to shoot trap doubles.

shooters stayed away from it like the plague. Pity, too, because the ST-100 was, and still is a fine trapgun, although expressly designed to be used on trap doubles.

In 1978, a then-revolutionary trap gun hit the market. Designed and imported by Leonard Pucinelli, the Italian-made I.A.B. was one of the first successful "unguns" and was offered in a wide variety of ensembles. Three barrel configurations were common with two single barrels and a set of over-under tubes. I had the pleasure of using one of these tri-barrel combos for almost a year and shot some exciting scores with it. There weren't many guns produced and used models pop up occasionally at near original prices. It's still a fine gun and worth a close look by a serious trapshooter in search of a "new" gun.

SKB trap and Skeet guns are still plentiful and have earned the "Seal of Good Reliability." In recent months, I've noted that asking prices for the over-unders is less than what they sold for when SKB pulled out of the American market. The 5700 series are exceptionally stoutly-made guns in both trap and Skeet versions. Their autoloaders resisted malfunctions and were a joy to shoot. The best doubles score I ever fired, a 99x100, was shot with an SKB Model 5700. Unfortunately, it was a "test" gun and I had to give it back to the importer. The Ithaca/SKB Century single barrel trap gun was dependable, nicely finished and inexpensive, yet it didn't sell well.

Another trap gun "sleeper" is the Gamba Edinburough, made by Gamba in Italy, and distributed by Steyr, Daimler, Puch of America. The gun is no longer for sale through normal outlets, but a few are still seen, "new in the box" at some gun shops. It is competitively priced and breaks targets with regularity!

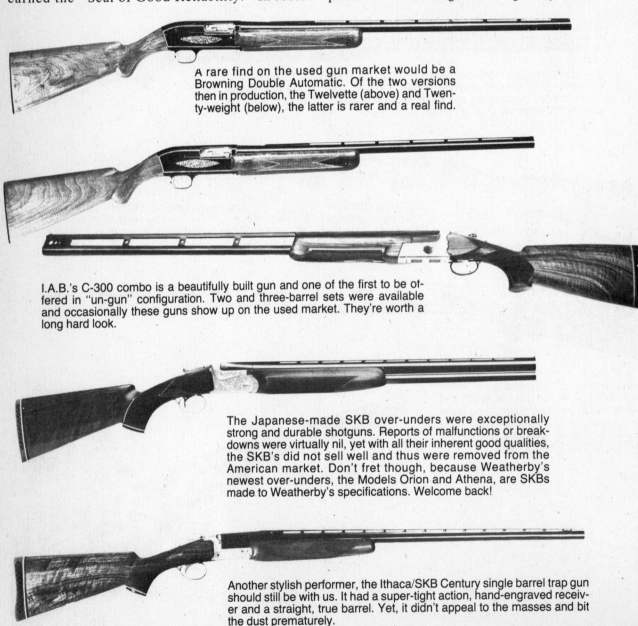

A rare find on the used gun market would be a Browning Double Automatic. Of the two versions then in production, the Twelvette (above) and Twenty-weight (below), the latter is rarer and a real find.

I.A.B.'s C-300 combo is a beautifully built gun and one of the first to be offered in "un-gun" configuration. Two and three-barrel sets were available and occasionally these guns show up on the used market. They're worth a long hard look.

The Japanese-made SKB over-unders were exceptionally strong and durable shotguns. Reports of malfunctions or breakdowns were virtually nil, yet with all their inherent good qualities, the SKB's did not sell well and thus were removed from the American market. Don't fret though, because Weatherby's newest over-unders, the Models Orion and Athena, are SKBs made to Weatherby's specifications. Welcome back!

Another stylish performer, the Ithaca/SKB Century single barrel trap gun should still be with us. It had a super-tight action, hand-engraved receiver and a straight, true barrel. Yet, it didn't appeal to the masses and bit the dust prematurely.

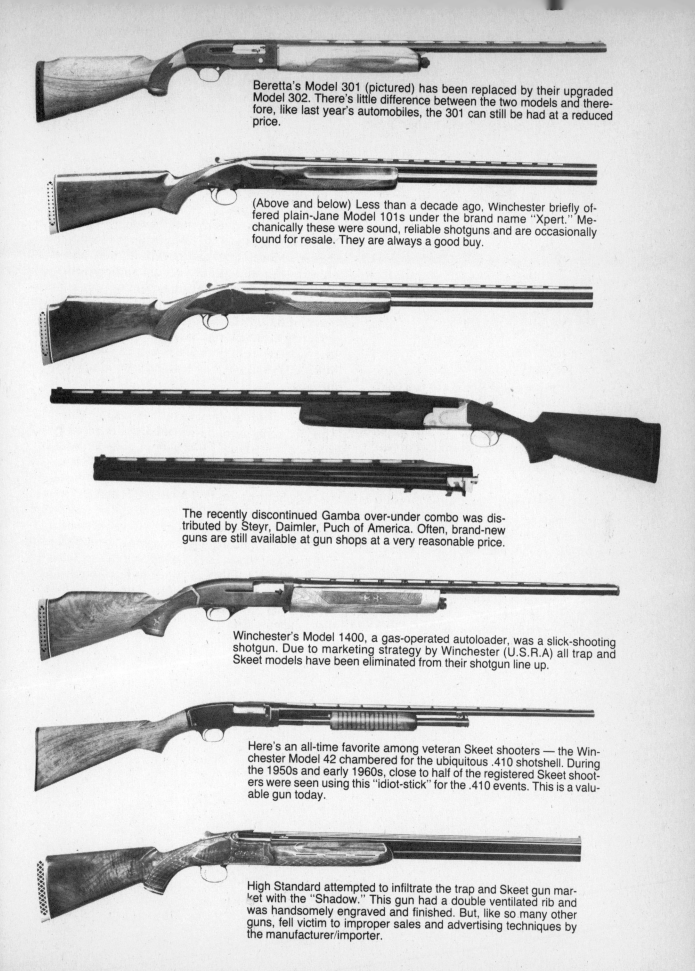

Beretta's Model 301 (pictured) has been replaced by their upgraded Model 302. There's little difference between the two models and therefore, like last year's automobiles, the 301 can still be had at a reduced price.

(Above and below) Less than a decade ago, Winchester briefly offered plain-Jane Model 101s under the brand name "Xpert." Mechanically these were sound, reliable shotguns and are occasionally found for resale. They are always a good buy.

The recently discontinued Gamba over-under combo was distributed by Steyr, Daimler, Puch of America. Often, brand-new guns are still available at gun shops at a very reasonable price.

Winchester's Model 1400, a gas-operated autoloader, was a slick-shooting shotgun. Due to marketing strategy by Winchester (U.S.R.A) all trap and Skeet models have been eliminated from their shotgun line up.

Here's an all-time favorite among veteran Skeet shooters — the Winchester Model 42 chambered for the ubiquitous .410 shotshell. During the 1950s and early 1960s, close to half of the registered Skeet shooters were seen using this "idiot-stick" for the .410 events. This is a valuable gun today.

High Standard attempted to infiltrate the trap and Skeet gun market with the "Shadow." This gun had a double ventilated rib and was handsomely engraved and finished. But, like so many other guns, fell victim to improper sales and advertising techniques by the manufacturer/importer.

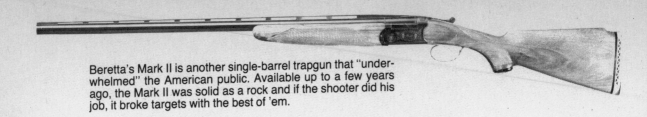

Beretta's Mark II is another single-barrel trapgun that "underwhelmed" the American public. Available up to a few years ago, the Mark II was solid as a rock and if the shooter did his job, it broke targets with the best of 'em.

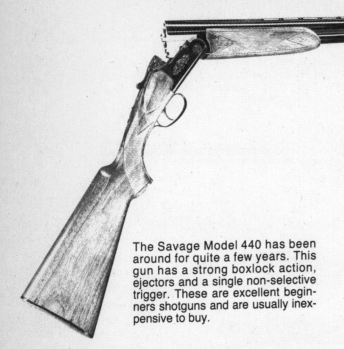

The Savage Model 440 has been around for quite a few years. This gun has a strong boxlock action, ejectors and a single non-selective trigger. These are excellent beginners shotguns and are usually inexpensive to buy.

Remember the Franchis? There was a raft of over-under combos around a few years ago in addition to a slick, soft-shooting autoloader. Where did they all go? Price-wise, they were then the best trap guns available for the dollar.

Winchester's old Model 101 was available in trap and Skeet models, but today's gussied-up versions fetch a much higher price than yesterday's counterparts. Olin's Xpert series of over-unders were available in trap and Skeet versions and were priced a couple hundred dollars under the Model 101. Where are they today? Winchester's Models 1200 and 1400 series were also available in trap and Skeet verions and proved to be competitive against more expensive guns. Since U.S.R.A.'s takeover, trap and Skeet guns are no longer part of this firm's laundry list.

During the late 1960s, Savage Arms offered an excellent over-under in both Skeet and trap versions. The Models 333 and 440 are near duplicates of today's Valmet guns.

Remington autoloaders have long been in favor on the Skeet fields starting as far back as the Model 11. This Browning Auto-5 look-alike was replaced by the slick-looking Model 11-48 with its rounded receiver. Recoil operated, like the Model 11, the 11-48 led a glorious life during the mid- to late 1950s. After the Model 11-48 came the transition Models 878 and 58, prior to the fabled Model 1100. All of these "8"-series guns were dependable and breakdowns were uncommon.

We could go on and on reminiscing about discontinued trap and Skeet guns, but space requirements demand that we stop now. I hope this brief interlude has created some fond memories for oldtimers, and for new "claybirders" it was nice to take you for a short stroll down memory lane.

Gun Fit 6

IF A PERSON needs his shoes repaired, he goes to a shoe repair store; the same holds true for other special service needs—go to the experts. Yet, unfortunately, a large percentage of shooters seek advice and help from non-professionals or quasi-stockmakers when they're looking for information about fitting their gun stock to themselves. After talking with dozens of professional stockmakers, to a man they confide that a staggering number of shooters tell them their ideas and dimensions without ever having been properly measured! This may sound astounding to you . . .but it's inconceivable to me!

There are literally dozens of custom stockmakers in the United States, professional and competent wood carvers who can accurately measure and fit a competitive shooter. To find these experts the shooter can scan ads in various gun magazines or trade journals. If there is one close by, either visit or call him on the phone. The important point here is to talk to him on a one-to-one basis. If there's any doubt that a particular stockmaker can satisfy your needs, ask him for references. If he's competent and proud of his work, he'll gladly offer you a hatful of names. If he hesitates or says he doesn't want to be bothered or has to prove to you that he knows what he's doing, then take a pass and find another who will comply with your wishes.

Choosing a stockmaker you can trust isn't unlike finding a doctor, dentist or lawyer. You'll need his services from time to time and when you do, you can be assured that it will cost you some bucks. So choose wisely.

An inherent problem associated with proper shotgun fit is that what is correct today, may be woefully wrong tomorrow, and there are many contributing reasons for this initially unforseen problem. Although trap and Skeet are shot year 'round, in reality attendance figures rise along with the temperature. Few of us enjoy shooting in cold, damp weather and as long as these games

Skeet shooting, for the most part, is a close-shooting game with targets rarely exceeding 25 yards. Gun fit is vitally important to World Class champions, but for the average Skeet shooter who wants to learn the game, most field-stocked shotguns are excellent "beginning" scatterguns.

Satterwhite, without the aid of a "try-gun" stock, can ascertain and fit most newcomers with incredible accuracy. This takes years of shooting experience and being able to communicate this information to neophytes is an art.

Proper stock fit for "doubles" shooting requires different dimensions than for guns used for singles and handicap events. The stock should usually be lower at the comb to compensate for shooting at the second target.

(Left) The old tale of measuring the length of pull from the crook of the shooter's arm to the trigger finger is a widespread misconception. Arm length is of less consequence to proper fit as the length of the neck, and distance between cheekbone and shoulder.

are avocations, we'll probably choose a different diversion on our days off when the wind is howling or there's 2 feet of snow on the ground. Dedication to a sport is commendable, but it often can border on the ridiculous.

Let's assume that you have a shotgun with a stock which seemingly fits you perfectly. It is comfortable to shoot, you've shot some excellent scores with it and you're 100 percent satisfied with it both mechanically and aesthetically. But under what conditions was the stock fitted to you? Chances are it was when you were wearing your favorite shooting vest, with a loose fitting sport shirt and a T-shirt. Let's suppose, for a moment, that at that time the length of pull was accurately measured to be 14¼ inches. The drop at the comb was 1¼ inches and the drop at the heel was 1¾ inches. These are typical trap stock dimensions. (I hope that Skeet shooters don't take offense at this time, but these dimensions are only stated for comparisons which will be changed for various reasons, as we'll find out.)

You're all signed up, squadded and ready to go when suddenly a storm gathers and the temperature quickly drops 20 degrees. What do you do? Typically, the average shooter would unthinkingly go back to the car, drag out a warm coat and trot back to the starting line, warm, but falsely prepared to shoot the best score of his career. Most of the time, this shooter will record a score from 10 to 12 points *less* than his average. Why? The coat was the culprit. The thickness of the coat will increase the shotgun's length of pull between ½- to 1-inch and this extended stock dimension will dramatically change the gun's handling qualities. Yet, it wasn't noticed by the shooter because the coat made the shooter warm and comfortable. So we now have a Catch 22. Does the shooter not wear a coat, brave the cold and at-

A properly fitted shotgun will allow the shooter to smoothly and effortlessly mount the gun in the correct place every time without the shooter even thinking about it. Improperly stocked shotguns are an insurmountable obstacle to overcome.

(Left and above) The 20 gauge shotgun is usually handed to a new shooter and it is an excellent choice. Most 20s from the factory are excellent Skeet "learner's" guns and their field stock dimensions serve — initially — quite nicely.

tempt to shoot under these conditions—or vice versa?

Another situation can occur ever so slowly with disintegrating scoreboard results. Many of us gain or lose weight throughout our lives. Some lose by diet, or illness and others gain by over-eating or possibly illness. Regardless, whether physical structure adds or depletes weight, the body changes shape and dimension. Two areas of change are important to a shooter—the amount and thickness of the flesh, fat or muscle in the shoulder and chest area and more important, the amount of flesh below the master eye in the area of the cheekbone.

There is no way to accurately measure how "thick" one's face is, nor to weigh the amount of flesh and muscle in the shoulder "pocket" area, so we'll have to use another means for measurement. In this case we'll use the shotgun stock as a reference. Once again, let's assume for a moment that you are shooting good scores

with your gun, it's comfortable, and you have all the confidence in the world while using it. At this time, accurately and precisely take the gun's physical measurements—the length of pull, drop at the heel and comb, pitch, and if possible the amount of cast-on or cast-off. Record these findings on a slip of paper and set them aside. An excellent location to preserve these important numbers is to remove the recoil pad or buttplate and inscribe them on the inside of the butt. These dimensions, taken today, could be very important to determine shooting problems—and solutions—in the future.

Six months down the shooting road, scores suddenly are beginning to deteriorate. Shooting averages, instead of going up are surely eroding. Why? If you have either lost or gained weight, then your face and/or body no longer correctly fit the stock dimensions. Obviously, something has to be altered to put things back in their

One of the world's finest shotgun shooters, John Satterwhite, is also a highly competent shooting instructor. With over 20 years of world-class shooting behind him, Satterwhite can correctly fit a shotgun to any trap or Skeet gunner.

correct position. It is theoretically possible to add face putty or body padding to correct for weight loss, but how do you immediately remove ⅛-inch of extra flesh from your cheekbone or ½-inch of fleshy tissue from the shoulder pocket? Realistically, neither can be done, so therefore the stock must be altered to once again correctly correspond to fit the semi-fixed dimensions.

Premiere shooters have learned how to adapt and compensate to varying conditions—both physically and emotionally. For physical alterations, there are numerous mechanical means. We won't go into the emotional conditions at this time, as we will cover this highly important subject in another chapter.

By now, we should realize and accept that all competitive shoots will not be held under ideal weather conditions. We'll encounter wind storms, rain squalls or fading light conditions throughout our shooting careers. Wind is the greatest influencing factor on the flight of the targets. An incoming (head) wind will always cause the target to rise in a higher arc than normal. A trailing (tail) wind, conversely, will lower the target's normal arc and force it to the ground faster than usual. For those selected few shooters who successfully shoot quicker than most, their ability to shoot fast will enable them to fire at targets before the wind can have any appreciable effect on them. During the initial 15 to 20 yards of the target's flight, the bird has not been influenced by wind conditions—it is still well under the influence of the momentum and speed dictated by the target throwing machine. Only a handful of shooters have been blessed with super-quick reaction time and reflexes. Most of us will be shooting at targets that have been influenced by the wind.

If our gunstock has been fitted to us and the shotgun's

(Left and below) Shotgun fit is perhaps a bit more important in trap shooting than in Skeet because of the distance the targets are being shot at. At longer trap shooting ranges, from 30 to 50 yards, slight errors are greatly magnified. Most Skeet targets are shot under 25 yards and a slightly imperfect stock fit goes virtually unnoticed.

pattern prints a 50/50 percentage, i.e., half of the shot swarm is above a common sighting point and half below, and we are shooting trap in a head wind, chances are we're attempting to break targets with only a half-pattern. Now this is really a handicap. It can be compared to attempting to hit targets by using shells containing only $\frac{9}{16}$-oz. of shot (maximum shot charge is 1-$\frac{1}{8}$ ozs. for all 12 gauge competitive events). If the wind continues to consistently blow in a set direction, wouldn't it be nice to be able to change the gun's point of impact—immediately and easily? There are ways!

The point of this scenario is that we must learn how to properly adjust to *all* the changing conditions around us if we are to become proficient trap or Skeet shooters. Up to now, we've only highlighted and pointed out problems, now its time to tell you some solutions.

One of the most respected gun stock makers in the world is Reinhart Fajen. Located in Warsaw, Missouri, Fajen has helped thousands of shotgun shooters with his unique ideas and innovative products. One of his latest, and most successful, is the Fajen Try-Stock. Initially intended to be used by other stock makers as a device to measure a shooter, this fully-adjustable stock has proven to be a boon for hundreds of competitive trap and Skeet shooters. Remember earlier in this chapter when we were discussing all the variables we will—or have—encountered and at that time wondered how we could compensate and make corrections for them? In most cases, the Fajen Try-Stock will serve the purpose and allow shooters to make necessary "fitting" corrections to compensate for varying conditions, either physical or weather-wise. The following was written by Reinhart Fajen and provides excellent insight from a leading expert on correct shotgun stock fit.

Distaff shooters need to be properly fitted to a shotgun more so than most men, due to greater physical differences. Ladies, as a rule, will begin to shoot a shotgun with a stock that is too short for them. After some experience, they'll realize the error of their ways and make proper corrections in length of pull.

Classes or shooting seminars are beneficial to learn how to shoot and more important, to determine how a shotgun should fit each individual for maximum shooting results.

Unless the shooter peers directly down the length of the shotgun barrel, he will encounter all kinds of problems which he can't define. To make corrections while shooting, the first requisite is a properly fitted gunstock — everything else will then naturally fall into place.

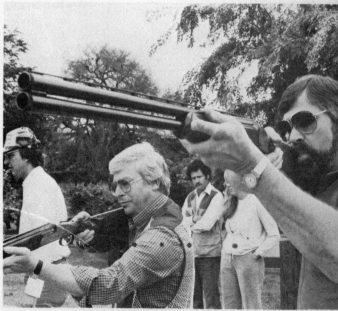

Gunstock Fit By Reinhart Fajen

"Our definition of a properly fitted gun can be simply stated by three rules, and if these are kept in mind, there should be no difficulty in arriving at the proper dimensions that are correct for any one shooter. This should also eliminate the thinking that certain features about a gunstock, outside these simple rules, will give some mysterious ability to never miss. A gunstock fits if: The shooter can *automatically* place the gun consistently in shooting position so that the barrel is pointing at the same object that he sees through or over the sights; secondly, he has complete control of the trigger; and thirdly, he feels no discomfort from recoil. Undivided attention can then be directed at the target, without the worry of deliberately lining up the sights, or anticipating the unpleasant effects of recoil. The shooter is then locked into a solid shooting unit, which can develop the confidence needed to make the best of one's ability.

"It is important that the three basic stock dimensions be determined in the following order: (1) Pull, or length of stock, is decided first, giving a base to properly determine (2) Drop and (3) *toe only* Cast at heel. The comb dimensions can then be developed precisely only after the first two are set correctly on the try stock. The length of pull is measured from the center of the trigger to the rear center face of the buttplate. The preceding is the procedure generally followed; however, it is more accurate to determine pull by measuring the distance from the rear of the trigger guard to the center of the buttplate, especially if the pull dimensions are used on various gun models. The rear of the trigger guard determines where your trigger hand and finger are located,

(Above and below) Master-hand placement and fit is critical to the control of a shotgun. The master hand does it all as the off-hand merely holds the front of the shotgun and controls the balance point. Photo above illustrates an improperly fitted pistol grip that causes the shooter to curl his little finger under the bottom of the grip to properly reach the trigger. Wrong! Photo below depicts the shooter's master hand firmly wrapped around the pistol grip and properly touching the trigger.

(Left) There must be at least 1½ to 2 inches of space between the shooter's thumb and his nose to prevent contact of these two points during recoil.

106

and this determines the *length-fit* of the stock. The trigger location within the guard can vary as much as 1-inch without having any effect on the stock fit. As one can see, if pull is measured on one gun with the trigger at the rear of the bow, and this same pull dimension is used on a gun with its trigger an inch forward, the *effective* pull, or *stock fit*, would be 1-inch different between the two guns. A uniform statement of pull can be given as: *The distance from the center of the rear of the buttplate to the rear center of the trigger guard bow, plus a nominal ½-inch to the front of the trigger.* This would give the same *fit* dimensions on guns whose trigger location varies within the bow.

"The 1929 catalog of the L.C. Smith Company, who at that time was making one of the better shotguns in the world, used this system of pull dimensions. The stock dimensions, and more importantly fit, could then be stated uniformly, regardless of whether the guns were equipped with single or double triggers. It is very likely that the commonly held notion that a shotgun should have an inch longer pull than a rifle, developed when the measurement was made from center rear of the buttplate to front center of the trigger on the rifle, and then made to front center of the *front* trigger of a double barrel shotgun, which was the most popular type at that time. This identical *effective* pull would then be incorrectly stated as an inch longer on the shotgun. This pull dimension will be determined by the shooter's physical measurements and his shooting stance, and not by one commonly held belief that proper pull dimensions should be determined by the distance from the first joint of the trigger finger to the inside of a bent elbow. If the shooter has a long neck and leans forward on the comb of the stock, a long pull is required. If he

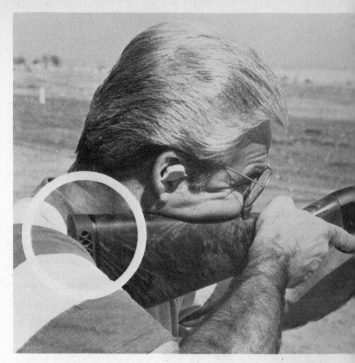

The top of the buttstock is above the line of the shooter's shoulder which clearly indicates improper stock fit. This shooter needs a gun stock with a Monte Carlo to lower the butt into the shoulder pocket while maintaining a comfortable head position on the comb.

(Left and above) Here the shooter is "crabbing" the stock in attempt to fit himself to the buttstock. All wrong! A higher comb and a Monte Carlo stock will enable the shooter to keep his head more erect and reposition the recoil pad squarely against the shoulder.

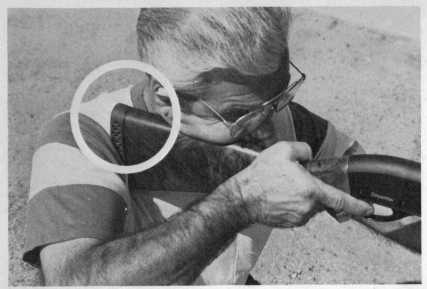

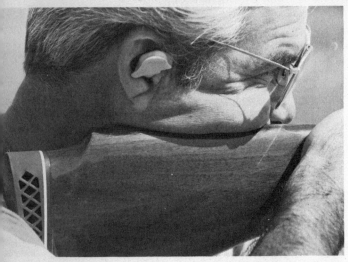

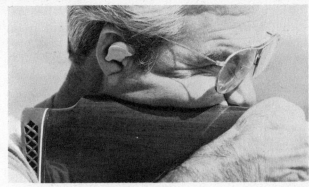

(Left, below left and below) For a shotgun stock to fit a shooter properly, it must enable the shooter to fit his cheek flush and comfortably against the top of the comb and at the same time the entire butt (recoil pad) must be square and in full contact with the shoulder pocket.

prefers to shoot with head erect, a shorter stock is in order. The length of the shooter's arms has nothing to do with proper length of stock, except that a person with long arms probably also has a long neck. The shooter should repeatedly mount his gun in normal shooting stance until a tentative length is set on the try stock. This length of pull must be initially determined independently of the other dimensions.

"In general summary, a stock is long enough if recoil does not jam the thumb into the nose, and short enough if the gun can be consistently placed into shooting position, smoothly and comfortably. This usually leaves room for choice of a suitable stock length if a level comb, such as found on a Monte Carlo style, is used. If however, the gun has a rather high comb, and slopes upward from heel to the point of the comb, and a firm contact is wanted, then a more precise pull dimension

must be determined. Simply stated, cheek pressure affects the relative height of the comb. This length of pull is fine for a shotgun or rifle with iron sights. The scope-mounted rifle presents another problem. The stock must be long enough, or the scope located, so that there is no danger of recoiling the rear of the scope into the eyebrow. This danger is increased as the angle of your shot goes up, which can happen in mountain hunting.

"After determining proper pull, the drop at heel, cast of toe and pitch should be determined. This is the distance from the sighting plane level, down to the top of the butt, and the vertical side angle of the buttplate.

"Generally, the shoulder muscles cover 2 to 3 inches of buttplate, and the drop should be such that this shoulder muscle takes recoil at about the center of the butt, so that the wide center part of the pad is centered on the shoulder. This avoids the hard top or bottom of

(Above and right) A shooter's particular style often dictates stock dimensions. Remember that the most important part of stock fit is to make the stock fit you, not the other way around. One exception to this rule is if your shooting stance is totally wrong, then a new and proper stance should be learned *before* going through the expense of a new stock. A qualified stockmaker will determine if your stance is totally wrong, needs marginal improvement or is acceptable to breaking targets.

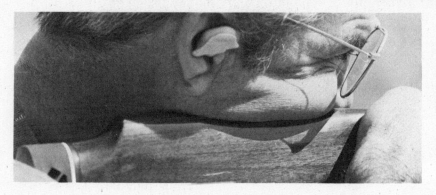

No two shooters are alike, either mentally or physically. Soft or "full" faced shooters will "spill" over the top of the stock comb and jam their face hard into the stock to make hard contact between the top of the stock and the cheekbone. Thin-faced shooters don't have to overcome excess facial tissue and may simply bring the stock to the face with little pressure to make proper contact.

the pad from punishing the shooter. In recent years, a trend is developing where the shooter prefers a normal upright stance rather than a head down and forward crawl on the stock. Many shooters are finding this position very effective. If the shooter prefers to shoot with the head erect, more drop at the heel is generally called for, using the Monte Carlo style of stock. This greater drop at the heel has been discouraged for many years, because of the painful experiences with most old time guns that came with stocks that had a lot of drop, and sharply rising combs toward the front. If the shooter had firm contact with the comb at the time of shooting, a bruised cheek would result. The painful kick was generally attributed to the excessive drop of the stock. Actually, the pain was caused by the upward slope of the comb, which was forcibly tightened against the side of the face as recoil jolted the gun toward rear, or by im-

proper contact of butt against shoulder. With the development of the level comb stock that fits properly, this upright stance works very well without undesirable effects from recoil, and lack of control.

"This erect position also permits the shooter who wears glasses to look at the target through the main part of the lenses rather than with head tilted down and forward, and looking through the top edge of the glasses at an angle. This posture could give a distorted view of the target location.

"Pitch, the vertical angle of the buttstock to the line of sight has been one of the problems with stocks that do not fit, and it's often not resolved. As a general rule, pitch should be zero to 1-inch down. This angle of the face of the recoil pad or buttplate should be about square with the force of recoil thrust, and fit flatly and evenly against the surface of the shoulder, so recoil is

This three-photo sequence illustrates a quick method to determine if a gun fits the shooter. (a) Hold the gun in both hands. (b) Focus both eyes on a particular object betwen 20 to 25 yards downrange. Then without moving head or body position, close both eyes. (c) Mount the shotgun, with both eyes closed. After the gun is mounted, open both eyes. If the gun isn't pointed close to the "aiming" subject, then gun probably doesn't fit well. Repeat this procedure a number of times until you can evaluate this procedure.

distributed through the full area of the wide center part of the buttplate, and absorbed through a like area of the shoulder. This eliminates painful jabs of the top or bottom of the buttplate, as well as sharp side edges of the butt where it would cut into the chest. Because of the firm fit, recoil is controlled and the gun remains in the same position before, during and after firing.

"A shooter who is full-chested or breasted may have the inside edge and/or toe of the buttplate dig into the chest and so prevent the center of the buttplate or recoil pad from fitting properly against the shoulder. Minor adjustments can be made by bevelling the inside edge of the recoil pad down through the toe, and dubbing off the toe itself. This, however, is not practical with a hard rubber or steel buttplate. In many cases this will not be adequate, so the *toe only* must be angled away from fullness to get that flat, full fit against the shoulder area,

and may be as much as an inch off center. This treatment will also correct a tendency to cant the gun off perpendicular. This proper fit aids in placing the gun in the same vertical no-cant shooting position each time and helps control recoil to a point where it is no problem.

"The proper length of pull and drop of heel have now been decided and set on the try stock. The next dimension to decide, and a very important one, is the drop of the comb at the point of contact with cheek and cheekbone. The instinct shooter probably wants very little cheek-stock contact and probably no contact with the cheekbone, especially in field or Skeet shooting. If you are not an automatic pointer, then you should have a positive fit at this point, and in our opinion, for field as well as target shooting.

"The comb at the contact area should be dimensioned so that there is a snug fit to the side of the cheek

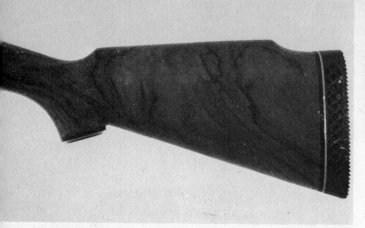

(Left and above) This stock for a Remington Model 31 is the author's "pet pumpgun" and was made by Pachmayr Gun Works from a piece of lightly grained English walnut. Not only was the stock custom fitted, but the fore-end was also carefully proportioned to provide proper balance and handling qualities.

(Below) The amount of drop at the Monte Carlo will be different for each shooter. Normal factory-made stocks will measure 1-inch of drop, whereas a custom stock maker might easily suggest 2 to 3 inches of drop depending on the shooter's physical dimensions and shooting style.

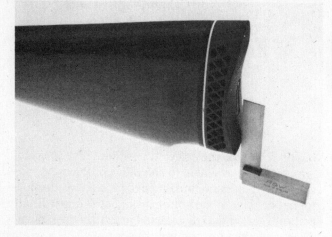

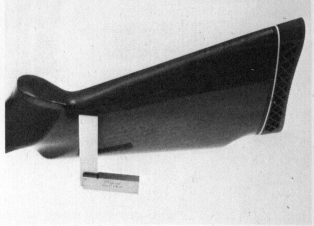

The drop at the comb is the single-most important measurement of a properly fitted shotgun stock. Because the shooter's eye is the "rear sight," head placement on the stock determines the correct and proper line of sight.

and under the cheekbone. The shooter can then, by feel, automatically line up with his sighting plane of the gun. For a more positive contact of the side of the face to the stock, a cheekpiece can be a big help. This firm contact of the cheekbone with the top of the comb can result in bruising that area if the conventional style stock is used which slopes upward from the heel, forward to the point of the comb. With this type of stock, the pressure to the cheekbone will increase as recoil jolts the gun to the rear. It requires very few of these bumps to cause pain and then flinching, with a common conclusion: 'This model, caliber, or brand of gun is not for me; it kicks too hard,' when the problem really is the upward sloping comb, or poor fit against the shoulder. Cast-off of comb and heel to a righthanded shooter can also result in tightening of the comb against face as recoil moves the gun to the rear. Good ear plugs, or

muffs, will cut down on muzzle blast which is sometimes confused with recoil, and eliminates a lot of the unpleasantness of recoil.

"For most shooters, the Monte Carlo type of stock, with lower heel, permits this snug positive fit without discomfort. The top of this stock style is the same height at the point of the comb, at the point of contact with the cheekbone, and at Monte Carlo (the raised portion at top rear). The comb tapers thinner toward the front and may slope downward toward the front slightly so as the recoil pushes the gun toward the rear, the pressure to the side of the face actually lessens, and there is no danger of discomfort and no reason for flinching. The level comb also allows a variation in horizontal contact with the cheekbone without altering the sight picture. This situation can develop when one changes the effective length of pull by wearing more or less clothing. This

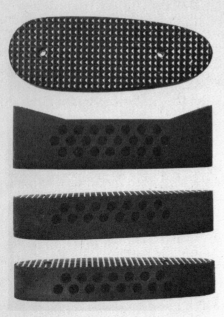

These recoil pads from Lujtic Industries are quite different than those supplied from Pachmayr, Supreme and others. The placement and size of the holes determine the amount of resiliency in the pad. The face design is also important and dictates the amount of "stick" to the shooter's shoulder.

A "try-gun" stock is the most beneficial aid to properly fitting a shooter to gunstock. Virtually every type of dimension can be adjusted to precisely determine a shooter's measurements — length of pull, comb height, heel height, cast, pitch, etc. By using one of these premiere measuring devices, much of the fitting technique employed by many stockmakers is left to qualified "guesstimates."

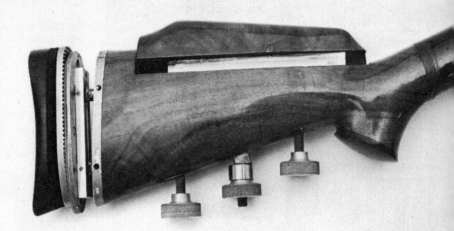

thickness of comb, rather than cast should be used to line up the shooter's eye laterally with the sights. For some shooters, the Monte Carlo style is not called for, because of physical dimensions and/or shooting stance, and the heel dimension can be the same as the level comb height. In a few instances, some stocks have been made with a reverse Monte Carlo where the heel is higher than the comb, so that the butt can be located properly against the shoulder.

"Accurate trigger control is very important for effective shooting. If the trigger is not pulled at the precise right instant, there is no hit. The shape and size of the pistol grip has a great deal to do with trigger control. Uniform trigger control can be had only if the trigger hand is in an identical, familiar and comfortable position on the pistol grip of the gun at each shot.

"It is very difficult to uniformly grasp the grip of most guns that have a half-moon shape far enough from trigger so that a giant would say: 'It fits.' This shape and size permits the *average* shooter to place the hand anywhere from close to the trigger guard to an inch or more toward the rear. Unless the shooter consciously and carefully places his hand in the same position each time, the trigger pull will be affected and a tight grip will be required to hold the selected position. Several custom grip styles are available to solve this problem. A more vertical grip, a thumbhole type, or the one with a locator tip, or curve at the bottom front of the grip will automatically locate the trigger hand in exactly the same position each time for uniform trigger pull. This also aids in holding the gun firmly against the shoulder, which is necessary for better recoil control without an overly tight grip of the trigger hand. This positive location of the trigger hand also avoids painful recoil bumping of the back of the trigger guard into the top of the middle finger.

"When these preliminary dimensions have been set, the Try-Gun should then be tried in actual shooting tests. Adjustments can then be made to suit between shots.

"Before the gun is fired, be sure the Try-Gun's two locking screws 'X' are set in the locking holes of the two pull adjustment rods, and all set screws snug only; do not over tighten, as this can easily damage the stock.

"After shooting enough to be satisfied that the proper dimensions have been arrived at, the various dimensions should be read and recorded. These dimensions can then be used to make a custom stock that fits."

Fajen's success with the Try-Gun stock has caused a great many trap and Skeet shooters to replace their present stock permanently with this unusual device—and for many, many good reasons. Earlier, we elaborated on different lengths of pull created by various layers of clothing. In the event that one wishes to shoot in a heavy, bulky jacket, then the try-gun stock's existing length of pull can be shortened to proper length. Ditto for angle of pitch. And for those who drastically and quickly lose or gain weight and it shows up in the cheek and cheekbone area, the height and cast off can also be altered easily with the try-stock.

The Fajen try-stock is a fiddler's delight, but its use can be overdone by a shooter lacking confidence in his or her particular style. The try-stock cannot break more targets, only you can do this. But, should shooting conditions vary and change from the norm, it can help you make necessary corrections. If you find that a certain set of dimensions work for you under certain shooting conditions—head wind, tail wind, wearing more than the normal amount of clothing—and if you perform reasonably well with these different stock dimensions—then write them down. Don't trust your memory, but make physical notes regarding the reasons why you made the changes and the results. And, don't forget that when weather and shooting conditions revert back to normal, re-adjust the stock back to its original dimensions.

For a seasoned competitor, it is difficult to change one's timing or placement of the gun to the shoulder. Yet, if we are to compete—and hopefully win—we must learn how to adapt to conditions. How many times have we heard our shooting comrades say, "I know I was doing it wrong, but I just couldn't stop it!" Non-

Gunstocks, for the most part, are made out of walnut although exotic and laminated versions are becoming popular. This pile of walnut ultimately represents over 3,000 shotgun stocks.

(Below) An engraved, skeletonized buttplate is a beautiful adornment and addition to any shotgun, but woefully wrong when found on a trap or Skeet gun. The time-proven rubber recoil pad is best for proper gun fit and if necessary, alterations.

This section of an English walnut tree will net nearly a dozen beautifully-grained shotgun blanks and fore-ends. Drying time will vary depending upon the moisture content of the tree, but there will be at least a 24-month wait until blanks can be sawed.

Shotgun blanks are layed out to make certain that the grain runs lengthwise with the stock for strength and beauty. These slabs, when eventually converted to shotgun stocks, are valued at almost $1,000 each.

From tree trunk to shotgun stock, if the stock does not properly fit the shooter, then all the graceful beauty in the world won't break targets!

sense. Bad habits can be broken easier than learning new techniques.

There are a couple of stratagems that may be used to compensate for sudden changes in the wind. For example, let's say that you are starting to shoot trap field number two and suddenly the day's gentle breezes drastically change into a forceful head wind. If you're familiar with your gun and you know where the center of the pattern prints in relationship to your line of sight, you immediately know that you'll have to "blot out" the higher rising target to compensate. This is a difficult bit of strategy to employ as covering the target eliminates it from view. This is "blind-side" shooting and is a fast way to disaster. A better technique is to lower the butt on your shoulder to where you see more space between the front and rear beads. This will cause the trap gun to shoot higher than your normal hold.

If the opposite wind conditions occur, then you can reverse the above procedure by raising the butt on your shoulder so that you'll see less rib exposed between the sights which will cause your gun to "flatten out," and you'll not shoot over the top of screeching "grass-cutters."

The best place and time to prove these tips is not on the firing line, but rather on a pattern board. Serious and dedicated trap and Skeet shooters spend as much time experimenting and making mental notes as they do shooting practice. Someone once said that great shooters don't think while they're shooting—but don't you believe it! The truly great shotgun shooters are thinking all the time and always expect the unexpected. More importantly, they know from previous experience how to cope with irregular targets or sudden changes in the weather.

Most trap and Skeet shooters have never had the opportunity to shoot a shotgun equipped with a try stock and that's a pity. These specially equipped guns have a completely adjustable buttstock that allows the "fitter" to dimension a stock tailormade for any shooter. A person really can't understand the utmost importance of stock dimensions until he or she shoots with a fully adjustable stock and can make corrections—during actual shooting conditions. The ability to immediately see the resultant differences is impressive and enables the new or experienced shooter to accurately judge how a shotgun stock should be properly fitted.

There's another way to determine if a shotgun stock properly fits you. Ask to try other shooters' guns. If possible, get permission to take one out to the range and fire a round or two with it—but, always use factory ammunition. It's in bad taste to use reloads in another person's pet gun just in the off-chance that something drastic should happen due to an improperly prepared reloaded shotshell. If you eventually "luck" into finding a gun that feels comfortable and you're breaking better than average scores, chances are that particular shotgun fits you better than your own. You have two options at this time: either try to buy the gun, or carefully measure and record the stock dimensions and compare it to your own. If there are any differences in length of pull, pitch, drop at heel or comb, cast, or if it is a Monte Carlo or straight stock design, write all this important information down. Then attempt to alter your existing stock by adding moleskin to the top of the comb to increase its height, or remove some of the wood on the comb to lower its height. Length of pull can be quickly and easily changed by adding cardboard spacers or sawing off a small slice at the butt, or by replacing the usual 1-inch thick recoil pad with a thinner version. Cast may also be altered by adding moleskin or removing wood in a similar manner as altering the height of the comb.

All of the above instructions are temporary "fixes" and will possibly require more attention as you gradually change the stock's dimensions until it fits you perfectly. While you are testing your "new" stock, record your scores for confirmation and future evaluation. Do not, repeat, do not at any time during this fitting process alter your original style of shooting. Remember you are making the gun fit you, not the other way around.

If your stock looks like a refugee from a remnant sale, don't be embarrassed. Only poor shooting scores will embarrass a shooter, never the appearance of the shotgun. One of the ugliest shotguns this writer has ever seen was an ancient, field grade Winchester Model 12 used by the fabled Arnold Riegger. The buttstock was fitted with a crude, lace-on pad to raise the comb to Riegger's preferred height and the small ring-tailed fore-end was out of place as "real" trapguns are equipped with the longer and extended fore-ends. On an aesthetic scale of one to ten, that old Model 12 would rate a minus three! But Riegger could have cared less, because it obviously fitted him to a "T" as his shooting records prove.

Once you've determined the proper fit, either by your own experimenting or with the aid of a professional stock maker/fitter, stick with the gun for at least a year of shooting, provided of course you haven't physically changed too much. Learn how to accept a minor shooting slump along with good scores. Even the best shooters have peaks and valleys—they're part of the great shooting games of trap and Skeet. Without them, we wouldn't come back to give it another go!

7 Trap Shooting Fundamentals

The shooter's weight is forward due to a slightly flexed left knee. Both feet must remain firmly planted on the ground. The entire upper torso, including a firmly positioned shotgun against the shoulder, all travel together in a single unit when swinging on the target.

I'M GOING TO let you in on a secret. There are three proven shortcuts to becoming an expert at shooting clay targets. In their order of importance they are: practice, PRACTICE and PRACTICE!

The best any tutorial can hope to do for you is to explain the basics, but, converting these instructions into a form that you can use is something you must do for yourself.

No matter how many books or photographs you've studied that illustrate proper shooting form or define leads and timing, none of these words of wisdom mean anything until you hit the target with regularity. And, that is something nobody else can do for you. It's been stated over and over by many competition shooters that given a shotgun, enough ammunition and money, even a chimpanzee could eventually become a AA, 27-yard trapshooter or a AAA Skeet shooter with all four guns.

The confusing aspect of trap shooting fundamentals is that there are so many of them. Trap shooting is divided into three separate segments: 16-yards (singles), handicap and doubles. For the most part, the shooter's stance and gun mount are about the same for all three events. There are a few nuances which we will discover a bit later, but for now we can state that a proper stance and gun mount for singles targets will work fine for handicap or doubles shooting.

To thoroughly understand gun mount and to learn the proper shooting stance, we should first break each of these segments into smaller portions for easier understanding.

The Master Eye

Before we become too involved in gun mount and stance, first we have to establish "eye dominance." People are classified as being right- or left-handed and the same holds true for eye dominance. Surprisingly, there is a large percentage of shooters who do not know which eye is dominant. For right-handed shooters the right eye is usually the "master" and vice versa for southpaws. But, unfortunately, nature sometimes

(Left, above and right) These three views of a proper trap-shooting stance enable the shooter to be comfortable and flexible. Compare these photos against what you look like while standing in front of a mirror. Check out foot position, slightly flexed left knee and elevation of arms and elbows.

makes mistakes and many righties are burdened with left eye dominance.

A quick and easy way to determine which eye is dominant is to place the index finger and tip of the thumb of the right hand together and form a circle. Pick a spot on the wall or any small object about 10 feet away. While keeping both eyes open, frame the target within your handmade "O" and extend your hand approximately 12 to 15 inches away from your face. After the target is centered, close the *left* eye. If the sighted object remains within circle, then the right eye is dominant. If the object has moved out of the circle, to the left, then the left eye is dominant. Go ahead and try it a couple of times, we'll wait for you . . .

Ready to go again? Fine! If you've discovered that your right eye is dominant and you're a right-handed shooter then all's well. The opposite would be correct

for lefties. But, if you've proven to yourself that your master side and master eye are 180 degrees opposed, then some corrective measures must be taken before any shooting lessons begin. Novices may at this time state what's the big deal, they "shoot pool" or participate in other hand-to-eye coordinating games with both eyes open and never run into any problems, why is trapshooting different?

The problem arises because the shooter must sight down the barrel and at the same time pick up the flight of the target, and this can only be done properly with both eyes working together. The master eye provides the shooter with a proper line of sight, while the "off" eye takes care of the depth perception and peripheral vision. It's really more complicated than that, and an optometrist could undoubtedly do a more detailed scientific explanation.

Now here are a couple of ways in which a right-handed shooter can overcome the problem of having to contend with a left master eye. First, the obvious method is to completely cover the left eye with either a patch over the eye or by blackening out the left lens of the shooting glasses. Neither is recommended, as eliminating one eye causes the other to do double duty and nature will make the single eye take on the added responsibility of providing depth perception which is primarily the role of the "off" eye. A better method is to merely diffuse the vision of the left eye by restricting its vision by placing a small ¾- by 1½-inch strip of Scotch Magic Mending tape directly on the left eyeglass lens, which will enable the left eye to "see out" but it will reduce its role from dominance to passiveness. Therefore, if only the right eye has clear vision of the target, it then will artificially assume the role as master eye.

Another method to compensate for "wrong" eye dominance is to have a special "cripple" stock made for the shotgun. John Amber, of GUN DIGEST fame, is one of the more notable shooters who has used this unorthodox system for many years, and anybody who has butted shotguns with this fine gentleman, knows that he's certainly not handicapped by using a cross-over stock. Briefly, this stock has an acute bend in it slightly behind the wrist (pistol grip) area which enables the right-handed shooter to place his head and cheek in a traditional position, but the stock's "bend" is approximately

the distance between the shooter's eyeballs. Therefore, the shooter retains his right hand dominance while peering down the barrel with his left eye. The making of one of these is only accomplished by a master stockmaker and one who can accurately select a stock blank with properly structured grain that will withstand recoil without shattering after a few rounds are fired.

In 1968, while competing in a 500-target, 16-yard marathon at Walla Walla, Washington, I witnessed a remarkable degree of success by a shooter overcoming the dreaded wrong eye syndrome. Throughout the 20 fields covered that day, this elderly gentleman had shot the entire 500-target event by placing the shortened buttstock on his left shoulder, grasping the pistol grip with his right hand and placing his left cheek against the right side of the buttstock. In essence, he was shouldering the gun left-handed, but shooting right-handed while using the only "good" eye he had. He later explained to me that he lost his eye in an industrial accident only 18 months earlier, had attempted to shoot left-handed, but as he was nearly 60 years old, he couldn't successfully make the drastic switchover. And yet, his score for the marathon was well into the 490s out of 500 and, as I recall, he won his class handily.

I've also seen trap guns equipped with add-on ventilated ribs attached to the left side of the barrel which enables the shooter to use a left master eye to peer down this secondary "railroad track." Shooters go to

Here are some exaggerated examples of how shooters hold their shotguns.

Photo "1" is a modified form of a rifleman's position and the elevated right elbow places too much strain on the shooter's neck muscles. The nearly vertical left arm causes the left shoulder to droop and brings it too far forward thereby upsetting the shooter's balance.

In photo "2," the shooter's right arm is improperly positioned as defined in Photo "1" and the left arm is too high which prevents the shooter from balancing the shotgun properly.

Photo "3" is the opposite extreme of photos "1" and "2" and the lowered right arm virtually eliminates the "pocket" formed at the shoulder when the arm is elevated to approximately 45 degrees.

great lengths to compensate for physical handicaps in order to stay in the game.

Gun Mount

Form or style in trap and Skeet shooting is probably more important than in most other hand and eye co-ordinated sports. To attain and retain the proper style of shooting, one must cultivate it early in the game, as there's nothing more difficult than to change one's style when it has virtually become a habit.

Most instructors much prefer to work with a total novice because they don't have to undo bad habits. That way they can start from page one and teach the new shooter the proper way to stand, shoulder the gun and learn about lead and sight picture.

There are only four physical points where the shooter is in contact with the trap gun—both hands, cheek and shoulder. Simply stated, gun mounting is the act of picking up the shotgun with both hands and bringing it up to the cheek and placing it against the shoulder. This seemingly uncomplicated maneuver has proven to be the downfall of many trap shooters before they really ever had the chance to become good shots. The biggest problem that I've witnessed over the years is the manner in which most tyros mount the shotgun.

For some inexplicable reason, the most common mounting error is when the novice brings the gun to his shoulder and then cants his head against the stock. This creates the following problems: First, as the shooter's head is not level to the ground, his eyes are also at an unnatural "cant." None of us walk around with our head tilted, yet too many competitors shoot in this most unnatural manner. Second, this position places undue stress and strain on the shoulder and neck muscles. In a very short time, these muscles will revolt by cramping and the obvious result will be lost targets. Proper stance, therefore, must first be comfortable and second, be within reasonable limits of total control of the shotgun through the various arcs of the target.

Stance

Granted, stance and style vary greatly from one shooter to another, and I've seen some exceptionally high scores recorded by shooters who employ a strange looking stance. But these same shooters are exceptions to the rules of stance and body control and a new shooter should not copy one of these "off-beat" stances just to look like a seasoned competitor.

Positioning of the feet in relationship to the anticipated flight of the target is also critical. The shooter must place his feet in a position to enable him to twist his body—from the waist—to any comfortable position within a 45 degree arc in relationship to the post on which he is standing. Earlier, there was a chart showing the legal flight path of a trap target—about 22 degrees on either side of a straight line drawn from the center

2

3

post or Station Three. Take another look at it for better understanding of "legal target flight path."

Tracking with the target is not done by swinging the shotgun from the shoulders and arms, but instead by pivoting from the waist and flexing at the left knee. The shotgun, arms, neck, shoulders, head and eyes should be locked together as a single, solid unit and move together when the shooter goes after the target. The left leg should be slightly bent at the knee which provides flexibility of the upper body and controls changes needed for elevation. In other words, rotating from the waist controls horizontal movements and the left (lead) leg directs vertical adjustments. The flexed knee also provides proper front-to-rear stability because recoil will shove the shooter backwards as soon as the shot is fired. The knee, therefore, also acts as a shock absorber and as the upper body is jolted by the shotgun's recoil, the left knee is automatically straightened and the shooter's balance is retained. Naturally, these two parts of the body must learn to work in perfect unison, but in time, and after a few hours of introducing Mr. Waist to Mr. Knee, they'll go together like ham and eggs.

The distance between the shooter's feet will vary because no two people are built alike. But as a guide, most shooters are able to hold their balance by spreading their heels about 9 to 12 inches apart. Wider stances seem to "lock up" a shooter and thus prevent a smooth approach to the target. Narrower stances tend to reduce the shooter's stability by creating a smaller angle of balance. Again, let me emphasize that the most important consideration is an individual's comfort. If the above dimensions are not natural, nor comfortable in their use, then disregard them—but only if you are breaking good scores and not having serious shooting problems.

By observing some of the best trap shooters, they seem to have an almost nonchalant shooting style. They always seem relaxed and under total body control, and they really are. They learned long ago that a proper and comfortable stance prevents fatigue and allows them to concentrate totally on the flight of the upcoming target. Correct stance and gun placement will, with enough practice, become an intuitive act. Achieving this perfection usually happens after a few months of shooting. Some psychoanalyst once noted, "If a person performs a physical or mental act the very same way for 21 consecutive times, predicated by thinking about it, the 22nd occurrence will happen automatically, without thinking about it," or words to that effect. Proper stance can be quickly learned, practiced and in a short time will become second nature.

Hand and Arm Position

The position of the shooter's hands and arms in relationship to the shotgun are part of stance and form. Let's first discuss the hands. The master hand—the one which grasps the pistol grip and manipulates the trigger

In Photo "4" the shooter is close, but no cigar as the left arm is still a mite too high and over a long shooting day cramp the left shoulder's muscles.

Photo "5" is just about perfect arm position for most shooters. The right arm is held high enough to form a proper "pocket" in which to place the shotgun butt while the left arm is in balance to hold the shotgun. To check your own shooting style against these photos, stand in front of a mirror and compare your own arms' position.

4

5

This shooter has assumed a good solid stance with weight slightly forward by flexing the left knee. Both feet are planted solidly on the ground and must remain in position while going after the target.

Here, the shooter is leaning forward only from the waist, which places his weight too far forward and the upper body is completely out of control when swinging after the target.

This position may be fine for "ducking under a swinging right-hand punch," but it places too much strain on the shooter's lower back and leg muscles. It also makes the shooter feel he is always shooting "uphill."

This shooter is too "stiff" and does not have any natural mobility in the upper torso. The left knee is not flexed and while it may look like a "classic" stance, it does little to break targets with any degree of consistency.

Which one of these five photos is correct hand placement for the "off" hand? If you said none of them, you'd be absolutely right! Let's find out why. In photo 1, the shooter's hand is too far forward on the fore-end and usually causes "underswinging." In photo 2, the hand is placed too far back which creates "overswinging" and the index finger is not pointed downrange. In photo 3, there's no control because the hand is merely holding the shotgun up—nothing more. In photo 4, the index finger is pointed downrange, but the hand is still located too far to the rear on the fore-end. In photo 5, the hand is too far to the rear and the index finger is not pointing downrange.

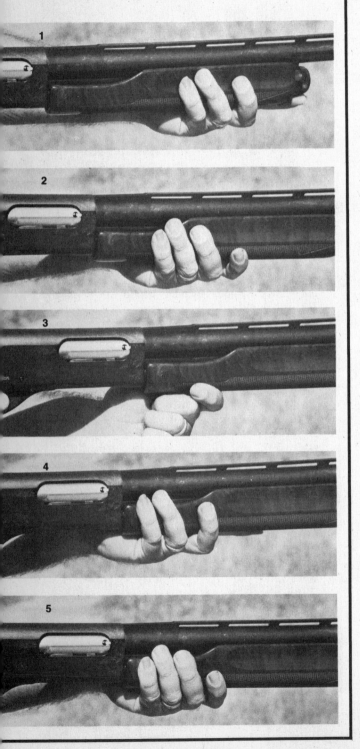

is the more important of the two. It should initially encircle the pistol grip firmly and just before firing the shotgun it should be squeezed tighter. The master hand controls the gun while the off-hand merely supports the front of it. There are those who preach and teach that the off hand controls the gun while the other hand merely pulls the trigger. Tain't so! Taking a firm grip on the shotgun with the master hand keeps the buttstock locked in position against the shoulder and also absorbs a great deal of the gun's generated recoil through anticipation of firing.

To prove this point, the next time you're out at the range try this enlightening experiment. Step up to the line, load a shell in the chamber and mount the gun, but don't pull the trigger. Instead, keep your trigger finger out of the trigger guard and ask a friend to step up along side of you and by using his thumb and index finger, have him pull the trigger at his discretion. By not knowing when the shotgun will go off, the full effect of recoil will be absorbed by your shoulder. Not only does this test dramatize the full effects of recoil, but it helps to establish the fact that the master hand does indeed absorb recoil.

The "proper" position of the trigger finger is relative to the shooter. I prefer to place the first pad against the trigger blade, probably due to early pistol training. This is the most sensitive area of the finger. Some shooters place the trigger blade in the first joint. Again, it's a matter of personal preference.

While talking about triggers, I would like to take on a "sacred cow." All too often we read that shotgun triggers should be "slapped," and that by definition means that the trigger finger should not touch the trigger until the instant of firing. The reasons given for this method are safety, overcoming heavy triggers and quicker response. Personally, I find that none of these explanations are valid. First, by stationing the finger away from the trigger until that sudden "moment of truth" is time consuming and it requires a complex series of instructions for the new shooter to learn. Like one of Parkinson's Laws, "More complex—sooner dead," therefore, keep movements simple and straightforward. Second, regarding excessive trigger pull weights, there's no reason for any competitive trap or Skeet shooter to use a shotgun with an inordinately heavy trigger pull weight. What is "inordinate?" In past years, most quality competition guns were set at the factory to release at between 3½ and 5 lbs. In recent years, however, many trap and Skeet guns have triggers "factory-adjusted" to meet specifications and restrictions set forth by the insurance companies that carry the manufacturer's liability insurance. For some inexplicable reason, known only to these underwriters, they have forced shotgun manufacturers to increase trigger pull weights to the point of being ridiculous. I've recently tested "competition"-type trap and Skeet guns with trigger pulls in excess of 10 lbs. which is at least twice as heavy as they

Keep the master hand down and around the pistol grip for maximum gun control and for proper reach to the trigger. The photo above is right and the photo below is obviously wrong.

butt than is made by using a "low" elbow position. The advantage of the "low" elbow is that it is more natural, thus comfortable, and is less tiring to the shooter over the long haul. Therefore, elbow position is a "choosie" proposition and the new shooter should initially try each style and eventually settle on the elbow position that works for him.

Muzzle Position

One of the most often asked questions by a beginner is where he should hold the shotgun in relationship to the trap house. To answer that question, I have to say that to become a skillful trap shooter, the tyro must pick up the flight of the target as soon as it leaves the trap house and second, shoot at the target as close to the

should be for needed sensitivity and quick response between shooter and shotgun.

Conversely, a trigger pull can be too light. Anything less than 3 lbs. is not recommended as it can cause premature release of the trigger by the shooter's natural tightening of the finger just before the shot is fired. Also, in the event that the shotgun is dropped to the ground with a live shell in the chamber, a light trigger could slip off its precarious perch and thus allow the hammer to release and strike the firing pin. I've been able to fire a shotgun with a lightened trigger—releasing at about to 2 pounds—by first, making certain that there was no shell in the chamber, and then from a height of 12 inches dropping the buttstock onto a hard surface. This is a controlled test, but nevertheless valid to determine if a shotgun's trigger pull is too light and unsafe.

Arm and elbow position is subject to suit a shooter's needs and comfort. Generally though, the position of the elbows should be about 45 to 50 degrees relative to the horizontal plane of the shotgun. Some shooters prefer a "high" elbow, similar to that style prescribed by rifle shooters. In this position a better fitting pocket is formed at the shoulder in which to place the shotgun

The tip or first pad is the most sensitive part of the finger, and therefore, it should be placed against the trigger (above). Shotgun triggers are designed to be pulled straight back, not from one side like photo below.

This ten-photo sequence illustrates the proper gun placement for each trap shooting post No. 1 through No. 5 from two different angles. The circle indicates where the shooter should align the shotgun's muzzle in relationship to the post he is standing on. At **Post #1**, the muzzle should be slightly above the roof of the traphouse and at the left corner.

house as possible. Therefore, the position of the gun muzzle in relation to the trap house is critical to performing these two important criteria.

Let's go through gun placement post-by-post, which will be the same for 16-yard singles or handicap shooting. We'll talk about doubles a little later in this chapter. Again, we're going to explain gun position for a right-handed shooter; in most cases, lefties will have to mirror these instructions.

At Post #1, most right-handed shooters swing better to the left than they do to the right on a right angle target. Swinging "better" means that the movement of shotgun and body is more natural due to the position of the arms and shoulders. Also, when the gun is moved to the left, the comb has a tendency to "stick" to the shooter's cheek because the master hand is forcing the stock to the face while moving the entire shotgun after the fleeing target. Let's take a break for a moment and try a little experiment.

Stand up and assume a shooting stance. Pretend that you have your shotgun cradled between your hands and assume a mounted position with the gun shouldered, placing your right hand up to your cheek and your left hand out where you would hold up the front part of the shotgun. Now, visualize that you have called for your

target and a left angle appeared. Quickly go after it. Did you notice that your right hand seemed to automatically press harder against your cheek? If it didn't, it should have, so try it a few more times. Now perform this same experiment pretending that you are moving for a tough right angle target. This part of the experiment should illustrate the tendency for a right-handed shooter to pull the stock and comb away from his face and cheek—not by design but due to muscular makeup. This body reaction is reflexive and like backing away from somebody who's going to throw a punch at you. The point of this is that if we can understand what our body is going to do before it does it, the brain can then make corrections to compensate. Now, back to the trap house.

Although the trap machine is supposed to be located dead-center within the trap house, quite often it isn't, but the shooter can quickly determine the machine's position by watching the target's flight on the preceding squad. If a "straightaway" target from Post #3 appears to be on a dead straight line with the 50-yard stake, then the machine is properly located. The correct starting position of the gun barrel in relation to the trap house for Post #1 would be to aim about 18 inches above the left corner of the trap house. At Post #2, the muzzle

At **Post #2,** the muzzle should be situated halfway between the left corner and the center of the traphouse.

At **Post #3,** the muzzle should be slightly to the right of center to prevent the muzzle from covering the view of a straightaway target.

At **Posts #4 and #5** (opposite page), a right-handed shooter should "cheat" a bit and start at a place well to the right side of the traphouse.

should be aimed at a point halfway between the left corner and the center of the trap house. Usually, most shooters are taught to hold dead-center on Post #3. I believe this is poor advice due to the flight of a straightaway target which seemingly comes out of the house directly under the barrel and therefore, the target's initial flight is obscured by the gun's barrel. I recommend a hold slightly to the right of center, about 9 to 12 inches, which will enable the shooter to quickly "read" a straightaway target. At Post #4, the barrel should not be pointed to a spot halfway between the right hand corner and center as prescribed for Post #2, but rather closer to the outside edge of the house. At Post #5, the shooter should "cheat" even more by starting at a point from 12 to 15 inches outside of the trap house's right hand corner. The reason a right-handed shooter should hold more to the right on Posts #4 and #5 involves what we discussed earlier in describing how and why a right-handed shooter swings better to the left and poorer to the right. "Favoring" the muzzle position on Posts #3, #4 and #5 helps the shooter to catch up with tougher right angle targets.

These "starting positions" are subject to change as wind conditions dictate. In the event of a head wind, which will quickly elevate targets, the shooter will find

RECOIL FACTOR WITH 30-34-INCH SHOTGUN BARRELS

3-DRAM, 1⅛-OUNCE		2¾-DRAM, 1⅛-OUNCE	
Weight Gun	Ft. Lbs. Recoil	Weight Gun	Ft. Lbs. Recoil
6.0 lbs.	20.2	6.0 lbs.	18.5
6.5 lbs.	18.6	6.5 lbs.	17.1
7.0 lbs.	17.3	7.0 lbs.	15.9
7.5 lbs.	16.1	7.5 lbs.	14.8
8.0 lbs.	15.1	8.0 lbs.	13.9
8.5 lbs.	14.2	8.5 lbs.	13.1
9.0 lbs.	13.4	9.0 lbs.	12.4
9.5 lbs.	12.7	9.5 lbs.	11.7

RECOIL FACTOR WITH 24-29-INCH SHOTGUN BARRELS

3-DRAM, 1⅛-OUNCE		2¾-DRAM, 1⅛-OUNCE	
Weight Gun	Ft. Lbs. Recoil	Weight Gun	Ft. Lbs. Recoil
6.0 lbs.	20.5	6.0 lbs.	18.9
6.5 lbs.	18.9	6.5 lbs.	17.4
7.0 lbs.	17.6	7.0 lbs.	16.2
7.5 lbs.	16.4	7.5 lbs.	15.1
8.0 lbs.	15.4	8.0 lbs.	14.1
8.5 lbs.	14.5	8.5 lbs.	13.3
9.0 lbs.	13.7	9.0 lbs.	12.6
9.5 lbs.	13.0	9.5 lbs.	11.9

that he should raise the muzzle and hold a "higher" gun. Depending on the velocity of the wind, a proper hold could range from 18 to 30 inches above the roof of the trap house. Conversely, should a tail wind appear, which drives targets down, a "lower" gun mount would be necessary, ranging from 6 inches below the roof line to 12 inches above it. If a cross-wind has an apparent effect on the target's flight, the wise shooter will make gun positioning adjustments accordingly.

Some shooters can quickly pick up the direction of the target as it leaves the trap house, while to others it only appears to be a flashing blur. As soon as you can determine and chart its course, move the muzzle ahead of the target and pull the trigger. Shoot as quickly as possible. Don't attempt to become too "fine" in your pointing. The longer you wait, the farther the target will travel. Never hesitate or "ride a target!" If you acquire this bad habit, it'll be very difficult to overcome.

Most new shooters are not told where to focus their eyes. Some stare at the front sight like rifle and pistol shooters, some concentrate on the trap house. The preferred method is to "look" down the barrel, but focus at an area about 17 yards past the trap house while looking for the target. The end of the barrel will automatically be in your peripheral vision and the muzzle will be natu-

COMPUTED LEADS FOR TRAP SHOOTING

Station	Target Position	16 Yds. Lead (in.) Horiz.	Vert.	21 Yds. Lead (in.) Horiz.	Vert.	27 Yds. Lead (in.) Horiz.	Vert.
1	1	0	7	0	10	0	15
	2	10	7	13	10	17	15
	3	19	8	25	11	34	16
	4	27	10	36	13	48	17
	5	35	12	45	15	61	19
2	1	10	7	13	10	18	15
	2	0	7	0	10	0	15
	3	10	7	13	10	18	15
	4	19	8	25	11	34	16
	5	27	10	36	12	48	17
3	1	19	8	25	11	34	16
	2	10	7	13	10	18	15
	3	0	7	0	10	0	15
	4	10	7	13	10	18	15
	5	19	8	25	11	34	16
4	1	27	10	36	13	48	17
	2	19	8	25	11	34	16
	3	10	7	13	10	18	15
	4	0	7	0	10	0	15
	5	10	7	13	10	18	15
5	1	35	12	45	15	61	19
	2	27	10	36	13	48	17
	3	19	8	25	11	34	16
	4	10	7	13	10	18	15
	5	0	7	0	10	0	15

rally guided to the target by your eyes.

Because we are shooting at a moving target, a "lead" is necessary. But how much? That is an impossible question for anyone to answer other than the shooter. No two people compute the same, especially in open space. What appears to be 12 inches may be 3 feet to another due to the speed of a shooter's swing. There is an accompanying chart nearby which defines both vertical and horizontal leads, at various yardages. This information is predicated on the shotgun's barrel moving at the

VELOCITY AND TIME OF FLIGHT OF TARGETS AT VARIOUS DISTANCES FROM TRAP HOUSE

Distance	Velocity (fps)	Flight Time
0 yards	85 fps	—
20 yards	47 fps	1.0 seconds
25 yards	43 fps	1.3 seconds
30 yards	40 fps	1.7 seconds
50 yards	31 fps	3.4 seconds

same visual speed as the target. Yet, under actual shooting conditions, some people are moving the gun faster than the apparent speed of the target, and some move slower. Therefore, a shooter with a faster swing would have to reduce his "lead" as prescribed from the chart; conversely, a person with a slower swing would be required to increase the prescribed amount of "lead."

Nobody said that trap shooting was an easy sport to learn, but once proper leads are emblazoned on a

shooter's mind, they're there forever, so don't fret if you're confused about leads and timing. They'll eventually both come to you with practice, PRACTICE, and more PRACTICE!

Let's discuss trap shooting's other event—Doubles. The shooter is required to shoot at two targets thrown simultaneously while standing on the 16-yard line. As a rule, the "straightaway" target is shot first and then the angle target. Sounds easy enough, doesn't it? Yet, doubles is trap shooting's most difficult game for the newcomer to learn. Unlike singles and handicap shooting, where only one target and shot is required, doubles demands specialized equipment. Single-shot shotguns are obviously not recommended. Most doubles shooters prefer using over-under shotguns for two reasons. First, the availability of two different chokes and second, their high degree of reliability. Some doubles contestants use autoloading shotguns, but their use is frowned on by other shooters due to the shotgun's ejection system. Unless the autoloader is altered in a manner to launch the empty hulls in a direction away from nearby shooters, the one using an autoloading gun not so equipped will often be asked to quit shooting—and rightly so. Being hit anywhere on the body from an ejected empty hull is very distracting and irritating. I don't recommend autoloaders for doubles events for this reason.

I also do not recommend that a newcomer to trap shooting jump into the doubles segment until he has become fairly proficient at both singles and handicap shooting. Shooting a poor score at doubles tends to lower confidence, and as a result, singles and handicap averages will plummet. Learn one segment at a time before advancing to a more difficult challenge.

Skeet Shooting Fundamentals 8

IT'S OFTEN been said that trap shooting is easier to learn but difficult to master and vice versa for Skeet shooting. The very first time I ever tried clay target shooting was at the old Aqua Sierra Gun Club located in Chatsworth, California. The year was 1957 and I was invited by a friend who recently discovered Skeet shooting and asked if I'd like to come along and give it a try. I said I would and off we went.

Armed with a well-used 12-gauge Browning Auto-5, my first crack at clay target shooting was at Skeet—supposedly an easier game or so I was told by all the "experts." For my first attempt at Skeet I recorded an embarrassing score of three out of 25. I was mentally shattered and quietly cursed my friend for talking me into this humiliating experience. Ready to pack it up and call it a day after a single shooting "lesson," one of the club members came up to me and asked if I'd like to shoot trap as he noticed that I didn't fare well on the

Skeet range. Under any other set of circumstances I would have politely begged off, but the interested shooter was none other than Frank Ferguson—a long time character actor in films and television and how could I refuse shooting with a "movie star!"

After listening to Frank's mini-clinic on how to shoot trap, I was fortunate enough to break a respectable 17x25, and from that point on I was smitten by the clay target bug.

The point to be taken is, should you not do well at your first attempt at either trap or Skeet, then try the other game. You'll quickly find that one or the other is initially best suited to your tastes and fits your "untrained" shooting style. You may switch to the other game later in your shooting career, but don't quit if you encounter a poor beginning—we all did!

The reason that Skeet is easier to "master" than trap is because the shooter knows ahead of time where the

Don't lean excessively forward while taking the shot. The shooter's weight should be slightly forward with both feet on the ground.

Comfort and flexibility are the two important ingredients which make a good, solid Skeet shooting stance. At each station (post) the shooter must fire at two totally different targets — an outgoer and an incomer. At stations #1, #2, #6 and #7, both of these targets are thrown simultaneously to make the game more interesting.

(Right) Prior to mounting the gun and calling for a target, collect your thoughts and mentally review the proper lead to break the target. Call it concentration or dedication, but all the best shooters are positive thinkers.

target is going to fly. Also, after some experience, he should be able to predict the exact spot where he'll shoot and hopefully hit the target. Therefore, stance and gun placement are the keys to breaking Skeet targets with consistency.

Regardless of the station the shooter is standing on, he should initially set up his stance to the approximate spot where he wants to break the target. After this is established by positioning the feet and body, he then twists only his upper torso in the direction of the trap house. Once the feet are positioned, they should not be moved until after the shot is taken.

The shooter's feet must be re-positioned for each target regardless of which station he is standing on because the outgoing and incoming targets should be shot at different locations in relationship to where the shooter is standing.

As in trap shooting, the shooter's stance must be comfortable with the shotgun snuggled tightly to the shoulder and cheek. The left knee should be bent slightly more than a trap-shooting stance because the Skeet shooter uses a more pronounced and longer swing.

(Above and below) A commonly made mistake by many Skeet shooters is lifting the rear foot by leaning too far forward into the gun. For best shooting results, keep both feet firmly planted on the ground — as they were intended — and shift body weight forward by bending the front knee.

This Skeet shooter uses the "finger-pointing" technique to help him guide his shotgun to the target. This is an excellent example of "good form" and will greatly contribute to better gun handling characteristics.

The positioning of the hands on the shotgun is very important as the "lead" or non-master hand controls the speed of the shooter's swing. For a properly balanced hand position, the lead hand is an equal distance from the shotgun's center of balance—usually where the barrel(s) meet the receiver—in relation to the master hand. Because the master hand cannot be easily moved fore or aft, as it must reach the trigger, the lead hand controls the balance of the shotgun. Usually, the proper position of the off hand is near the middle of the fore-end. If a Skeet shooter finds that he is swinging too slowly, he can merely slide his left hand back a touch which automatically increases the swing speed as the center of balance is altered and makes the gun muzzle heavy. Conversely, moving the left hand out—or, forward—on the fore-end usually reduces muzzle speed.

Many well-intended Skeet instructors preach that the target should be broken where it crosses the middle stake. In actual shooting, however, top shooters rarely break the target at this location. Both incoming and outgoing targets are shot at as close as possible. If you were in a duck blind, wouldn't you rather shoot at a fast-flying teal at 20 yards than 35? An African "white hunter" once told his client that the secret to bagging big-game animals is to sneak as close as possible and then slip up 10 yards closer! The old tale about waiting for a target to get downrange to make better use of the spreading shotgun's pattern is poor advice. You should always shoot outgoing targets *before* they cross the middle stake and incoming targets *after* they cross it.

There are three distinctly different types of leads Skeet shooters employ. First, the overwhelming majority of Skeeters use a **sustained** lead. Simply, the shooter tracks the target with the shotgun's muzzle at

(Left and above) Skeet targets are shot at close range — rarely exceeding 21 yards and, when possible, even closer. The old tale about waiting on the target so that the shotgun's choke has a better opportunity to "open up" is misleading. You should always attempt to shoot outgoers before they reach the middle stake and incomers after they pass this mid-point. The closer the better!

Most tournament Skeet shooters use a sustained lead by which they track the flying target with the end of the shotgun's muzzle at the same speed as the target and when the lead seems about right, pull the trigger. If done properly, a puff of black smoke will fill the air!

the same speed as the target is moving and when the sight picture appears to be right, pulls the trigger and continues moving the muzzle after the shot to promote follow-through. The second type is **swinging through** where the shooter points the muzzle slightly behind the target and subconsciously "whips" the muzzle past the target and pulls the trigger. I've asked successful Skeet shooters who employ this method what various leads they see for different targets and they state that all leads are the same, but the swinging through motion of the gun at varying speeds provides the proper lead. This is a very difficult thing to learn. And, third, there is the **spot** shooting technique where the shooter aims at a location where he believes the target will fly, shoots well in advance of the target meeting this spot and hopefully the target will intercept the shot swarm. This style isn't as inefficient as one might think; in fact on calm, windless days, spot shooters usually beat the pants off their competitors who are using either of the other two styles. Where the spot shooter gets into trouble is when the wind is blowing and the flight of the target is both erratic and unpredictable.

I shall not attempt to tell you how to lead a target because this subject is conjecture. The actual amount of lead for each target is fixed and calculable, but what appears to me to be 2 feet at 20 yards, may look like 6

Watch the target being broken with the shotgun properly mounted against the face and shoulder. Pulling the gun away too quickly will eventually create follow-through errors.

(Left) The Skeet shooter must employ a longer swing and follow-through than the trap shooter. Therefore, his stance must be more flexible. The left leg should be bent to provide a smooth pivot point for the entire body and smooth swing.

inches to you. Remember when you were a youngster heaving rocks and stones at anything that moved. It didn't take you very long to realize that you had to throw well in front of a moving object to assure a hit. Nobody could explain to you how much to lead your target—only by trial and error experience did you learn the feel.

Picking up the flight of the target as soon as it leaves the trap house is of great importance in shooting good scores. There are two places to initially look for the target—at the opened window of the trap house or down the gun barrel until it comes into view. But, under no circumstances should you ever shoot at a target when it isn't perfectly clear and sharp in your line of vision. The initial flight of the target will appear to be blurred because the eyes cannot focus on such a fast moving object. Wait a fraction of a second until the target is distinctly recognizable and its relationship to the end of the barrel are in proper perspective. Then pull the trigger and if everything was done correctly, a black puff of smoke will appear in the sky!

Newcomers to the marvelous world of Skeet shooting have a tendency to mimic the styles of champions, hoping that if they look good, they'll shoot good. To a degree, this isn't a bad idea if the "imitatee" has good form, stance and a smooth fluid motion. One of the

Some Skeet shooters use an exaggerated form of swinging through after the shot is fired — if this works for you and you're comfortable, use this style. But don't mimic others just because they look good to you — develop your own style and stick with it.

Think before you call for the target! Try to make a mental picture of what your lead should be before you mount your shotgun, then call for the bird. Mental preparation — before the shot is fired — greatly improves one's score on the Skeet.

problems that often crops up is how the tyro mounts his gun. Some of the world's greatest Skeet shooters have been playing the game for decades and when they started, the "dropped stock" was mandatory. By definition, "dropped stock" means that the butt must be off the shoulder when the target is called for. A "mounted stock" means that the shooter places the gun against his shoulder, cheek firmly touching the comb, and then calls for the target. Even though the rules were subsequently changed in the mid-1950s, to permit a mounted gun, the old-timers continued to shoot in their accustomed manner.

Unfortunately, many newcomers see these great shooters still using the dropped stock method and mimic them. In effect, they are placing an additional burden on themselves as a mounted gun position is not only legal, but it helps to eliminate mounting problems so often encountered by the neophyte Skeet shooter. Take full advantage of the rules set down by the NSSA, learn them, and more important, abide by them.

Tyro shooters should start out by using a mounted gun (left) instead of the dropped stock (below) position. All too often, newcomers will attempt to mimic a top Skeet shooter's style instead of learning how to develop their own shooting form.

The only "easy" targets on a Skeet field are the ones you break — all the others are difficult and some more so than others. Right-handed shooters often find High Deuce (outgoers from post #2) are troublesome targets due to the righty's natural swinging problem. Newcomers should try a bit harder on this particular target until they get it down "pat." It eventually becomes a confidence builder.

Tyros should initially avoid shooting smaller gauge shotguns like the .410 bore and 28 gauge until they master the 12 gauge. Until you can consistently score in the mid-90s out of a 100 with the 12 gauge avoid these little troublemakers.

Are there any "easy" targets on the Skeet field? Yes, the ones you break—all the others are difficult. Some may be labeled easier than others, but until you can break every target, from every station, every time you shoot, you'll be better off believing that they are all tough targets. For a right-handed shooter, some targets are more difficult than others, as records kept on this subject so prove. A righty seems to have the most difficult time with High Deuce, which is the outgoing target from Station Two. As we explained in an earlier chapter, the right-handed shooter does not swing to the right as effectively as he does to the left. Knowing, understanding and accepting this as a fact of life, the smart student will bear down a bit harder on this particular target and after a few sessions of concentrated effort, he'll be able to turn this very difficult target into a confidence builder.

Shooting from Station Eight puts fear in the hearts of newcomers. They just can't imagine how they'll ever be able to hit the target that is so close and flying so fast. As any seasoned Skeet shooter will verify, the closer the target is, the better chance you have of hitting it. Where the tyro goes wrong is in the position he places the gun's muzzle before calling for the target. If possible, stand directly behind the shooter ahead of you and watch the flight of the target—but don't watch the shooter's barrel. You'll see that the target clears the house very rapidly and that its path is consistent. I have found that the

If possible, stand directly behind the shooter on the station and observe the flight pattern of the target. If the wind is blowing, you'll be able to learn from the preceding shooter's experience, and you'll convert his problems into your advantage.

best place to point the muzzle is about 18 inches outside of the window and slightly below it. This barrel position enables you to see the target clearly as it leaves the house and by placing the barrel outboard it cuts down on the distance you have to move the barrel to catch the target in flight. Actually, all you have to do to hit the target is to flip up the front end of the gun and pull the trigger. This same technique works for either the high or the low house Station Eight targets.

Like blonds, Skeet shooters have more fun than trap shooters. This fact is evident in the way a Skeet shoot program is written—for the shooters, whereas many trap shoots are seemingly held for the benefit of the host club. At most major Skeet shoots, there are many concurrent events which add spice to a program. There are two-man teams, husband and wife teams, two-in-a-family teams, five-man teams, zone teams, etc. The list is almost endless, and all of this helps to stimulate and promote Skeet shooting. Whereas major trap shoots employ five classes in singles events (AA,A,B,C,D), comparable Skeet events wisely make up to eight separate classes (AAA,AA,A,B,C,D,E and N/C (non-classified). This method of sharing the wealth among the masses has helped Skeet to increase both its membership and attendance at registered shoots at a faster rate than trap shooting in the past decade or so.

Skeet doubles are part of the game and must be learned by the tyro almost immediately. Though it is possible, while shooting practice, to politely ask the puller to throw doubles targets—one at a time—you'll soon learn that shooting a pair in the air isn't all that difficult. As long as you shoot your outgoing target before it reaches the center stake, you will have plenty of time to pop the incomer. Doubles are shot from four stations—#1, #2, #6 and #7 except in special doubles events where all the posts, except #8 are used. Also, some clubs use "doubles from all stations" to eliminate lengthy shoot-offs. There is a problem associated with this type of tie-breaker because the competitors are not shooting the same game at which they previously participated. It's like asking a bowler, who tied another kegler to break a tie by shooting pool. Shooting doubles from all the stations is an entirely different version of Skeet, and one that demands a great deal of practice to learn because of the radically different leads as they are not related to shooting singles.

With the advent of better ammunition and improved shotguns, today's "average" Skeet shooter must break every target thrown for him just to get into a shoot-off.

At the 1983 World Skeet Championships held in San Antonio, Texas, there were some incredible scores recorded. Phil Murray, one of Skeet's premier shooters,

(Above and left high house station 8. **Opposite page:** low house Station 8) Most newcomers to Skeet shooting initially believe that Station #8 targets are extremely difficult to hit. The "trick" to consistently hitting these targets is to "cheat" and place the muzzle approximately 12 to 18 inches outboard of the opening. When the target appears, all the shooter has to do is elevate the muzzle slightly and pull the trigger.

The only difference between good shooters and great shooters is how they approach the Skeet game. Class C shooters are said to shoot one event at a time — Class B one field at a time — Class A one post at a time and Class AA one target at a time! Don't count misses, but instead, maintain positive concentration of the upcoming target.

This Skeeter is using an over/under with 30-inch barrels — about 2 inches too long for this shooting sport. Barrel length for Skeet guns should be not more than 28 inches and many are 26 inches and sometimes even less. The shotgun's balance is usually determined by barrel length.

Smaller gun clubs are usually warm and friendly towards both new and seasoned shooters.

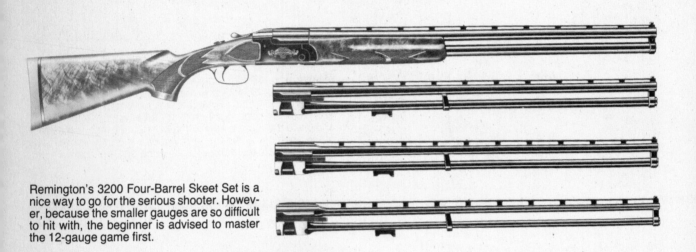

Remington's 3200 Four-Barrel Skeet Set is a nice way to go for the serious shooter. However, because the smaller gauges are so difficult to hit with, the beginner is advised to master the 12-gauge game first.

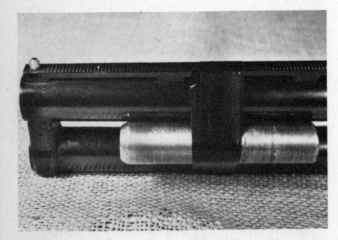

Adding weight to the shotgun's barrel at the muzzle will smooth out a herky-jerky swing and also help to reduce muzzle rise between shots while firing at the elusive "doubles" targets.

fired a perfect 650x650 which included 250x250 in the 12 gauge, 100x100 in each of the other three gauges (the 20 gauge, 28 gauge and .410 bore) and capped off this extraordinary shooting exhibition with a perfect 100x100 in doubles!

Tournament Skeet often will hold separate events whereby the contestant must shoot shotguns smaller than the 12 gauge. There are four gun classifications: the 12 gauge (all-bore where a contestant can shoot any shotgun whose ammunition does not exceed 3 drams equivalent of powder and 1⅛ ozs. of shot. A shooter using a smaller gauge gun is doing so at his own risk); the 20 gauge, 28 gauge and the .410 bore. Until a newcomer learns Skeet's demanding basics, and can consistently shoot in the mid-to high 90s with the 12 gauge, I would advise him to stay away from the smaller gauge games. It's very tempting to jump right in by entering 28 and .410 bore events, but don't do it. Learn the 12 gauge first, then the 20 gauge and ultimately, you'll taper down to the .410 bore.

Although trap and Skeet are both clay target shooting games, there is quite a bit of difference in the personality of the two sports. Skeet, for the most part, is

(Above) Although these Skeet shooters are engaging in a friendly round of practice, the man standing behind the shooter on the station is prepared to "back him up" by shooting at the target if missed. This is a poor practice and is definitely a *No-No!*

(Above right) It's not proper etiquette to stop the squad by picking up empty hulls during the shoot. Wait until after the event and then go back and pick up your empty hulls — never during the shoot.

(Right) Never leave a shooting post with a closed gun. You may know that it is "safe," but your squadmates don't!

shot for fun, although in recent years there has been a renewed interest in purses, options, giant jackpots, etc., which are supposed to pique a shooter's interest by shooting for money. Trophies, awards, brassards, medals and other non-monetary rewards are what the Skeet shooter goes after. The opposite holds true for trap shooting which is a game, designed from its inception, with cash awards. Therefore, the attitude of a trap shooter is different toward his sport than the Skeet shooter's. The Skeet participant shoots for fun, while the trapman shoots for "blood."

If you're "next-up," stand close enough to the shooter on the post so that you can watch the targets, and when its your turn to shoot, all you have to take is a few steps.

I don't mean to over-generalize by saying that Skeeters are a more gregarious group than trap shooters, but the atmosphere at a major trap shoot is more austere than what I've witnessed at Skeet events over the years. Either of the two sports appeal to an individual's own personality, and eventually, a newcomer to clay target shooting will comfortably settle into one or the other. Rare is the shooter who consistently partakes of both games. As Indy and stock cars are to racing, trap and Skeet are to clay target shooting; they are greatly different and are enjoyed by different people.

9 Purses, Options and Pay-Offs

TROPHY PRIZES versus cash purses and optionals. There has long been a dispute among trap and Skeet shooters whether it is more enjoyable to shoot for money, trophies or just for the fun of it. So that you can better understand and be able to decipher a shoot program, we'll go into greater details regarding the various purses and options.

The very first trophy a new shooter wins in competition becomes a prized possession throughout his life, and practically all trap and Skeet tournaments offer trophies for the winner in the various categories of competition. Quite a few years ago, I was privy to shooting on a Skeet squad with an elderly and obviously affluent gentlemen who was attending his first registered Skeet shoot. Now, in the late 1950s, it wasn't uncommon for the sponsoring gun club to put up enough trophies which placed down to Class D, 3rd place.

You guessed it, that new shooter won that prestigious trophy, which stood at least 6½ inches high. He beamed from ear to ear as though he had just won the "Nationals." A few weeks later I saw him again at the local gun club and asked the condition of his trophy. He proudly stated that he "built a room around it"—a trophy room, and predicted that in a few more years it would be filled up. And, he was right, because that first trophy led to a fantastic shooting career and to date he has won well over 150 Skeet shooting trophies.

There will always be new converts coming into both trap and Skeet shooting and to these new competitors their first trophies will always have greater intrinsic value than any cash prize.

The majority of trap shooters, however, have for generations shown a decided preference for cash-pay events and it is considered opinion of many who have followed the game for years, that this feature has kept trap shooting active and growing during both good and hard times.

Skeet, on the other hand, has grown steadily and become firmly established in the shooting world as a trophy game. Time, however, brings many changes and the majority of Skeet programs today offer competition for cash optionals along with trophies and brassards.

In both trap and Skeet, many shooters who have attended tournaments for sport, recreation and friendly competition have won more trophies than they have use, or room, for. These same men and women, however, show an avid interest in the event-by-event payoff and will stand in line at the cashier's window to collect what they have won in the division of the money.

Shooting programs must appeal to new shooters as well as to the crusty campaigners to be successful in drawing a cross section of both trophy and money shooters.

Class Shooting

In the early days of tournament trap shooting, all contestants competed in one group and the top scorers were the winners. This method was all in favor of the best shooters, and the men who could not protect their

There's hardly a sport in which man participates that there's not a great deal of "off-track" wagering going on. Since its inception, trap shooting has been a natural breeding ground for bookies and betting.

While the majority of Skeet shooters prefer to pit their skill against their peers for trophies, lately there has been more interest generated at Skeet shoots due to "optionals." A modest entry fee by the shooter earns semi-meager returns when compared to trap shooting rewards for money play.

Two of trap's greatest—Dan Orlich (left) and Tom Frye (right) discuss the merits of shooting for money versus trophies. In the mid-1960s, trap shooting in the state of Nevada was at an all-time high, thanks to the Sahara Gun Club in Las Vegas and Harold's Gun Club in Reno. Both attracted all the best "money-shooters" in the country and often entries were limited to 1,000 shooters due to lack of time and space.

Singles, or 16-yard trap shooting events don't generate high interest in purses and optionals these days. A few decades ago, there were no official "classes" and each shooter shot against another, regardless of ability, with high score overall declared the winner.

Skeet shooting has been built on the premise of fun for trophies. The attitude of the average Skeet shooter is more complacent than that of a "play-for-pay" trap shooter. Regardless of the shooter's attitude, both sports develop a sense of fair play among the competitors.

In most 16-yard classes at major shoots, a 99×100—even though it's a good score—will not make the purse or optionals. There're just too many entrants in each class for a 100×100 not to be shot on any given day of competition.

The board reads:

S-100 200-16 YDS.   PRELIMINARY DAYS   SUNDAY, AUGUST 13, 1978

HAYNES, FRANK	AA	BETHALTO, ILL	99
STITT, JAMES	B	PIQUA, OH	99
MCKINLEY, LARRY	AA	RICH HILL, MO	100
WILEY, MELVIN JR.	AA	FT. WORTH, TX	99
CARVILLE, BRUCE	A	N. ATTLEBORO, MA	99
JASKOSKE, JIM	AA	W. CHICAGO, IL	99
WILHELM, CARROLL	B	DELPHOS, OH	100
HARRISON, LEO	AA	HANNIBAL, MO	99
BLATT, ART	AA	N. HOLLYWOOD, CAL	97
FOSTER, FRANCIS	AA	SPARTANBURG, SC	97

entry through their shooting ability either withdrew from competition or entered "for targets only."

Tournament shooting could not grow under the one-class system so this brought on the classification method based on registered target averages, and known ability, as it prevails today.

Shooting by classes has broadened the base of the sport, and especially, built up the interest of the lower percentage groups. At the same time it has added to the burden of tournament office detail and lessened the interest of many high percentage shooters in the 16-yard portion of the program.

The standard system whereby shooters are classed in accordance with their known ability and official 16-yard averages is shown below:

Five Classes

97% and over	AA
94% and under 97%	A
91% and under 94%	B
88% and under 91%	C
Under 88%	D

Four Classes.

95% and over	A
92% and under 95%	B
89% and under 92%	C
Under 89%	D

Three Classes

95% and over	A
91% and under 95%	B
Under 91%	C

Only the largest tournaments can maintain good interest in five classes. The average sized tournament of 75 to 100 shooters usually calls for four-class competition, which means there are four separate trophy and money divisions running concurrently on the same 100 or 200 target program.

At most trap shoots the class system works out to the satisfaction of all groups except Class AA. The other groups generally have sufficient entries to make an interesting race in the events as well as on the total score, but the AA shooters sometimes have less to show for a perfect 100x100 score than a Class D entrant who barely shoots his average.

For example, let's take a hypothetical case with 100 entries and five classes. The following example shows what often occurs: AA entries—6, A entries—14, B entries—33, C entries—31, and D entries—16.

Optional entries are refunded when there are less than five entries in any one class (entered for the money). It is obvious in this example, there are enough entries in each group to create competition but Class AA will have a dull event money-wise.

Shooting by class groups stimulates competition and creates action for trophies as well as for money, for those who want it. Trap and Skeet tournaments could not have gained their present size and shooter interest without the class system.

Yardage Handicaps

Over the years of registered trap shooting, four of the most important changes in the rules have been aimed at reducing the chances of top-flight shooters of maintaining anywhere near their 16-yard average in their handicap shooting. These changes in their sequence were:

1. Elimination of plated shot in target loads.
2. Limitation of powder charge to 3 dram equivalent.
3. Reduction of shot load from 1¼ ozs. to 1⅛ ozs.
4. Extension of the extreme yardage, first from 23 to 25 yards, and eventually to 27 yards as at the present.

The official ATA average books will show that the man or woman who can maintain a handicap average from 23 yards or farther within 5 to 7 percent of his 16-yard average is the exception rather than the rule.

Shooting handicap targets from the back yardage positions (25 to 27 yards) is a much different game than singles from 16 yards. Some of the variables that must be taken into consideration are:
1. Greater leads, especially from extreme distances.
2. Longer distance of shot travel to target zone.
3. Reduced density of shot pattern.

Even under perfect weather conditions, when the score sheets are totalled for the squads standing back of 22 yards in handicap events, they average five to ten percent more "zeros" than when the same shooters are shooting at 16-yard targets.

Based on averages and known quality, the top gunners can almost be named before shooting starts in the 16-yard program, but in handicaps the folks who participate in the division of the High Gun Money invariably shoot above their season's average in that event.

New shooters must shoot at 1,500 registered 16-yard or handicap targets before they are issued their permanent handicap card. The tendency of handicap committees, generally, is to start newcomers at 22 yards.

Handicap shooting is in a very healthy condition and is a growing segment of the trapshooting game. Evidence of this is found at every state shoot where the yardage events usually bring out the largest entry lists of the entire shooting program. The three main handicap events at the Grand American attest to shooter's desire to play the money in the "big" handicap events.

Percentage System

The method that is most widely used today for dividing the cash purses in trap shooting events is "percentage," where tie scores divide the proceeds. The system offers the chance of some shooter hitting a lucky payoff—a jackpot so to speak—where a lone 25 straight in the optionals can result in a substantial payoff. There are numerous recorded payoffs where a single "straight" on a particularly tough field has paid a whopping $1,200 for a $2 entry. It is a rare occurrence, but,

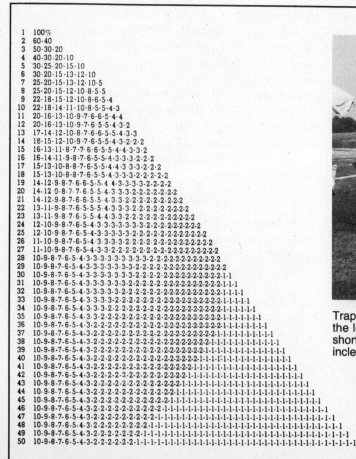

1	100%
2	60-40
3	50-30-20
4	40-30-20-10
5	30-25-20-15-10
6	30-20-15-13-12-10
7	25-20-15-13-12-10-5
8	25-20-15-12-10-8-5-5
9	22-18-15-12-10-8-6-5-4
10	22-18-14-11-10-8-5-5-4-3
11	20-16-13-10-9-7-6-6-5-4-4
12	20-16-13-10-9-7-6-5-5-4-3-2
13	17-14-12-10-8-7-6-6-5-5-4-3-3
14	18-15-12-10-9-7-6-5-5-4-3-2-2-2
15	16-13-11-8-7-7-6-6-5-5-4-4-3-3-2
16	16-14-11-9-8-7-6-5-5-4-3-3-3-2-2-2
17	15-13-10-8-8-7-6-5-5-4-4-3-3-3-2-2-2
18	15-13-10-8-8-7-6-5-5-4-3-3-3-2-2-2-2
19	14-12-9-8-7-6-6-5-5-4-4-3-3-3-3-2-2-2-2
20	14-12-9-8-7-7-6-5-5-4-3-3-3-2-2-2-2-2-2-2
21	14-12-9-8-7-6-6-5-5-4-3-3-2-2-2-2-2-2-2-2-2
22	13-11-9-8-7-6-5-5-5-4-3-3-3-2-2-2-2-2-2-2-2-2
23	13-11-9-8-7-6-5-5-4-4-3-3-3-2-2-2-2-2-2-2-2-2-2
24	12-10-9-8-7-6-5-4-3-3-3-3-3-3-2-2-2-2-2-2-2-2-2-2
25	12-10-9-8-7-6-5-4-3-3-3-3-3-2-2-2-2-2-2-2-2-2-2-2-2
26	11-10-9-8-7-6-5-4-3-3-3-3-3-2-2-2-2-2-2-2-2-2-2-2-2-2
27	11-10-9-8-7-6-5-4-3-3-2-2-2-2-2-2-2-2-2-2-2-2-2-2-2-2-2
28	10-9-8-7-6-5-4-3-3-3-3-3-3-3-3-3-2-2-2-2-2-2-2-2-2-2-2-2
29	10-9-8-7-6-5-4-3-3-3-3-3-3-3-2-2-2-2-2-2-2-2-2-2-2-2-2-2-2
30	10-9-8-7-6-5-4-3-3-3-3-3-3-2-2-2-2-2-2-2-2-2-2-2-2-2-2-2-1-1
31	10-9-8-7-6-5-4-3-3-3-3-3-2-2-2-2-2-2-2-2-2-2-2-2-2-2-2-2-1-1-1
32	10-9-8-7-6-5-4-3-3-3-3-2-2-2-2-2-2-2-2-2-2-2-2-2-2-2-2-1-1-1-1
33	10-9-8-7-6-5-4-3-3-3-2-2-2-2-2-2-2-2-2-2-2-2-2-2-2-2-2-1-1-1-1-1
34	10-9-8-7-6-5-4-3-3-3-2-2-2-2-2-2-2-2-2-2-2-2-2-2-2-2-1-1-1-1-1-1-1
35	10-9-8-7-6-5-4-3-3-2-2-2-2-2-2-2-2-2-2-2-2-2-2-2-2-2-1-1-1-1-1-1-1
36	10-9-8-7-6-5-4-3-2-2-2-2-2-2-2-2-2-2-2-2-2-2-2-2-2-1-1-1-1-1-1-1-1-1
37	10-9-8-7-6-5-4-3-2-2-2-2-2-2-2-2-2-2-2-2-2-2-2-2-1-1-1-1-1-1-1-1-1-1
38	10-9-8-7-6-5-4-3-2-2-2-2-2-2-2-2-2-2-2-2-2-2-2-1-1-1-1-1-1-1-1-1-1-1-1
39	10-9-8-7-6-5-4-3-2-2-2-2-2-2-2-2-2-2-2-2-2-2-1-1-1-1-1-1-1-1-1-1-1-1-1
40	10-9-8-7-6-5-4-3-2-2-2-2-2-2-2-2-2-2-2-2-2-1-1-1-1-1-1-1-1-1-1-1-1-1-1-1
41	10-9-8-7-6-5-4-3-2-2-2-2-2-2-2-2-2-2-2-2-1-1-1-1-1-1-1-1-1-1-1-1-1-1-1-1
42	10-9-8-7-6-5-4-3-2-2-2-2-2-2-2-2-2-2-2-1-1-1-1-1-1-1-1-1-1-1-1-1-1-1-1-1
43	10-9-8-7-6-5-4-3-2-2-2-2-2-2-2-2-2-2-1-1-1-1-1-1-1-1-1-1-1-1-1-1-1-1-1-1-1
44	10-9-8-7-6-5-4-3-2-2-2-2-2-2-2-2-2-1-1-1-1-1-1-1-1-1-1-1-1-1-1-1-1-1-1-1-1
45	10-9-8-7-6-5-4-3-2-2-2-2-2-2-2-2-1-1-1-1-1-1-1-1-1-1-1-1-1-1-1-1-1-1-1-1-1-1
46	10-9-8-7-6-5-4-3-2-2-2-2-2-2-2-1-1-1-1-1-1-1-1-1-1-1-1-1-1-1-1-1-1-1-1-1-1-1-1
47	10-9-8-7-6-5-4-3-2-2-2-2-2-2-1-1-1-1-1-1-1-1-1-1-1-1-1-1-1-1-1-1-1-1-1-1-1-1-1-1
48	10-9-8-7-6-5-4-3-2-2-2-2-2-2-1-1-1-1-1-1-1-1-1-1-1-1-1-1-1-1-1-1-1-1-1-1-1-1-1-1-1
49	10-9-8-7-6-5-4-3-2-2-2-2-2-1-1-1-1-1-1-1-1-1-1-1-1-1-1-1-1-1-1-1-1-1-1-1-1-1-1-1-1
50	10-9-8-7-6-5-4-3-2-2-2-2-2-1-1-1-1-1-1-1-1-1-1-1-1-1-1-1-1-1-1-1-1-1-1-1-1-1-1-1-1-1

Trap shooting's long-yardage (25 to 27 yards) shooters over the long-haul cannot expect as many cash pay-offs as the short yardage (24 yards or less) shooters, especially during inclement weather which takes its toll on the "back-fencers."

This chart illustrates the percentage system breakdown. The left hand column indicates the number of places of "pays" and the rows of numbers for each pay-off spot always equals 100 percent.

143

Some states have life-long awards. The author (right) is receiving the California President's Medal for a combined score of 196×200 for singles and handicap shooting in a single day.

nevertheless, it has happened and every shoot is capable of providing these bonanza payoffs.

Tournament shooters are a sporting crowd and one of the best advertisements any program can have, when the shoot is concluded, is to have shooters talking about "lucky-pay spots" that they lucked into. High-pay tournaments are never forgotten as evidenced by famous "Pot 'O Gold" shoots in the mid-1960s where trap shooters could win as much as $10,000 for a 200 target handicap race.

There is a vast difference between "40-30-20-10 percent, High Guns," and "40-30-20-10 percent, Percentage (ties divide)," so the program must state explicitly what shoot management has in mind to avoid any possible misunderstanding at payoff time.

Reduced to the easiest possible explanation on a single 25-target event, if the program reads 40-30-20-10 percent, *High Guns*, and four shooters break 25 straight, they win whatever money is in the pot, with 25 percent going to each man. Whereas, when the program reads 40-30-20-10 percent, *Percentage*, all who break scores of 25, 24, 23, and 22 are assured of participation in the money division if they entered "for the money."

With 40-30-20-10 percent, Percentage, scores of 22 or higher in 25-bird events pay off, and shooters who average 88 percent or better can expect to share in the money division when they "shoot their average" in a 25-bird event.

There are many variable sets of figures that can be used for the percentage division and we show 40-30-20-10 percent only as a basis of illustration.

Changing the figures to 50-30-20 percent gives 10 percent more to the high scorers and limits the payoff from going below 23x25, or 92 percent average. A 60-40 percent does not pay scorers below 24x25, or 96 percent average. To pay on scores as low as 21x25 in events, the figures 30-25-20-15-10 percent are used. In any instance where there does not happen to be a 25x25 score among the shooters who entered the event for money, the top pay goes to the 24's, and the payoff extends one score further down the list.

High Gun System

The High Gun System is widely used to pay off on the total score in handicap events especially, and with the percentage points broken down into much smaller units as you will note in the following table.

High Gun System Example

If 67 shooters enter for an event and pay $5 per man to be divided High Gun System on the total score, with one-money to each five entries, there are 14 High Gun "pays," scaled as follows: 18, 15, 12, 10, 9, 7, 6, 5, 5, 4, 3, 2, 2, 2% to divide the total purse of $335 (67 entries at $5 each).

		Score	Pays
18%	$60.30	98	$60.30
15%	50.25	97	45.225

It is imperative that the shooter understand and know what is stated inside a shooting program before casually putting up his hard-earned money hoping to hit the big jackpot.

12%	40.40	97	45.225
10%	33.50	96	33.50
9%	30.15	95	24.55
7%	23.45	95	24.55
6%	20.10	95	24.55
5%	16.75	94	16.75
5%	16.75	93	13.40
4%	13.40	93	13.40
3%	10.05	93	13.40
2%	6.70	92	6.70
2%	6.70	92	6.70
2%	6.70	92	6.70

On the same basis, if there were 126 entries, then $630 would be divided among the 26 High Guns on the following percentage table: 11, 10, 9, 8, 7, 6, 5, 4, 3, 3, 3, 3, 2, 2, 2, 2, 2, 2, 2, 2, 2, 2, 2, 2, 2, 2%.

This system works out to the satisfaction of most shooters in dividing the money purse on the total score in large or small handicaps as the yardage method of handicapping is the most equitable way so far devised to equalize the abilities of a field of shooters.

To increase or decrease the number of payoffs is easy when the gun club knows exactly what they want to do and the program so clearly states.

When 100 entries are in the High Gun options and the program reads, "one-money to each five shooters or fraction thereof," the first 20 High Guns participate in the division of the monies and the following table is used: 14, 12, 9, 8, 7, 7, 6, 5, 5, 4, 3, 3, 3, 2, 2, 2, 2, 2, 2, 2%.

When 100 entries are in the High Gun options and the program reads, "one-money to every seven entries or fraction thereof," the division is on the following basis—with 15 pays to the 15 High Guns as follows: 16, 13, 11, 8, 7, 7, 6, 6, 5, 5, 4, 4, 3, 3, 2%.

The Lewis Class System

The Lewis Class System is only used for money or trophy division on total scores. It is in wide favor in certain areas of the country and in these sections there seldom is a program offered to the shooters that does not include several Lewis Class options. Rarely found on the West Coast, the Lewis Class is extremely popular east of the Rockies.

This system offers the excellent feature of permitting any contestant to make a long shot bet on his own score and many tournament shooters play the Lewis option, if nothing else. The playing of the Lewis class is close to being a lottery as "winning" scores are not decided until after the shoot is finished.

Under the Lewis System, a shooter whose official classification is AA and whose handicap card shows 27 yards, can emerge as a Class #3 winner because the number of targets broken in that particular program designate the shooter's Lewis rating for that program.

As strange as it may seem, a shooter may be in Class #1 today and Class #3 tomorrow. Both may contradict the official classification card in the shooter's wallet,

PRELIMINARY DAYS

THURSDAY, AUGUST 11, 1983
Starting Time: 12:00 Noon
EVENT NO. 1 — HALL OF FAME SINGLES
100 TARGETS

Targets & Shooter Service	$16.00
Shells (compulsory)	$19.00
Maintenance Fund	$ 1.00

Lewis Class Option — Five Classes
$10.00 on the 100, divided 20-20-20-20-20, high gun in each class.

Class Options —
$5.00 on each 50, divided 40-30-30%. $10.00 on total 100, divided one money for each five entries, high gun.

Trophies —
Trophy to Winner in each Class AA-A-B-C-D, Trophy to Lady, Trophy to Junior, Trophy to Veteran, Trophy to Industry.

EVENT NO. 2 — GEORGE S. McCARTY HANDICAP
100 TARGETS

Targets & Shooter Service	$16.00
Shells (compulsory)	$19.00
Maintenance Fund	$ 1.00

Options — Open - - - - Purse—Yardage Group
$2.50 on each 25, divided 60-40%. $5.00 on each 50, divided 40-30-30%. $10.00 on total 100, divided one money for each five entries, in each yardage group, Grand American Point System. $1.00 on total 100, one money, divided high gun.

Lewis Class Option — Five Classes
$10.00 on the 100, divided 20-20-20-20-20, high gun in each class.

Trophies —
Trophy to Winner and Runner-up, Trophy to Lady, Trophy to Junior, Trophy to Veteran, Trophy to Industry.

FRIDAY, AUGUST 12, 1983
Starting Time: 10:00 A.M.
EVENT NO. 3 — ROBERT MUNSON SINGLES
100 TARGETS

Targets & Shooter Service	$16.00
Shells (compulsory)	$19.00
Maintenance Fund	$ 1.00

Lewis Class Option — Five Classes
$10.00 on the 100, divided 20-20-20-20-20, high gun in each class.

Class Options —
$5.00 on each 50, divided 40-30-30%. $10.00 on total 100, divided one money for each five entries, high gun.

Trophies —
Trophy to Winner in each Class AA-A-B-C-D, Trophy to Lady, Trophy to Junior, Trophy to Veteran, Trophy to Industry.

EVENT NO. 4 — CHET HENDRICKSON HANDICAP
100 TARGETS

Targets & Shooter Service	$16.00
Shells (compulsory)	$19.00
Maintenance Fund	$ 1.00

PAGE 13

Both Lewis Class and Optionals are available at most of the major trap shoots around the country. The Lewis Class is virtually a "luck of the draw" event, while optionals only reward the shooter who breaks perfect or near-perfect scores.

but nevertheless, everything is entirely legal and thoroughly understood by the shooting fraternity when the Lewis Class System is brought into play.

Thus, with the Lewis System, a top-notch shooter can place a $2 or $5 "hedge" bet on himself and should he shoot a poor score that places him far out of the optionals or purse in his own class, he can still hit a lucky spot in the Lewis class that would put him "even" for that day of shooting. It's much like making an "any craps" insurance bet when a large sum of money is on the Pass Line on a crap table. By the same reasoning, many low-percentage shooters play the Lewis on the outside chance their score may "hit" where the Lewis pays, well knowing in advance of their shooting that this is their only chance to have a "run for their money" under the average program offered.

Many veteran tournament shooters, who long ago discarded any idea of regular participation in optional entrance events, play the Lewis knowing perfectly well they are making a small bet that will require some luck rather than pure shooting ability to walk to up the cashier's window and collect a few bucks for their day's efforts.

The Lewis System is variable and works out in any program either by stating how many shooters will make up a class, or that the entry will be divided into two, three, or four or more equal groups. For establishing trophy or merchandise winners at a shoot where there are unknown and non-classified contestants, the Lewis System is at its best. Every contestant places himself in class automatically by his score in that particular event and long runs from either end of the event, or the long run within each individual score, can be used to break ties.

At tournaments smaller than State or Zone shoots, where there is no classification or handicap committee officiating, Lewis Class has wide acceptance in doubles events and the division used is usually 50-30-20 percent High Gun in each Lewis class group.

In greater detail, here's how the Lewis Class options work. The Lewis Class System is based on the final scores as they are posted when the shoot has been completed and gives every contestant an equal chance to win, no matter what his shooting ability.

Before the shoot starts, the management should determine how many classes there will be and how many prizes in each class. If this is too difficult to forecast with any degree of accuracy, the program might state that "there will be one class for every ten entries" or "one class for every 15 entries," and that there will be "three winners in each class," etc.

When all the shooting has been completed, the scores are listed in numerical order from the highest to the lowest. They are then divided into as many groups as there are classes. For example, if there were 30 entries and five classes, there would be six scores in each class. The highest score in each class would then be the winner.

Since there will be odd numbers of entrants and tie scores on the dividing line between the classes, the following rules have been established:

1. Where a "short" class is necessary, due to the odd entry list, the short class or classes shall head the list.
2. Where the line of division falls in a number of tie scores, the contestants are assigned to the class in which the majority of the scores appear.
3. Where an equal number of tie scores appear on either side of the dividing line, contestants shall be assigned to the head of the lower class.
4. Where the original division is changed, due to the tie scores, this change shall apply only to the

Class 1 Brackets represent assignment of scores according to Rules 2 and 3.	⎰100 99 98 98 96 96	**Winner Class 1**		Class 4	⎰90⎱ 90⎱ 90⎰ 89 89 88 86	Rule 2 places all 90's in Class 4 and they are winners of this class.

Horizontal lines represent division of all entries into classes according to Rule 1.

Class 2	⎰95⎱ 95⎰ 94 94 93 93 93	**95's tie for Class 2**		Class 5	⎰85⎱ 85⎰ 84 80 79 75 74 70	Rule 3 places both 85's in Class 5 and they win this Class.

Class 3	⎰92⎱ 92⎱ 92⎰ 91 91	Rule 2 places all 93's in Class 2 and therefore 92's tie for Class 3

In case of ties, the winner may be decided by the toss of a coin, by the largest number of consecutive targets broken, etc. Where the Lewis System is used to divide money, the winnings are usually divided into equal parts.

This illustration is an example of a Lewis Class pay-off and breakdown sheet. The Lewis Class is a pure lottery and if a shooter's score falls in the right place, he'll take home a nice paycheck.

Two-hundred 16-yard target races are naturals for all kinds of options and purses. Lewis Class, Rose options and Miller System are just a few of the many being offered by major gun clubs around the country. There's only one requisite to cashing in on them—an exceptional display of good shooting!

classes directly affected and the original division shall continue in the other classes.

To cite an example, we will take a shoot containing a 100-target program in which there are five Lewis classes and 33 contestants. Since the short classes are placed first, there would be six shooters in Classes #1 and #2 and seven shooters in Classes #3, #4 and #5. The final scores are arranged from the highest to the lowest and the lines drawn in between the classes.

In case of ties, the winner may be decided by the toss of a coin, by the largest number of consecutive targets broken, etc. Where the Lewis Class System is used to divide money, the winnings are usually divided into equal portions.

The Rose System

The Rose System of money division places a definite point value on every pay spot and totally eliminates any chance for a lucky pay-off.

A Rose program with points valued at "4, 3, 2, 1, each 25," means that scores of 25 are worth four points, 24s are worth three points, 23s worth two points and 22s worth one point. At the conclusion of the event, all points won by the contestants who entered for money are totalled, then this total number of points is divided into the amount of money available from the entrance fees and added money to establish the value of a single point.

Thus, if all pay scores total 200 points and there was $400 in the purse to be divided, each point would have a

Arnold Reigger, truly one of modern trap shooting's winningest competitors, always weighed his investment against the odds against losing. His shooting exploits are well documented in ATA shooting records. He was one of trap's earliest and true "professionals."

value of $2 and, therefore, a 25 straight would be worth $8, 24s would pay $6, 23s would pay back to the shooter $4 and even a common 22 would earn $2.

There's a variation of the Rose system on the 25 options and that is called the Rose Accumulation Points. The point value is established at the conclusion of the program rather than on each 25-target sub-event. With this method, the cashier totals the points won on each event, and a 100-straight score would be paid on the basis of having won 16 points when the points have a 4, 3, 2, 1 value.

There is no limit to the point value combination and it is possible and logical to establish point value on the total score, rather than sub-events. Such a combination, to bid for participation by all classes would appear in the program somewhat as follows:

Each Class Shoots For Their Own Entrance
And Pro-Rated Added Money.

100-Targets, 16 yards, or All-Gauge Skeet

Class AA points worth 3, 2, 1	- on total score,
Class A points worth 4, 3, 2, 1	- on total score,
Class B points worth 4, 3, 2, 1	- on total score,
Class C points worth 5, 4, 3, 2, 1	- on total score,
Class D points worth 6, 5, 4, 3, 2, 1,	- on total score,

Even though it entails conducting five separate tournaments on the same 100 targets, such a program would not add to the cashier's duties as it would entirely eliminate figuring event pays and the payoffs on the total scores could be quickly arrived at. An entry of 150 shooters, fairly evenly divided as to classes, might show some merit in this plan, especially where there is every reason to feel that scores will be high, and the shoot management feels that with each class shooting separately the payoff should not be governed by luck but by good scores.

Because the Rose System is as methodical as the mul-

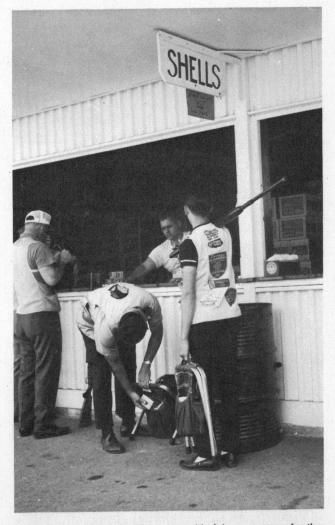

Whenever shooting for big money, it's false economy for the shooter to use reloads. There's the off-chance that a single "blooper" could cost the shooter several hundreds of dollars because of a single lost target.

One of the prime sources of "Added Money" is from the sponsoring gun club soliciting advertising from gun-related companies and putting a major portion of that income into the added money fund.

tiplication table and eliminates lucky pay-offs, this seems to be the only reason why this method of paying on point value has not been more widely accepted. Shooters seem to prefer to have some sort of "luck of the draw" aspect in programs.

The Phil Miller System

The Miller System has all the necessary ingredients to increase interest in purse competition at either 16-yard singles targets or All-Gauge Skeet events. Also, the Miller System rewards the shooter for firing scores usually well above his normal average. The pay-offs are higher percentage-wise than most other play-for-pay systems.

Example:

50 Targets 16-Yard Singles or All-Ga. Skeet

100 shooters, Entry fee $5 = $500 purse

Class AA shooters must break 50×50 to qualify.
Class A shooters must break 49×50 or more to qualify
Class B shooters must break 48×50 or more to qualify.
Class C shooters must break 46×50 or more to qualify.
Class D shooters must break 45×50 or more to qualify.
Class E shooters must break 44×50 or more to qualify.

The cashier figures the payoff as follows:

2-Class AA shooters qualify
4-Class A   shooters qualify
4-Class B   shooters qualify
2-Class C   shooters qualify
4-Class D   shooters qualify
4-Class E   shooters qualify

Recap: 20 shooters qualify for Purse Money Division—$25 to each shooter. If 40 shooters qualify for Purse Money Division, then $12.50 to each shooter.

For a 100-Target event, these are the recommended minimum scores to qualify for payoff in each class:

AA—98×100 or more
A —96×100 or more
B —94×100 or more
C —92×100 or more
D —90×100 or more
E —88×100 or more

For a 200-Target event, these are the recommended minimum scores to qualify for payoff in each class:

AA—197×200 or more
A —193×200 or more
B —190×200 or more
C —187×200 or more
D —184×200 or more
E —181×200 or more

These recommendations were established quite a few years ago, and noting the shooting averages have risen in the past few years, the minimum qualifying score could be raised by a target or two depending on the decision of the gun club management. There are many proponents of the Miller System and some of its advantages over other singles and Skeet purses are:

1. Lower class shooters have the advantage, and there are usually more of these shooters partaking in any event than "hot-hammers."
2. Each shooter is betting on himself in that he can shoot better than his average. If he does, he knows that he'll earn a slice of the pie, if he doesn't, well, there's always tomorrow!
3. There's no dropping of targets for "place" bets, which virtually eliminates "sandbagging."
4. Purses are equal, regardless of the number of entries in each class which favors the AA and A shooters as they are less in number. Any added money is divided equally among the winners.
5. The cashier's task is greatly reduced and this system is preferred by many gun club managers.

Added Money

Usually, at least a portion of the money shown in the typical program as "Added Money" is paid into the

FOURTH DAY...
THURSDAY, AUGUST, 18, 1983
Starting Time: 9:00 A.M.
EVENT NO. 16 — PRELIMINARY HANDICAP
100 TARGETS

Targets & Shooter Service	$16.00
Shells (compulsory)	$19.00
Maintenance Fund	$ 1.00
HALL OF FAME CONTRIBUTION	$20.00
Ford Purse	$ 5.00
Purse	$25.00
High Gun Purse — 30-25-20-15-10 High Gun	$50.00

PURSE (Open to those who enter the purse)
The purse entry will be divided one money for each five entries, Grand American Point System, yardage groups (17-18-19) (20-21) (22-23) (24-25) (26-27).

HALL OF FAME CONTRIBUTOR AWARDS — $3,000 GUARANTEED
The above $20.00 contribution is required for qualification; added money will be paid five Lewis classes, 50-30-20 high gun in each class.

OPTIONS (All Yardages Participate)
$2.50 on each 25 divided 60-40%. $5.00 on each 50 divided 40-30-30%. $1.00 on each total 100, one money, divided high gun.

Lewis Class Option — Five Classes
$10.00 on total 100, divided 20-20-20-20-20, high gun in each class.

Preliminary Handicap
The generous contribution of $6,000 by **Budweiser** has enabled the A.T.A. to award the following added money.

****

SPECIAL ADDED MONEY
$6,000.00*
Compliments Budweiser

Champion	$1500
Runner-up	$1200
3rd Place	$ 900
4th Place	$ 780
5th Place	$ 720
6th Place	$ 600
7th Place	$ 300

*Awarded with the trophies ties do not divide

****

Trophies —
Trophy to Champion, Runner-up, Third Place, Fourth Place, Fifth Place, Sixth Place and Seventh Place. Trophy to Lady Champion. Trophy to Junior Champion. Trophy to Sub-Junior Champion. Trophy to Veteran Champion. Trophy to Sr. Veteran Champion. Trophy to Industry Champion.

One of the major contributors of additional funds to promote trap shooting in recent years has been Budweiser beer. A hefty $6,000 in special added money at the 1983 Grand American created a lot of good will amongst the shooters.

shoot by the contestants as target entrance money. This is standard practice and the gun club does guarantee that the money will be placed in the program as stated.

Every well-operated club, therefore, should know the laid-in cost of their targets and run a preliminary cost audit on their entire tournament operation. (Target costs vary throughout the country as they are bulky and freight is a big cost item.) The following example will show how easily a club can overestimate the amount of money available to "add" to their shoot. In this hypothetical case the club management desires to create an interesting handicap event and add all they possibly can over and above their target cost. They might figure 2 cents per target will be available for this purpose over operational and target costs.

Example:
100 Targets Handicap — $15 Entry Fee
Target trapped at 6¢ each,
$9 goes into High Gun Purse.
$300 "added" to purse by gun club.

At least 150 shooters were expected and the club planned to regain the Added Money from the sale of 15,000 or more targets. Bad weather, however, cut the entry list to 100 shooters so the club overestimated their target income by one third and added $100 more than their income from target sales permitted. Not a fatal loss, but in the wrong direction for a successful business.

Other Sources of Added Money

Many tournaments do not have added money far in excess of any profit they might figure to derive from the sale of targets. Some of the sources of this actually "Added Money" are:

Regardless of the type of purse or option the shooter enters, it all boils down to one simple task—"break targets." Sometimes it's not so simple and if a shooter can't afford it, he or she shouldn't put up hard-earned cash chasing money.

1. At State Shoots where the state association gives back to the shooters a set portion of the fees they have charged at registered events for the express purpose of creating a substantial amount of added money for the state tournament.

2. Where successful gun clubs, organized on a non-profit basis, have funds in their treasury beyond their needs for operating expenses and decide to return this money to the shooters as added money to create interest in their own tournament.

3. Through the sales of ads in gun club program from club supporters and local business firms advertising the tournament.

4. Where commercial operators of large gun clubs "beef-up" their program with added money far above what they expect to show as profit on target sales, as an advertising medium to draw tournament shooters who will travel long distances to attend major events held in locations that have attractions other than shooting targets.

Guaranteed Purses

Some well-established annual tournaments have been built up to their present size through Guaranteed Purses. These clubs now have experience that guides them in preparing their programs and knowing the drawing power they have created, they can accurately forecast their expected attendance. Clubs that do not have this experience should be aware of the fact that Guaranteed Purses pyramid the club's chances to win or lose money on the overall shoot.

Example:

$100 Target Handicap — $15 Entry Fee — $1500 Guaranteed Purse

$300 to High Gun
$200 to 2nd High Gun
$150 to 3rd High Gun
$100 to 4th High Gun
$75 to each next two High Guns
$50 to each next eight High Guns
$25 to each next eight High Guns

Using the same figures as the "Added Money" program described above, the club expects at least 150 entries. From the 2¢ per target that might normally be used as Added Money, they plan on $300. In this event, however, the $300 goes into a guarantee along with $9 from each entry, and the club has a fund of $1,650 against their $1,500 guarantee. The club is well satisfied along with smiling faces on the shooters.

Many gun clubs state in their program "All purse money collected in excess of the guarantee will be paid back to the shooters in additional cash purses at $25 each." In this instance, 166 entries at $9 each would be necessary before the gun club regained their guarantee from purse entrances.

Now for the rub. What would happen if the entry list drops to 100 shooters? One hundred entries at $9, plus $200 (collected at 2¢ per target on 10,000 targets) would create a fund of $1,100 against the guarantee of $1,500. The club has overextended itself and must dig up $400. Guaranteed Purses draw shooters, but on the other side of the operating ledger have an added degree of risk for the sponsoring club.

Wolf Shoot

Many major tournaments, especially those conducted throughout the West offer a Wolf Option. It's usually offered to those who want to place an additional $35 optional on their ability to break big handicap scores.

If you have entered the purse or options, pay close attention to your recorded scores on the scoresheet. After the event is over, errors cannot—and will not—be corrected. It is your responsibility to make certain that they are correct. Failing to do so, could cost you hundreds or even thousands of dollars for a single target "lost" when it was actually "dead."

This is an A.T.A. Shoot and Their Rules will govern same.

A.T.A. fee of $2.00 will be collected on First Event each day.

Watch your score, because it cannot be changed after leaving shooting post. Your score will be called at the end of each five targets.

Management reserves the right to change, modify, postpone, or call off any event due to bad weather, darkness or other causes at their discretion.

THE CHAIRMAN OF THE SHOOT HANDICAP COMMITTEE RESERVES THE RIGHT TO INCREASE THE YARDAGE OF ANY SHOOTER WHO HAS NOT REGISTERED A MINIMUM OF 1000 HANDICAP TARGETS.

Trophies to Hi-Lady, Hi-Vet, Hi-Jr. in each event with 2 or more entries in their category.

All purses are non-compulsory. Shooter must enter to be eligible.

Winners of 16 yard classes will advance one class next day.

WOLF OPTIONALS ON 200 HANDICAP
(SEE EVENT NO. 3)

Total amount of entrance money will create a purse on a per entry basis which will be divided 50-30-20% percentage system in each of the following divisions:

$2.00 on 1st 50	$5.00 on 1st 100
$200 on 4th 50	$2.00 on 3rd 50
$5.00 on total 200	$5.00 on 2nd 100
$2.00 on 2nd 50	

This option will run concurrently with Events 3 & 5. No extra outlay for shells and targets. Scores in said 2 events shall provide basis for payoffs in this event. Fifteen shooters will be required to fill. No refund of entries will be made after Event 3 has started.

ONE TROPHY PER EVENT

PLENTY OF PARKING SPACE
For Self-Contained Trailers, Campers and Motor Homes.

The Wolf optionals are usually offered for trap shooting handicaps and are run concurrent within a 200-target race. Payoffs have been known to equal or surpass regular Purses awards.

This is usually presented as follows:

Wolf Event On 200 Handicap Targets
Entry Fee — $35
with $5 on each 50
with $5 on each 100
and $5 on total 200

Division 40, 30, 20, 10% (percentage) on each of seven events.

This adds an interesting feature and as the event is run concurrent with the regular program, it doesn't require additional expenditure for targets or ammunition. Some exceptional pay-offs have resulted when a shooter happens to have the good fortune of turning in two excellent handicap scores back-to-back.

Ford Purses

O.N. Ford was one of the finest trap shooters and a great booster of the sport. He originated the Wolf Shoots, the Ford Purses and the Pacific International Trapshooting Association (PITA), all very much in evidence today.

Ford Purses call for an entry fee of $1 or $2 per event, usually optional, that is paid-out on a winner-take-all basis. They run concurrent with the 25-target sub-events and total score in handicap and doubles programs and payoff at longshot odds to the lucky winners. At the Grand American trapshooting tourney, a lone Ford Purse win usually assures a shooter that his Vandalia trip has been successful!

The printed program should specify if there is to be any limit on the number of Ford Purses one shooter can win, otherwise a lone 100-straight can claim all five Ford Purses.

Tie scores are shot-off on the next following 25-target sub-event and the purses split between those still tied at the end of the fourth sub-event unless the program states "ties on the first day's purses will carry over onto

Those shooters who can live up to this slogan are certain to cash in on some of the financial rewards at either a trap or Skeet shoot. Surprisingly, 100-straights are not all that uncommon today, and most of the time this exemplary shooting will only get the shooter into a tie-breaking shoot-off.

the next day's handicap events for shoot-off." If reverse scores are to be used to break any ties the program should definitely say so. Ties on the total score purse cause the purse to be split among those involved in the tie.

Example:

If the program stated that no shooter could win more than one event purse and the total score purse and ties that could not be settled by next sub-event, scores would be divided between the shooters involved. The following will illustrate the working out of five Ford Purses on a 100-target handicap race. (Ford Purses on 16-yard singles events have proven to be unsuccessful.)

Scores By Sub-Event For a Shooter	Total Score	
25-25-23-22	95	Winner Sub-event #1
25-24-25-21	93	Winner Sub-event #3
25-25-22-25	97	Winner Sub-event #2 and ½ Total Purse
25-24-24-24	97	½ Total Purse
24-22-23-25	94	½ Sub-event #4
21-22-23-25	91	½ Sub-event #4

The original Ford Purse Plan was for first-time winners to get $25 and repeat winners to be paid the entire accumulated amount except the original $25 which was held back to keep the purse alive in the name of its original donor. Repeat wins, however, in the same handicap occurred so infrequently that Ford Purses today are handled on the above basis.

ATA Point System

The ATA point system is a high-gun system which means the more targets the shooter breaks, the more he or she wins. One money for each five entries means that one-fifth of the shooters will be winners. Low score in the money will receive one point, next higher score will receive two points, etc., except the difference between the first and second high scores will be four points and the difference between second and third high scores will be three points instead of one point. The total points awarded will be divided into the total money to determine the value of each point. The amount the shooter will receive will be the value of each point multiplied by his or her total number of points.

Optionals—25s & 50s

Virtually every trap shooting program written offers these "optionals" for handicap shooting events. So that they are thoroughly understood by new shooters, let's take a closer look at them and see if they're a "good buy."

The "25" options are usually a $2.50 bet per field and are split 60/40 percent on a percentage system. Simply, this means that the highest score on each field will share the 60 percent portion of the pot and the second highest scores will share the 40 percent portion of the pot. For example, all entrants shooting a 25 straight on Field #1 will share the 60 percent portion of the pot equally. All shooters scoring a 24×25 on Field #1 will divvy up the 40 percent portion of the entry money. If there are no 25×25s recorded on Field #1 by any of the entrants, then the next highest recorded score (assuming that a 24×25 was fired by someone) would move up to the top spot, and of course, a 23×25 would move up as well. As 100-target events are usually shot over four fields, each "25 option" is an event within itself.

The second most common option is similar to the "25s," and is played on the "50s." Some gun clubs offer two 50 options, based on Fields #1-#2 and Fields #3-#4. Recently there has been a trend to offering three 50 options, with the middle two fields (#2 and #3) making up the trio of "50s" options. Fifty straight in handicap—from any given yardage—is a difficult feat and therefore, a 50 straight usually pays quite well. Some years ago, I was attending a Winter Chain trapshoot in California and while viewing the pay-off sheets saw a lone 50×50 straight. This paid a smiling trapshooter over $1,900 because it was the only 50 straight recorded on the first two fields.

The reason for this incredible payoff for a $5 wager

A shooter should study and read a program before entering any event. Unless he knows how to read a program, he's probably better off shooting for targets only. Education doesn't come cheap and most trap and Skeet shooters have played the money when they shouldn't and vice versa.

TROPHY PURSE

Payment of the trophy purse will be based on official order of finish in all events and one place will be paid for each 25 entries (or any fraction) in class. $4 from the trophy purse will be returned to shooter's class in the .410, 28 and 20 gauge events, $5 in High Overall events. $8 will be returned in the 12 gauge event.

Champion and Runner-up are not eligible for class money but are guaranteed a minimum purse of $350 to Champion, $250 to Runner-up in the .410, 28 and 20 gauge events. For the 12 gauge event, Champion will receive a minimum of $650, Runner-up $450. The HOA Champion will receive a minimum of $1,000; Runner-up, $750.

Division of trophy purse monies in class will be according to the following table:

Number in Class	Split
1-25	one money
26-50	60/40
51-75	50/30/20
76-100	40/30/20/10
101-125	30/25/20/15/10
126-150	30/20/15/13/12/10
151-175	25/20/15/13/12/10/5
176-200	25/20/15/12/10/8/5/5
201 & over	splits posted at cashier

CONTRIBUTOR'S AWARDS

NSSA Charities Foundation, Inc. and the Olympic Training Center will express their appreciation to shooters who make TAX DEDUCTIBLE CONTRIBUTIONS on the basis of $5 to each shooter in class. This $5 token of appreciation will be distributed as follows:

Number in Class	Split
1-10	one money
11-20	60/40
21-30	50/30/20
31 & over	40/30/20/10

DOUBLES CLASS TABLE

Class	Doubles
*AAA	97% and over
AA	95% to 96.99%
A	91% to 94.99%
B	85% to 90.99%
C	80% to 84.99%
D	Under 80%

Major Skeet shooting events are now offering quite a few "optionals," and are starting to generate more interest in this once "shoot only for fun" game.

was the inclement weather. With over 400 shooters in attendance, and many of them playing the purse and options, this lucky shooter hit it big as none of the other entrants were able to put together their own 50 straight on the same two fields.

Calcuttas

Calcuttas are in wide use for golf events. Practically every country club sponsors one of these money-makers and they are made up of enthusiastic players and buyers. Officially frowned upon by the ATA, Calcuttas nevertheless are an integral part of trap shooting. Often referenced as a "Special Event" in programs or by some other ambiguous name, the Calcutta is a wagering event that allows non-shooters to get into the act. Here's how it works.

Each shooter who wants to enter the Calcutta usually pays an entrance fee of $5 or $10. This enables him to have his name listed on the tote board. As his name is announced by an auctioneer, anybody in the audience makes a cash bid for him or her. The highest bidder then claims his "horse." At the conclusion of the auction, all the monies are added up, including the shooter's entry fee, and are placed in a giant Calcutta pot. Payoffs may be made on either a High Gun or Percentage system, and usually the auctioneer will ask the potential "buyers" how they want the pot to be split. A count of raised hands will dictate the type of payoff.

Regardless of the type of payoff — high gun or percentage — the "buyer" will receive 70 percent of his "horse" if he comes in and the shooter ("horse") will receive 30 percent of his share of the pot. In the event that the shooter "buys" himself, then he would, obviously, receive the entire 100 percent of his share of the pot.

The Calcutta is a favorite "special event" sponsored by many gun clubs. Based on its success at golfing events, the Calcutta enables non-shooters to get into the "action" by purchasing "horses" (shooters) and collecting excellent returns on their investment.

To break it down more graphically, let's take a closer look at a typical Calcutta event. There are 100 shooters entered at $10 per entry fee for a beginning pot of $1,000. These 100 names are posted on a large blackboard and the auction begins. Adjacent to the shooter's name is the buyer's name and the amount paid for the shooter.

Let's say that the total income for the auction was $5,000 which averages out to a $50 bid per shooter. Now there is a grand total of $6,000 in the Calcutta pot.

Most Calcuttas pay three places—50% to the Highest score, 30% to the runner-up score and 20% to the third highest score. Now this is where there is a large difference between the High Gun and Percentage pay-off system comes into play. If the High Gun system was voted by the "bidders," then the three highest scores—including ties—would share the Calcutta pot. To define this last statement, let's assume that there was a lone 99 and a pair of 98×100s recorded. The 99 would take the 50 percent portion of the pot and the pair of 98s would take the 30 and 20 percent portions and divide it equally with each 98 receiving 25 percent of the Calcutta fund.

With the Percentage system invoked, the lone 99 would still take the top 50, the 98s would share the 30 percent portion and any 97s would divvy up the 20 percent allotment. With the Percentage system, more shooters have the opportunity to sneak into the payoff picture, but the amount of dollars in the pot is spread quite a bit thinner than offered by the High Gun system.

Now let's go back to the $6,000 pot and see who gets what. As you recall, our first example was the High Gun system, and therefore the lone 99 takes 50 percent of the $6,000 pot for a $3,000 pay-off. The buyer receives 70 percent of this amount—$2,100—and the shooter receives 30 percent—$900. The two 98s take runner-up and third places, split it, and each receives 25 percent of the pot or $1,500 per shooter. And, like the champion, buyer and shooter must split the proceeds 70-30 percent, respectively.

If the Percentage System was voted in, the single 99 score would not be affected, but the two 98s would share only in the 30 percent portion of the pot and each would receive 15 percent or $900. Third place, or the 20 percent portion, would be shared by the 97s, and if there were four 97s shot, then each would be entitled to 5 percent of the pot or $300.

Unquestionably, the reason main reason for trap shootings popularity and longevity is shooting for money. And, being at the right place at the right time can reward the shooter with huge monetary payoffs. On the other side of the financial coin is the amount of money invested to enter a single race and play all the purses and options. For example, at the 1983 Grand American Handicap event it would cost the shooter $172 for targets, ammunition and playing all the options and purses as shown below:

Targets & Shooter Service	$16.00
Shells (compulsory)	19.00
Maintenance Fund	1.00
Hall of Fame Contribution	20.00
Ford Purses	5.00
Purse	30.00
High Gun Purse	50.00
25 Options	10.00
50 Options	10.00
100 Options	1.00
Lewis Class options	10.00
Total	$172.00

Medals, pins and brassards are bits of nostalgia that linger in a shooter's mind far longer than a pay-off check. But for the shooter who has more trophies than he or she could ever need or want, the incoming cash reward for a fine day's shooting is tough to beat.

This is quite a bit of money to expend for a single day's event, but if one was a gambling man, then this would be the time and place to make this wager. The number of entrants at the Grand American Handicap event has averaged over 3,800 shooters in the past 6 years—and remember, this is accomplished in a single day! It's the world's largest single-day shooting event.

Recorded pay-offs at the Grand range from fantastic to pitiful depending on the weather conditions. With thousands of competitors playing the money, normally "excellent" handicap scores in the high 90s often net the shooter less than what he has wagered. On the other hand, if poor weather conditions prevail and scores are sub-par, then the few high scores may reap the benefits to the tune of $25,000 to $40,000 in total pay-offs. Not exactly chicken-feed!

Playing the money at the larger trap shoots is like playing $1 or nickel slot machines. The winner will receive back in proportion to what he invests. Somewhat smaller in attendance, but still considered major shoots around the country are the various Zone and State shoots along with the mini-Grands like the Spring Grand, Mid-West Grand, etc.

Until Harold's Club in Reno folded its tent a few years ago, the State of Nevada was known for its "big-buck" trap shoots. The fabled Golden West Grand in Reno attracted all the name shooters as did Bob Taylor's Ranch House and the Mint/Sahara shoots in Las Vegas. The 1960s and 1970s produced some record-shattering entry lists along with fantastic cash awards, but in recent years, only a few Nevada-based shoots are really bonanza-type events.

Some shooters—both trap and Skeet—can't handle the pressure of money shoots. To these individuals, it is best to enjoy yourself and shoot for "targets only." And don't kick yourself in the seat of your pants if you should "accidentally" shoot a big score which, "if" you had played the money, you would have made out quite well. Someone once said that "hindsight vision is always 20/20," but in trap and Skeet events where cash is "on the barrel-head," you pay your money and you take your chance!

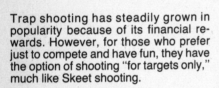

Trap shooting has steadily grown in popularity because of its financial rewards. However, for those who prefer just to compete and have fun, they have the option of shooting "for targets only," much like Skeet shooting.

Handling the Adversities 10

ADVERSITY . . . an interesting word to discuss in conjunction with the shooting sports of trap and Skeet. The classic definition of the word as listed in the dictionary goes something like this, "An event or series of events that oppose success."

All new shooters are protected by beginner's luck, but when that cup runs out, watch out! Don't make early predictions about how easy trap or Skeet shooting is or you'll eat your words sooner than you think.

If you've been a clay target shooter for some time, you can undoubtedly rattle off any number of "happenings" that have led to the downfall of your shooting success. If, however, you've recently taken up trap or Skeet shooting, you may well be protected, so to speak, by the "beginner's luck" syndrome that allows many newcomers to the sport to make statements like these: "It's such an easy sport. How can anyone miss those clay targets?" Or, "With all those BBs in the air, you can't possibly miss!"

Newcomers also bring a snicker to veteran shooters when they make forecasts like: "I don't think it'll take much time at all before I reach the 27-yard line." Or, "The way I'm shooting now, I'm sure by the end of my first year I'll be able to hold a high 90s average in all four gauges."

You'll hear no bold statements like these coming from the mouths of experienced shooters because they've learned the hard way that "adversities" of trap and Skeet shooting are not to be taken lightly. Much like Murphy's Law, they can come into play ever so swiftly, making your attempts at shooting a good score all but impossible on any given day.

What are these adversities that can so drastically affect your shooting style? Unfortunately, there are quite a few and we'll discuss some of the more important ones. As we begin, keep in mind the list we present here is by no means the complete series of adversities that you'll encounter out on the range. After this discussion, however, you should be able to correct some of the more common shooting problems that plague both new and old shooters.

Adversity 1
Proper Gun Fit/Mounting/Basic Stance
"The Mythical Average Shooter"

Though this subject has been covered in detail elsewhere in this book, it must be mentioned here because improper gun fit is trap and Skeet shooting's number one, most commonly committed error. If you strive to be more than a once or twice a year shooter, you must

Strength and body conditioning are important elements of becoming a top-notch competition shooter. The arm, shoulder and neck muscles need to be conditioned, not only prior to a shoot, but every day of the week to keep them tuned.

become "as one" with your gun. If your scores are to improve, you must achieve consistent gun placement (mounting), along with proper gun fit, plus the proper position of your body and gun in relationship to the upcoming target.

How many times have you heard it said, "The average gun comes from the factory with dimensions to fit the average shooter?" Guess what? There is no average shooter and it behooves each one of you to determine how your gun must be modified so that it fits you and not the other way around. Seek the help of a professional and determine what the correct length of pull should be. Find out if the comb is too high or too low. Double check the relationship between the sight beads, the rib and the point of impact.

If you're concerned about messing up a pretty piece of wood on your fine such-and-such tournament gun, you have your priorities mixed up. Your first and foremost objective should be to pulverize more targets, not preserve the good looks of a piece of wood. Too often, a new shooter will show off the cut of wood on his gun proclaiming that it's a real work of art. Next, you see

A competition shotgun is designed expressly to serve a single purpose—break targets. If the shotgun doesn't fit you properly, then your score will suffer the consequences.

Most of today's production shotguns are designed with stock cast for a right-handed shooter. If you're a lefty, you'll need some corrective stock work to make the shotgun work for you.

Proper gun fit is the single most important ingredient for a newcomer's attempt to become a proficient Skeet or trap shooter. Regardless of inbred talent, a new or old shooter cannot overcome a poorly fitted shotgun.

that shooter take his museum-quality piece out on the firing line and tuck it in here or pull it there so he can see the target better, or position it a bit lower on his shoulder because "it breaks targets better that way."

Try not to forget that the function of a trap or Skeet gun is to destroy clay targets. If you have a really fine piece of wood that doesn't fit and you don't want it marred, buy another "using" stock for your gun and store the fancier wood. They don't give extra targets for good looking guns.

Correct mounting of the gun is an another "adversity" that takes its toll. One hard-and-fast rule . . . if it doesn't feel good, you can bet all the change in your pocket it isn't mounted correctly, and chances, are, you'll miss that next target out.

Basic stance and barrel placement in relationship to the target is yet another of the adversities that can ruin some of your fun during a shoot. Reread the section on stance and muzzle position elsewhere in this book and keep in mind that the slightest deviation from the material presented will have a profound effect on your ability to break clay targets effectively and effortlessly.

We all learn from watching. Instead of spending idle time at the beer bar or coffee shop, look at as many top-notch shooters and see how they shoot. You'll be surprised at all the "free" advice you'll gather for your well-spent time.

Shooting Skeet at Station 8 demands proper gun fit. If the stock is too short or long, you are placing an additional handicap on your shooting.

A good tip is to have a friend take a few snapshots of you while you are shooting. Compare your stance and shooting position against some of the top shooters. Don't emulate them—only study their gun mount and follow through.

Adversity 2
Bad Instruction
"Everybody's an Expert"

Visualize this scenario, if you will. A new shooter walks into a Skeet club, says he is a beginner and asks if there is anyone around that might give him a few pointers on how to shoot Skeet better. If you've ever seen a situation like this played out, you know what happens next.

"Instructors," converge (usually in droves) to the aid of this bedeviled novice and what follows is a glossary of every shooting term ever heard—"you're shooting too high, too low, you're behind the target, you're in front of it, your stock is too low, your stock is too short"—and on and on. Of course, the student becomes so confused at the end of his lesson that what little he thought he knew prior to the "everybody's a qualified instructor" experience has long since been modified or forgotten.

There is only one way to get qualified instruction.

First and foremost, *pay* for professional help. How and where do you find it? Subscribe to or borrow the magazines that deal with either trap or Skeet shooting. In them you'll find ads from various instructors around the country who give what they refer to as "clinics" for a predetermined amount of dollars. If you want the best instruction available, clinics are the best way to go. Call the instructor that seems to fit your needs the best and discuss his requirements for a clinic. Normally for one of these shooting experts to come to your area, a certain number of students must be guaranteed, etc. That is the Cadillac approach to receiving instruction.

If you're a little lean in the wallet or there are no clinics in your area, follow this next approach. Visit all the gun clubs in your area and start asking the club managers who they'd recommend to give you trap or Skeet lessons. Next, watch an actual lesson by each of the instructors and determine for yourself which one you would like to teach you. If you're having some difficulty coming up with names, then borrow a year-end average book from either of the three clay target associations—National Skeet Shooting Association (Skeet), Amateur Trapshooting Association (trap) and the Pacific Inter-national Trapshooting Association (trap). Look for the shooter with the best overall average that lives in your area and ask him directly if he will give you lessons.

Adversity 3
Switching Guns
"Don't Do It"

Do you have any idea how long it takes to learn the nuances of a trap or Skeet gun well enough to seriously start improving your scores with it?

Many top trap and Skeet shooters say it takes at least a year *if you do a lot of practicing* with it and longer if you practice infrequently. Plan on burning up a lot of shells with a new gun. It will take that long just to sort out the correct stock fit for your style of shooting. It will also take a while to discover which reload or factory round works best in your new gun.

When you've committed to shooting a certain gun, *stay with it!* If you shoot some bad scores, forget them. They aren't signals to change to another gun. It's mind-boggling to see how many shooters switch guns and how frequently they do it. Want some incentive? Look at the better shooters. Do they switch guns? Hardly ever . . .

A new shooter is strongly advised to seek help from a professional instructor. A good one will charge and a poor one will give advice for free. You get what you pay for.

and that's the message. Stay with your gun through good scores and bad for at least a year or two before you determine once and for all that you can't achieve your shooting goals with it.

Adversity 4
Patterning
"My Gun Throws Great Patterns"

If you were given a nickel for every shooter out of a thousand who took the time to pattern a newly acquired gun to determine (a) what shotshell worked best in it and (b) where and how it printed its pattern, before committing himself to buying it, you probably wouldn't end up with enough cash to buy a bag of beans. Yet, when it comes to adversity in shooting trap or Skeet, this is a very big problem.

How many times have you suspected one load patterns better than another in your gun? You know it does better because you can see it pulverizing targets. On the other hand, you've shot some factory shells or reloads that seem to perform less efficiently. Then too, there are times when you are shooting and you're convinced you were smack dab in the middle of each target, yet you were only getting a small piece of the bird. That's when doubt in your ability creeps in and you begin to wonder whether your gun is shooting where you've pointed it.

A session at the pattern board will answer your questions. But failure to pattern your gun can lead to some serious doubts about your loads, your gun, your ability—or all three. There's no quicker way to improve your scores than by determining what load (factory-new shells or reloads) performs best in your gun. The difference between various brands of shells and reloads and their patterning ability in your gun can be dramatic.

By patterning your gun, you'll also determine whether it is shooting where you are pointing. If not, it is a simple matter for a competent gunsmith to alter the point-of-impact with a stock modification or choke work. It is a time consuming task that will have you counting pellet holes in large pieces of paper until you're blue in the face. But worthwhile work it is and remember, to do the job correctly, you'll have to fire a minimum of ten rounds of each shell to establish what combination works best in your gun. The rewards are worth the effort.

Clay targets are meant to be broken. Use the best ammunition you can buy or only use top-quality reloads. Losing a target due to faulty ammunition because of economics is an unforgivable sin—the few pennies saved could cost you big bucks.

Don't take any target for granted. Remember, the only "easy" target on the trap or Skeet field is the one you hit, all the others are tough and demand your total concentration.

If you travel any distance to a registered shoot, make certain that you check weather forecasts before you leave and take appropriate clothing along with you.

Skeet and trap shooting are outdoor shooting sports and you can't control the weather, but to become a top-notch shooter, you must learn how to cope with changing conditions.

Once you've determined the right shell combination, you'll see a noticeable increase in your ability to break clay targets, whether they be at a trap or Skeet shoot or a weekend fun event. Take the time to pattern your gun and you'll remove even more adversity from your clay target shooting efforts.

Adversity 5
Flinching
"It Goes with the Territory"

Everybody, has flinched at one time or another. An occasional flinch is something you can expect. An occasional flinch can be tolerated and when it happens, you can only hope to luck out and break the target. But when that flinch becomes more frequent, then it's truly an adversity that will have to be remedied quickly or it just might destroy any and all shooting ability you've acquired.

Flinching, when it is epidemic, is horrible to see. As you may know, flinching is the body's reaction to the constant pounding of recoil produced every time the gun is fired. When flinching is bad, it can literally cause a shooter to abandon the clay target sports all together. Is flinching curable? Yes, in many cases it can be totally and completely eliminated by taking one or all of the following measures.

The attack on the flinching problem is usually four-

fold. First, a shooter should try the use of recoil devices in his stock. Another suggestion is to switch to an autoloading shotgun with its somewhat drawn out recoil curve. Custom barrel work from a competent gunsmith is yet another way to go. You can have the forcing cone of your chamber lengthened along with back boring the entire barrel. These two steps will also reduce recoil. Another benefit from these modifications is that they should also improve the patterning of your gun. Porting your barrel is another modification that can be made to lessen recoil. Reloads should also be seriously researched. A good 1-oz. load will recoil remarkably less than a regular 1⅛-oz. target load.

Finally, if all of the above fails to eliminate flinching, then possibly it's time for a release trigger. That is to say, a trigger that fires the shell when it is released rather than pulled. The release trigger will probably go down in history as the one device that has cured more flinches than anything else. However, it is something you should only consider after all the above remedies have been tried first.

All of the adversities mentioned so far can be considered to be mental problems and may be solved by mechanical means. There is, however, a completely new set of adversities that are more difficult to overcome. Let's look at them, see what causes them and find out how to counteract them.

162

Watch the wind—if it is at your back then the targets will fly in a lower trajectory and the opposite holds for an incoming wind—you must make mental and mechanical corrections to compensate.

Both trap and Skeet shooting require a few important accessories. Shooting glasses, hearing protectors, shell carriers, hats, etc. are integral to good shooting.

Adversity 6
Bad Weather

Skeet and trap shooting are outdoor sports. Therefore, to become a champion or earn the revered title of a "consistent" competitor, one must shoot in all kinds of weather. It is rare when a trap or Skeet shoot is called off because of torrential downpours, hurricane-speed winds or sub-zero temperatures. Like show business, the game usually goes on. That factor alone makes both of these shooting sports both unique and challenging.

Neither game is seasonal, as both registered and fun shoots are held around the calendar in all parts of the country. Shoots are held in Montana in March when shooters are bundled up like eskimos searching for seals. Conversely, trap and Skeet events are scheduled in California and Arizona when the mercury will often top 110 degrees! Shooter comfort has never been a criterion for scheduling an event!

Learning how to shoot well in inclement weather is the mark of a champion. I'll not forget one prime example when attending a trap shoot sponsored by the Mint Gun Club held in Las Vegas, Nevada. It was in February, and traditionally the weather is cold with a prevailing wind out of the north. Shooting conditions on that particular day were dreadful—bitter cold with tempera-

tures hovering around the 40 degree mark, the wind was gusting from 10 to 30 knots, and to make matters completely sour, a light drizzle was falling.

Simply venturing out in this weather was a challenge—shooting in it was an experience and shooting a good score would seemingly be preposterous. To a man, everyone was complaining about the weather and accepting defeat before chambering a shell. Comments like, "Hope I can break an 80," or "Why bother!" were commonplace among them. Yet, a handful of shooters looked at the rain-soaked flag, half-frozen and standing at attention with smiles on their faces. This is what they came to Las Vegas for—*bad* weather!

That small group knew that they had the odds in their favor. Although "handicap" trap shooting is theoretically supposed to be the equalizer between average and outstanding trapshooters—because of the yardage differences—in reality, most 27-yard trap shooters maintain a higher handicap average than the majority of short- or middle-yardage competitors. How did these superlative shooters get to the "back fence?" Not by ducking out of shoots that were held in bad weather. They've learned not only how to cope with "adversities," but to actually benefit from these normally distracting circumstances.

Anyway, back to the Las Vegas trapshoot. There were well over 175 squads of shooters who signed up for

163

Learn from watching. If targets are flying erratically due to weather conditions, make a mental note of these unusual flight patterns. Don't allow yourself to be surprised by an unusual flight pattern by the target—expect the unexpected!

Double and triple check your equipment and other important shooting accessories before it's your time to toe the shooting line. There's always enough time to do this before the shoot—and never enough time during the shoot.

the handicap event. Often, there were so many shooters in attendance, that the Mint Gun Club would have to cut off entries due to time and space problems. But, the bad weather made its mark. Squad after squad would have "missing" shooters, those who pulled out of the event assuming that they were beaten before they even started. They usually went back to town for the luxury of a hotel suite and a toddy. Of the 800 shooters who originally signed up for the event, actually less than 700 "toed the line." And as anticipated, scores were very, very low. Normally "good weather" shooters were breaking scores in the high 60s, low 70s and boasting that they weren't the lowest on their squad.

Scanning the score board, I noticed that once in a while someone would record a score of 90 or so posted, and immediately the "gather-arounders" would shake their heads in dismay and moan, "Don't know how they did it!" Suddenly, there was a roar of total amazement throughout the line. Somebody shot a perfect 100x100! Incredible, yes indeed . . . surprising, not at all! The shooter was Dan Bonillas, trap shooter par excellence. Not only did he shatter 100 targets, but he did it from the maximum handicap distance of 27 yards. No, the weather did not clear up suddenly when Bonillas was shooting, as scores by his squadmates proved. And it wasn't just a "lucky" day for him. His shooting records prove that when the weather is at its worst, Bonillas is at his best! He makes the weather work for him because

he doesn't change his shooting style.

The reason most shooters fail miserably in foul weather is that they believe they have to radically change their shooting style—or timing—when conditions vary from the norm. This is a common mistake made by both newcomers and veteran shooters alike. Good competitive shooters learn how to cope and adapt their shooting style to a particular shooting hazard . . . they don't drastically alter their timing, stance or gun mount. They stay with the style that made them great shooters. As a rural sage once said, "You dance with what you brung."

How does the average shooter learn how to cope with bad weather? There's only one way and that's to shoot in it. However, you have to prepare for it before you shoot, not after the event is over. If it's cold, don't try to wear every stitch of clothing you own—you may be warm on the inside, but all those clothes will hamper your shooting ability and drastically change your gun mount position. Either of these happenings will virtually guarantee failure for that given event. Wear as little clothing as possible that will affect normal gun mount position. If you're accustomed to wearing a shooting vest and medium to lightweight shirt, then try to stay as close to these dimensions as possible. The more clothing you wear alters not only the length of the gun's pull, but it also impedes the freedom of movement in your shoulder and chest muscles.

To eliminate any surprises regarding the flight of the target on windy days, stand behind the trap you're scheduled to shoot on and study the target flight. Pay close attention to the wind and let it work for, not against you.

Trapshooting's revered location is the coveted "27-yard line." Shooting handicap targets from this distance is the most difficult of all shooting events as yearly averages prove.

Typically, a round of trap takes less than 12 minutes to complete on a single field. Skeet shooting takes a bit longer, but experienced and fast shooters can complete a round in about the same time. It's advisable, therefore, to keep a warm jacket nearby and only slip into it *between* fields. This way, you'll have an opportunity to warm up between events and bring your body temperature back to normal. Remember, the body has great resilience and can cope with bad weather better than the mind.

Many shoots are held during rainstorms. Here again, you must either brave the elements in normal shooting togs or slip into a lightweight rain suit. A jacket will only provide protection for the upper body, but rain pants will keep the legs dry and warm. A quality rain suit is expensive, usually running upwards of $50 for a ventilated nylon version. It is probably the most expensive piece of apparel you'll ever wear considering the costs versus the number of times it'll be worn. But when hundreds or even thousands of dollars—or a championship—is at stake, the rain suit is an inexpensive insurance policy. Take it with you as religiously as you would ear plugs and ammunition.

Predicting weather is somewhat of a science—regardless of what the local weatherman says on the evening news. If there's a storm in the area where you're going to shoot, take enough of the correct clothing to be able to dress as comfortably as possible, regardless of condi-

tions. And, if you're away from home and you pack extra shirts, gloves, raingear, etc., don't leave them in the motel room! Too many times, I've seen shooters scurrying back to their rental car only to remember their warm, lightweight down jacket is resting on a comfortable hanger inside a motel room closet. Scratch one shoot fee!

OK, now you're properly dressed for the occasion and the wind is still blowing and the rain is beating a tune on the metal roof of the clubhouse. It's time to take some mental precautions and evaluate the situation. If possible, go out on the shooting line and study the bird's flight—long before it's your turn to step to the line. There's nothing more demoralizing than to be surprised at the flight of the first bird out of the house, and, 99 times out of a hundred, you'll miss it. If there's a tail wind, you can be certain that the bird will be driven down long before it reaches the "setting stake." But, if you know this in advance of the actual happening, you're both mentally and physically prepared for its unorthodox flight.

Mentally, you know in advance what to expect. Instead of receiving a normal "regulation" target on your command, you'll be presented with a lower-flying "diver" that will smash into the ground somewhere between 10-15 yards short of the stake, depending on the intensity of the wind. But remember, unless the wind is of gale force or at least running 25 knots or more, the speed of

165

the target will not be increased. It is set—with properly maintained trap machines—to leave the trap arm at about 40 miles per hour. By the time the bird travels 40 yards or so, it has slowed down to 25 mph.

Conversely, if a head wind is blowing, the target will rise drastically from the trap house. This type of ill-wind will only have some effect on the target *after* it has traveled about half its regular prescribed distance. Therefore, the first half of the target's thrown arc is rarely affected by the wind's velocity or direction. It is during this flight time of the target that the shooter must begin to make his millisecond calculations. If a shooter totally concentrates on the target when it first leaves the house, his or her mind will automatically make the necessary corrections to present a correct sight picture, and the result is a smashed target! And that, fellow shooters, is the name of the game!

Adversity 7
Trap Pullers
"He fast pulled me!"

Good shooters have reasons for missing a target—poor shooters use excuses. Unlike most other competitive sports where there is money involved, or at least semi-expensive trophies, the shooting contestant is dependent on another person's ability to perform. Poorly

trained target pullers are the norm and knowing this in advance is what the shooter must learn to accept, tolerate, and overcome. If one "blows his cool" over a trap puller's inconsistency, then all he's done is to greatly dilute his or her concentration on the target.

There are many ways to prevent this from happening. Remember earlier when it was suggested to preview the targets *before* it was your turn to shoot? At the same time, you should pay close attention to the trap puller's personality and timing. If quite a few targets were turned down by shooters on the squad you were watching, you know in advance that the puller was either badly trained or just having a bad day. We all have bad days, so why not give that teenager the benefit of the doubt and allow him the same consideration.

As a rule, trap and Skeet help are youngsters, ranging in age from 10 to 18 years old. These junior-age workers are usually paid minimum salary—and in some instances less, depending on the gun club's management. Why? Simple economics. In any event, these kids are doing a job, not because they enjoy it, but rather because they have to work and earn a few bucks on their own. As a group, it's certain that they would all rather be off on a beach somewhere, enjoying themselves with their peers. Instead, they're constantly being scowled at, scolded and taking the abusive brunt of the inconsid-

If the trap puller inadvertently "fast pulled" you, don't accept that target and don't shoot at it. There's nothing in the Skeet or trap shooting rules that says you must shoot at mis-pulled targets.

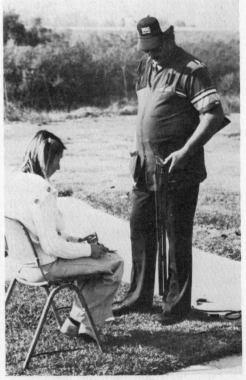

As a matter of practice, whenever passing by the puller/scorer, take a cursory glance at your scores while the sub-event is in progress. Any errors must be caught and changed at that time.

erate shooter's personality.

While pre-checking your upcoming field's targets, look for tell-tale signs of poorly trained or inattentive trap help. If an unusually high percentage of targets is rejected by shooters, walk up to the field to determine whether the puller or shooter is to be blamed. Many, many shooters don't call for the target in a clear, decisive voice. Grunts and groans are fine for wrestlers, but clay bird shooters must develop sharp, distinctive "calls" for the target. If you can't hear the shooter's call for the target, then odds are the trap puller couldn't either. But, if you can clearly hear the shooter's call and the puller doesn't respond quickly, then you have a good idea who the culprit is in this scenario. Another method to determine if there is a mental or mechanical problem regarding the puller is before you begin to shoot, politely ask the puller if you can test the "pull cord" yourself. You'll rarely be denied. Go ahead and pull a couple of targets; if there's a delay or a pause between the time you punch the button and the bird is released, that field probably has a faulty cord or button and it *must* be replaced with one in proper working order. This happens quite frequently and any time the pullers are blamed for equipment failures, its up to you to determine the source of slow pulls.

What is an inordinate number of "rejected" targets by the shooters? First, we know that there are five shooters on a squad and each person fires at 25 targets for a total of 125 targets per field. If 10 percent of the targets are rejected—12 to 13—that means that each shooter, on an average, would turn down two to three per field. That is an objectionable and unacceptable number of shooter refusals. Three to 5 percent would be a tolerable and acceptable count.

If you are convinced that the trap puller is not paying attention to his job, then there are some things you can do. First, talk to the puller and tell him your findings in a calm, orderly manner. If he apologizes and says he'll do better, then go ahead and take your place on the field. Chances are you and your squadmates will receive excellent pulls and the problem is quickly and easily solved. But, in the event that your initial conversation with the puller isn't to your liking, and with the backing of your squadmates, then go to management or the range master and request a puller replacement. Most of the time, a heads-up range master knows which trap line personnel are going to create problems and which aren't. You'll rarely get a squawk-back when a "bad kid" is reported. Yet, you'll probably get a bunch of static if the puller you "snitched on" has a proven track record with the range master.

As the weather can greatly influence your shooting, it

If you get a fast or slow pull, don't break your concentration by scowling at the trap puller. Not only will it disrupt your concentration, odds are you'll upset the puller and the result will be more "problem pulls."

Don't get involved in other shooters squabbles and discussions with trap personnel. Stay away from these distractions unless they pertain to you. It is often better to squad up with a group of strangers than close shooting buddies for this reason.

Changing stations is an excellent time to relax your mind and let it wander to any thoughts past the trapline. A successful shooter only has to concentrate for 10 seconds before and during his time to shoot at a target. Sound easy? Hardly!

The scoreboard is a favorite gathering place to find out how shooters have done—but don't look at the scoreboard until *after* you shoot. Knowing that a 98 or 99 is already posted in your class puts extra pressure on you.

The rewards of shooting are not only mental, but many clubs award 100-straight pins to those shooters who excel. Not terribly important at the time of presentation, they do become significant bits of memorabilia as the years pass.

also affects trap personnel. Whereas you have the opportunity to seek some relief from wind, rain or heat, the poor puller and trap setter usually have to work under these conditions with little or no break for long periods of time. No wonder that shooters occasionally receive bad pulls for no apparent reasons.

The most often heard excuse is, "I shot at a fast (or slow) pull." Immediately, a shooting buddy will side with the griper and claim the same blame for his misses. There's no reference in any of the clay target shooting rule books that states the shooter must accept and shoot at a target that has been "fast" or "slow" pulled. This is the shooter's option to either take it or turn it down. Those who are in control will almost always refuse improper "pulls;" those who can't control their actions and thoughts seemingly get stuck with all the "bad luck." Accepting and shooting at ill-timed calls and pulls is part of both trap and Skeet shooting games. One

has to learn early-on how to control these misfortunes. Here are some ideas how to cut-down on bad pulls:

1. Develop a sharp, distinctive call. Don't mumble, grunt or yell. It is better to make your call a tad louder than necessary than to make the trap puller strain his or her ears to hear you.

2. Become consistent in your call. Don't change it from one day to another. If you use the word "Pull!" . . . stay with it. If you prefer a "Hup!" or a "Pulit!" use the same call throughout your shooting career. Just because you once heard a super-shooter bellowing "Eeeeyooah!" and he always breaks a 97 or better, that doesn't mean that his call is breaking the targets. Say whatever is comfortable for you, and over the years it'll become a natural action for you . . . you won't even think about it. To verify if your call is proper, ask a trap puller—either between stations or at the end of the round—if he can hear your call distinctly and clearly. If

(Left) All too often, a new shooter is only interested in his own targets. Pay close attention to the flight of the other four targets which will help you decide your plan of attack on other birds.

(Right) Relaxed concentration is a style that one must constantly work on to overcome upsetting emotions. The single-most important adversity you have to overcome is your own mental attitude.

It is imperative that you check the scoresheet before you leave the field. If there is a mistake on your score, it must be corrected before you leave—otherwise it stands!

he can't, you can rest assured that he'll tell you, and in no uncertain terms. This is one of the few times that a trap puller can "get even" with a shooter, but in a nice way.

3. Don't get into an argument with trap personnel over scoring of targets. Remember it is your responsibility to verify that they record what you shot. During a trap tournament, scores will be called out after each post. Typically, the scorer/puller will simply say; "Change 5,5,4,5,3." Meaning, that shooters 1, 2 and 4 broke 5 out of 5 targets, while shooter 3 broke 4 out of 5 and shooter 5 broke 3 out of 5. If you have any questions about your score, the time to voice them is during the changing of the posts. Afterwards is too late! In the event that you thought you broke five targets and the scorer/puller called out a four, you'll have to have the backing of at least two squadmates to convince the scorer/puller that he or she made a mistake

and he'll have to change your score. This rarely happens, but in the event that you can't convince fellow squad members and the scorer that your score is incorrect, it will stand as originally stated. This is the time you have to gather yourself together and control your emotions. If you can't or don't, then you'll probably miss the next two targets as your thoughts are still back at the score sheet. Like baseball hits, they'll even out over the long haul and undoubtedly, somewhere down the shooting line, a scorer/puller will see a minute piece come off your target when you knew it was a "lost" target.

The purpose of this chapter is to acquaint the new shooter with a few of the pitfalls he'll encounter in both trap and Skeet shooting. The more you shoot, the more experience you'll gain. We all learn from experience and mistakes, but a wise man also learns from other people's mistakes!

11 Tournament Preparation

"TO BE forewarned is to be forearmed," a sage once said and this bit of advice is especially true when it applies to tournament preparation. This chapter will deal with some of the problems you'll eventually incur if you shoot long enough.

Trap and Skeet shooting has a fairly high amount of participant turnover. If you stay away from the competitive fields for a few months, there will be many new faces on the firing line when you come back. To these newer shooters we shall direct our comments; the "vets" will smile and nod their heads in agreement, as they, too, have paid their "dues" and experienced similar problems.

Preparing for your first, 17th or 250th tournament should be a ritual, one which demands the shooter's to-

tal concentration for success. If a business transaction entailed a Board Meeting, the successful businessman would be well schooled and prepared in advance of the upcoming meeting, right? Yet, all too many trap and Skeet shooters take their shooting too casually and hide behind the excuse that, "I only do this for fun. If I want to work hard at something, I'll do it at my job." At best, this is pure nonsense. Show me a shooter who enjoys himself when he shoots a lousy score and I'll wager that this same individual is eating himself up inside.

People shoot registered trap and Skeet for the competition between themselves and their peers. If they are strictly shooting for fun, then they would only shoot practice where scores are meaningless and their names would never be listed on the club's scoreboard.

When Dan Bonillas' career is completed, he'll own every major trap shooting record in the book. His 100-straights in doubles approaches 40 in number — the number of 100x100s from 27 yard shot by him surpasses the number of times the majority of trap shooters have broken a like score from 16 yards.

Industry representatives, like Bob Oxen, who worked for Federal Cartridge Co., were willing "experts" to help shooters solve a myriad of inbred problems. Today's "reps" are more sales oriented than pure trap and Skeet shooters, but are willing and able to help newcomers in the sport.

A rare photo indeed — Arnold Riegger on a Skeet field! With this man's ability, and if he had chosen to shoot Skeet competitively, his name would be enshrined in Skeet's Hall of Fame.

Mental Attitude

Tournaments are no different physically than practice rounds. There's no difference in the flight of the targets, and the same guns and ammunition are used to shoot practice or tournament targets. The rules are the same — if you miss a target, a "0" is recorded on your score sheet. However, the major difference between practice and a tournament is mental attitude and advance preparation.

One of the reasons for the popularity of trap and Skeet is the lack of physical advantage of one person over another. Just because a super-strong male can bench-press 500 lbs. of weight doesn't mean he can shoot more accurately than a 13-year-old young lady. There's little correlation between physical strength and a winning attitude. There are a few exceptions, of course, when 500- or 1,000-target marathons or time-consuming shoot-offs occur and one shooter's better physical condition lets him outlast "weaker" competitors. As a rule, however, physical condition is of little consequence as witnessed by shooters of both games, and in all age groups, who come through as winners. Haven't we all envied and marveled at scores posted by sub-juniors and Senior veterans?

Most tournament shooters use virtually the same equipment — shotguns, ammunition and shooting techniques vary little. Like most sporting endeavors, the first 90 percent of a person's aptitude is made up of learning the basics, equipment and perfecting a proprietary technique. The remaining 10 percent is mental

Trap and Skeet shooting boils down to one simplistic rule — break the target. Virtually all of the stumbling blocks in the path of a shooter are self-inflicted. Stringent self-control techniques are a must as both games are 90 percent learning the basics, equipment and technique and 10 percent mental preparedness.

preparedness. If one can totally concentrate on perfecting the basics to where no mistakes are made, then a perfect 100x100 will be the resultant score.

No shooter can force another to make errors under normal conditions. Every shooter pulls his own trigger and blunders in judgment are self-inflicted. The game of tennis has two scoring rules that are unique — forced and unforced errors. Forced errors are caused by one

Arnold Riegger, a tremendous trap shooter during the 1950s, was able to master the difficult feat of total concentration. His secret was not to concentrate for the entire 100-target event, only for a brief period of 10 seconds at a time — 5 seconds before the target was released and the 5 seconds it took him to shoot and follow-through. Now that sounds easy doesn't it?

Skeet and trap shooting have no "gray" areas, and unlike horseshoe pitching and tossing hand grenades, close doesn't count.

player to make an unreturnable shot against his opponent. Unforced errors are those, which in the eyes of the scorer, should have been made and would be classified as "easy." One of tennis's premier women players is Chris Everett Lloyd. She rarely makes an "unforced error" as she calmly stands on the baseline and returns every shot. In effect, she is letting her opponent make all the mistakes. Her attitude towards tournament tennis play is "aggressive defense," thereby encouraging her opponent to make the mistakes en route to defeat.

Competitive trap and Skeet shooting, outwardly, doesn't seem to inspire this type of play, yet inwardly, all of the better shooters understand this psychology. Winning is striving for inner perfection and letting your opponents make the mistakes. Champions can only control their own game plan, not their opponents and if they shoot their best — which is a 100x100 — they've done their job. Perfect scores are commonplace at most of today's trap and Skeet shoots, but what exactly is "commonplace." Literally translated, it would mean

There's often a long wait between events. Some shooters prefer to gather in the coffee shop, others stand around and "chew the fat," while others take a needed siesta to gather their thoughts.

(Right) It's a good idea to prepare for a tournament by getting to the grounds early to watch the trap personnel set the machines for the day's events. Doubles targets are especially demanding and unless the shooter knows exactly where the target will fly, he is under a distinct handicap.

Dan Bonillas (center) soon realized the importance of mental preparation and his attitude toward shooting is to make the other fellow beat himself. Bonillas rarely makes a mental mistake and his incredible shooting feats in recent years are already legendary.

that over 50 percent of the entrants break a perfect score. In the real world, that simply isn't true. At a 16-yard trap shoot or a 12-gauge Skeet event, if there are 100 competitors firing, four or five "straights" would be about par. Now that's only 4 or 5 percent of the shooters that put it all together. Hardly "commonplace" to those who didn't break them all!

If one were to interview those shooters who broke 'em all, when asked how they did it, to a man they would say it was because of good mental emotional control. A certain gun or a different brand of ammunition is rarely credited with a victory, but is often the accused culprit and excuse for failure, when in reality the shooter's mental attitude makes up that important "10 percent" to which we earlier alluded. Those shooters who can control that all important "10 percent factor" are the champions; those who cannot are called participants.

Mental toughness is a term composed of two opposite meaning words — "relaxed concentration." Every suc-

Regardless of how long a shooter has been at the sport, he must learn to swallow his ego and seek professional help to improve his shooting if it doesn't come about naturally through time and effort.

Shooting practice is no different than shooting a registered event. The targets and equipment used by the shooter are the very same, only the mental attitude is different. Practice fields should be better used by the shooter to "dream up" shootoffs and compete against other pre-shoot contestants, whether they know it or not.

Only a qualified instructor can help a shooter out of a shooting slump. Their keen, trained eyes can quickly spot a shooting problem created by numerous reasons, but generally the slump is caused by the shooter's inability to use proven and practical shooting form and style.

Mental toughness — or relaxed concentration — can be practiced both on and off the Skeet field. Many of the greatest shooters visualize the target before it is released and establish the proper mental image before pulling the trigger.

Pump guns can often be a bit temperamental and are affected by a build up of dirt and grime. Mental preparation prior to a tourney is important, but so is attention to equipment to preclude mechanical problems. Of the two uncertainties, mechanical troubles are easier to prevent from happening.

cessful competitor, just prior to and during the shooting event is in a state of "keyed-up" emotional tension. Instead of allowing the pressure of the shoot to play havoc on his nerves, the seasoned — and again, successful — shooter makes this mental condition work for him. How? Through desire and enthusiasm! Haven't we all scratched our heads when reading about the outstanding exploits of trap and Skeet champions shoot after shoot? How do they manage to keep their interest level high enough to be consistent winners? Again, it's an over-simplified case of mind over matter. They not only have a stronger desire to win, but in keeping with the tradition they have built among their fellow shooters, they are expected to win! And, usually do.

Now that we've convinced you that mental preparation is 90 percent of a winning attitude, what's the other 10 percent? Most prominent clay target shooters will agree that equipment makes up 10 percent of either game. We've all witnessed shooters using "inferior" equipment and beating the pants off their competition

Preparing your gun and equipment before the event starts will help loosen up tension caused by tournament jitters. Busy hands are happy hands and when it's time to shoot, you'll be better prepared both physically and mentally.

armed with expensive guns and costly accessories.

A prime example of this was back in the mid-1930s, when a youngster was driving past the ATA home grounds in Vandalia, Ohio, while the Grand American Tournament was being conducted. Noting that a trap shooting event was being held, he wheeled his Model T pickup into the parking lot, signed up for the event, purchased his shells and went to work. After the smoke had cleared, guess who's name was at the top of the list? Right. Our farm boy, who was using the only shotgun he ever owned, a field-grade Winchester Model 12 in 16 gauge! Obviously, nobody took the time to tell our hero that he didn't stand a ghost of a chance armed with a 16-gauge, field-grade shotgun and especially not properly attired because he was wearing bib overalls!

Granted, this is a wonderfully true story and one that has been repeated numerous times, but it does provide a moral. Equipment only contributes — it is not of primary importance to winning.

Yet, at the same time, a shooter properly preparing and maintaining his equipment will give himself some beneficial peace of mind while standing on the firing line. There's nothing more distracting than when subconsciously worrying about one's shotgun or ammunition. If, therefore, the shooter thoroughly cleans and oils his pet scattergun before the event and makes certain that his ammunition is the best he can make — or buy — then he has set his mind to a winning attitude.

Paying close attention to other equipment is equally important. All trap and Skeet shooters should wear shooting glasses, both for protection and to improve eye sight. What would happen if you accidentally dropped a pair of glasses and cracked a lens? Do you carry a back up pair to handle this emergency? If not, then the extra investment for a spare pair of glasses could prove to be an inexpensive insurance policy.

The same back-up policy holds true for any special accessories used and needed during a competitive event, such as ear plugs or muffs, devices to hold ammunition like a pouch or holder to attach a full box of

While shooting tournament trap or Skeet, it's advisable to have a spare set of all your important shooting accessories — shooting glasses, ear plugs, shooting pouch, etc. Like Murphy's Law, if something can go wrong, it will. Pre-shoot preparation will pay off for those who do it, and for those who don't, they always fall back on the old cliché . . . "Sure wish I didn't do that."

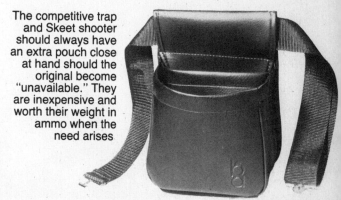

The competitive trap and Skeet shooter should always have an extra pouch close at hand should the original become "unavailable." They are inexpensive and worth their weight in ammo when the need arises

Preparation for a tournament demands proper attire. A shooting vest is a valuable piece of equipment because it holds fresh ammunition, empty hulls, and all sorts of important carry-along accessories. The vest should fit comfortably and not cause any binding across the back or chest areas. If you look good, you'll generally feel good about what you're doing.

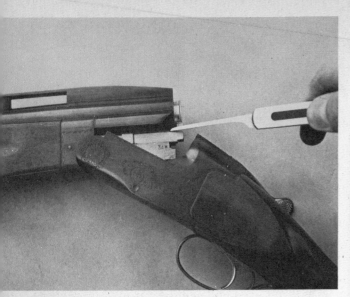

(Left) Guns and equipment *must* be kept clean and lubricated. Attention to details before the tournament starts will reward the shooter with a clear and uncluttered mind while the event is on.

Etiquette is an important aspect of learning how to participate in trap and Skeet shooting. Be considerate of other shooters and the trap pullers by restricting loud talking and "horseplay."

(Left) If you perspire profusely during hot, muggy days, be certain that your shooting glasses fit properly and have them adjusted so that they stand away from the forehead and eyebrows. Perspiration will then merely fall off the face and not onto the glasses which could impair vision. If you can't see'em, you can't hit'em!

ammunition on the shooter's belt. "Blinders," which attach to the sides of shooting glasses are generally made from cardboard and after a couple of shoots are badly disfigured by perspiration. Is there a reserve set close by? The use of blinders prevents wind from entering the shooter's eyes and also helps the concentration factor as it creates "tunnel vision."

On hot, muggy days, perspiration can — and does — hinder many shooters. Droplets of sweat on shooting glasses is more than a hindrance. Anticipating this problem, a sweat band wrapped around the forehead will prevent perspiration from staining the glasses, thereby allowing clear vision at all times. Another solution to this problem could be solved by refitting shooting glasses to stand off from the shooter's forehead and eyebrows.

Trap shooting, more so than Skeet shooting, creates havoc with shotguns due to the build up of heat. In trap, the time between shots is usually less than a minute as a typical fast-shooting five-member squad will run

through a field in 12 to 15 minutes. This sparse amount of time between shots doesn't allow the gun to cool down between shots and many shooter's are victimized by heat waves coming off the top of the barrel. If this common problem affects your shooting, then carry a water-soaked towel to artificially cool down the barrel between stations. I for one, have used this technique for many years, as heat waves bother me to the point of near-hysteria.

On And Off-Field Etiquette

Etiquette on and off the shooting field is just as important to know and learn as sight picture, gun placement and any other "basic" of shooting. Just how important is etiquette? Plenty, as it can greatly influence your final score.

Nobody wants to associate with a poor sport or braggart, regardless of his vocation or avocation. Like any small group, and competitive trap and Skeet is considered to be a minor sport, the "word" quickly spreads

(Left) Heat waves often bother and hinder a shooter's performance. Trap's newest innovation — the "Un-Gun" — prevents this vexing problem as the normally installed top barrel on an over-under is replaced with a high-posted ventilated rib.

On and off-field etiquette is as important to learn and practice as sight picture, gun control and other shooting techniques. Proper etiquette is demanded by ATA and NSSA rules.

(Left) Low-ribbed trap and some Skeet guns don't allow ample ventilation between the rib and barrel to dissipate heat. Barrels can be quickly cooled — between stations — by applying a wet towel to the area just forward of the chamber, where most of the heat is accumulated.

like wildfire as to how a person handles himself on and off the field. One of the first rules a new shooter must learn is let the score speak for itself. It is the only yardstick for measuring a shooter's performance on a given day. Don't make up mundane excuses and don't place the blame on others for a bad day. Absorb the aches and pains of an "off" day and try to do better on the next outing.

What are the "no-nos" when shooting competitive events? There are many, but just a few of the more serious violations are:

1. **Tardiness.** There's nothing more irritating to fellow squad members than being late when your squad is called to the line. And there's little excuse for being late unless you just drove into the parking lot, jumped out of your car, grabbed your shells and shotgun and came a puffin' up to your awaiting field. This rarely happens and most of the late arrivals are those inconsiderate individuals who were "tied-up" chewing the fat with their cronies…while their squadmates were put on hold.

Don't be a complainer. Accept "lost" and "dead" targets equally. Losses are part of the game and there's never been a shooter to come down the pike that has hit them all — nor will there ever be!

2. Excuses. There are literally hundreds of excuses that trap and Skeet shooters have developed over the years, and so far none of them have ever been the real reason for the shooter's inability to break the targets. These evasions of the truth range from "fast or slow pulls," "bad ammunition," or other physical "defects," to more sophisticated morsels like, "I just wasn't ready for it" or "the pressure got to me." Now, some of these excuses may be valid and truthful — in your own mind — but your fellow shooters really don't want to hear about them. They, too, have their own problems and don't care to offer a sympathetic ear. Keep your dirty laundry at home and don't hang it on the line.

3. Gripes. If you have a complaint about the condition of the shooting field, tell it to the gun club manager. Ditto for an excessive number of broken targets, inattentive trap help, parking lot conditions, etc. All of these problems can only be solved by the person in charge of the shoot, not by other shooters.

4. Talking. There's absolutely no reason to talk to fellow squad members while on the field and the shoot is in progress. Not only does it disturb the person you are talking to, but others as well. Keep your on-the-field comments to yourself until you're off the field. And then, if possible, only after the final field is shot, unless they are important to the safety or well-being of a squad member.

5. Advice. Don't give it unless asked. If you've never missed a target, then you are the expert. But if you have missed a target somewhere along the long shooting road, then you are not an expert unless solicited by a fellow shooter. Don't walk up to a buddy who had a bad field and tell him that you observed that he was shooting behind the targets. Don't you think he knows that? Of course, he does. But, if you're the sage that you think you are, then explain to him how not to shoot be-hind targets in three words or less. Can't be done, you say? OK, then pass this assignment.

6. Loud Talking. One of trap and Skeet shootings most vexing problems to other shooters are those people awaiting their turn and running off at the mouth. These inconsiderate shooters can and do cause a great deal of distraction, not only to those on the line but to the puller as well. Most shooters wear some form of hearing protection, but trap personnel don't and can't because they have to listen to the shooter's call for the target. All too often, fast or slow pulls are caused directly by distractions from the crowd that adversely affect the puller's concentration. Human nature being what it is, people have a tendency to listen to other's conversations while attempting to do their own task at hand. If you and a buddy are engrossed in telling/listening an off-color joke, chances are the trap boy is listening as well. Trade places at that moment with the shooter who is about to call for his target — guess what kind of "pull" he'll receive? Be considerate of those at work.

7. Gun Handling. In all the years and millions of rounds of shotshells expended at registered trapshoots, there's never been a single recorded fatality. Why? Trap and Skeet shooters are a fanatical group of safety-conscious shooters and won't hesitate "jumping" a fellow shooter whenever there's a gunhandling violation. Not only are there specific and enforced rules regarding gun safety in both the ATA and NSSA guidelines, individual shooters, referees and trap personnel are constantly keeping a watchful eye on those who break these rules. Even "bending" them can cause the culprit quite a bit of embarrassment. Never point a muzzle at another human being, unless, of course, you expect to be shot in return!

8. Shooting Out Of Turn. Now this may sound

If, while waiting your turn to shoot and you see another shooter about ready to call for his target, keep quiet. Any loud talking or disturbances will surely cost the shooter a target. Be considerate of others.

strange, but it happens more often than one would expect. Generally this disturbance happens in a trap shooting event and more times than not, it is when the shooter standing on Post #1 calls for a target when in actuality the target belongs to the shooter on Post #5. To lose the count between shots is easy to do, especially if one lets his mind wander. Usually a sharp trap puller will realize the error, stop the squad from shooting, and tell the "out of turn" shooter it's not his shot. In the event that one does shoot out of turn and hits the target, no score is recorded nor is the shooter in violation penalized — only ostracized!

9. Stopping a Squad. Unless there are mitigating circumstances, like gun breakdown, sudden sickness or such, stopping the flow and timing of a squad is demoralizing to the other shooters. There are inexcusable circumstances like not having enough shells to complete a round or (in the event that one needs an extra shell due to firing a broken target and that shot must be retaken) asking a fellow shooter for an extra shell, each shows a lack of preparation and consideration.

10. Pulling Out. In the event that a shooter must leave a shoot for various reasons, ill health, sudden emergency or such, then he or she should make an attempt to let other squadmates know in advance that he cannot attend. Also, the departing shooter should tell the "squadder" (that person who makes up the squad sheets) that he must leave the grounds and that his spot is open. The shoot cashier and squad maker will attempt to fill this void. Less critical in Skeet than trap, shooting "short" greatly alters the rhythm and timing of a squad due to the nature of the game. Regardless, though, if one declines to shoot because of bad weather or unusually high scores already posted after officially entering an event, this is a classic example of a "fair-weather shooter."

These 10 classic examples only scratch the surface of clay target "don'ts." There are many, many, more but space limits us to these 10 most "popular" ones. Competitive shooters are a condescending lot and will forgive both new and veteran shooters an occasional violation. But for those who don't heed advice and continue to make problems for fellow shooters, one will have a tough time scratching up a squad on which to shoot. I've seen classic examples of where a "problem shooter" is entered and squadded and when his mates find his name on the scoresheet, all four pulled off the squad and formed a new one! Now that's a message to be learned.

Competitive shooting is not a popularity contest, but one's attitude and conduct does seriously affect those around him. Be thoughtful, courteous and enjoy yourself, but not at the expense of others.

Squadding

Picking squadmates is like choosing a wife. Difficult, but not impossible. We are all affected by those around us and if we enjoy the company of a certain individual, we have a natural tendency to associate with him on and off the shooting field. Should this association be extended to the trap or Skeet squad? Not in my opinion and I feel that it is a mistake to squad-up with a close friend. Most shooters on a squad are cognizant of how other squad members are doing. This is a natural act of paying close attention to your own targets, but to other's as well. You can accept a lost target better than your buddy will and his, "Gee, I'm sorry for Joe" attitude will ultimately and adversely affect your friend's score. Try to deliberately squad yourself with associates — never close friends.

If you're a lower class shooter, make a diligent effort to be placed on a squad of higher classified shooters. Their style of shooting will positively influence your

If possible, don't squad with a close friend as a bad day by either of you could greatly influence the other's concentration. There's a natural tendency among shooters to subconsciously "count" the other fellows score, and none of us enjoy seeing a good buddy "go down the tubes."

own capabilities. Most of your higher ranked (AA or A) trap shooters have developed a fast shooting rhythm which promotes better scores. Shooting with these "race cars" will bring out the best in you and most likely you'll shoot several points above your average. You still may be the low man on your squad score-wise, but you'll have learned a valuable shooting lesson.

Like frogs and ponds, 'tis better to be low man on a "big" squad than big man on a "low" squad. The novice and low-average shooters are plagued and characterized by poor timing and non-rhythmic shooting techniques. Merely trying to "keep up" with experienced and rhythmical shooters will automatically improve a new shooter's gun handling techniques and score. Therefore, poorer shooters will mostly benefit from shooting with a better squad, and conversely, a better shooter will suffer when "stuck" on a squad of slow-shooting novices.

Shootoffs — How to Handle Them

Shootoffs are an integral part of competitive trap and Skeet shooting. Not only do they determine the winner and losers of a certain event, but this unique part of the game showcases shooters and either brings out the best or worst in all of us. There's quite a lot of pressure on those participating in a shootoff and the only way to overcome, or at least learn how to cope with it, is to shoot. There's no other way to overcome sweaty palms, shaky hands or attacks of unusual nervousness. No matter what is said in this chapter or other books, nothing effectively describes the inner feelings one gets when his or her name is called for a shootoff.

Shootoffs are mainly psychological and are no more difficult than the main event. In fact, they're easier. After all, your score tied only a few others or maybe even a lone shooter. Therefore, you already beat most of the field, so overcoming a smaller hurdle like those involved in the shootoff with you should be a snap. A positive attitude is the single most important aspect of winning a shootoff.

Many years ago, I was involved in a Skeet shootoff with a single shooter. This veteran knew all the psychological tricks to keep his opponent worried. When we went out to Station One, I noticed that he had a shell carrier with four full boxes of ammo neatly stacked. I asked why he carried all that ammunition with him. He looked me coldly in the eye and said, "Sonny, I don't plan on missing *any* targets!" Scratch one shootoff as I

The tension created by attending a major shoot like the Grand American is overwhelming, regardless if the shooter has attended one or 20 "Grands." This gathering of the clans draws over 5,000 shooters in 10 action-packed days of hot and heavy shooting.

(Right) Shoot-offs are part of the great games of trap and Skeet shooting. The author (left) was left smiling only because that was all he received for his efforts. Walt Weaver (right) won the shootoff and the awards for 100x100 in the overtime event.

blew High One and true to his word, my antagonist went straight!

Shootoffs are always called at the end of the shooting day and usually conditions are different from what they were when the regular event was being shot. Lighting conditions are generally poorer and often a late afternoon wind comes up at many clubs. Be prepared for these changes. If, when you were shooting the sun shone brightly, but now it is slowing falling in the west, discard sunglasses for clear lenses. Take a good look at the flight of the late afternoon targets, and if you shot on an early squad and there's been a long delay, say a couple of hours or more, go ahead and shoot a practice round to get yourself warmed up again.

At some of the larger events, shootoffs may be held after dark and under the lights. If you've not shot much during these conditions you'll find that night-shooting is much more difficult. Again, the only way to learn how to shoot at night is by doing it. Most gun clubs offer night shooting, so make it a point to learn how to shoot after dark, anticipating important after-hours shootoffs.

Experienced shooters can literally "eat up" a new shooter during shootoffs. I've shot against one of America's top-notch high-average shooters who will deliberately attempt to alter his competitor's timing and rhythm by changing his cadence and call. One target he'll shout "Pull," the next "Hup," and perhaps another "Ugh." The reason for this is to attempt to make the other fellow worry about what the next "call" will sound like, instead of keeping total concentration on his own targets. All too often, this ruse works! The lesson to be learned is to ignore this clever bit of shootoff strategy, although it's easier said than done for the newcomer.

Another "dirty trick" I've seen used by unscrupulous shooters is to "accidentally" have their gun discharge just before calling for their first target in a shootoff, blaming nervousness, gun malfunction, etc. In reality, it was done deliberately in attempt to unnerve his opponent. A difficult performance to prove, but nevertheless this deception is commonplace around the country.

Another shootoff enigma is the jinx. Some years ago, my ex-wife Marcie Blatt was involved in at least a dozen shootoffs with a lady trapshooter named Irma Allison. On paper, their averages were about the same. Yet, Irma had a jinx on Marcie that was so strong that when the two of them locked horns, Marcie "knew" she was

Night shooting is a totally different game. Because there is no background for reference, many shooters have a difficult time with under-the-lights-shooting. You should practice after-hour shooting because many major shoots hold shoot-offs after dark due to a large number of entrants.

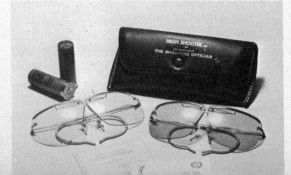

Most shootoffs are held at the end of the shooting day and lighting conditions are drastically reduced. The forewarned shooter will keep a spare set of clear-lens glasses to use for near-dusk or after-dark shooting conditions.

Shoot-offs are part of trap and Skeet shooting. Learn how to be both an appreciative winner and a gracious loser and you'll enjoy these sports that much more.

Tournament shooting is not without its rewards. Here, Chuck Poindexter (left) accepts the California President's Medal for high combined score for single and handicap events in a single day.

beaten before a shot was fired. The law of averages never made itself known when these two butted heads and Irma always won!

Everyone remembers their first shootoff, regardless if they won or lost. My first in trap was during a Winter Chain shoot at the Kingsburg Gun Club in central California. The year was 1961 and I shot my first 100x100 in the singles race. But I was not alone and tied the venerable George Ross. The early 1960s were George Ross's "heydays" and a tougher competitor and more formidable foe couldn't be found. Going head-to-head against Mr. Ross at that time would have made me a 100-to-1 longshot bet to beat him. The first field, we both went straight. I then realized that he wasn't going to beat me, regardless of the number of shots needed to be taken. I wasn't going to miss, recalling that previous experience I related to during a Skeet shootoff. It took three rounds (75x75) to defeat this great champion, and as a relative newcomer to the trap lines, I left the field 12 feet tall! Even the 10-inch "iron-man" trophy weighed 84 pounds and turned into solid gold to boot.

One of the most difficult shootoffs for a newcomer to handle is in trap doubles. The lead-off spot is the hardest position for shooters to learn as they don't have an opportunity to preview a pair targets for a new post. They must put in their mind the "approximate" and "anticipated" position of the target's flight. New shooters, unfortunately, when involved in a shootoff and those who have never, or rarely been squad-leaders during a doubles event, have a most difficult time when thrust into the lead-off position for the very first time.

To avoid this traumatic experience, a new shooter should occasionally sign-up as squad leader on a doubles event to gain this invaluable experience.

Shootoffs are memorable occasions and if you prepare ahead of time for them, you'll do very well. Keep a positive attitude and above all, mind your own affairs and break targets in the same manner that put you in the shootoff in the first place by not changing your style, timing or rhythm. Winning a shootoff is when preparation meets opportunity.

Shooting Slumps

Although not truly part of tournament preparation, shooting slumps are part of both shooting games. When is a shooting slump? It is difficult to categorize because it is only measurable in degrees. If a known AAA Skeet shooter "only" breaks a 98x100 in a 12-gauge event, is he in a slump? A minor one perhaps, but an occasional sub-par score doesn't make a shooting slump. We all have good and bad days, and our scores will fluctuate with the stars, biorhythms or position of the moon in relationship to Venus. Shooting slumps are like baseball players going "oh for thutty." Shooting slumps, however, cannot be directly traced to luck, either good or bad. If a baseball player smacks a line drive directly at an infielder, he is bestowed with the title as being "unlucky," yet he is still declared out. Golfers, too, can be both victims and beneficiaries of good and bad luck and their scores can reflect how dame fortune smiles on them.

There are hardly any "gray" areas in trap and Skeet shooting. Near misses are still misses and unlike horse

Shooting slumps are to be expected. Usually these unforseen happenstances occur when the competition shooter suddenly develops a flaw in his mechanics and subconsciously blames it on the shotgun, ammunition, etc. In reality, most slumps can be avoided by continued practice of shooting basics.

shoe pitching and hand grenade throwing, close doesn't count. Attempting to prevent a shooting slump from occurring throughout a shooting career takes a lot of mental preparation. Personally, I have never known any shooting champion who hasn't been affected by this bugaboo. It happens to the very best, so don't be discouraged if it happens to you.

If your misses are fairly well distributed in terms of a specific target or station, then improving your concentration is the only way to better your overall score. But, should you realize that you're missing a particular target, say High Deuce on the Skeet field or a screaming right angle from Post Five on the trap field, you immediately classify this particular target as "difficult." In reality, there's no such term as a "difficult" target — only the shooter has acquired the difficulty. Almost all the time, the reason for missing a certain target is due to the shooter's loss of proper shooting technique. For some unknown reason to the shooter, he cannot break a certain target under certain conditions. This is what leads to shooting slumps.

Worrying about a particular "problem" bird will lead you to missing "easy" targets and soon your level of confidence is lowered to the point that virtually every target suddenly becomes "difficult." You start flinching, lifting your head off the stock, or any of the other disastrous happenings which will reflect in lost targets. Your confidence and poise are gone and in attempting to regain these vital ingredients you start to make artificial corrections. Some shooters switch guns, install release triggers, alter stock dimensions, etc. These meth-

ods are extremes and should not be employed as they were not part of the recipe that elevated you to your shooting status before the "slump" stuck you. What then caused the slump and more importantly, how do you get out of it? Seek outside advice. There are many competent instructors offering sound, expert counseling — at a price, of course. Remember, advice is only worth what you pay for it — if it's free, odds are that it isn't worth listening to.

Qualified shooting instructors agree on one proven method to reverse the affect of a shooting slump, and that is to coach the student all the way back to the basics. Emphasis is stressed on stance, body and head position, lead, timing and all the "learned" variables that somewhere along the way, the shooter either never knew or simply forgot. Like the forest and tree analogy, the shooter is too close to the problem and it takes an outsider with a keen and trained eye to spot the problem. Physical malfunctions lead to mental malfunctions which, in turn, are recorded on the score sheet.

Another way to eliminate a shooting slump is to quit shooting for a period of time. All too often, shooters who are experiencing difficulties are practicing their mistakes instead of performing the basics, which reduces mistakes. Take a couple weeks or months off and try a new hobby. Get shooting out of your head and let it clear for a while. When you return, you'll find that your level of enthusiasm is high, you'll enjoy kibitizing with shooting cronies and shooting again will be fun!

I can recall on two separate occasions when I was unable to shoot registered ATA singles events. After one

Sometimes a layoff from trap or Skeet shooting is beneficial. After a year's absence from the registered firing line, the author (left) recorded a 100x100 in singles and tied two veteran shooters, Max Faeth (middle) and Dick Howe (right).

12-month absence the next time out I miraculously broke a 100x100. Again, and only a few months ago while this book was being written, I was away from registered competition for nearly 2 years and again the "Big Shooter In The Sky" rewarded my efforts with a 16-yard straight. Reflecting on these blessed events, I found that my renewed interest in trap shooting was piqued and that my scores, just before semi-retirement, were at their lowest ebb. Layoffs, for the most part, have proven to be beneficial for shooters mired in the midst of a slump.

To become a proficient shooter, you have to learn the basics the hard way as there are no shortcuts to success. But, you also must to learn how to *retain* the basics while advancing forward. This is called the learning process and we all are guilty of letting previous knowledge slip through our fingers which invites problems. Remembering is vital!

International Shooting **12**

INTERNATIONAL SHOOTING receives little attention and publicity here in the United States. The few dedicated shooters who represent our country during the three major world shooting events, the Olympics, the Pan American Games and the World Championships, are indeed a drop in the proverbial bucket when compared to the thousands of domestic trap and Skeet shooters. Yet, it is these same selected few who get the "heat" if our International Trap and Skeet teams do not fare well against other nations, especially those within the Communist Bloc.

Since the end of World War II and starting with the Olympic games held in Helsinki, Norway, strong political overtones have been part of these games. Perhaps this non-athletic aspect of the games originated in the 1936 Olympiad in which Nazi Germany attempted to use the games as a springboard for world-wide propaganda. Regardless of when and where all this started, it is now too late to take politics out of world-wide competition and perhaps it is just as well if we leave it in, because it's still better to swap insults across a conference table than to exchange gunfire.

Regardless of the political games played during the Olympics, and as foolish as they are, the main purpose of the games is to showcase the athletes and their respective talents.

What follows are brief descriptions of our two subject events, just to give you an idea of how tough and demanding they are.

International Skeet

Strangely, International Skeet shooting is simply a return to Skeet's original game which was devised by Messrs. Davies and Foster, as explained in an earlier chapter. The main differences between today's International Skeet and the days of yore are the distance and

Representing and accepting a medal at any of the major world-class championships has to be the highlight of any shooter's career. There are no monetary rewards for International shooting, but standing on the podium and listening to the National Anthem being played will definitely put a lump in the winner's throat.

In Europe, there are many publications dedicated to International-type shooting. European trap and Skeet shooters are better known there than they are in the U.S. as both the contestants and results are widely publicized in both newspapers and periodicals. Pity that our own press doesn't consider shooting sports a worthy theme.

International-style Skeet demands that the contestant start from a low-gun position. The buttstock must be at waist level and there cannot be any gun movement until the target is released. This type of shooting places emphasis on smooth and extremely fast gun mounting techniques.

Accepting a gold medal for Skeet shooting during World Class events has been the highlight of John Satterwhite's illustrious career. Stepping up on the center platform and listening to the National Anthem while Old Glory flutters in the background is ample reward for the countless numbers of hours and thousands of dollars of personal funds, just to be one of the privileged few.

International Skeet can be described in one word—speed! Both the flight of the target and the shooter's reaction are about twice as fast as required for domestic Skeet. International Skeet is more difficult and challenging than domestic Skeet. Unfortunately, like International Trap, there aren't many facilities in the United States at which to practice either of these "different" clay target shooting games.

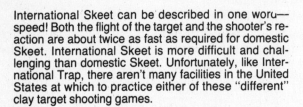

speed of the target.

The International target must fly about 11 yards farther than the flight of the original 60-yard target (which incidentally, is still being used in domestic Skeet). There is no discernible difference between the domestic and International Skeet field. The clay targets used are slightly thinner in profile than domestic targets and are much harder to withstand the added stress necessary to throw them not only faster, but farther as well.

And, like Skeet's original rules, targets are released after the shooter's call with variable delays of up to 3 seconds. Along with the delayed target, the other major difference between American (domestic) and International Skeet is the starting postion for the gun. In International competition, the shotgun butt must be either in contact with the shooter's hip or at a level line with it. An on-the-field referee watches for infractions of this rule more than any other. Also, the shooter can't move

the gun butt until the target has cleared the trap house. In the event that a shooter calls for the target and starts to raise the gun off his hip and onto the shoulder before the target is presented, a "lost" target is declared by the referee. The ref's decision is final and not subject to rebuke or challenge by the shooter.

There's no disputing that International Skeet shooting is a more demanding game than the indigenous version. The speed at which the target flies makes bringing the gun up quickly and precisely from its "low" position tricky and somewhat unpleasant. It can best be described as semi-controlled snap-shooting and therefore, International Skeet guns and ammunition are necessarily quite a bit different than those used in American Skeet.

For openers, the dominant type of gun used for International Skeet is the over-under because it is more reliable than autoloaders or even pump-action repeaters,

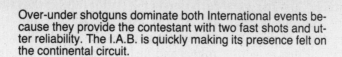

Over-under shotguns dominate both International events because they provide the contestant with two fast shots and utter reliability. The I.A.B. is quickly making its presence felt on the continental circuit.

Beretta's Model 680 over-under trap gun is used by many of the Italian trapshooters. One of the main reasons for the Italian domination of the International shotgun shooting scene is because of subsidizing of their best shooters. Major industrial firms pay for all entrance fees, practice expenses, ammunition and guns. All the shooter must do is shoot well and win! If he doesn't, there's always someone waiting in the wings to step into his spot.

(Left) Speedy presentation of the shotgun to the shooter's shoulder can—and must be—continually practiced to become proficient at International Skeet shooting. The over-under shotgun is this game's overwhelming favorite due to the excellent handling characteristics and proven high degree of reliability.

(Right) These shooters were the U.S. representatives for the 1977 World Championships held in Antibes, France. Our trap and Skeet teams both garnered medals.

and it's faster between shots. Granted, there are some shotgun virtuosos who can make multiple shots from a pump gun sound like nearly one roaring boom, but even exhibition shooters like John Satterwhite who use pump guns in their act, switch back to the over-under when serious International target work is encountered.

Stock dimensions are quite different from those found on "domestic" Skeet guns. As a rule, there is considerably more pitch and drop at the comb and heel. Unless the gun is mounted perfectly every time in a swift, fluid-like motion, the shooter doesn't stand a chance against these ultra-fast targets. Fast and correct gun mounting techniques are the single most important part in learning how to shoot International Skeet, at least successfully.

The chokes on the guns for this speedy game are virtually wide open and many are really "chokeless." The Tula-type choke is the predominant favorite among

shooters world-wide as it helps to create a garden-hose like pattern at relatively short range. Contributing to the shooter's need to have a quick-opening pattern is special ammunition made by both Federal and Winchester. Federal's T-122 has no shot protector built into the wad column and is loaded with 1⅛ ozs. of #9 shot with a muzzle velocity approaching 1,200 feet per second. The T-123 cartridge is loaded with 1⅛ ozs. of #10 shot (slightly smaller) and exits the muzzle 100 fps faster at 1,300. Both shells are loaded with soft shot, which has a tendency to spread the pattern more than shells loaded with hard shot.

Winchester's International Skeet loads are "hot" and record about 1,330 fps, pushing 1⅛ ozs. of #9½ size shot. And, like Federal, Winchester's International loads don't have a built-in shot protector and use card and fiber filler wads and an umbrella-type over-powder wad.

There are those proponents of International Skeet who claim that their game is closer to duplicating similar shots taken in the field, but I doubt this. Most of the upland game bird hunters I have seen rarely carry the gun butt at their hip, but elevated quite a bit higher and thrust out away from their body for fast and smooth mounting. International Skeet is different than American Skeet, but so is International Trap as compared to the American rendition. Each of the four games has its own set of rules and idiosyncrasies and they should stand on their own set of merits. They can not — and should not — be pitted aginst each other, nor should there be any hard and fast conclusions drawn from these comparisons. Let each sleeping dog lie.

International Trap

Whereas there are some similarities between International Skeet and American Skeet, there's hardly any common bond between International and American trap shooting. International Trap is shot in all worldwide competition — the Olympics, the Pan American Games and the World Championships.

In International Trap, a trench below ground level houses 15 separate traps, three for each of the five posts. The shooting stations are 15 meters behind the traps and a squad consists of six shooters, five of whom each stand on a station; the sixth is the "rover." After each shot is taken, the shooter moves over one station to his right until eventually all 25 shots are taken. The angles and distance the International Trap target is thrown are greater than American trap with 70 meters being the minimum legal distance. Angles and elevation vary greatly between each trap and range from 1 to 4 meters high when measured 10 meters from the trap. For example, a 4-meter target leaves the trap at nearly a 45-degree angle and must land at least 70 meters downrange. A 1-meter target travels on a near horizontal line with the ground and is difficult to break.

During tournament competition, each of the 15 traps within the bunker are re-set in a different location for each day of the tournament. In case you're wondering, International trap machines do not oscillate either horizontally or vertically but remain in a fixed position for a given day. As each shooter stands on a post, one of the three machines beneath his feet will release a target — but he doesn't know which one. A programmed com-

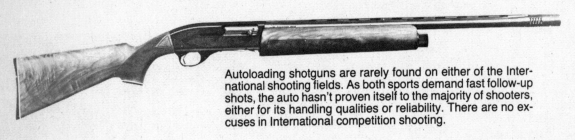

Autoloading shotguns are rarely found on either of the International shooting fields. As both sports demand fast follow-up shots, the auto hasn't proven itself to the majority of shooters, either for its handling qualities or reliability. There are no excuses in International competition shooting.

In 1967, this Air Force shooting team broke a resounding 497x500 while shooting shoulder-to-shoulder at the Tucson, Arizona Winter Chain trapshoot.

International trap necessitates the use of 15 machines per field, making maintenance a major problem. A well-organized and properly managed gun club always has back-up machines in the event of breakdown which keeps down-time to a minimum.

puter takes care of all that mystery-solving and at the end of a 100, 200 or even a 300-target race, every shooter will have received the exact same combination of birds as did each of the other entrants. Now, that's what I call *fair!* Just another reason why International trap is perhaps the finest clay target game played today.

To cope with these most difficult targets, participants are allowed two shots at each bird and it makes no difference in scoring if the target is broken with the first or second shot, or both shots for that matter. Virtually all of the more seasoned International Trap shooters routinely fire both barrels, attempting to hit a large piece if the first shot broke the target. This two-shot sequence keeps the top-notch competitor sharp and prevents "lulling" should he start to break *too* many targets with the first shot. That may sound strange, but if a shooter is doing well, and makes most of his "breaks" with the first shot, human nature takes over and the all-important back-up shot is not only unneeded, but ignored. Then, should the shooter miss his first shot, his reflexes have been drastically slowed to the point that the second shot is taken, but usually too late to hit the target. That is "lulling."

Olympic trap is a difficult game to master and unquestionably, in my opinion, the most difficult of all the formal clay target games. There are only a handful of sites in the United States that have these expensive "trenches," and most of them are found on military bases — Lackland Air Force Base, Texas and Fort Benning, Georgia, to name a few, and a handful of civilian installations. All totaled there are only about 10 separate sets of International Trap shooting facilities. In comparison, this type of trapshooting is *the* game in Europe and especially Italy. Shooters on the other side of the pond are sponsored by many of the larger industrial firms and the ranges are more like country clubs where members are required to join and pay annual dues, just for the privilege to pop primers over the trench.

The civilian sector, therefore, has had a difficult time in being able to place any non-military shooters on the official United States Shooting Teams because there are so few places to shoot.

About 20 years ago, the ATA, along with some help from the NRA, decided to solve this lack of shooting facilities problem. A new game was inaugurated and appropriately named Modified Clay Pigeon which utilized

Gun clubs in Europe have a country club-like setting and cater mainly to affluent shooters. Trap and Skeet shooting in Europe is expensive; virtually all of the "hot-hammers" are sponsored by major industrial firms who foot the bill.

This Winchester-Western trap machine has been modified to throw targets as prescribed for Modified Clay Pigeon events. This single trap simulates all the various angles and elevations of the targets thrown by those in a 15-trap trench layout used in International trap.

189

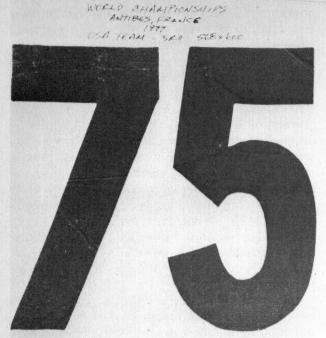

A bit of memorabilia from Jim Poindexter's archives—a photo of his assigned shooting number at the World Championship games held in Antibes, France in 1977. The U.S. trap shooting team placed third that year with a team total of 568x600.

a standard American trap field and a specially-modified trap machine that would propel targets at speeds and angles somewhat approximating International Trap targets. Those who have shot this "practice" sport, to a man, state that it's better than nothing, which ultimately means that it's a poor substitute for the "real thing."

Equipment-wise, over-under shotguns dominate this tough shooting game. As two shots may be taken at each target, speed between shots is extremely important. The target leaves the arm of the trap machine in excess of 60 miles per hour, therefore, if the shooter hesitates, due to indecision or a slow functioning shotgun, he can kiss the target goodbye, especially on a "grass-cutting" 1-meter bird. Watching some of the finest International trap shooters is an exhilarating experience. Jim Poindexter's fast shooting style is poetry in motion and when he points and pulls the trigger on his 30-inch barreled Krieghoff, the two shots sound like one — BAbang, not Bang-Bang.

Ammunition plays a big part in the shooter's overall performance for an International Trap event. Once shooters get "locked-in" to using a certain brand, dram equivalent and size of shot, switching ammunition can and has proved to be disastrous. There are no restrictions on the "power" of the shell as any dram equivalent is permissible. There are two restrictions regard-

Winchester's Grand European trap gun is capable of producing big scores in the hands of competent bunker shooters. Excellent balance combined with trouble-free operation are the two most important criteria that make a shotgun suitable to withstand the vigorous use given to it by International Trap shooters.

Gathering momentoes like these brassards from both International and domestic trap shooting is always at the shooter's own expense—little return for years of toil and thousands of dollars to cover shooting costs.

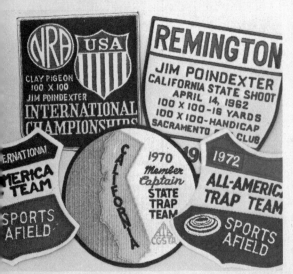

Modified Clay Pigeon trap shooting is really a practice game for International bunker style shooting. It is as close to duplicating the flight of the "trench-target" as possible and is conducted on a standard American trap field. The trap machine used here is highly modified to throw the target over 70 yards.

ing the size and the amount of shot — #7½ and 1¼ ozs. is the legal allowable maximum. Most of the American shooters I've talked to prefer 3¼ drams and 1¼ ozs. of #7½ shot for the first barrel and 3¾ drams and 1¼ ozs. of #7½ shot for the second barrel. Both of these loads are about on par with what the average hunter would use for ducks and pheasants. How would you like to shoot a couple hundred shells with this wallop in a single day? Its not pleasant and that is why most International Trap events are held over a 3-day span.

Typically, a 200-target race would be shot over 2 or 3 days, depending on the sponsoring club's facilities, with 75 targets on the first and second days and 50 on the final day. In comparison, it is not unusual to find most American trap clubs hosting 300 — or more — targets in a single day. Who says a shotgun's recoil isn't an influencing factor?

International Trap is a much better spectator sport as the action is fast and furious and the shooters are constantly moving from one post to another. But, perhaps the best or worst, depending on your point of view as a shooter or spectator, is when a shooter misses a target a blast from an air horn chills the air for all to hear. If I were seriously shooting this game, I'd get the rules changed to a have the referee muffle a simple "Lost," instead of that intimidating and embarrassing fog horn!

Jim Poindexter is now retired from shooting due to a middle ear problem contracted at the height of his long career. Jim competed in both American and International trap competition for over 22 years and has garnered many trophies and awards including a 5th place finish at the 1972 Olympics held in Munich, West Germany.

This five-man United States Air Force squad shot against both domestic and foreign competitors in the mid 1960s. From left to right: Chuck Poindexter, Ken Jones, Col. William Marriott, Howard Vendrick and Dick Loffelmacher.

13 Reloading

AS A SHOOTER becomes more deeply involved in competitive shooting, it is inevitable that the subject of reloading will rear its head. The sight of all those empty shells that have been scrupulously gathered, brought home, and are now residing in a large box or two will be a temptation that is hard to resist. A shooter's thinking usually goes along the line of, "I have all these hulls just sitting there, doing me no good. Why not reload them, save myself some money and put them back in action?" Why not, indeed?

There is an abundance of fine reloading tools on the market from which to choose. Components are readily available at prices that seem to offer a huge saving in the cost of finished ammo over what must be shelled out for factory fodder. But, before embarking on a shopping expedition for reloading gear, a shooter should take a careful look at some of the facts of reloading life.

Reloaders of ammunition for rifles and handguns generally have hopes of producing cartridges that will be a bit better than factory loads. With careful planning and good reloading techniques, it is entirely possible that a special combination of powder, primer and bullet can be found that will definitely give better performance. Certain guns will shoot more accurately with ammo that has been "fine-tuned" to suit their individual taste. Special bullet sizes and shapes may be utilized that are not offered by commercial ammunition sources. Velocities may be also increased (or decreased) to meet the requirements of a particular shooting situation. In other words, leaving money out of the picture for the moment, it is quite feasible for the rifleman or pistolero to create a loaded round that is superior to factory ammo in one way or another. Does this same reasoning apply to reloading shotshells? Perhaps disappointingly, the answer is a qualified "No."

The goal of the rifle cartridge reloader is flat trajectory, combined with pinpoint accuracy—at ranges of 100 yards and more. This requirement does not exist for

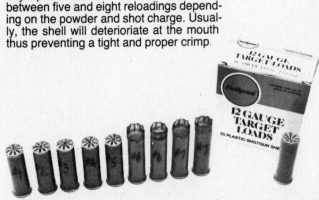

Recycling empty hulls past their point of effectiveness is false economy. Most of today's plastic hulls have a reuseable life of between five and eight reloadings depending on the powder and shot charge. Usually, the shell will deteriorate at the mouth thus preventing a tight and proper crimp.

(Left) Trap and Skeet shooting demands total concentration on the target. If the shooter/handloader has even the smallest inkling that his home-brewed ammo is not up to snuff, then this mental distraction will cause the shooter to lose targets somewhere along the way.

It's not difficult to learn how to put the empty hull in your pocket before it hits the deck. If you're shooting a pump gun, simply take it off your shoulder before cycling the action and eject the empty shell into your hand. For some strange reason, many trap and Skeet shooters have the tendency to pump the gun immediately after the shot is taken. Perhaps this is from earlier "field" training which demands fast follow-up shots on fast moving game.

(Left) If you wish to reload your empty hulls, make certain that you catch them before they hit the ground. Many gun clubs have rules saying that whatever hits the ground stays on the ground! Also, interrupting your squad mates by bending down and picking up empties can be very distracting to those on each side of you.

(Right) If a shooter believes that he can concoct ammunition superior in performance to what the factory can, he's kidding himself. Unlike centerfire metallic ammo, where the handloader can — and often does — create loads far superior to factory fodder, the trap and Skeet shooter is governed by ATA and NSSA rules and cannot exceed stringent limitations.

shotshells. A shotshell used for trap or Skeet must deliver a pattern of shot that covers a rather large area at target distances generally no greater than 50 yards. "Accuracy," in a rifleman's terms, is meaningless as applied to shotshells. Accuracy in shotshells is defined in terms of pattern size and pattern density. Loading techniques undoubtedly affect patterns, but pattern size is largely a function of the gun and its barrel choking.

Competition trap and Skeet shooters have little or no choice when it comes to projectile weight or powder charge, because the rules limit total shot weight to no more than 1⅛ ozs., and shot size is likewise restricted to 7½ shot or smaller. Powder charges can be no greater than 3 drams equivalent.

Given the above limitations of shot weight, shot size and powder charge, it is most unlikely that a reloader could develop a load that would perform better than factory ammunition. Indeed, the opposite is more often the case because factories have development facilities and research capabilities far more elaborate than any reloader could possibly duplicate. Years of experience and the combined knowledge of a host of experts are

Handloads are fine for practice or non-registered events, but whenever hard-earned cash is on the line for shoot-for-pay events, it's false economy to use handloads instead of fresh factory ammo.

Over the years, the author has found that factory-loaded ammunition is the best to use for a number of reasons. First, it eliminates any mental distractions which can be caused by shooting reloads that do not equal the consistency and performance of factory fodder. Second, once-fired empty hulls can be sold to handloader for a hefty $4 to $5 per hundred. This return on investment greatly reduces the cost of factory ammo making the few dollars savings per case questionable.

behind every shotshell leaving the assembly lines of any major ammunition manufacturer. A reloader who thinks he can put together a shotshell that will produce higher scores than factory shells on trap or Skeet fields is probably indulging in a little ego-flattering fantasy.

If a shotgun has been properly patterned, and shoots to point of aim, scores will be made by the shooter, not the ammo he uses. The most meticulously loaded shotshell in the history of the world cannot break a clay target unless the man holding the gun places the shot load in the path of the target. Fastidious reloading cannot improve scores. Only practice can raise one's average. It takes years of hard, dedicated work and thousands of rounds of ammunition to become a proficient tournament shooter—there really are no shortcuts.

If homemade shotshells are no better than factory ammo, why do competitive shooters spend large amounts of money for equipment, then sit for countless

hours at a bench, making thousands of shells, year after year? Most reloaders will point out that they're saving bags of money by re-cycling their ammo. Though there is no doubt that reloaded shells cost less than factory ammunition, the actual saving may be somewhat lower than might initially be thought.

Depending on the area in which one lives, it costs between 8¢ and 12¢ to reload a 12-gauge shotshell with 1⅛ ozs. of "hard" shot—not including the cost of the empty hull. For comparative purposes, let's take an average and say that it costs $2.50 to reload a box of shells, or 10¢ per shell. On the surface, then, it would seem that reloading is a pretty profitable enterprise, since a case of Winchester AA shells sells for about $80, or $4 a box. This adds up to a clear profit of $1.50 per box, or $30 a case. But, wait a minute! There is more to the economics of this business than meets the eye.

Suppose that the reloader didn't refill all those used

Reloading shotshells isn't an avocation designed to save the shooter great gobs of money, due to initial cost of equipment and maintaining an inventory of components. Why do we then reload? There are some important reasons, but it's mostly for the fun of doing it.

hulls, but sold them to another reloader instead. Empty plastic shells bring from $4 to $5 per hundred on the open market, or $20 to $25 per case. The actual net cost of factory ammo becomes not $80 per case, but $80 minus $20 to $25 for the empties, or $55 to $60 per case. Remember that the cost of reloads was set at $50 per case, so the net saving drops to $5 to $10, if empties are sold instead of being reloaded. Hold on, the whole story hasn't been told yet.

How about the money invested in equipment and inventory? Reloading equipment is not exactly cheap. High-speed shotshell loaders range in price from about $300 to $750 or even more. A working inventory of powder, shot, primers and wads can eat up a lot of dollars. There are also numerous little gadgets that make reloading life easier, yet still represent money expended. Total investment in equipment and materials can quickly add up to $1,000 or more. Amortized over a period of time, it takes a lot of reloading to recover this investment. What if the money tied up in reloading gear were placed in a high-yield savings account? Interest on this amount would just about pay the remaining difference between reloads and factory ammo. Net financial gain from reloading? Virtually *zeee-roe!* And remember, we haven't said a word about the value of the time involved that might be spent more profitably.

As the condemned man said just before the trap was to be sprung to hang him, "You can't argue with facts." So much for the economics of reloading shotshells. It simply doesn't pay—at least enough to make it worth the effort. Then why, in the face of this fact, do experienced shooters reload their own ammunition? For one thing, it is a good way to escape the pressures of modern society and spend a few hours now and then alone with

Empty hulls can quickly pile up in a normal day's shooting, but not so in this particular instance. The author and accomplice, Dave Hetzler, while conducting a durability test on Weatherby over-unders fired over 1,500 rounds of ammunition in less than 60 minutes using three guns. Incidentally, there were no malfunctions with either guns or ammunition.

If you are reloading Winchester AA hulls, then use only Winchester reloading components — ditto for Federal or Remington ammunition. Staying with each manufacturer's recommendations will not only keep the inventory of components to a minimum, but you'll be able to produce reloads that have been proven by the factory's ballisticians.

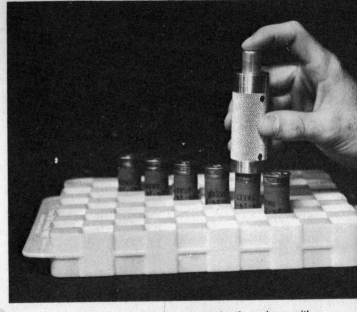

This handy little device marks the primer with a dab of colored paint to identify, through a color code, the type of handload as to dram equivalent, the size and amount of shot.

Recently there's a trend in 12 gauge ammunition touting the effectiveness of 1-oz. loads. Trap and Skeet shooting is tough enough using 1⅛-oz. legal and maximum loads, so why should a competitor place additional hardship on himself by using sub-par loads? The author recommends "full-house" loads for all the various trap and Skeet events.

one's thoughts. There is also a certain satisfaction to be derived from making something with one's own hands that will later bring pleasure in return.

If reloading is for pleasure and not profit, so be it! Nowhere is it written that all things must be done for financial gain. No man lives for money alone—or shouldn't. We shoot for fun, and we reload for fun. That's reason enough.

Now that the facts of reloading life are firmly in mind, let's get down to some of the basics. There is one word that is the key to quality reloading—*consistency*. Regardless of the load that a shooter selects as his standard, it must be consistent from one loading session to the next. Remember, there's no shotshell load that will shoot around corners or dip in the middle of its flight path when the elusive claybird hits a chuckhole in the air. There will be times when targets will be missed, es-

pecially on windy days, through no fault of the shooter. These things happen to us all. But there is no excuse for missing due to faulty reloads. That is where consistency comes in. The shotshell and its charge or pellets must perform the same way every time, so that shooter knows with certainty exactly where the shot will go when the trigger is pulled.

The most practical and easiest method of producing best-quality reloads is to follow factory recommendations. If a shooter prefers a certain brand—be it Federal, Winchester or Remington—stick with the factory components. If Peters Blue Magics work best, use only factory-manufactured or recommended components. This includes wads, shot and primers. If one leans toward Winchester AA hulls, then he should achieve excellent results using Winchester components.

Reloaders who deviate from factory recommendations are not taking advantage of the factory's expertise and knowledge. Huge ammunition companies hire full-time ballisticians and use test equipment that is not available to the general public to both prove and dis-

196

prove all types of shotshell loadings. Munitions makers have been successfully turning out millions of shotshells for decades with few, if any, problems. Can any reloader equal this record? So, instead of ignoring the advice found in factory instruction sheets and attempting to develop your own "superload," stick to the numbers supplied by the real experts. Does this mean that good reloads can't be made using mixed components and non-standard loading techniques? Of course not. But the amounts of time, money and effort given to working out all the nuances of your own original reloads are likely to be greater than most shooters are willing to expend.

Assume now that we have a batch of choice, clean, empty cases with matching components, all ready to load except for the shot. What size shot should be used? And how much? Some shooters use different loads for 16-yard trap and handicap trap, yet another for doubles. Is this sort of specialization really necessary?

Recently, there's been quite a bit of conversation about 1-oz. trap and Skeet loads for 12-gauge shotguns. Proponents of the 1-oz. load claim many advantages: Reduced recoil, lower cost and better patterns. The first two claims are valid, but the third is suspect. If we are governed by rules and regulations from both the ATA and NSSA which allow 1⅛ oz. of shot, no larger than No. 7½s, why not play the game to the hilt? Why should we purposely handicap ourselves? The game is difficult enough without introducing artificial obstacles. The 1-oz. load may be great for upland game, but for claybirding, load all the shot that you legally can use.

How about shot sizes? Let's borrow a quote from a fabled white hunter who was asked by his client, "Why do you carry a .600 Nitro Express?" The professional replied, "Because they don't make a .700 Nitro Express!" The same holds true for both trap and Skeet shooting—bigger is better in the long run. How many times have we all shot at a target and hit it, and it continued on its merry way leaving a puff of dust in its wake? Most of the time this common occurrence happened because the shooter felt that he had made a mistake and either mispointed his gun or had used the wrong load. Often, the culprit in this scenario is the target. Ten years ago, practically all clay targets were left in their natural black color. Today, most target manufacturers and gun clubs offer colored targets. All of these colored targets are painted in various hues of white, yellow, green, orange or red. A coat of paint on a target makes it harder to break—during manufacture, packaging, transporation and in the air. Today's harder targets have helped gun clubs to reduce their operating costs by lowering the breakage factor, and target manufacturers have eliminated a large portion of their protective packaging requirements. To overcome the target hardness problem, the largest size shot legally allowed (7½) should be used for both trap and Skeet. A single 7½ pellet has 30 percent more energy at 40 yards than a single No. 8 pellet. Believe it! Todays' targets require a good deal of energy to break them.

Long experience has taught the value of using maximum loads for both trap and Skeet: 3 drams equivalent with 1⅛ ozs. of 7½ shot. The same load is equally effective for both trap and Skeet. Using the same load for all events has certain other advantages as well. By using the identical load at all times, you get to know just exactly what to expect from it, with the result that scores should show an uptrend. Loading everything the same way means only having to buy one brand of wads, powder, primers and shot. An added plus is that the reloading equipment never has to be readjusted from one loading session to the next.

Reloading has, if nothing else, a couple of things going for it. First, it offers a psychological edge to some shooters who think that with their better loads they will improve their scores. Secondly, there is a perceived edge of saving money, and therefore having more shells to shoot. There is no doubt that shooters who load a lot will shoot a lot. And that is probably the best reason of all for getting into reloading in the first place. Gobs of ammunition means the shooter will get plenty of practice, and that's the true secret of successful tournament shotgunning.

Once a decision has been made to start reloading, you must select a loading press that will meet your personal needs. A rundown of some of the presses available might be helpful to beginners trying to wade through the maze of equipment that is offered on the market today.

In selecting a shotshell loading press, the reloader

Lee Load-All

Lyman 100 SL

Polar Bear 600

MEC 600 Jr.

MEC Sizemas

may choose a tool that will produce handloads at rates from 10-20 per hour to 500 or more per hour. Prices range from a few dollars to $700 or more. Generally speaking, the more expensive the press, the greater its production rate. The simpler tools are adequate for the occasional shooter who loads shells only now and then, but for trap and Skeet shooters who burn up large volumes of ammo, some type of progressive press is needed that will turn out at least a couple of hundred finished shells an hour. A careful reloader, using a modern progressive reloading tool can produce reloaded shells second to none in quality. Single station presses can turn out good ammo, too, but it takes longer and the operator must be aware of the limitations of such equipment.

By far the simplest press, and one of the least expensive, too, is the Lee Load-All. The Load-All will load plastic or paper shells with 6 or 8 segment crimps. Dies are made of nylon, and shot and powder measures have built-in baffles. Each step of the loading process ends on a positive stop. There are no wad pressure adjustments. The press is supplied with a charge bar and 24 replaceable shot and powder bushings. Complete with load data, the Lee Load-All is made for 12, 16 and 20 gauge.

The Lyman 100SL press is one of the fastest single-station presses. It provides full length resizing of high or low brass without adjustments. A 100-primer reservoir

MEC Grabber

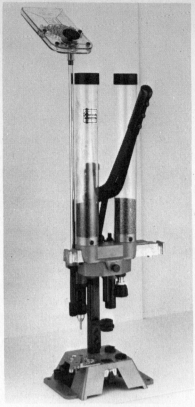

Pacific 155

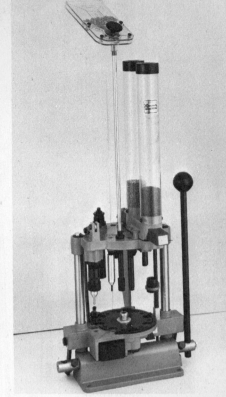

Pacific 336

Ponsness-Warren
Du-O-Matic 375

is optional. It has a floating wad guide, a clear view pressure indicator, and a floating crimp starter. The crimping die applies a uniform crimp to each shell. It's made in 12 and 20 gauge only.

Bear brand loading presses come in several models, from the simple Bear Cat II to the semi-automatic Polar Bear that can produce up to 600 completed shells an hour. It handles both paper and plastic cases, and has fully adjustable wad pressure with an indicator. An automatic primer feeder is included.

MEC offers a single-stage press, the 600 Jr., that can produce 200 to 250 shells an hour. A cam-actuated crimper is a main feature. The Mec Sizemaster handles all types of cases, and is made for all gauges. It has an automatic primer feed and a charge bar window. Crimpers are included for 6 point, 8 point or smooth cone. Mec's Grabber is a six-station progressive press that turns out a finished shell with every pull of the handle. Resizing, primer feed, and charge bar cycling are all automatic. Crimping is cam-actuated for uniformity, and the Spindex Crimper Head changes inserts in seconds. This press is particularly adaptable to loading for trap and Skeet. The Grabber is made in 12 gauge only.

Pacific's Model 155 is a multi-station press that sizes case rims and heads before loading, and the rest of the case after. Capable of loading over 200 shells per hour, it comes with an automatic primer feed as an option. The Pacific Model 336 is a progressive tool that has an

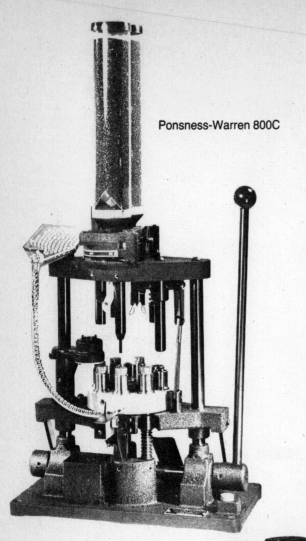

Ponsness-Warren 800C

automatic turntable and swing-out wad guide in addition to many other high-production features. Eight shells move around the turntable, and eight different operations are performed at each stroke of the operating lever. After loading, the finished shell is ejected. All the operator has to do is place an empty hull on the shell plate and insert a wad into the machine. Pulling the handle does the rest. About 500 to 600 shells may be loaded per hour with ease on this press.

The Ponsness-Warren Du-O-Matic is a single stage press that requires only four moves to produce a loaded shell. It is made for 12, 16, 20 and 28 gauges and .410. Ponsness-Warren's Model 800-C Size-O-Matic is a semi-automatic press that handles all cases. Shells remain in one of eight sizing dies that are permanently affixed to the die cylinder that indexes automatically to position the shells for each operation. A carrier receives and positions wads for seating. Wad pressure is adjustable from 10 to 130 lbs. With the aid of a helper to keep components moving, up to 700 rounds per hour are possible. The P-W Mult-O-Matic 600-C is designed especially for trap and Skeet shooters. A single operator can crank out 500 finished shells in an hour with ease. It is available in all gauges, (except 10) with a choice of 6 or 8 point crimp starter.

Redding's Super 32 Shotshell loader is a turret-type press capable of producing 300 shells per hour. All loading operations are done at one station to eliminate shell handling. It has fully adjustable wad pressure, a foolproof charge bar, and a tilting top for easy change of

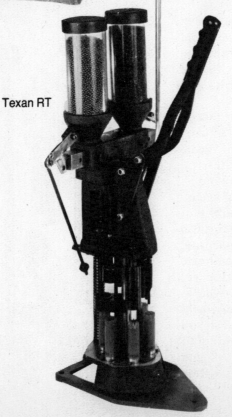

Texan RT

Texan FW

powder and shot. Available in 12, 16, 20 and 28 gauges plus .410 bore.

The Texan Model FW resizes for high or low brass without adjustment. The wad guide automatically lowers and raises for easy and fast insertion of wads. The crimp starter seeks out original folds in the case mouth for perfect crimps. Of the double column design, this press is quite rigid and strong. The Texan Model RT is a six-station progressive press with adjustable wad pressure. The shot drops while pressure is being applied, and the press has a self-aligning crimp starter. It has powerful double-link leverage, and indexing turret and a primer catcher. This one has high speed production capability, and is ideally suited to competition shooters. Available in 12 or 20 gauge.

Specific information concerning loading data should be obtained from publications issued by companies producing components, or from manufacturers of reloading equipment. Instructions included with each press will give a new reloader step-by-step directions that, if followed, will result in a perfectly loaded shotshell. Additionally, *Reloading for Shotgunners,* available from DBI Books, Inc. contains much useful information.

If, after an introduction to the whys and wherefores of reloading and a brief look at some of the equipment available, a shooter has the desire to jump into reloading on his own, we wish him luck and good shooting. A reloader may not save a lot of money, but he'll have a lot of fun and derive a great deal of satisfaction in doing something constructive to help along his hobby.

Redding Super 32

A wealth of valuable reloading information can be found in a number of books, in addition to those loading manuals published by the ammunition and component makers.

There is a wide variety of powders to choose from for shotshell reloading but it pays to stay with manufacturers' data for safety and best performance.

14 Know Your Shotgun Barrel

ONE OF THE MORE critical aspects of trap and Skeet shooting is a three-word phrase, often misunderstood or misinterpreted—namely, *point of impact*. It's well accepted that the shotgun's point of impact is not always in line with the shooter's *point of sight*. So, if a shooter is looking at the target in a certain relationship and the gun throws its shot charge in a different location, the obvious result is a lost target.

All too often, many shooters will go along with this great self-imposed handicap by adjusting their shooting style to conform to the shotgun's point of aim. A few talented shooters can make necessary mental calculations to correct this problem, but the majority of shooters cannot.

You can make book that today's "hot-hammers" in both trap and Skeet shooting have tailored their gun to print a pattern *exactly* where they are looking. Even though we humans are supposed to be smarter and wiser than a piece of machinery, there are those stubborn shooters who can't stand the thought of altering their prized shootin' iron just for the sake of performance. Well, to those unyielding individuals, I can only offer sympathy and thanks. Sympathy for being such good losers and thanks for contributing entrance fees for my winner's share of the purse!

To those shooters who are having a problem breaking all their targets—and how many of you maintain a 100% average—it will behoove you to stop what you're doing and carefully analyze your gun's point of impact.

To ascertain exactly where your shotgun is shooting

(Left) Any newcomer to trap or Skeet should first gain valuable shooting experience before attempting to solve the mysteries surrounding shotgun patterning. After some of the initial exuberance has worn off, it's then time to delve into patterning and point-of-impact determination.

(Right) As simple as it may sound, many shotguns do not place the shot swarm where the shooter is looking. Unfortunately, many shooters will not take the time to determine why. If they did, they would find a remarkable increase in their scores — after corrections were made.

(Left) Today's Skeet guns are regulated by the factory to shoot a tad high. Not too many years ago, this built-in elevation "lead" was thought to be unnecessary, but most of today's better Skeet shooters have found — and proved —that a 6 o'clock hold enables them to view the target at all times.

There're a number of ways to build a pattern board. This simplistic approach is fine if the wind isn't blowing too strongly, but a better method is to tape the pattern paper onto a nonflexible backing which will hold up in the wind. Solid steel pattern boards are worthless for accurate testing as counting pellet hits is virtually impossible. (Courtesy Shotgun Sports)

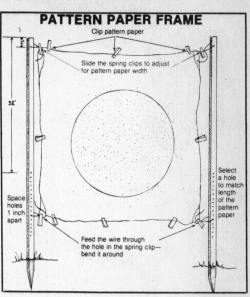

PATTERN PAPER FRAME

Clip pattern paper

Slide the spring clips to adjust for pattern paper width

32"

Select a hole to match length of the pattern paper

Space holes 1 inch apart

Feed the wire through the hole in the spring clip— bend it around

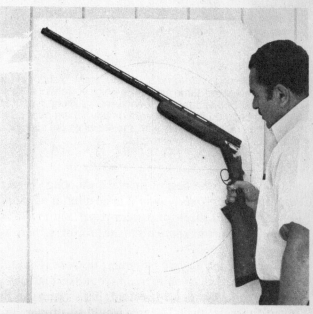

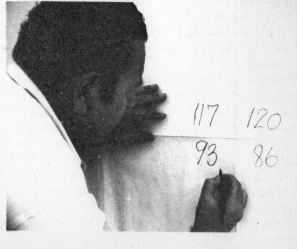

117   120

93   86

Folding a pattern test sheet in quarters (above and above right) will enable the shooter/tester to quickly determine the point of impact of a shotgun. Counting every pellet hole in each quadrant (right) will numerically determine how and where a shotgun shoots in relationship to the shooter's line of sight. For optimum results, the line of sight and the gun's point of impact *must* be in direct relationship to each other — otherwise the results will be a bushel basket full of "lost" targets.

While conducting pattern tests, it's important to shoot at the paper targets in the same manner in which you shoot at flying clay targets. Don't attempt to "bench-rest" a shotgun or draw too fine a bead on the center spot on the pattern paper. Assume a natural shooting position and fire when the shotgun's front sight touches the aiming spot.

they use in tournament use. This is a mistake. Only shoot the same brand, dram equivalent and shot size as what you'd use in a registered event. If you use reloads for 16-yard shooting, go ahead and use them for these point of impact tests. But, if you only use factory shells for handicap events, then you'll have to use duplicate ammo for conclusive results. Shotguns are somewhat like rifles and handguns as they will perform differently with various brands, types and loads.

Another test requisite is that you assume a shooting stance exactly like you do during a competitive event. You should not shoot from a sitting or braced position, but rather from one which closely duplicates your natural stance. "Bench-resting" a shotgun doesn't duplicate your usual shooting position, so stand up on your "back legs" as you'd normally shoot.

If you're a two-eyed shooter, then make certain that you aim at the center spot with both eyes open. Many shooters/testers make the mistake of closing the "off" eye to draw a finer "bead" on the aiming spot. Wrong! Try to fire the test shots as similarly as you would on a flying clay for accurate test results.

If possible, have a helper change the paper for you and *don't look at the targets until you're finished.* Human nature, being what it is, if you sneak-preview your first one or two shots, you'll have a tendency to try and correct or compensate for any of the gun's point of impact failings. Don't fall into this trap. *This important test is not to determine your ability to correct where the shotgun is shooting, but to find out where your shotgun's point of impact is in relationship to your line of sight!*

will require a great deal of time and shooting. To perform this task properly, you'll need a lot of ammunition, at least 20 sheets of pattern paper and much patience. There are no shortcuts to the process, so here we go.

The regulation 40-yard patterning distance is not relevant for this test. If you're testing your Skeet gun, then a distance of 25 yards is to be used. If it's a trap gun for 16-yard targets, then 32 yards would be proper. For handicap shooting, add 16 yards to your assigned yardage, i.e., 38 yards for a 22-yard shooter, 40 yards for a 24-yard shooter, etc., and you'll have your optimum test yardage.

Pattern paper should be large enough to contain the entire shot swarm, a sheet about 40-inches square will work satisfactorily. A sighting dot, at least 4 inches in diameter, must be placed dead-center in the pattern sheet as this will be the spot where you'll point the gun's front sight. After the pattern paper has been tacked to a backing board or pattern board, step back to the measured yardage and fire at least 10 separate patterns.

There will probably be a tendency for shooters who perform this test to use ammunition different from what

If the shotgun doesn't throw its shot charge in exactly the location the shooter thinks it will, then nothing else matters. Memorizing and visualizing where the shot charge will print at a given range is critical to breaking consistently good scores.

Don't scoff at shooting a shotgun with a scope. There are a number advantages to using an optical sighting device over traditional methods. Comb height never needs to be altered — you simply dial in correction on the elevation screw. Cast-off a problem? Not with a scope-equipped shotgun; just make an adjustment with the windage turret. Scopes do take some getting used to, but for shooters with serious problems, they could be the solution.

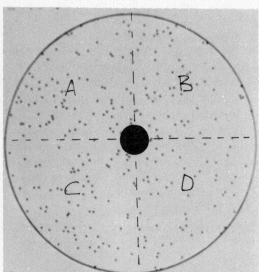

(Left and right) By shooting at a pre-set aiming dot about 4-inches in diameter, the shooter/tester can easily determine where the gun shoots in relationship to his line of sight. This determines the shotgun's point of impact. Dividing the pattern paper into four equal quadrants — after the test shot is fired — will facilitate pellet counting and determining the shotgun's vertical and horizontal ratio from dead center. Top to bottom, 60/40 vertical, 55/45 horizontal (left to right).

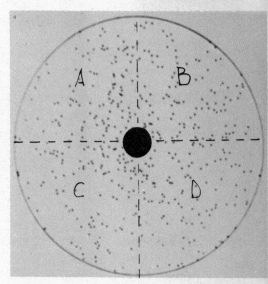

Also, if you have the benefit of a helper, ask him to "call" your shot for you. After mounting your shotgun in your natural stance, let him holler "Pull, Shoot" or any other command. Place the gun's front sight on the target and pull the trigger. If you feel that you've "pulled the shot" in one direction or another, ask your helper to mark your predictions on the test pattern. If, on the other hand, you believe that your sight picture was correct, then don't say anything and assume that the shot was "zeroed."

As stated earlier, you should fire a minimum of 10 shots on 10 separate clean sheets of paper which will average out for any sighting errors. If you only shoot at two or three targets and you inadvertently pull off the target spot, you'll have the tendency to initially and incorrectly blame the gun when in reality you were at fault for a poorly aimed shot. With this 10-shot rule, both good and bad sightings will even out and a true picture can be analyzed from the results.

Now, let's assume that you've fired your 10 pattern sheets and it's now time to make that most eagerly-sought discovery. The most important determination is whether your shotgun shoots left or right of dead center. Simply eyeballing the pattern sheet is not good enough. For proper evaluation, fold the pattern sheet in quarters from the center spot, then count the pellet hits in each square. If the upper left square has more pellet holes than the upper right square, this indicates that your gun places it's main shot charge left of center. Optimally, all four squares would have an equal pellet count, but realistically this is a near impossibility as a shotgun will never produce identical patterns from shot to shot regardless of the type of ammunition. The ultimate method to determine the gun's point of impact is to count each square for all 10 pattern sheets, calculate the average and then go back and look at the results on each sheet. For example, let's assume that the total pellet count for the upper left square on the 10 test targets was 1500 hits. Therefore, if this figure is divided by 10, each target would average 150 hits in this square. Going back and reviewing each target, it is easily determined whether or not that particular pattern sheet falls within this calculated standard.

Dividing the target paper into four separate sections will allow the tester to determine both "windage" and "elevation" results of his test gun. A similar structured evaluation can be made to determine how high—or low—the shotgun's point of impact is. If more than half of the shot swarm is above the center line, then the shotgun shoots high. If more than half of the pellets are printed on the lower half of the target paper, then, obviously, the shotgun can be classified as shooting low.

In recent years, there have been quite a few references by gun scribes as to how a shotgun prints its patterns. Terms 50/50, 65/35, etc. have been bandied about and with few exceptions, there have been very few explanations of what these numbers mean. Simply, these formulas relate to the amount of shot hitting the paper above and below a predetermined sighting point. A 12-gauge shotshell loaded with 1⅛ ozs. of 7½ size shot contains approximately 393 pellets. If, for example 235 of the pellets were found to be above the center line and 158 below it, then simple arithmetic (235 divided by 393) would calculate to a pattern of 60/40. See the accompanying chart for approximate pellet count for a given charge.

Remember, determining the exact point of impact

therefore, we'll concentrate on elevation.

Only in the last decade or so have trap and Skeet guns been designed by the factory to shoot high. Many old-time scatterguns produced 50/50 or 40/60 patterns. Shooting at fast-rising trap targets requires a "higher" shooting gun. A like analogy holds true for Skeet shooters, as most of today's "hot-shots" advocate a 6 o'clock hold enabling the shooter to keep the target in view at all times. Although most trap and Skeet shooters rarely admit it, the majority of "lost" targets are the result of shooting *under* them. Yes, even missed low-house Skeet targets fall to this shooting hazard. To measure or calculate a shotgun's barrel (percentage-wise) can also be accomplished with actual pellet count, as previously mentioned, or by carefully measuring where the exact center of the pattern impacts on the pattern sheet. The accompanying chart will help you "classify" your shotgun barrel's performance.

Now that we've determined a proper method to evaluate and accurately judge the shotgun's point of impact, let's assume that there is a windage problem to solve. Again, we must use a hypothetical case. After performing the 10-target shooting test, the 10 different pattern sheets were viewed and calculated, and it was obvious that the shotgun produced a pattern that strongly leaned to the left of the aiming point. The horizontal ratio was calculated to be 60/40. (So not to confuse this issue, we'll leave out the vertical ratio at this

Approximate Number of Pellets in a Given Charge

Shot Size	½ oz.	¾ oz.	⅞ oz.	1 oz.	1⅛ oz.
#7½	175	262	306	350	393
#8	205	308	359	410	462
#9	292	439	512	585	658

Note: Only the above loads and shot sizes conform to both ATA and NSSA rules.

Point of Impact Relationship at Known Yardages

30″ Pattern Test at 42 Yards		30″ Pattern Test at 32 Yards		30″ Pattern Test at 22 Yards	
Pattern	Distance	Pattern	Distance	Pattern	Distance
0/100	15″ Low	0/100	14″ Low	0/100	13″ Low
10/90	12″ Low	10/90	11″ Low	10/90	10″ Low
20/80	9″ Low	20/80	8″ Low	20/80	7″ Low
30/70	6″ Low	30/70	5″ Low	30/70	4″ Low
40/60	3″ Low	40/60	2″ Low	40/60	1″ Low
50/50	Center	50/50	Center	50/50	Center
60/40	3″ High	60/40	2 ″High	60/40	1″ High
70/30	6″ High	70/30	5″ High	70/30	4″ High
80/20	9″ High	80/20	8″ High	80/20	7″ High
90/10	12″ High	90/10	11″ High	90/10	10″ High
100/0	15″ High	100/0	14″ High	100/0	13″ High

from these results is not a science, but rather a calculated estimate. Unlike rifle shooting, where there is a single projectile for simpler evaluation and measurement, the shot charge has hundreds of projectiles and each are subjected to deformation which alters flight characteristics. The problem is further compounded as each pellet is not *exactly* the same as its brethren.

After scrutinizing the results of your tests, let's assume that windage is right on (if it's not, we'll tell you a little later in this chapter how to make corrections), and

time.) There are three methods to re-zero the shot swarm and put it in dead-center to the line of sight. First, the front sight could be moved slightly to the left. This would be a task for a gunsmith as the old screw hole must be filled and the front sight remounted within a new hole that has been drilled and tapped. This is not an impractical job for a shotgun equipped with a ventilated rib on top of the barrel, as most trap and Skeet guns today are so equipped. The second method is to alter the cast on the buttstock, and there are a couple of

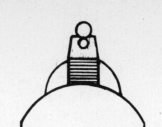

Sighting flat down rib gives true P.O.I. of the barrel.

Figure 8 is preferred by most shooters.

Sight picture seen after bending barrel or raising comb.

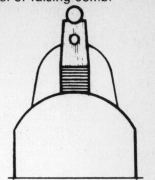

Unquestionably, the most important test for shooter and shotgun is to determine the shotgun's point of impact. Without knowing exactly where the shot swarm will strike downrange, shooting is being done by luck and guesswork — neither of which is conducive to breaking many targets. (Courtesy Shotgun Sports)

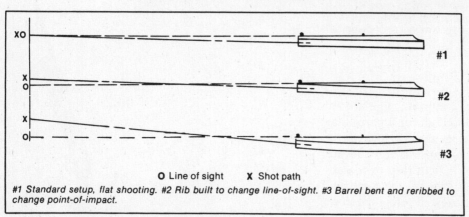

O Line of sight   **X** Shot path

#1 Standard setup, flat shooting. #2 Rib built to change line-of-sight. #3 Barrel bent and reribbed to change point-of-impact.

The ventilated rib on the shotgun controls the shooter's eye enroute to the target. It is advisable to alter the stock dimensions rather than bending the barrel or rib because after a few hundred shots, the barrel will revert back to its original position — slowly, but surely.

Shotguns may be mechanically corrected to change the line of sight to correspond to the point of impact by altering the position of the rib, but the author does not agree with the "barrel-bending" theory. (Courtesy Shotgun Sports)

ways to do this. If the amount of cast-off (for a right hand shooter) has to be reduced, which means to reduce the angle of the buttstock in relationship to the line of the barrel, a commercially made lace-on or slip-on pad can be used to increase the width of the comb. When the shooter then lays his cheek against the buttstock, the cast-off has been artificially reduced. The other method is to have the stock "bent." This is a delicate job that can only be undertaken by a skilled stockmaker. The best at performing this precarious process is Pachmayr Gun Works. The buttstock is immersed in hot oil—near boiling temperature—for a predetermined time (only known to the "immerser") until the wood is pliable enough to accept a bend at the wrist. Sometimes a stock will break, and the customer is informed ahead of time that there is this possibility. In that event, the customer loses a stock and Pachmayr loses a job. If the operation goes as planned, after slowly cooling down, the stock will retain a "set" and the cast alteration has been made. This same technique can also be used to raise or lower the stock.

And, finally, the last preferred method is to employ a stockmaker to slice off part of the comb, shim and reglue it, or replace it with another piece of wood which closely duplicates the existing stock's grain structure.

By now, some of you may be wondering why we haven't offered the "barrel-bending" method to adjust and change an incorrect point of impact to line of sight. Here, I'll take a firm stand and oppose this method for a brace of reasons. First, any time metal is bent "cold" it places stress and fatigue at the location where the bend is made. Second, "cold bending," is not permanent and after an unknown number of shots, the barrel will revert to its original position due to the memory of the steel. While this reversal process is taking place, the barrel's point of impact is gradually returning to where it originally was and the shooter will be slowly "bleeding to death" by missing targets and not realizing the cause.

Also, anytime a ventialted rib barrel is bent it will create a sharp line of near-breakage on the top of the rib. This will weaken the rib at worst and create a distorted sight picture at best.

Should a shooter determine that he needs a replacement stock for his pet scattergun, some of the larger shoots are visited by gun dealers who usually have a large inventory of extra stocks and aftermarket accessories. The ability to install a new gunstock and then go out and shoot with it is the best way to determine if the new stock properly fits the shooter. If it doesn't, then go back and try another!

Patterning is a lengthly, drawn-out exercise and requires nearly a full day's effort to thoroughly test and properly evaluate performance. No less than 10 separate pattern test sheets must be shot to accurately determine results. Less than 10 will not do for a complete picture as sighting errors will not be averaged out and will incorrectly reflect shot dispersal and aiming points.

Altering the vertical point of impact is a relatively easy task. If the pattern is too high for a particular shooter's style, then the top of the comb is lowered by physically removing a small dimension of wood, no more than $\frac{1}{16}$-inch at a time. A light rasp or coarse-grade sandpaper can be used to "lower" the comb and test shots should be fired and evaluated before the stock is completely refinished.

If the pattern prints too low for a particular shooter, then a reverse process must be applied and the comb must be raised—again, only in increments of $\frac{1}{16}$-inch at a time. There are also various types of artificial combs on the market. One of the more popular ones is from Meadow Industries, Dept. 50S, Forest, VA 24551. Dubbed "Convert-A-Stock," this kit has interchangeable spacers and is held securely in place by Velcro fasteners. Six to 11 different comb heights are available that can raise the height of the comb from $\frac{1}{16}$-inch to $\frac{5}{8}$-inch.

For the thrifty "do-it-yourselfer," simple moleskin, the type that is used for foot protection, can be laid on the top of the comb until the desired height is obtained. Ultimately though, most shooters will only use these methods to act as a measuring system and then either have a new stock made or alter the existing chunk of wood for a permanent fix.

Another method to raise the comb height is to locate a competent stockmaker and have him reshape the inletting at the junction of the stock to the back of the receiver. Some "smittys" do an excellent job on this intricate task and some don't. If this seemingly easy, yet difficult to properly perform task is not done with precise mating of the entire inletted surface to the receiver,

then the stock will undoubtedly crack or even shatter due to recoil after a few shots are fired. Take heed if you opt for this frangible process.

As you can see, the importance of proper stock fit cannot be underestimated. And, unfortunately, the greater majority of trap and Skeet shooters are using shotguns that do not fit them. There are all kinds of rationales—"What's the big deal, I'm only shooting for fun!" But, wouldn't you have more fun if you broke more targets? Or, "I can't afford to have that done!" If you blew out a tire on your automobile, you'd buy a new tire, wouldn't you? Or would you drive around on three wheels?

There are certain "costs" that are mandatory to becoming a top-flight trap and Skeet shooter. The first and most important is stock fit. And, besides, your first "big win" will probably give you a giant dollar or equally valuable intrinsic return on your stock-altering investment.

Long yardage handicap trap shooters are generally shooting their targets between 43 and 50 yards. This is "stretching" the barrel, especially while restricted to light target loads. Therefore, shooting at these extended ranges requires that the shooter be right on. Prior knowledge learned by a few sessions on the pattern board will impress on the shooter's mind the size and dimension of his gun's pattern.

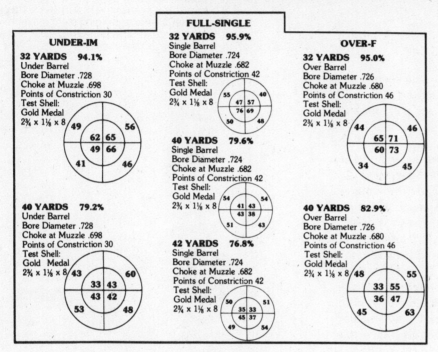

FULL-SINGLE

UNDER-IM

32 YARDS   94.1%
Under Barrel
Bore Diameter .728
Choke at Muzzle .698
Points of Constriction 30
Test Shell:
Gold Medal
2¾ x 1⅛ x 8
49 | 56
62 | 65
49 | 66
41 | 46

32 YARDS   95.9%
Single Barrel
Bore Diameter .724
Choke at Muzzle .682
Points of Constriction 42
Test Shell:
Gold Medal
2¾ x 1⅛ x 8
55 | 47 | 57 | 40
76 | 69
50 | 48

OVER-F

32 YARDS   95.0%
Over Barrel
Bore Diameter .726
Choke at Muzzle .680
Points of Constriction 46
Test Shell:
Gold Medal
2¾ x 1⅛ x 8
44 | 46
65 | 71
60 | 73
34 | 45

40 YARDS   79.2%
Under Barrel
Bore Diameter .728
Choke at Muzzle .698
Points of Constriction 30
Test Shell:
Gold Medal
2¾ x 1⅛ x 8
43 | 60
33 | 43
43 | 42
53 | 48

40 YARDS   79.6%
Single Barrel
Bore Diameter .724
Choke at Muzzle .682
Points of Constriction 42
Test Shell:
Gold Medal
2¾ x 1⅛ x 8
54 | 54
41 | 43
43 | 38
51 | 43

40 YARDS   82.9%
Over Barrel
Bore Diameter .726
Choke at Muzzle .680
Points of Constriction 46
Test Shell:
Gold Medal
2¾ x 1⅛ x 8
48 | 55
33 | 55
36 | 47
45 | 63

42 YARDS   76.8%
Single Barrel
Bore Diameter .724
Choke at Muzzle .682
Points of Constriction 42
Test Shell:
Gold Medal
2¾ x 1⅛ x 8
50 | 51
35 | 33
45 | 37
49 | 54

These series of shotgun patterning tests are more valid and informative than using the 40-yard standard which, over the years, has proven to be more pertinent for hunting and field shotguns. (Courtesy Shotgun Sports)

Patterning

Why should trap and Skeet shooters pattern their shotguns? I've known countless numbers of shooters who absolutely refuse to shoot a pattern in fear of finding out that their gun produces a poor pattern on paper, yet they do reasonably well with it on the score sheet.

There are numerous stories—and probably all true—regarding competitive shooters who read some interesting article in a gun magazine describing how and why they should pattern their shotgun. The typical reader would suddenly become enthusiastic about this testing procedure and go through the mechanics of locating a place to conduct these semi-exhaustive tests, scrounge pattern paper, etc. Unfortunately, the majority of the time these tests were based on the "40 yard" standard. Shotgun makers and ammunition manufacturers closely adhere to the standards set down by the Society of Ammunition and Arms Makers Institute. For many years,

SAAMI has set the shotgun patterning range at 40 yards as their "standard." For hunting or field guns, that is fine, but, unfortunately, trap and Skeet shooters rarely fire at a target that is always 40 yards downrange. Therefore, trap and Skeet gun pattern evaluation distances must use a different "standard" to determine optimum results.

In the case of Skeet guns, the standard is no more than 25 yards. Most of the time, Skeeters are firing at targets closer than 25 yards and many shots are taken at 10 to 15 yards, especially second shots on doubles and those on Station Eight. Some Skeet shooters prefer to set "their" standard at 21 yards, which is exactly halfway between the high and low house. A fast Skeet gunner genrally shoots at his targets at ranges under 20 yards, therefore his standard should be reduced to mimic his shooting style. The advantages of "standards" is that there are so many of them, if you get the point. If not, we'll explain a bit further.

(Left) For handicap trap shooting, the shooter's standard is based on his assigned yardage plus 16 additional yards, which is about average for most shooters. Thus, if a shooter assigned 23 yards shoots at a pattern board 39 yards away, the results on the pattern sheet will closely duplicate the effects when shooting at the clay target.

(Below) Because Skeet is a close-shooting game, with many shots being taken as close as 7 to 10 yards, a standard somewhat less than the typical 21-yard patterning point must be used to determine pattern density and point-of-aim references.

Just because you read an article or hear someone explain how he patterns his shotgun doesn't necessarily mean that this "standard" is correct for everyone—not by a long shot. (Pardon the pun!) Every shooter, trap or Skeet, employs different timing and therefore, should pattern his shotgun at the range he normally shoots at a target. Novices, or newcomers to the Skeet field, as a rule are considered "slow shooters" and fire at outgoing targets well past the center stake. Remember, the center stake is located mid-point between the two houses at an equal distance of 21 yards. So, if a newcomer is shooting at a target 5 to 6 yards beyond the stake, then he should set his standard for 26 to 27 yards for outgoing targets. Conversely, the same shooter will probably be shooting at incoming targets a bit too late and at ranges 7 to 10 yards out from the muzzle. Now we have a Catch 22 situation. Does the tyro set his standard for 26 yards to predict results on outgoing targets or 10 yards for incoming targets at 10 yards? Neither. I don't recommend newcomers to Skeet to fret about patterns until he or she is accustomed to this unique shooting game and develops a serious attitude and more importantly, establishes a predictable style and timing.

Remember, Skeet shooting is a fun game. Becoming too involved, technically, can quickly dilute the new shooter's enjoyment of this sport. Shoot it for a few months without worrying about the subtle idiosyncrasies. Then, and only then, if you wish to pursue it further, learn all about its finer points. But until that time comes—just enjoy!

After establishing your own personal "standard," it's time to do some serious pattern work. Earlier in this chapter, we discussed the point of impact, and how to test and evaluate its results. The Skeet shooter could also use the POI test to determine pattern percentages and scan the pattern sheet for "holes." These are areas illustrated on the pattern sheet which are presumably large enough for a target to slip through unscathed.

Even though there may appear to be many of these voids, in the real shooting world it is such a remote possibility of this happening, it's not worthy of consideration. One of the major drawbacks to "reading" a pattern sheet is that the flat piece of paper does not relate to length of shot string. As we stated earlier, shotgun patterning is still an unsolved mystery due to its many, many variables. All we can do, at this point, is to ascertain with the evidence we have at hand and attempt to make an accurate judgment. And, at best, this is merely a logical assumption, but it is a guide and reference point.

So, therefore, even if a pattern sheet graphically indicates these "black holes" of infinity, don't become unduly worried or alarmed—especially if you and your

To determine a standard for 16-yard (singles) shooting, the proper distance is 32 yards. If the shooter's timing is average, he'll break targets about 15 to 17 yards from the traphouse.

Every shotgun is marked in some manner and in varying locations as to the type and amount of choke in the barrel. This Browning BT-99 shows a single asterisk (*), meaning Full choke. Some makers roll-mark the top of the barrel with their identifying marks; others "hide" it inside the action.

shotgun are consistently breaking targets. The crux of these pattern tests is to imbed in your mind the actual size of the diameter of your shotgun's pattern at a given distance along with the percentage of shot contained within a 30-inch diameter circle. If you can visualize what your shotgun pattern looks like at 21 yards, it will help you immensely in your quest to break 100 straights with regularity.

Learning and memorizing what a shotgun pattern looks like can often become a two-edged sword. Some shooters, after finding out that their gun produces a nicely rounded pattern of nearly 30-inches in diameter become sloppy in their pointing technique, rationalizing, and thinking all they have to do is be "close-enough" to break any target. Wrong! Pretend, instead that the pattern is only the size of a pie plate. This way should the shooter misjudge the lead of the target, the ring of shot outside this imaginary 10-inch circle will become the insurance policy and hopefully "chip" the bird to record a "dead" target on the score sheet.

Another problem many Skeet shooters develop is to aim instead of point the shotgun. They want to become too fine and careful in their shooting style. Shotguns, as we said earlier are always pointed, never aimed. Aiming the shotgun is the surest way I know to stop the learned swing and acquired mandatory methods to hit a flying object, especially one so small as a clay target. Often, you'll hear shooters complaining to one another that they are starting to aim at targets and suddenly their scores plummet to new depths. The aiming syndrome often arises when a Skeeter is mired deep in a shooting slump. Good things happen one at a time—problems crop up in bunches!

Another reason for patterning a Skeet or trap gun is to verify that it is choked as marked on the barrel, or in the case of over-unders, barrels. Some manufacturers use ambiguous marking methods, some use abbreviations and letters, while other makers clearly mark the barrel Full, Improved Modified, Modified, Improved Cylinder, Skeet, or Cylinder. The tables listed will help decipher the manner in which some of the shotgun makers mark their barrels pertaining to choke.

Identification of Ambiguous Choke Marking Terms

Maker: Browning

Marking Symbol	Choke	Percentage
*	Full	65-75%
*_	Improved Modified	55-65%
**	Modifed	45-55%
**_	Improved Cylinder	35-45%
**S	Skeet	30-35%
***	Cylinder	25-35%

The use of inside calipers will measure the shotgun's bore and choke area accurately. Constriction is calculated by subtracting the measurement at the choke from the inside dimension of the shotgun barrel.

To properly determine the results of pattern tests, it's important to shoot the same ammunition as one would use in an event. If reloads are used for competitive shooting, fine, use them. But, don't use reloads for testing and factory-fodder for competitive events. Like apples and oranges, the two cannot be favorably compared.

Maker: Beretta
On the upper barrel of most over-unders, the choke markings are usually marked "F/M" for "Full and Modified" with the upper letter indicating the top barrel and the lower letter for the bottom barrel. Thus, S/S equals "Skeet and Skeet," "IC/M" equals "Improved Cylinder and Modified," etc.

Maker: Perazzi
This company marks their shotguns in two manners for the European and American markets. U.S. barrels are clearly marked "Full," "Modified," etc. For guns used in Europe, Perazzi uses a series of "zeros" to indicate chokes as follows:

00	= Full
000	= Improved Modified
0000	= Modified
00000	= Improved Cylinder

Maker: Winchester
Many Model 101s are double marked with both a series of asterisks and abbreviations as follows:

*(Full)	= Full
**(Imp. Mod.)	= Improved Modified
***(Mod.)	= Modified
****(Imp.Cyl.)	= Improved Cylinder

Although shotgun manufacturers do have good intentions, occasionally a barrel won't produce the pattern as marked. For these rare occurrences, we must, therefore, prove the barrel's performance and to determine, if in fact, it will throw a pattern close to what the barrel

is marked. Choke markings should not be taken for granted. Assuming that a barrel marked "**S" or "Skt" will *always* produce Skeet patterns is a pitfall that shooters can prevent from happening by actually testing and evaluating the results from a session on the pattern board.

This same important confirmation test should also be done with trap guns. These are more difficult to pattern and regulate than Skeet guns because of the varying distances to the target. If all the targets were shot at a precise and consistent distance, then trap shooters could "tailor" a shotgun's barrel to produce a "perfect" (if there is such an entity) pattern for a known range. But, alas, target distances vary from shot-to-shot and again a compromising "standard" must be established.

For a trap shooter to properly evaluate the patterning performance of his shotgun, he too, like the Skeet shooter, must disregard the SAAMI 40-yard patterning standard. For singles or 16-yard shooting, the average trap shooter will break targets approximately 15 to 17 yards out of the trap house. By adding the distance the shooter stands from the traphouse (16 yards) to the "breaking site" of the target which adds up to 32 yards, then the trap shooter should fire on a string of 10 pattern targets from 32 yards to evaluate his gun's performance.

For the handicap (not handicap*ed*) trap shooter, adding 16 yards to his yardage, i.e., 22 + 16 = 38 yards, 26 + 16 = 42 yards, etc. should determine the proper patterning "standard." Again, like any pattern testing, at least 10 shots should be fired on clean pattern paper for accurate determination and evaluation of the results.

Some shooters go one step farther and place their trust in bore "constriction." Constriction is merely the result of actually measuring the shotgun bore in two locations and subtracting the smaller number from the

Shotgun patterning is still a bit of a mystery to many shooters regardless of the many books and articles written on this vexing subject. No two shotguns will pattern alike, nor will a single gun produce consistent patterns from shot-to-shot due to the many variables in ammunition.

larger, which is then defined "constriction." For example, if—and most are—a 12 gauge shotgun's bore measures .729-inch at its widest point inside the barrel (not including the chamber area), and the measurement at its narrowest point (at the end of the choke area) is found to be .689-inch, then subtracting the latter from the former set of measurements will determine the amount of constriction, and, in this case .040-inch.

These calculations can only be accomplished with an accurate set of inside calipers or by using a bore gauge. These measurements are an excellent guide to determine whether or not a barrel has been altered, but again, not an "absolute" as to the type of pattern it will produce. See the accompanying table for more detailed information on shotgun bore constrictions.

Calculated Constriction For Various Gauges*

Designation	12 ga.	20 ga.	28 ga.	.410** bore
Full	.040	.034	.030	.020
Imp. Mod.	.030	.025	.023	.018
Modified	.020	.017	.015	.010
Skeet	.015	.012	.011	.006
Imp. Cyl.	.010	.008	.008	.002

* These numbers are intended to be used only as a guide as virtually every shotgun manufacturer will develop a constriction factor which works best in their own particular product.

**In reality, there have been instances where certain .410 shotguns have produced near-Full choke patterns even when the barrel was clearly marked "Skeet."

In closing this chapter, there is one more criterion that we haven't talked about which can—and will—influence pattern performance, namely the size and hardness of the shot pellet. There are three rules that seemingly prove themselves every time a shotgun is

patterned: Hard shot, that which contains at least 5 percent antimony, will produce a tighter pattern than Soft shot, which contains a lower percentage of antimony. The reason for higher percentages with harder shot is that the pellets are not as badly disfigured and distorted after leaving the barrel. Therefore, a round(er) pellet travels on a straighter plane than one which is flattened on one side or badly misshaped, which will cause it to fly in an irregular direction. The other rule is that velocity of the shot swarm leaving the barrel will have a calculable effect on the pattern. As a given rule, higher velocities tend to open up a pattern more than lower velocities. A 12-gauge shotshell that is loaded to a 3-dram equivalent and contains 1⅛ ozs. of #8 shot will produce a more open or larger pattern than its counterpart loaded to a 2¾-dram equivalent. And finally, larger size shot will tend to produce tighter patterns than smaller sizes. A gun shooting #7½s will produce slightly smaller (tighter) patterns than #8 shot. The disparity is negligible because the difference in shot diameters is rather miniscule as indicated by the chart below:

#7½ shot = .095-inch in diameter
#8 shot = .090-inch in diameter
#9 shot = .080-inch in diameter

By now, you must be wondering if patterning a shotgun is very important. Yes, it really is, but there are few absolute conclusions which can be drawn from these lengthy tests. Over the years of testing and evaluating shotgun patterns, combined with reading and studying other tomes written on this controversial subject, I can conclude this chapter by making one positive statement—patterning is not the perfect evaluation of a gun's presentation of pellets to the target, but at this time, it is still the best method which we have to offer.

15 Accessories for Guns and Gunners

THERE ARE ONLY two things a shotgunner absolutely needs for participation in trap or Skeet competition — a shotgun and a good supply of shells. (Plus a fair amount of money to pay for other expenses, of course.) Unquestionably, this is a true statement, as far as it goes. However, an aspiring scattergun champion will soon find that there are several other items of equipment that he will either need or want, in addition to the basic necessities.

By carefully observing veteran clay-bird shooters in action, and by talking to them after the day's shooting is over, a newcomer to the sport may quickly learn what extra gear is considered essential. Not everyone will agree when it comes to choosing accessories, of course. Personal opinions and experiences influence the selection of auxiliary equipment. Experience has shown, however, that certain items not only help in improving scores, but make life on clay-pigeon fields safer and more convenient.

Personal safety should be a shooter's prime concern. Not gun-handling safety — that's another subject — but protection of sight and hearing. Shooting glasses are necessity number one. The possibility of being struck in the eye by a flying particle is a very real hazard when operating any firearm, but a shotgun is perhaps potentially the most dangerous of all. Stray bits of unburned powder, ricocheting shot, fragments of broken targets — all these and more could cause a serious eye injury. Accidents of this sort don't happen often, but a little forethought will prevent a lot of misery if an unexpected mishap should occur.

Shooting glasses should be large enough to cover the entire eye area, so that there is ample protection above, below, and to each side of the eye. It is particularly important that lenses extend above the eyebrow, since proper shooting stance forces you to look well above the normal line of sight through the glasses. Glass lenses should be chemically hardened or heat-treated to resist breakage. Plastic lenses are highly impervious to breakage without further treatment. There is no such thing as a completely unbreakable lens. All lenses can be broken if they are hit hard enough, but a blow of such intensity would not be stopped by glasses alone anyway. If a corrective lens is needed to ameliorate a visual problem, shooting glasses may be ground to individual prescription.

Hy-Wyd glasses by Decot (P.O. Box 10355, Phoenix, AZ 85064) have long been a favorite of shotgunners all over the world. Hy-Wyd lenses are made of scratch-resistant CR-39 plastic, and may be had in any of the following colors: orange, purple, bronze, vermilion, gold, fleshtone, green, brown, yellow, gray, and photo-gray (glass only.) Available in three sizes, Hy-Wyds will fit almost any face. Decot Hy-Wyds can be furnished in either single vision or bifocal prescription form, as well as regular plano (no power.)

Jim Sheffield of Oak Lawn Optical (100-C One Turtle Creek Village, Dallas, TX 75219) makes **High-Shooter** glasses that are similar in appearance to Decot Hy-Wyds. Making use of Armorlite plastic lenses, High-Shooters come in all popular colors, in both plano and prescription. A case is included, and there is a warranty on both frame and lenses.

Doctor Yochem Shooting Glasses (334 N. Azusa Ave., West Covina, CA 91791) are of a slightly different shape from the majority of shooter's spectacles. They give ample coverage, with adequate ventilation to prevent fogging. Don Yochem will send a brochure describing these lightweight glasses to any one requesting it from the above address.

Another shooting glass that has maintained its popularity over the years is made by **Bausch and Lomb**. B&L shooting glasses are available in most good gun shops and sporting goods stores in non-prescription form. Any optometrist should be able to provide them with prescription lenses if a visual correction is necessary. Standard lens colors are gray, brown, yellow (kalichrome,) photogray and photobrown.

Tasco makes a very nice non-prescription shooting glass, available in a variety of tints including a polarized lens that does much to eliminate bright spot glare. **Zeiss** also produces high quality shooting glasses, but not in prescription. Zeiss colors are yellow, grey, green and vermilion. Both Zeiss and Tasco glasses should be available through gun shops and sporting goods stores.

Good shooting glasses may be obtained from other sources, as well, but care should be taken that lenses are of first quality, and that the frames are sturdy enough to withstand the rigors of active use. There is nothing so annoyingly uncomfortable as a spectacle frame that will not stay in adjustment.

Some shooters are bothered by distractions seen in the peripheral visual field. Blinders attached to temple pieces of shooting glasses block vision to the side, and may be helpful in such cases. **Derek Partridge** now markets leather blinders with integral clips that serve the purpose quite well. Homemade cardboard blinders work, too, but Partridge's products have a certain touch of class that is lacking in do-it-yourself devices.

All shooters should wear some form of hearing protector. Shotguns don't have quite as loud a muzzle blast as big-bore pistols or high-powered rifles, but constant exposure to shotgun discharges will inevitably cause some degree of hearing loss. Only a fool will play the "tough guy" who feels that hearing protectors are for sissies. Ask any old timer in the shooting game (in a loud voice, of course) what he thinks about the subject, and he will, without doubt, most firmly say that he who does not use a noise reducing device while shooting is an idiot.

Ear muffs, of the type produced by Safety Direct Inc., (23 Snider Way, Sparks, NE 89431) are one of the most effective means of attenuating harmful noises. Muffs from Safety Direct bear the **Silencio** label, and are made in two models. One version has plain vinyl cushions and a head band that may be worn behind the head, over the head, or under the chin. Another model, similar in appearance, has ear cushions filled with liquid to afford maximum protection with a minimum of discomfort.

Shooting glasses are a must, not only for vision enhancement, but for safety. The possibility of eye injury from flying particles is very real when shooting clay birds.

Clay target shooters need more than a shotgun and a box of shells to be competitive. This veteran shooter is properly attired with cap, shooting glasses, ear protectors and a vest with pockets for shells. A comfortable shirt, loose-fitting pants and adequate footwear complete the ensemble.

Decot Hy-Wyd shooting glasses have long been a favorite with trap and Skeet shooters. They fit high on the forehead for good vision when the head is tipped forward in the shooting position. Lenses are impact-resistant CR-39 plastic.

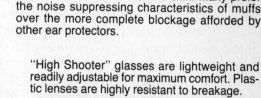

Silencio ear muffs may be worn over the head, behind the head or under the chin. Many prefer the noise suppressing characteristics of muffs over the more complete blockage afforded by other ear protectors.

"High Shooter" glasses are lightweight and readily adjustable for maximum comfort. Plastic lenses are highly resistant to breakage.

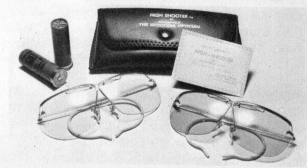

SDI ear plugs from Silencio are made from a soft, pliable material with an inner air cushion that provides a comfortable seal. One size fits all. A handy carrying case is included.

(Right) Bob Allen's hot weather vest has a ventilated back of nylon mesh, extended leather shoulder pad, and open-top bellows pockets for shells. A lightweight vest adds to comfort on steamy summer days.

(Right) Deluxe 50-shot pouch holds either loaded rounds or empties. A single pouch of this type may be combined with a shell-box carrier to provide space for both full loads and empties.

Some shooters find that ear muffs interfere with mounting the stock firmly against the cheek. If muffs ride too heavily on the gunstock, scores can be adversely affected. For those who find the muffs to be annoying, ear plugs are perhaps a better choice. These vary in design from simple foam plastic cylinders that may be discarded after use to custom fitted units that are contoured to fit individual ears. Silencio "SDI" plugs are soft air-filled plastic that mould themselves to the ear's shape and sharply limit noise input. A slightly better design is the Silencio **Silent Partner** plug. Made from silicone rubber, these are a bit more comfortable to wear, and they form a somewhat tighter seal in the ear canal.

The Norton Co. (16624 Edwards Road, Cerritos, CA 90701) makes an ear plug with a small valve that closes against loud noises, yet allows normal conversation to be carried on with practically no interference. The **Norton Sonic II** is an up-dated version of the Lee Sonic ear valve that was on the market for many years. The Sonic II is an excellent choice for shooters who object to ear muffs. The Norton Company also makes an ear muff, called the **Gun Muffler,** that is quite effective in reducing shotgun muzzle blast.

David Clark Co. (360 Franklin St., Worcester, MA 01604) is a pioneering firm in the field of hearing protection. Clark offers a full line of audio suppression equipment, including newly-designed **Flow Fit Ear Seals** for their top-of-the-line muffs. Clark protectors have

been a favorite with shooters for decades.

Once the budding clay-bird buster is equipped with adequate eye and ear protection, he will find that he desperately needs at least one other piece of personal gear. It soon becomes obvious that there is no convenient place to carry ammunition. Pants and jacket pockets are awkward places to stow shells, and 25 of them take up more space than is usually available in clothing not designed for the purpose.

One of the better solutions to the problem is a shell pouch that is designed to hold a full box of shells, and hangs from the belt. Either the regular trouser belt may be used or a special one for the pouch may be worn over outer clothing. With a full box of ammo handy, there should be no more of the fumbling that experienced shooters find so bothersome. If empty shells are to be kept for reloading, a second pouch may be hung below the one holding fresh ammo into which fired shells may be easily dropped. Instead of carrying two pouches, some shooters prefer a larger divided pouch that holds live rounds in one compartment, and empties in another.

Bob Allen, (214 S.W. Jackson St., Des Moines, IA 50317) makes a full line of pouches and shell carriers in both vinyl and nylon that should satisfy the needs of any clay target shooter. **The Hunter Corp.** (P.O. Box 467, Westminster, CO 80030), makers of holsters and other fine leather goods, offers several leather pouches and

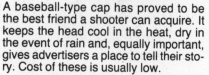

(Left) Light, airy summer vest of polyester mesh gives maximum ventilation. Flared international shoulder pad extends to the waist and is made from tightly woven cloth for coolness.

Western styling accents this shooting coat by Bob Allen. It provides adequate warmth without sacrificing all-important freedom of action.

A baseball-type cap has proved to be the best friend a shooter can acquire. It keeps the head cool in the heat, dry in the event of rain and, equally important, gives advertisers a place to tell their story. Cost of these is usually low.

carriers for shooters who prefer that material over plastic. **The Maverick Leather Company** (P.O. Box 12305, El Paso, TX 79912) also makes a handsome oil-tanned leather shell pouch with matching belt that holds 50 loaded rounds and 50 empties in two separate compartments. **Pachmayr's Mark 5 Shooter's Bag** attaches to a special belt loop with Velcro fasteners. There is room for a full box of shells in an inner pouch, along with a larger outer pouch for empties. Loops are also provided for five extra shells. **Pakit** from Pachmayr is a stainless steel clip that slides into the bottom of a factory ammo box. Attached to a leather belt loop, this simple gadget turns the ammo box into a shell carrier. Simply slip a box onto the Pakit clip, tear off the box top and, behold! A shell carrier is born. The Pakit belt loop also holds a spare shell ready for instant use.

Another solution to the problem of where to carry the shells is a shooting vest or coat with pockets large enough to hold both loaded and empty shells. Vests are made in many styles and weights for either summer or winter wear. Most have shoulder pads, and some are equipped with an "International-style" pad that extends from shoulder to waist to ease the motion of mounting a gun held at hip level for Olympic type events. Left-handed shooters are not left out in the cold, since padded left shoulders are offered by almost all manufacturers of clothing. The theory behind wearing a vest instead of a full jacket is that the arms are left free of restraint, except for a light and loose shirt.

In cold winter weather, there is no choice but to wear a coat of some sort, but it must be made so as to allow maximum freedom of movement for both arms and shoulders. Whereas a rifleman can use a coat as a recoil absorbing device on the target range, a shotgunner can't tolerate any restriction of his upper body. An ordinary winter jacket may be fine for warmth, but a trap or Skeet shooter should have a coat that is designed specifically for the purpose. **Bob Allen,** among others, makes a complete line of coats and vests that should satisfy any reasonable need.

A hat of some variety is worn by most serious clay target shooters. Though some prefer to shoot bareheaded, there is considerable merit to having some protection against sun glare and weather. On a windy day, shots can be spoiled by hair blowing in the eyes, and a proper hat can prevent this sort of interference. A shooting hat ought to cover the head, protect the eyes from glare, and yet not interfere with mounting the gun or sighting. For these reasons, a simple billed cap is the head gear usually seen on trap or Skeet fields. Hats of all kinds are available everywhere. Style and fit are an individual's own choice, since comfort and convenience are more important than appearance. In really cold weather, a cap with ear flaps can provide warmth and comfort without interfering unduly with one's shooting stance. Unless a hat has a heavy sweat band, perspira-

217

Bob Allen's adjustable-back gloves have Velcro fastener for snug fit. Perforated for ventilation, these capeskin beauties absorb perspiration.

(Below) The "Shootin' Shoe," designed by Bob Allen has non-skid sole with built-in insulation for maximum coolness with sure footing. Gun toe rest snaps onto laces and may be removed if desired.

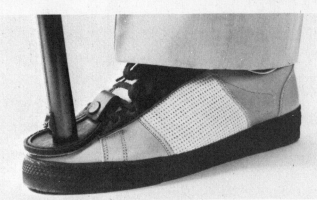

This hot weather shooting shirt from Bob Allen is all mesh Dupont Zelcon that absorbs moisture like cotton. The shoulder pad is quilted polyester.

tion can be a problem on hot summer days. Nothing is quite so disconcerting as having drops of sweat suddenly appear on shooting glasses to blur your vision at a critical moment. A cotton sweat band, of the type commonly worn by athletes, can keep those annoying droplets out of the eyes.

If there is just no way to resist braving wintry blasts for a round or two of trap or Skeet, gloves are an absolute necessity. Frozen fingers do not for good shooting make. Gloves should be designed specifically for shooters, because regular ones don't allow enough freedom for the trigger finger or for loading shells. Incidentally, some shooters wear lightweight gloves even in the summertime, for much the same reasons that racing drivers wear them — to absorb perspiration and improve grip.

Shirts should be loose and comfortable. If a shooting vest or coat is worn, any sport shirt is adequate that meets these standards. For those who shoot in shirtsleeves, special shooting shirts are made with shoulder pads, pockets, shell loops, etc. **Bob Allen** has as fine a selection of shirts for shooters as can be found anywhere.

Trousers are a matter of personal choice. The only thing to be aware of is that they must be loose enough not to bind when swinging on a target. Special pants are made for shooters, but it is really not necessary to go to this extreme just to be correctly dressed for trap or Skeet.

Shoes are an item to which many claybirders don't

give much attention, yet good firm footing is important to scoring well at clay target sports. Footwear that provides good ankle support together with non-slip soles is preferred by many, although special shoes purposely designed for clay target work are available from **Bob Allen** that are lightweight, with low tops for those who would rather have an athletic-type shoe. When waiting their turn to shoot many shotgunners rest the muzzle of their unloaded gun on the toe of one shoe to take some of the weight off their arms. For those who make a practice of this, a pad is available that clips over the shoe laces and covers the toe of the shoe. It's a simple thing, but it can save a lot of wear and tear on both feet and shoes. **Hunter Corp.** offers a nicely made leather toe guard that has a raised rim to keep the gun muzzle from slipping off the foot.

A minor item, but a welcome one on hot summer days, is a towel for wiping perspiration off hands and gun. **Bob Allen** makes a neat towel with an elastic strap that clips on the belt so that it is out of the way, yet always ready when needed. Any old rag will do, of course, but it's nice to have equipment with that little extra touch of class.

As trap or Skeet shooting becomes more or less a way of life, claybirders find that they habitually carry a rather large number of small items with them. Things like cleaning materials, gun oil, small tools, extra shells, a couple of candy bars, or maybe a bottle of aspirin inevitably show up along with other, more important shoot-

Shotgun butt pads are made in a bewildering array of shapes and sizes. This selection includes only a few of those made by Pachmayr Gun Works of Los Angeles.

(Above) Zippered utility bag for shooters folds flat for convenient storage when not in use. Ideal for carrying both shells and accessory gear. Handles are reinforced to stand the strain of heavy loads. This offering from Bob Allen is made in black or chestnut brown leather-grain vinyl.

Zippered case for take-down shotguns holds stock and barrels in separate padded compartments. Extra space is provided for sunglasses or small accessory items.

ing gear. A bag of some kind to carry all these ancillary items is almost a must. A brown paper bag might serve the purpose but, face it, that's tacky. A utility bag for shooters is the answer here.

Bob Allen, who has carefully researched the special needs of shotgunners, makes an excellent utility bag that will hold practically everything a shooter might require at the range. **Dan Titus Shooting Specialties** (872 Penn St., Bryn Mawr, PA 19010) can supply a handsome top-grain cowhide case with room for eight boxes of shells plus space for accessories. The **Case-Gard Model S-175,** from MTM Molded Products Company (P.O. Box 1438, Dayton, OH 45414) is a sturdy plastic case that holds up to seven boxes of 12-gauge shells, with room left over for storage of other items. A handy shoulder strap leaves the shooter's hands free. **Ed Scherer Custom Leather Craft** (W30059 Woodcrest Dr., Waukesha, WI 53186) makes carrying bags, shell pouches and belts in either plain leather or beautifully hand-tooled finishes. Scherer's leather-goods are among the very best to be found. There is no need to be ashamed of your luggage if all your gear is lodged in a smartly designed carry-all. It isn't essential to good shooting, but it's neat.

A good gun case, however, is another story. Not only does it protect a valuable gun from miscellaneous dings and scratches, but other shooters, and spectators, feel more comfortable when a gun is carried on and off the shooting line in a case. A soft, padded, zippered case is probably the most convenient type, although if one is traveling a long distance or by public transportation, a substantial solid case might be preferred.

If guns are to be transported by common carrier, such as an airline or railroad, a hard case with good locks is absolutely necessary. A big, heavy case not only affords protection to a valuable firearm, but it discourages petty thievery — at least as much as possible.

There are so many fine gun cases on the market that it is impossible to even begin to mention all of them. All better sporting goods stores and gunshops display a selection of cases to fit every need and budget. It usually pays in the long run to buy a case that is as well-made as you can afford. It is false economy to house a gun costing several hundreds, or thousands, of dollars in an inadequate, ill-fitting case.

If one may judge by the number of gun accessories on the market, few shooters are satisfied for long with a shotgun just the way it comes from the factory. Each claybirder seems to have his own ideas as to what it takes to make a good gun better. Some after-market add-ons are of dubious value, while others are unquestionably helpful in one way or another. Shooters would be wise to discuss comtemplated additions or alterations with others who may have had experience with a particular product or service.

The most sought-after accessory for shotguns is some device that will reduce recoil, or at least diminish its effect on the shooter. An adequate recoil-absorbing butt

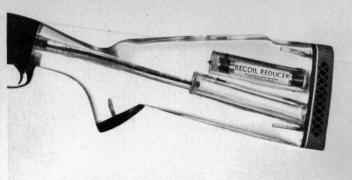

(Above) Edwards Recoil Reducer works on the principle of a weighted piston suspended between two springs inside a metal cylinder. When properly "tuned" for a particular gun, felt recoil is significantly reduced. Two units may be fitted inside a stock for double effectiveness.

Action Cheek Saver consists of an outer covering of suede over a pad of Akton energy absorbing material. Facial discomfort due to recoil is greatly reduced.

Counter Coil is a hydraulic shock absorber fitted to a gunstock in place of the regular recoil pad. It is adjustable for various loads and gauges. MBM Enterprises' recoil reducer adds about 8 ozs. to a gun's overall weight.

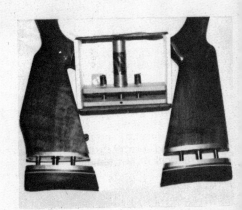

pad is a virtual necessity on a shotgun used for trap and Skeet. Without some degree of protection, shoulders can quickly become uncomfortably bruised. Though many guns today are fitted with butt pads at the factory, a shooter may find that a different thickness or contour will prove more to his liking. The easiest pad to install is a slip-on, such as the one supplied by **Supreme Products.** It is made from Neoprene and comes in three sizes, one of which will fit almost any shotgun. Supreme also makes a variety of screw-on pads in several thicknesses. **Pachmayr Gun Works,** (1220 So. Grand Ave., Los Angeles, CA 90015) has been a major source of recoil pads for over 37 years, and they make pads in various sizes and ribbing styles to suit all shotgun applications. Several recoil pads on the market today are practically carbon copies of earlier Pachmayr products. See your gunsmith or write for a catalog.

Morgan's adjustable recoil pad allows a shooter to quickly alter drop, pitch and recoil absorption as conditions dictate. A good-looking accessory, these pads are made by **Morgan Adjustable Recoil Pad Co.** (4746 South Ave., Youngstown, OH 44512).

There are many other makes of butt pads available that are also entirely satisfactory. Whatever the choice, a butt pad must be properly installed — usually a job for a competent gunsmith. Remember, too, that a pad that is thicker or thinner than the original will change the length of pull (the distance from trigger to butt.) It may be necessary to cut off the stock, or add spacers, to achieve a pull that is right for a particular shooter.

Accessory cheekpieces are used by some shooters, not only to reduce recoil effect against the face, but to alter the height of the comb. Cheekpieces are not normally attached permanently, but are fitted in place with laces or Velcro fasteners. Leather is the material most commonly used, although some modern plastics are equally satisfactory. Meadow Industries (P.O. Box 450A, Marlton, NJ 08053) makes the **Convert-A-Stock** pad that attaches with Velcro fasteners and allows the shooter to select up to 11 different heights for better control of pattern impact through cheekpiece adjustment. A new device that does a superb job of relieving recoil shock to the face is the **Action Cheek Saver** by Action Products (22 N. Mulberry St., Hagerstown, MD 21740). Made of a thin layer of Akton, a shock absorbing plastic material, it is covered with a soft suede outer layer that is remarkably comfortable. Action Products also makes a pad of Akton that may be fitted into the shooting shirt or coat and has a pocket built into the shoulder pad. Impact absorption of Akton is little short of miraculous. It must be experienced to be believed. This space age material should have a whole host of applications in all shooting sports.

Over the years, many shooters and tinkerers have dreamed up all manner of gadgets to be attached to shotguns (and rifles) for the purpose of defeating basic

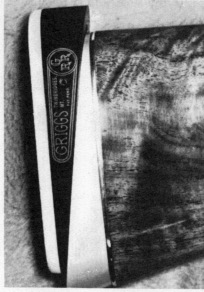

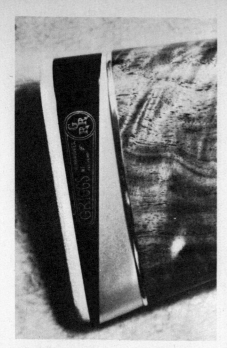

(Above and right) Griggs Recoil Redirector consists of a two-piece sliding buttplate that causes the gun butt to move downward as well as to the rear in reaction to firing. Springs inside the unit quickly return it to its original configuration.

(Above) Mercury Recoil Suppressor relies on 6 ozs. of mercury inside a sealed steel tube to absorb shock of firing. Units may be installed inside butt stock or in an unused chamber of a double-barreled gun. A third type (not shown) fits into the magazine tube of an autoloader.

laws of physics as applied to recoil. A majority of these devices proved to be nearly totally useless, but some actually do reduce felt recoil to a great extent. What most recoil-reducing attachments do is to spread reaction of gun discharge over a longer period of time, thus changing a sharp shock into more of a pushing sensation.

A relatively new recoil absorber that actually works was developed by Rod Brakhage, of Stillwater, Oklahoma. Known as **Counter Coil,** Rod's device consists of a hydraulic unit that replaces a gun's regular buttplate. It is adjustable for various gauges and loads, so that a shooter may take full advantage of its effect. Counter Coil cuts the level of felt recoil by about 50 percent. It should be installed by the factory or a good gunsmith, although templates are supplied if a gun owner wishes to do the job himself. Some wood must be trimmed from the butt-stock in order to retain desired length of pull. Counter Coil adds from 4 to 8 ounces to a gun's overall weight, which is not enough to make any appreciable difference in balance, in most cases. Counter Coil is available from MBM Enterprises (715 East 46th St., Stillwater, OK 74074). Current cost of the basic unit is $105, plus $20 for installation.

Perhaps the best known recoil reducer was developed by Jesse Edwards, of Alton, Illinois. Called simply the **Edwards Recoil Reducer,** it consists of a tube about 1 inch in diameter in which a weighted piston is suspended between two springs. Weight, spring tension and length (from 3½ to 4½ inches) are varied for best results with different guns and loads. A 1-inch hole is drilled from the rear of the buttstock for installation. Additional absorption of recoil effect may be gained by use of two units placed one above the other. A claimed advantage of Edward's system is that muzzle jump is tamed so that second shots at doubles are more easily made. Many leading trap and Skeet shooters endorse the Edwards Recoil Reducer, and it is in use by shotgunners worldwide. Standard Edwards reducers retail for $45.00, plus installation.

Another method of recoil reduction using a movable weight is found in the **Mercury Recoil Suppressor,** made by C & H Research (115 Sunnyside Dr., Lewis, KS 67552). This is a hollow steel tube, ⅞-inch in diameter, that is partially filled with mercury and then permanently sealed. Instantaneous movement of liquid mercury is said to absorb much of the shock of recoil. Overall weight is 11 ounces, including 6 ounces of mercury. Units are made for buttstock installation or insertion in a magazine tube. A third type may be fitted into the unused chamber of a double-barreled gun. All models sell for $47.50.

A different approach to the recoil problem is taken by the **Griggs Recoil Redirector.** It operates on the principle of changing the force of recoil from a backward thrust to a downward motion through a sliding buttplate mechanism. On firing, the buttstock moves down and

221

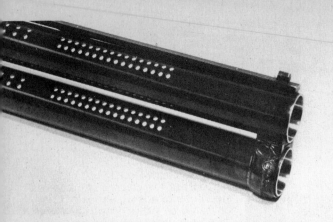

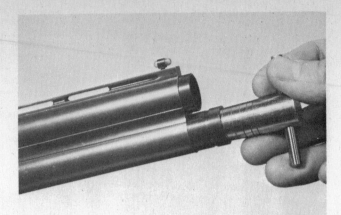

Porting of these Krieghoff barrels was done by Len Evans III of Precision Porting. A total of 152 holes were drilled in the two barrels to achieve desired downward thrust.

A special wrench is used to install choke tubes made by Pro-Choke, Inc. Only ¼-inch of the choke extends beyond the muzzle, leaving the appearance of the gun essentially intact. Precision machining and threading of the muzzle is critical in this modification.

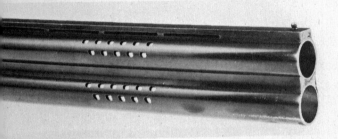

(Left) Pro-Port vents are directed upward and outward at an angle of 45 degrees on the upper barrel of this over-under double. For added stability and effectiveness, ports on the lower barrel are angled at 60 degrees from vertical.

away from the face as well as to the rear. Springs within the unit return it to its original position almost immediately. The Griggs sliding buttplate weighs little more than the pad it replaces. Price is $59.95 from Griggs Recreational Products (200 S. Main, Twin Bridges, MT 59754).

Reduction of felt recoil may also be achieved by the addition of a muzzle brake or by porting the barrel near the muzzle to vent propellant gases upward. Muzzle brakes enjoyed a certain popularity in times past, but the current consensus seems to be that they do not work sufficiently well and that they have an adverse effect on shot patterns. Barrel porting, on the other hand, accomplishes the same purpose without any of the problems connected with muzzle brakes. Although porting is now done by many gunsmiths, the method originated with Larry Kelly, of **Pro-Port, Ltd.** After almost 25 years of research, Kelly devised a means of cutting 11 compound ellipsoidal ports into each side of a barrel by use of electrical discharge machining. This type of "drilling" leaves no tool marks or damage to surrounding metal. Upward venting of gases counteracts muzzle lift and lowers perceived recoil by 20 percent, as well as reducing turbulence at the muzzle. Pro-Porting costs $65 for a single-barreled gun and $110 for an over-under. From Pro-Port, Ltd., 41302 Executive Dr., Mt. Clemens, Michigan 48045.

Len Evans, of Evans Tool and Die (157 N. Salem Rd., Conyers, GA 30208), drills a series of small round holes on each side of a barrel near the muzzle that direct gases up and to the sides for recoil reduction. Although the exact number of vent holes varies with gun and gauge, a sample **Precision Porting** job on a Krieghoff had a total of 76 holes in each barrel. Evans charges $50 per barrel for his work.

Porting is done by many gunsmiths, but care should be taken in having a porting job done to see that no burrs are left around the holes or that barrel contours are not altered, or else patterns may be adversely affected.

Variable choke devices, such as the venerable **Cutts Compensator** that was in widespread use many years ago, have gone out of fashion. Add-on adjustable chokes have been superseded by screw-in interchangeable choke tubes. Some gun makers, such as Winchester with their **WinChoke** system, offer screw-in chokes as standard equipment. Owners of guns lacking such modern conveniences who would like to experiment with different chokes will have to rely on various specialty shops as a source of this item. **Briley Manufacturing, Inc.** (1085-C Gessner, Houston, TX 77055) has added screw-in chokes to their line of products. **D&M Enterprises** (Box 118, Soda Springs, ID 83276) specializes in this sort of work. **Stan Baker** (5303 Roosevelt Way N.E. Seattle, WA 98105), one of the first to make screw-in choke conversions, has equipped the guns of many of the nation's top shooters with chokes of his design. Stan has a booklet describing his work that is free for the asking. There are numerous custom gunsmiths

(Left) The acknowledged master of tubemaking is Claude Purbaugh. His patented insert tubes simply slide into 12 gauge barrels. Inserts are chambered for 20, 28, and .410 shells. This concept has become increasingly popular in the last decade for two reasons—reduced cost as opposed to interchangeable barrel sets, and by adding weight where a Skeet gun needs it—in the barrels.

Weatherby's "Multi-Choke" system is typical of factory installed choke tube inserts. Tubes add practically no weight to the gun, since metal must be removed to accommodate them.

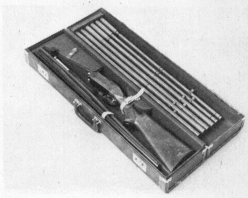

Cased set of Purbaugh insert tubes in all gauges for a standard Krieghoff shotgun. Tube system is designed so that overall weight of the gun remains the same regardless of gauge.

who do choke work, and any good gunshop should be able to direct a scattergunner to a specialist for this critical modification.

One of the better screw-in choke systems is made by Mike Bruce, of **Pro-Choke, Inc.** (2760 N.E. 7th Ave., Pompano Beach, FL 33064). Pro-Choke bores out muzzles to exact concentricity with the gun's barrel. Muzzles are then threaded to accept a choke tube, that is installed using a special wrench that is supplied. Only ¼-inch extends beyond the original muzzle, so the general appearance of the gun is not changed to any appreciable extent. The system has been extensively tested, and has been found to be perfectly safe and effective. Choke tubes are available in Skeet, Improved Cylinder, Modified, Improved Modified and Full. Sets are furnished in a nicely finished wooden box that includes a fitting tool and three tubes of a buyer's choice. Pro-Choke units pattern well and vastly increase the versatility of any shotgun. Current price is $159.95 plus postage and handling for single barreled guns, and $209.95 for doubles.

Skeet, of course, is shot with guns in four different gauges, but how about using the same gun for all four events? It's definitely possible if one uses an over-under 12-bore with insert tubes for the smaller gauges. Many years ago, Claude Purbaugh made up a set of inserts in 20, 28 and .410 gauge for a 12-gauge Browning and met with considerable success. Since that time, tubes have been improved to the point where they are being used by Skeet shooters everywhere. Purbaugh tubes, the

choice of many champion shooters, are available from **Multi-Gauge Enterprises** (433 W. Foothill Blvd., Monrovia, CA 91016).

After the initial acceptance of Purbaugh's invention, Larry Kolar, of New York, began making his own version using titanium chambers in 28-gauge, which did much to equalize weights of .410, 28 and 20-gauge installations. Kolar later sold his business to Don Mainland, of Racine, Wisconsin, who operates **Target Arms** company. Today's Kolar tubes are made in combinations of titanium and stainless steel, with integral extractors that fit over the regular 12-gauge extractors. A weight is added to the gun when in 12-gauge configuration to equalize overall weights of all four gauges, so that there is no difference in feel, balance or trigger action when changing from one gauge to another. **Target Arms** (1951 S. Memorial Dr., Racine, WI 53403) offers several possible combinations of tubes at varying prices. Tubes are not cheap, but the total cost is quite a bit less than for four separate guns.

Jess Briley, of Houston, Texas, also makes matched sets of tubes with extractors that compete most favorably with Kolar tubes. Briley's tube sets come in a custom fitted case that makes a very handsome piece of equipment.

For those who would rather have complete interchangeable barrels, several gunmakers offer this option. All barrels in a set weigh exactly the same, so that there is no difference in feel between one gauge and the

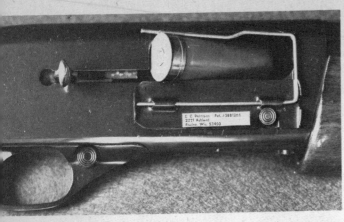

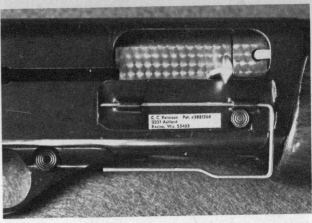

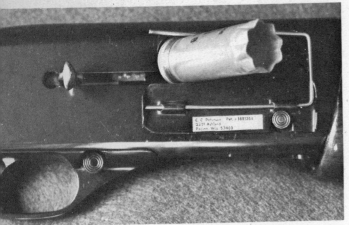

(Left, above left and above) Save-It shell catcher does not interfere with loading, and empties are easily removable. Shell catcher folds down out of the way when shooting doubles. Unit attaches to the gun by two-sided adhesive tape.

Pachmayr "Snap Caps" allow the gun owner to safely lower the shotgun's firing pin without cause for breakage.

others. Four-barrel sets are made by **Browning** for their Citori and Superposed models, by **Remington** for the Model 3200, by **Shotguns of Ulm** for the K-80, and **Perazzi**. Prices range from around $2500 for the Citori to $10,000 or so for the Perazzi. Barrel sets are also produced by various custom barrel makers to individual order. Gunsmiths who specialize in shotguns are the best source for this kind of work.

Shooters who reload will probably want to try one of several shell catchers that are designed for attachment to autoloading shotguns. The simplest of these is made by **C. C. Petersen** (2221 Ashland Ave., Racine, WI 53403). It is a wire spring that fits over the ejection port, doesn't interfere with loading, and may be turned down out of the way when shooting doubles. Two models are available to fit most self-loaders. It fastens to the side of the receiver with two-sided adhesive tape. **T & S Industries** (1027 Skyview Dr., West Carrollton, OH 45449) makes a shell catcher that clips onto a receiver below the ejection port. Instant installation and removal adds to the utility of the T & S Shell Catcher.

Standard factory triggers are notorious for their poor actions because the pulls are often gritty, over-long and heavy. A bit of judicious gunsmithing can frequently clean up a factory trigger to acceptable levels, but for those who want the best trigger possible, it is sometimes necessary to install a custom assembly. One of the better makers of trigger groups for regular-production

shotguns is **Allen Timney** (13524 Edgefield St., Cerritos, Ca 90701) who makes replacement units for Remington 1100s and 870s. Timney triggers have enjoyed an enviable reputation among both shotgunners and riflemen for many years.

Some shooters prefer a release trigger over a conventional "pull" type. Release triggers are noted for their function as a last-ditch cure for inveterate flinchers, but that is not their only attribute, by any means, since many claybirders simply shoot better scores with them. **M. L. Schwab** (4910 N. Alicia, Tuson, AZ) specializes in release triggers for several of the most popular shotgun models used on trap and Skeet fields.

Shotgun firing pins are surprisingly fragile, and nothing does them more harm than dry-firing. To avoid damage that could be caused by dropping a hammer on an empty chamber, snap caps are the answer. These are dummy shells that take up the impact on a firing pin so that inertia loads don't overstress it to the point of breakage. **Pachmayr** supplies an exceedingly sturdy snap cap, as does **Shootin' Accessories**. A minor investment in one or two of these little firing pin savers could eliminate a potential problem that has long been a plague for all shotgunners.

An excellent source of miscellaneous small accessory items for shotgunners is **Shootin' Accessories, Ltd.** (P.O. Box 5400, Reno, NV 89513). The following are a few of the goodies offered by this company. A screw-

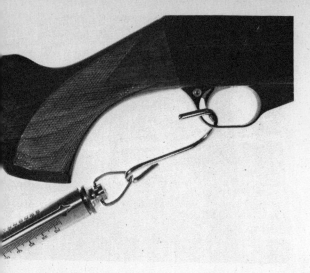

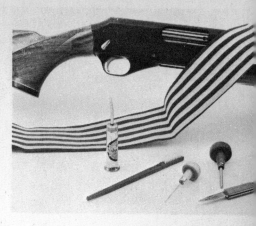

Some of the items from Shootin' Accessories include a gun sock to prevent wear of a gun's metal surfaces, a leakproof oiler, a brush to clean those hard-to-reach places, wooden-handled punches for trigger group pins on autoloaders, and a small knife made in the form of a shot shell.

A trigger pull scale should be used from time to time to assure consistency of trigger weight. Changing of trigger pull due to wear is a prime cause of lost birds on trap and Skeet fields.

(Right) A dial indicator gauge can be useful in ascertaining the precise dimensions of a choke, or the inside diameter of a barrel.

driver set that has sizes to fit most gun screws is something every shooter needs. How many times does a shooter wonder if his trigger pull has changed? A trigger pull gauge just like gunsmiths use will tell the tale. Owners of Remington 1100s or 870s will definitely want a punch that fits the pin holding the trigger assembly — a wooden-handled punch is available that matches the pin precisely and virtually eliminates scratched receivers. A small, leakproof oiler takes up little space in a shooter's utility bag, yet provides the critical drop or two of oil needed to make things run smoothly. Lastly, a handy little folding knife made in the shape of a shotgun shell could be clever addition to any shooting kit.

A product that is not exactly a shooting accessory, but one that we think has practical applications in shooting sports, is the **EasyTalk** personal radio. Made in two models, one with a body pack for the main transceiver, and the other completely integrated into the headset. Potential use of this device is as a training aid, so that a coach could tell a shooter precisely what he is doing, right or wrong, without having to shout or distract the trainee in any way. Microphones on these incredibly light-weight units are voice activated, thereby making it possible for a shooter to respond to instruction without having to press a mike button. EasyTalk could readily be installed in a muff-type hearing protector, or simply worn over one ear with a sound attenuating plug in the other. Radio range is about half a mile —

enough for our purpose. Price is a modest $79.95 per unit, from Porta Phone (P. O. Box 506, Wakefield, RI 02880).

After a day's shooting, guns must be cleaned. Cleaning equipment is available at all gunshops and sporting goods stores, as well as by mail order from many firms. A good, solid cleaning rod made especially for shotguns is needed, plus proper brushes, swabs, patches and solvents. Excellent materials are available from **Outers** and **Hoppes,** both specialists in this field. A new cleaning system, originating in Germany, is now marketed by **Beeman's** (47-TS Paul Drive, San Rafael, CA 94903). Beeman's unit consists of a sturdy rod plus scrubbing and oiling patches that are made to precisely fit the bore. A rod guide prevents damage to the muzzle or chamber mouth while removing deposits from the barrel. The Beeman kit is perfect for those meticulous shooters who wish to give their highly-valued guns the best kind of care. **RIG Products** (Box 1990, Sparks, NV 89432) manufactures a handy cleaning rod that is made in sections small enough that the entire unit may be carried in a pocket or shell carrier without taking up a great deal of space. RIG also makes an excellent line of cleaning solvents and gun oils.

Though they're not accessories in the generally accepted sense, books, periodicals and other printed material can be invaluable to shooters in keeping them abreast of developments, as well as serving to improve

Just a few of the many publications that are most helpful to clay bird shooters. Reference books like these are a ready source of information when needed.

Specialty magazines keep a scattergunner up to date on latest developments in equipment and techniques, as well as on competitive events and their results.

their shooting abilities. Most of the top shooters have extensive libraries, and avidly read current publications to gain more information about their beloved sport. Magazines such as *Sports Afield, Outdoor Life* and *Field and Stream* regularly run articles of interest to shotgunners. Strictly gun magazines, including *Guns and Ammo, Shooting Times, Guns, Gun World* and *The American Rifleman* frequently contain information of great interest to scattergunners. Other periodicals catering exclusively to shotgun sports are *Skeet Shooting Review, The American Shotgunner, Shotgun Sports, Scoreboard West, The Skeeter* and *Trap and Field.* All these shotgun magazines are slanted toward clay target shooting, and anyone at all interested in these activities should take time to peruse them. Brochures and catalogs are another source of information that should not

be overlooked.

Literally dozens of books have been written about shotgunning, and many of these are advertised in current magazines. For hardcover books that are either out of print or hard to find, **Ray Riling Arms Books** (6844 Gorsten St., Philadelphia, PA 19119) is undoubtedly the country's leading dealer in firearms books. The names of other dealers and publishers of gun books may be found in the directory section of *Gun Digest.*

The accessory items mentioned here have only scratched the surface of what is available to shotgunners. A complete and comprehensive listing of all makers and products is more than we have room for in this book, but we have at least given the reader some idea of what sorts of things a shooter might need or want in order to make life easier on trap or Skeet fields.

Appendix

Amateur Trapshooting Association
Rules and Guidelines

I
Organization Of The
Amateur Trapshooting Association

The following is an informative summary of the organization of the Amateur Trapshooting Association. Complete details are contained in the Articles of Incorporation and the By-Laws of the Corporation which are contained in a separate booklet. The Official Trapshooting Rules of the ATA govern the shooting of registered targets, the conduct of shooters and the duties of shoot management. The ATA has the responsibility for the formation, regulation and enforcement of these Rules.

A. Purpose Of The ATA

The purpose of the ATA is to promote and govern the sport of amateur trap shooting throughout the world.

B. Membership

Membership is divided into two classes, both of which have full shooting rights and privileges. The membership year runs from October 1 through September 30.

Life members are issued at a charge of $150 and pay no annual dues. Only life members may hold office in the ATA.

Annual members pay yearly dues of $10. They are allowed to vote for state directors and officers, but may not hold office in the ATA.

C. Target Year

The target year, on which averages are kept and compiled by the ATA headquarters starts on October 1 and ends on September 30. Scores, however, shot at any tournament that ends after September 30, regardless of starting date, will be included in the following year's averages.

D. State Organizations And Delegate Elections

Shooters in the various states and provinces are organized into state and provincial associations which control shooting in their own territories and conduct state and provincial championship tournaments. Such associations receive aid from the A.T.A. in the form of trophies and cash refunds. This aid is covered in detailed set of written rules.

At each annual state or provincial championship tournament sanctioned by the A.T.A., a business meeting must be held on a date and time specified in the program for the tournament. The date of the meeting must be one of the last three days of the tournament. The time of the meeting must be no earlier than 8:00 a.m. and no later than 9:00 p.m., except that if the meeting is held on the last day of the tournament, then the meeting must commence no later than 12:00 noon. All members of the A.T.A. residing in that state or province who are present in person at the meeting and who are also members of their state organization, are entitled to vote for the state or provincial delegate to the A.T.A. and for not more than two alternative A.T.A. delegates, all of which must be

Life Members as a prerequisite to such election. Selection of the state or provincial delegate, and the alternate delegate (s) should be given the utmost consideration. As delegates, in a properly called meeting, constitute the Board of Directors of the Amateur Trapshooting Association and as such have the responsibility of overseeing the operation of the Association. Only those persons who are responsible, dedicated individuals should be considered.

E. Zones

The zones are comprised of the following territories:

Central: Illinois, Indiana, Michigan, Iowa, Minnesota, Nebraska, North Dakota, Ohio, South Dakota, Wisconsin and the provinces of Manitoba and Saskatchewan in Canada.

Eastern: Connecticut, Massachusetts, New Hampshire, New York, Pennsylvania, Rhode Island, Vermont, New Jersey and the provinces of Quebec, Canada and the provinces in Canada lying east thereof.

Southern: Alabama, Florida, Georgia, Kentucky, Mississippi, North Carolina, South Carolina, Tennessee, Virginia, West Virginia and the Canal Zone.

Southwestern: Arkansas, Colorado, Kansas, Louisiana, Missouri, New Mexico, Oklahoma and Texas.

Western: Alaska, Arizona, California, Hawaii, Idaho, Montana, Nevada, Oregon, Utah, Washington, Wyoming and the provinces of Alberta and British Columbia in Canada.

F. Executive Committee And ATA Manager

1. The Executive Committee consists of a representative from each of the five zones elected each year to the Executive Committee at the annual meeting of the Board of Directors. One member of this Executive Committee is designated President and the other four are designated Vice-presidents.

2. The Board of Directors has delegated direction of the affairs of the ATA between annual meetings to the Executive Committee.

3. The Executive Committee employs a manager to handle the daily affairs of the ATA under its supervision. The ATA Manager implements the policy set forth by the Board of Directors and/or the Executive Committee and follows their directions.

4. The main office and records of the ATA are located at Vandalia, Ohio.

G. Board Of Directors

The Corporate Powers of the ATA, under Delaware law, are vested in the Board of Directors which consists of a delegate from each affiliated state or province. The Board of Directors meets annually during the Grand American Tournament.

H. Constitution And By-Laws

The ATA is organized under the Corporate Laws of the

State of Delaware and has a Delaware charter and corporate by-laws formulated in accordance with Delaware laws.

I. Jurisdiction
The ATA has jurisdiction over all affiliated associations regardless of location.

II.
Information For New Shooters

A. Procedure For Joining The ATA
1. Annual Members
Application for annual membership may be made at any registered shoot by filling out an application which requires two Life Member's signatures and the payment of $10 dues to the ATA. A temporary receipt will be given to the shooter, upon receipt of a proper application. The temporary receipt should be retained as evidence of payment and be used in lieu of a membership card until the membership card is received. The ATA will issue an annual membership card in the usual course of business. This card will be marked to indicate the shooter's handicap yardage.

Annual members have all the shooting rights and privileges of Life Members, but may hold no office in the ATA. Annual members are entitled to vote for the state delegate and alternates to represent their state, or province, at a meeting of the Board of Directors of the ATA.

Annual memberships are renewable by mail on or before October 1st. Send your complete name, address, including zip code and $10 to ATA, Vandalia, Ohio 45377 to renew, if you do not receive a renewal form from the ATA.

2. Life Memberships
Life memberships are obtained by the submission of a proper application and the payment of $150. Upon approval of the application, the ATA will issue a Life Membership certificate.

From the $10 annual membership, $2 is returned by the ATA to the state organization. From the $150 life membership, $75 is returned to the state organization over a 10 year period and part is retained in a special ATA emergency fund. From the $1 Daily Fee you pay, 20% is returned to the state organization.

B. ATA Membership Insurance Benefits
All active dues paying members of the ATA are entitled to the following benefits:
1. Membership liability
The ATA provides $1,000,000 of personal liability for all members for any claims arising out of injuries at an ATA registered club regardless of whether or not it is a registered shoot. Coverage is on a per claim basis and is excess of any other insurance.
2. Return of Dues Program—Annual Membership only
ATA provides each annual member with full reimbursement of all dues paid from October 1, 1979 to the individual member's death. Members, however, must have a record of continuous dues payment.
3. Accidental Death and Dismemberment
ATA provides each member with $10,000 of Accidental Death and Dismemberment coverage. Dismemberment includes the loss of any hand, foot, or eye. Coverage is provided while traveling to, while at and while returning from any ATA registered shoot.
4. Life Insurance Plan
As an optional membership benefit, the ATA offers each member and/or his spouse the opportuntity to apply for up to $100,000 of low-cost, group life insurance. Dependent children are each eligible for $1,000 in coverage.
5. Catastrophe Major Medical Insurance Plan
As an optional membership benefit, the ATA offers each member and/or his spouse and unmarried dependent children, under age 25, the opportunity to apply for up to $1,000,000 Catastrophe Major Medical group insurance

Note: Any incidents or notice of claim should be given to the ATA Insurance Administrator: Albert H. Wohlers & Co., 1500 Higgins Road, Park Ridge, Illinois 60068 or call (toll free) 800-323-2106.

C. Target And Membership Year
The target year and membership year runs from October 1st to September 30; however, scores shot at any tournament ending after September 30, regardless of starting date, will be included in the following year's averages.

D. Handicap Yardage For A New ATA Shooter
1. New Lady Shooter
New lady shooters will be assigned a Handicap of 18.0 yards.
2. New Sub-Junior Shooter
A shooter who has not reached his or her 15th birthday will be classified as a sub-junior and will be assigned a handicap of 18.0 yards.
3. New Male Junior Shooter
All male shooters between the ages of 15 and 18 will be assigned a handicap of 19.0 yards.
4. New Male Shooter
A new male shooter, 18 years of age or older, will be assigned a handicap of 20.0 yards.
5. A new member who had previously been a member of another trapshooting association must shoot their last assigned yardage in that association unless he has received an ATA 1,000 target review and been granted a yardage reduction.

It will be the responsibility of the new member to notify the handicap committee of his last assigned yardage in that association.

E. Classification Of A New Shooter In Singles (16-Yard) And Doubles Events
A new shooter may be assigned to any class in 16-yard yards and doubles events until the shooter establishes his known ability.

F. Rules Of Conduct Of An ATA Shooter
Know the ATA rules, so that you know your rights and duties and follow them as you expect other shooter to do.
1. It is your duty to have your card punched if you win additional yardage before leaving a shoot. If you leave a shoot prior to the completion of a handicap event, it is your duty to find out if your score qualifies you for a yardage increase. It is your responsibility to neatly and accurately record all registered scores on the score card before leaving the shoot and keep the 16 yard and doubles average in the column provided up to date for use by classification committees. Scores in 16 yards, handicap, doubles and ATA International should be recorded accurately on the basis of the number of targets shot in that event.
2. When making your entry at any registered shoot, produce your plastic identification card and your average card so that your name, address and membership number are properly noted and errors in records prevented. Shooters not having a plastic card should always list their entire name and address on the event cards.

The score card is intended for the purpose of providing the classification committees at the shoots with up to date data on your shooting ability. Shooters not having their cards up to date may be put in a higher class or otherwise penalized.

Failure to accurately record scores, or falsification of scores, can lead to suspension from the ATA.

3. Veterans are defined as ATA shooters 65 years of age or older. Senior Veterans are 70 years or older. Sub-juniors, Juniors and Veterans will be required to change their status on the date of their birthday, e.g. on the day a sub-junior turns 15 any event shot on that day will be shot as a junior. When a junior reaches 18, on that day he or she must shoot as an adult. Veterans will qualify for veteran's races on their 65th birthday. The only exceptions are as follows:

a. When considering for High-Overall or All-Around when there is no sub-junior, junior or veteran's trophy the contestant's age on the first day that qualifies him for said award must be utilized.

b. In the Grand American, when qualification for sub-junior or junior is determined at the state level, he may be able to participate in the Champion of Champions event based on his age at the state shoot.

4. A contestant is duly notified to compete when his name is called by the scorer, or other person authorized to do so by the management. If a squad hustler is furnished, it is a matter of courtesy only and does not relieve the contestant from his responsibility of reporting when his name is called by his referee, scorer or other person authorized to do so. Shooters not responding when duly notified may be disqualified by the management.

5. Every person entering the competition agrees to all official decisions and to abide by these rules.

6. A contestant may hold his gun in any position when it is his turn to shoot. He must in no manner interfere with the preceding shooter by raising his gun to a point or otherwise create a distraction.

7. It is the duty of the contestant to see that his score as determined by the referee is correctly recorded. In case of error, it shall be the duty of the contestant to have that error corrected before he has fired the first shot at the succeeding position or before he leaves the trap if the target concerned was within the last five targets of that sub-event. Otherwise the score must stand as shown on the score sheet.

G. Renewing Membership In The ATA

Any shooter reapplying for membership in the ATA who had been assigned a previous handicap yardage shall resume shooting at that yardage. The only exception is if he was assigned a yardage based on age, because of present age he may be required to shoot at a longer yardage. Failure of a shooter to shoot his previously assigned yardage will result in disqualification and winning scores and prizes forfeited.

III
Official Rules Of ATA Tournaments

In these rules, the word "State" is intended to include province or other similar territory having an affiliated association.

A. Registered Shoots

The ATA governs the conduct of all shoots registered with it. Only clubs affiliated with their state association will be permitted to hold registered shoots.

To constitute a registered shoot at least five (5) or more persons must compete and compete each event, and provided that they first become members of the ATA and pay the registration fee of $1 for each day of competition at each shooting location, and such state association fees and dues as may be charged.

No daily fee charges shall be permitted except those assessed by the ATA, the Zone, or the State in which the tournament is being held.

B. Who May Participate

Only members in good standing who have paid their annual dues or are Life Members may participate in a registered ATA shoot.

C. Events And How Shot

In official ATA usage a sub-event is any number of targets shot on any one field at one time, with one full rotation on all five stations by each shooter, such as 25 singles or handicap targets or in doubles 25 pairs, 15 pairs or 10 pairs. An event is the total targets of a specific type (16-yard, handicap, doubles, or ATA International) such as 200 16-yard targets, 100 handicap targets, etc. for which separate entry is made. Therefore, an "event" consists of two or more "sub-events." Events of less than 50 targets may not be registered.

1. 16 Yard Singles

This event must be shot five shots at each post from 16 yards (14.6m) with each shooter in order shooting at one target until all have shot five times, and then rotating in a clockwise manner to the next station.

2. Handicap Targets

This event must be shot five shots at each post from 17 to 27 yards (15.5 to 24.7m) with each shooter in order shooting at one target until all have shot five times, then rotating in a clockwise manner to the next station.

A contestant must stand on the highest whole yardage punched on his or her card. For example, if a card is punched 20.5 yards, the shooter will stand on 20.0 yards. However, if one half yard is then earned, the card must be punched to the 21.0 yards and the shooter must stand on the 21.0 yard line.

A shooter may not stand on a higher yardage than he is punched, unless assigned penalty yardage by the shoot handicap committee.

If there is a 200 target race, the second 100 handicap event must not begin prior to the awarding of earned yardage based on the first 100 target event.

It is not permitted to have more than one 50 and/or 75 target handicap event in a registered tournament in any one day.

3. Doubles

This event must be shot from 16 yards (14.6m), with each shooter in order shooting at two targets thrown simultaneously from the trap house until all have shot the specified number of times, then rotating in a clockwise manner to the next station. (A doubles event will be shot by having each squad shoot successive alternating 15 pair and 10 pair sub-events on the trap or traps being utilized, or a club may elect to throw Doubles in sub-events of 25 pairs.)

It is not necessary to change traps after each sub-event.

4. ATA International Targets

The event must be shot at 22 yards (20.1m), two shots per target, five targets per station, 25 targets per sub-event and the event must be no less than 50 targets. Traps which simultaneously oscillate automatically in both horizontal or vertical directions shall be used. The maximum angles thrown by the trap in its oscillation shall be approximately 45 degrees right and left of straightaway. In a vertical plane the target should vary from 4 feet (1.2m) to 12 feet (3.7m). It is suggested that targets be thrown at 55 yards in still air.

ATA rules regarding ammunition, misfires, dud shells, broken gun, dead target, lost target, broken target, no target and applicable doubles rules shall apply.

D. Classification, Handicapping, And Special Designations

1. For 16 yard targets and Doubles, shooters should be placed in 3 or more classes, according to their known ability.

a. To arrive at "known ability" the following should be taken into account as far as such information can be made available.

(1) Official registered targets. (Abnormally low scores should be disregarded.) Averages of all registered shooters

are compiled and published annually.

(2) Non-registered scores including shootoff scores, non-registered events, practice scores, etc.

(3) Any other information bearing on a shooter's ability to shoot and break targets.

b. For 16-yard events the following systems are suggested:

Five Classes

97% and over	AA
94% and under 97%	A
91% and under 94%	B
88% and under 91%	C
Under 88%	D

Four Classes

95% and over	A
92% and under 95%	B
89% and under 92%	C
Under 89%	D

Three Classes

95% and over	A
91% and under 95%	B
Under 91%	C

c. For Doubles events the following systems are suggested:

Five Classes

93% and up	AA
89% and under 93%	A
85% and under 89%	B
78% and under 85%	C
Under 78%	D

Four Classes

90% and up	A
85% and under 90%	B
78% and under 85%	C
Under 78%	D

Three Classes

89% and up	A
83% and under 89%	B
Under 83%	C

d. Any club desiring to use a different classification may do so by printing the desired classification in the program of the shoot.

e. For better classification of shooters it is suggested that the following method be used.

(1) If the shooter has less than 500 targets on the current year's score card, use the previous year's average and known ability.

(2) If the shooter has between 500 and 1,000 targets (inclusive) on his current year's score card, use the current average and known ability or the previous year's average and known ability, whichever is the higher.

2. *Recommended 16 Yard Punch System*

a. This system is to be utilized for clasification at only the Grand American, ATA Zone Championships, State Championships, Golden West Grand, Spring Grand, Midwestern Grand, and Southern Grand tournaments. Cards shall not be punched at any other than the above shoots.

b. Classification at all other shoots shall be decided by the club shoot classification and handicap committee.

c. All scores equaling or exceeding those of champions, runner-ups, and the respective class winners will receive one punch. This will apply only to the singles champion-

ships when at the above mentioned shoots.

d. The shooter's average card will be printed providing for two punches in each of the five ATA classes. When a shooter has one punch it indicates he has won that class of one of the above shoots. A shooter with two punches in a class should be advanced.

e. It will be the shooter's responsibility to see that his card is properly punched prior to entering any of the above listed tournaments.

f. The intent of this system is to inform classification and handicap committees of prior wins. Punches indicating these wins may be disregarded by the classification committee if they so choose.

3. A shooter will be handicapped between 17 and 27 yards at the highest yardage punched on his card, unless he is required to shoot Penalty yardage. (Section 5.)

4. *ATA International*

a. For ATA International targets shooters will be divided into three classes. Class 1, Class 2, Class 3.

b. For ATA International events the following system based on assigned Handicap yardages is suggested:

Class 1............................24-27 yard
Class 2............................21-23 yard
Class 3............................17-20 yard

5. *Penalty Classification*

The management of registered shoots may establish penalty yardage, and penalty classification for 16 yard targets and doubles, if said conditions are printed in the program. In no event shall any shooter be assigned a handicap of less than the minimum yardage appearing on his handicap card.

6. *Special Categories*

Ladies, Juniors, Sub-Juniors, Veterans, Sr. Veterans and Industry shooters shall be so designated.

a. All female shooters shall be designated as Ladies, though because of age they may also be designated as Juniors, Sub-Juniors, Veteran or Sr. Veterans.

b. A shooter who has not reached his or her 15th birthday will be designated as a Sub-Junior.

c. A shooter who is 15 but has not reached his or her 18th birthday will be designated as a Junior.

d. A shooter who is 65 years or older will be designated as a Veteran.

e. A shooter who is 70 years or older will be designated as a Sr. Veteran.

f. Industry personnel shall be so designated and may shoot for only those championships and trophies so designated.

E. Squadding

1. In all ATA events contestants shall shoot in squads of five except:

a. When there are less than five contestants available for the last squad of any program.

b. When yardage differences in handicap events make it impossible or unsafe.

c. When there are withdrawals from a squad after the competition has begun and squads scheduled.

d. When in the opinion of shoot management, the harmony of the shoot may be enhanced by squadding less than five contestants.

2. It is illegal for more than five shooters to be in a squad.

3. The squadding of practice shooters with those shooting registered events shall not be allowed, nor shall anyone be allowed to shoot registered events on a non-registered basis.

4. The shooter in position 1 is the Squad Leader and should:

a. ascertain that all members of the squad are ready before commencing the event or sub-event.

b. initial the score sheet at the end of each sub-event.

c. the Squad leader *only* may call for one target before starting his squad to shoot in a regular event.

5. If a broken or irregular target is thrown, the contestant in turn may ask to see another target; if there is a delay due to trap or gun trouble the contestant in turn, may ask to see another target. If during a sub-event a contestant is consecutively thrown two illegal or broken targets, the contestant shall have the right to see a legal target before he resumes shooting.

F. Official Scoring

1. Procedure

a. The official score is the record kept by the scorer on the sheet furnished him by the management for said purpose and shall show in detail the scores made in the event or sub-event for which furnished. It is recommended that the score sheet shall not be smaller than 10 inches by 28 inches and the box provided for each score not smaller than ¾ by ¾-inch. Score sheets on which more than one sub-event is recorded may be carried from trap to trap by the squad leader. Such score sheets must be left at the last trap to be handled by club personnel from that point.

b. The scorer shall keep an accurate record of each score of each contestant. If he calls dead or lost, the scorer shall promptly mark 1 for dead and zero for lost. His record of the competition shall be official and shall govern all awards and records of the competition to which it relates.

c. The scorer shall call all targets, or only the lost targets, as directed by the managment.

d. Should more targets be fired in a sub-event than the event calls for, then the excess targets of the sub-event will not be scored.

e. It is the duty of the referee to see that the shooters change firing points at the proper time; however, any targets shot after failure to move at the proper time shall be scored.

f. The official score must be kept on a score sheet in plain view of the contestant. If contestant's view of the score sheet is obstructed for any reason, he may refuse to shoot until he has an unobstructed view of the score sheet.

g. It is an error if the scorer fails to mark the results of any shot in the section of the score sheet where the results should have been recorded. In such cases it is the duty of that contestant to have that error corrected before he has fired the first shot at the succeeding position or in the case of his last post before he leaves the trap. Failing to do so he shall be held to have lost the target not scored, the management of the competition shall so record it as lost.

h. Every contestant in a squad shall be permitted to examine his score before the sheet is sent to the bulletin board or to the cashier's office. The score sheet should be initialed by the squad leader.

i. Errors in the details of the official score can only be corrected in strict accordance with aforementioned rules, but an error made in totaling said details shall be corrected whenever same is discovered.

j. The referee shall distinctly announce "lost" when the target is missed and "no target" when a target is thrown broken.

2. Broken Or Dead Target

A broken target (called dead) is one that has a visible broken piece from it; or one that is completely reduced to dust. The referee shall declare such target dead when it is so broken in the air. A "Dusted Target," is a target from which there is a puff of dust, but no perceptible piece is seen; it is not a broken target.

3. Lost Target

The referee shall call "lost":

a. When the contestant shoots and fails to break the target whether missed completely or when only dust falls from it.

b. When the contestant flinches and does not shoot.

c. When the shell is defective but no part of the over powder wads or shot remains in the barrel.

d. When a whole target appears promptly at command of contest and is within the legal limits and the contestant does not shoot.

e. When the contestant after calling "pull" fails to shoot because his gun was unloaded, uncocked, not properly closed, because the safety was on, or was faulty, or jarred back whether from his oversight or not, *except* that some vital part of the gun has suddenly broken so that it cannot possibly be made to function without repairs, or that he has an allowable misfire.

f. When an illegal target, or a freak target is shot at and missed. Contestant may refuse illegal targets, but if he shoots, the results must be scored.

g. If a contestant has more than two misfires in any sub-event of 25 targets (or other number in case of doubles) and did not change guns or change to the other barrel of a double barrel gun, or change shells as outlined. If these changes are not made, any misfires shall be called lost.

h. When a contestant voluntarily withdraws from, or is disqualified, and takes no further part in a sub-event after having shot at one or more targets called for by said sub-event and thereby does not shoot at the total number of targets called for by such sub-event, the referee shall declare all targets which the contestant did not shoot at in the sub-event to be lost targets and they shall be scored accordingly.

i. When a score sheet shall come into the office with one or more targets that are not scored at all, they shall be scored as lost targets by the management.

j. If a contestant uses a shell after it has misfired, he shall abide by the result obtained through the use of that shell.

k. If after an apparent dud shell or misfire the contestant opens his gun before the referee comes to him to make a decision, the target shall be called "lost."

4. No Target

a. To better apply the following rules, these definitions are given:

(1) Misfire (Dud Shell): failure of a shell to fire when the primer is struck with the firing pin or when evidence is present that the hammer did fall even though the primer shows no indentation, or a shell which lacks a live primer or one in which the primer fires, but through failure of the shell or lack of components, and which consequently leaves part of or all of the charge of shot or wad in the gun. A soft load, in which the shot and wad leave the barrel, is not a misfire.

(2) Malfunction of a gun: failure of the gun to function, or work as it was designed to do. Malfunction of a gun applies only to a second shot of doubles.

(3) Broken gun: a gun in which some vital part has broken so that the gun cannot be made to fire without repairs.

b. It is a "no target" and the referee shall allow another target under the following conditions:

(1) When the target is thrown broken, regardless of the results of any shots fired.

(2) When a contestant shoots out of turn.

(3) When two contestants, or a contestant and non-contestant shoot at the same target.

(4) When the trap is sprung without any call of pull, or when it is sprung at any material interval of time, before or after the call of the shooter, provided the contestant does not shoot. If the shooter shoots, the result must be scored, unless the shot is fired after the target has struck the ground.

(5) When in single shooting two targets are thrown at the same time, regardless of whether the shooter fires.

(6) When an "illegal" target is thrown, a target that is more than 25 degrees outside of the prescribed limits of the an-

gles in single-target shooting, or what is known as a "flipper" or "freak" target that may have slipped out of the carrier of the trap or one not properly placed on the trap provided the contestant does not shoot at it. If he shoots, the result must be scored.

(7) When a target, whose color is markedly different from that of the others, is thrown and the contestant does not shoot. If he shoots, the result must be scored.

(8) When firing, the contestant's feet must be behind the firing mark assigned to him. He must stand with at least one foot on the imaginary line drawn through the trap and firing point, or have one foot on each side of the line. Exceptions to the rule contained in the second sentence of this paragraph may be granted by the referee due to inequalities in the shooting platform. Should a shooter fail to observe this rule the referee shall call any target shot at and broken a "no target," but if shot at and missed, the result shall be scored accordingly.

c. When the contestant has a misfire shell or apparent misfire, he, without opening his gun or removing the shell or shells, must forthwith allow the referee to inspect his gun before making his decision. If the shooter opens his gun before the referee comes to him to make a decision, the target shall be called "lost."

d. If a contestant has a second misfire in the same sub-event of 25 targets (or other number in case of doubles) he shall be warned by the referee. The shooter must at that time demonstrate to the referee that he is either (1) changing guns or changing to the other barrel of a double barreled gun, or (2) that he is changing shells. If he fails to do one of these things, all succeeding misfires in that sub-event will be called "lost."

e. If, after the change of guns or of shells, the shooter has another misfire in the same sub-event, he must make the other change of the option for the remainder of the sub-event or be disqualified for interfering with the harmony of the shoot. Management shall also disqualify him on the same grounds of interference if he persists in using the same gun or guns, or shells on succeeding sub-events with resultant misfires. To avoid disqualification he may withdraw from the sub-event, have the gun repaired or shells replaced, and finish the sub-events as directed by the management.

f. In addition, in Doubles shooting, the referee shall declare "no target" under the following conditions:

(1) When only one target is thrown.

(2) When more than two targets are thrown.

(3) When both targets are broken by one shot.

(4) When there is an allowable misfire on either shot.

(5) When the gun breaks down so either shot cannot be fired.

(6) When there is a maximum of one (1) gun malfunction for the second shot of any one trap per sub-event, whether the sub-event consists of 10, 15 pairs. In sub-events of 25 pairs two (2) gun malfunctions are allowed. If the shooter changes guns, he will be allowed another malfunction per sub-event. However, if the shooter does not change guns, any subsequent malfunction shall be called "lost." Misfires are not considered malfunction.

(7) When one or both targets are thrown broken even though the shooter fires at one or both targets.

(8) If one or both targets are not within the prescribed angle or height limits and the shooter does not fire either shot. If the shooter shoots at an illegal first target and the second target is legal, he must also shoot at the second target. However, a shooter is not required to shoot an illegal second target even though he shot at the first target which may have been either legal or illegal target.

(9) Both targets shall be called "lost" if the shooter deliberately shoots at the same target twice. This rule is not applicable to a gun "doubling" or Machinegunning," these are malfunctions and are not deliberate second shots.

G. Shoot Offs

The management of a tournament may rule that ties shall be carried over to the first (or more if needed) sub-event of the next like event. However, when there are ties in a handicap event and any tying shooter earns yardage and consequently will be shooting farther back in the subsequent handicap event, all tying shooters must agree to the carry over.

Competitors qualifying for a shoot off in case of ties during regular event may see two targets at 16 yards, handicap, and ATA International and two pairs of doubles prior to the commencement of the shoot off.

All ties whenever possible shall be shot off and in such a manner as the management of the competition shall designate. Unless otherwise specified by the management, ties on singles events shall be shot off in 25 target events and doubles in 10 pair events.

Ties for All-Around championships shall be shot off on 20 singles, 10 handicap, and 5 pair of doubles. Ties for High-Overall shall be shot off in such a manner that the shoot off represents as closely as possible the same proportion of singles, handicap and doubles targets as the High-Overall program contains but keeping the shoot off to 50 targets or less. The singles, handicap and doubles portion of the shoot off shall be in order that the event occurred in the program.

When squadding shooters for shoot offs for High-Overall and All-Around the shooting order shall be in the order in which they shot in the last event involved except where such order would be inadvisable or dangerous because of yardage differences, and this order shall remain through subsequent shoot offs. In subsequent shoot offs the position shall be rotated in a clockwise manner, with the shooter from position 1 advancing to position 2 and the shooter from position 5 rotating to position 1 or to the position dictated by the number of shooters remaining, but always in the clockwise rotation.

The following method shall be used for rotation of shooters: Starting firing points to be used shall be as follows — except where handicap yardage make it unsafe.

If one shooter — firing point number 2.

If two shooters — firing points numbers 2 and 4.

If three shooters — firing points numbers 2, 3, and 4.

If four shooters — firing points numbers 2, 3, 4, and 5.

If five shooters — firing points numbers 1, 2, 3, 4, and 5.

If more than five shooters are involved in the tie, they shall be divided as equally as possible into two or more squads as directed by the management.

H. Safety

1. It is the shooter's responsibility and the shoot management's responsibility to conduct a shoot in a safe manner.

2. It is the shoot management's responsibility to remove any competitor who is conducting himself in an unsafe manner (repeat violators should be reported to the Executive Committee for further action).

3. It is the shoot management's responsibility to instruct the trap help in the proper and safe conduct of their respective duties.

4. All trap help must have a flag or other warning device to warn of the trap boy's exit from the trap house.

5. Trap personnel should be totally instructed in the potential danger of the trap (particularly the target throwing arm).

6. Movement and exposure on adjacent traps should be kept to the minimum.

7. The practice of tracking targets behind a shooting squad is unsafe, disconcerting to the shooter and is not permitted.

8. Alcohol impairs judgment and the ATA rules pertaining to alcohol must be enforced by club management.

9. In singles and handicap shooting, only one shell may be inserted in the gun at one time; in doubles only two shells may be inserted in a gun at any time.

10. In handicap there shall be no more than two (2) yards difference between adjacent shooters in the squad, *and no more than a total difference of three (3) yards in a squad.* When squadding 17, 18 and 19 yardages, there shall be no more than one yard difference between adjacent shooters in the squad, and no more than a total difference of two yards in a squad.

11. In case of failure to fire, where the referee is needed, shooters must remain in position with the gun pointed toward the target area and the referee must go to the shooter.

12. A gun may be loaded only when the shooter is on the firing station and the gun must be empty when shooter is moving from station to station.

13. All guns must be unloaded with the action open at all times except on the firing line or in a gun rack. Violators subject themselves to immediate disqualification, without recourse, with dismissal from the grounds. Repeat violators will be notified of a 30 day suspension upon second violation, third violation will receive a 90 day suspension and continuing violators will be reviewed by the Executive Committee for further disciplinary action.

14. As a safety precaution test shots will not be permitted.

15. A contestant shall load his gun only when at firing point facing the traps. In singles shooting he may place only one shell in his gun at a time and must remove it or the empty case before moving from one position to another. In changing from one post to another, the shooter should not walk in front of the other competitors. All guns used by contestants must be so equipped and so used as not to eject empty shells in a manner to substantially disturb or interfere with other contestants. The management may disqualify a contestant for violation of these rules.

I. Guns And Ammunition

A contestant cannot use:

1. A gun whose bore is larger than 12 gauge. Only 12 gauge shotguns and ammunition may be used at the Grand American Tournament; guns of smaller gauges are permissible in other registered shooting, but no consideration shall be given to that fact in handicap and classification.

2. Any load other than lead shot. This includes tracers, copper, and nickel coated shot.

3. Any load heavier than 3 drams equivalent of powder or 1⅛ ounces of shot be standard measure struck, or any load containing shot larger than number 7½.

4. Any shell loaded with black powder.

Any shooter violating any of these rules shall be barred from competition. Any such violator shall be referred to the Executive Committee for possible further disciplinary action.

J. Firing Position And Shooting Order

1. There shall be 5 firing points, numbered 1 to 5, left to right, spaced 3 yards apart, and 16 yards from B (Diagram II). At all positions the contestant's feet must be behind the firing mark assigned to him, and he must stand with at least 1 foot on the imaginary line drawn through the trap and the firing point, or have one foot on each side of the line.

The 16 yard (14.6m) position shall be 16 yards behind the center of the trap in the traphouse. The distance that the target shall be thrown shall also be measured from this point.

2. All contestants must shoot in regular order or sequence according to his or her position in the squad. A contestant who does not shoot in regular order is "out of turn" and the results

are not scored.

3. When the referee calls no target for any contestant, the next contestant is not in order until the preceding shooter has shot and the referee has ruled dead or lost.

4. The referee shall not throw a target unless all contestants are in the correct positions.

5. To preserve the harmony of the competition, no member of a squad shall move toward the next firing point until the last shot of the inning has been fired.

6. At any registered trapshooting competition, no person shall be permitted to "shoot up" that is, enter and take a part in any completed or partially completed event or events after Squad No. 1 shall have completed sub-event No. 1 of any new event to be shot on Trap No. 1.

7. At tournaments which are not "section system" with several squads, starting at the same time on several traps, such procedure shall be construed for purposes of this rule to be the same as if all squads started on Trap No. 1.

K. Trap Machine

An automatic trap machine which throws targets at an unknown angle shall be used. All trap machines used to throw ATA registered targets shall be so manufactured as to interrupt irregularly the oscillation of the trap or otherwise assure the unpredictability of the flight of substantially all targets thrown.

L. Traphouses

Traphouses must adequately protect the trap loaders and shall not be higher than necessary for the purpose. Traphouses constructed after January 1, 1956, shall conform to the following specifications:

Length: not less than 7 feet, 6 inches (2.3m), nor more than 8 feet, 6 inches (2.6m).

Width: not less than 7 feet, 6 inches (2.3m), nor more than 8 feet, 6 inches (2.6m).

Height: not less than 2 feet, 2 inches (.7m) nor more than 2 feet, 10 inches (.9m), the height to be measured from the plane of the number 3 shooting position.

Firing points. The firing points shall be 3 yards (2.7m) apart on the circumference of a circle whose radius is 16 yards (14.6m).

M. Targets

No target shall measure more than four and five-sixteenths (4⁵⁄₁₆) inches (10.94cm) in diameter, not more than one and one-eighth (1⅛) inches (28.58mm) in height, and shall weigh 3.5 ounces (99.23g) with an allowable variation of 5 percent from this figure.

N. Flights And Angles

Targets, whether single or doubles, shall be thrown not less than 48 yards (44m) nor more than 52 yards (48m) measured on level ground in still air. The recommended distances for the throwing of any target shall be 50 yards (46m).

Targets, whether single or double, shall be between 8 (2.4m) and 12 feet (3.7m) high, when 10 yards from the trap. The recommended height is 9 feet. The height at a point 10 yards (9m) from the trap is to be understood to mean height above an imaginary horizontal straight line drawn through the firing point and the trap. (See Diagram II.)

In singles shooting the trap shall be so adjusted that within the normal distribution of angles as thrown by the trap, the right angle shall not be less than a straightaway from firing point 5. To help in determining legal angles, stakes should be placed on the arc of a circle whose radius is 50 yards (46m) and whose center is the trap. One stake should be placed where a line drawn through firing point 1 and the base of the trap intersects this arc and another stake placed where a line drawn through firing point 5 and the base of the trap intersects the arc. These lines and stakes will assist in determining the required angles, but it is to be understood that the angle specifications apply when the target is from 15 to 20 yards (14-18m) from the trap rather than where the target strikes the ground. However, no target is to be declared illegal unless it is more than 25 degrees outside the angles prescribed.

In doubles target shooting the recommended method of throwing targets shall be such that the right hand target shall be an approximately straightaway from firing point number 1 and the left hand target shall be an approximate straightaway from firing point number 5. However, no target shall be declared illegal unless it varies more than 25 degrees from these recommended angles.

Distance Handicaps. The distance handicaps when used shall be prolongations of the lines given in Diagram I, commonly known as fan shaped. The distance between firing points at 16 yards (14.6m) shall then be 3 yards (2.7m).

A common misconception is that once the first squad of an event has shot over a trap the trap cannot be reset unless it is throwing illegal targets. This is not true. Should, for some reason, a trap be throwing targets that, though not necessarily illegal, are so poorly thrown that it will appreciably affect the shooters score, any shooter may request that the management reset the trap. It will be the management's responsibility to decide if the trap(s) should be reset.

O. Trophies, Aids, And Requirements For States And Zones

1. Residence

No person, amateur or industry representative, may compete for ATA Trophies or titles in state or zone tournament, unless he or she for the preceding 6 months has been a bona fide resident of said state or zone. However, he or she may return to the former state or zone residence and compete for trophies.

In case there is a dispute with respect to the residence of a shooter attending a state or zone tournament, it shall be the duty of the state association or the zone officials in which the shoot is being held to rule as to said shooter's right to compete as a resident shooter. The ruling of the state association or zone official shall be final.

2. Targets Only

At all state and zone championship events in which ATA trophies are donated, contestants who are residents of that state or zone must be allowed to shoot for targets only, plus payment of ATA and state registration and/or zone fees in those events and be eligible to win ATA trophies and the respective championships.

3. At all shoots where ATA trophies are furnished a line referee must be provided by the host club or State Association.

4. Compulsory Purses

No compulsory purse and/or option shall be permitted at the Grand American and/or championship events at the State, Zone or Provincial tournaments.

5. State Aids

The ATA in its program of building strong state associations aids them financially. From the $10 membership, $2 is returned to the state organization. From the $150 life membership, $75 is returned to the state organization over a ten (10) year period and part is retained in a special ATA emergency fund. From the $1 daily fee you pay, twenty percent (20%) is returned to the state organization.

These are made to the state association 10 days prior to the State Tournament, provided such tournament is held and provided the state turns in to the ATA at least $200 from annual membership dues and registration fees. From this refund, there will be deducted an amount equal to that which is represented by "unpaid cards" of shooters from that state who shot in registered shoots without payment of annual membership dues, and any fines due because of late shoot reports. On or before January 1 of each year the ATA shall inform the secretary of each state of the approximate amount of refund to be paid to that State and this information must be printed in program for that annual State Tournament.

6. State ATA Trophies

The ATA will also donate to each state association trophies for the winners of the championships in singles, doubles, handicap, all-around and five (5) classes in either the Class or Singles Championships.

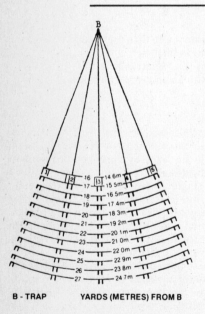

B - TRAP   **YARDS (METRES) FROM B**

Diagram I

Trap and Firing Positions

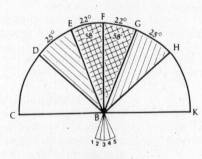

Diagram II
Legal Target Flight Area for 16 Yards and Handicap Shooting

1 to 5—Firing Points spaced 3 yards (2.7m) apart.
B—Trap.
CDEFGHK—Fifty yards (46m) from Trap.
BDEFGHB Shaded—Area of Legitimate Target.
BEFGB—Cross Hatched—Most desirable area in which to throw target.
3BF—Imaginary straight line through Trap and No. 3 Firing Position.
CBK—Imaginary straight line through trap at right angles to No. 3BF.
EF, FG—The distance between these points shall be a straight line 58 feet (17.7m) long.
Target elevation 8 to 12 feet (2.4 to 3.7m) above number 3 firing point at point M 30 feet (9m) in front of trap. Target distance 48 to 52 yards (44 to 48m).

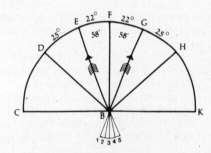

Diagram III
Double Target Shooting

1 to 5 Firing Points spaced 3 yards (2.7m) apart.
B—Trap, 16 yards (14.6) from Firing Points.
CDEFGHK—Fifty yards (46m) from Trap.
3BF—Imaginary straight line through Trap and No. 3 Firing Position.
CBK—Imaginary straight line through Trap at right angles at 3BF.
Arrows indicate recommended flight of target.
Distance of Targets' Flight—48 to 52 yards (44 to 48m).
EF, FG—The distance between these points shall be a straight line 58 feet (17.7m) long.
Elevation of target 8 to 12 feet (2.4 to 3.7m) above number three firing point at a distance of 30 feet (9M) in front of the trap.

The ATA will also donate trophies to the winners of the Ladies, Juniors, Sub-Juniors, and Veterans Championship 16 yard events. Nothing shall prevent a lady, junior, sub-junior or veteran champion from winning other ATA state championship trophies in the same or another event. *However, when there are both trophies, junior and sub-junior ATA trophy, the junior must take the junior trophy, and the sub-junior must take the sub-junior trophy regardless of the high score between the two of them.* Winners of ATA Championship trophies are not eligible for ATA class trophies in the same event. These rules should not be construed as governing trophies from other sources.

7. Championship Events At State Tournaments

The four state championships mentioned above shall be determined on the following:

Singles — 200 targets
Doubles — 50 pair
Handicap — 100 targets
All-Around — the sum of the above, 400 targets.

Ladies, Junior, Veterans, Sub-Junior, and any other championships, not included in the four mentioned above may be determined on a lesser number of targets at the discretion of the state shoot management.

8. Zone Aids

Zone officials may determine the division of the ATA added money for zone tournaments in the singles and doubles class championships and in the championship events of singles, handicap, and doubles. It shall be made available to all ATA registered shooters regardless of location. Unless the money is specifically restricted to zone residents at the discretion of the various ATA zones and it must be so stated in the zone programs.

9. Zone ATA Trophies

The ATA will donate trophies to the winners of the championships in Singles, Doubles, Handicap and All-Around. The ATA will also provide 5 Class trophies for Class Day and 5 Class Doubles for the Doubles Championships, and to the winners of each five classes in the Singles Championship events at each of the five ATA Zone Tournaments. Trophies will be presented to lady, junior, sub-junior and veteran zone champions in the Singles championship event.

Nothing shall prevent a lady, junior, sub-junior, or veteran from winning other Championship trophies in the same event. *However, when there are both junior and sub-junior ATA trophies, the junior must take the junior trophy and the sub-junior must take the sub-junior trophy regardless of the high score between them.* Winners of Championship trophies are not eligible for class trophies in the same event.

10. Championship Events At Zone Tournaments

Zone championships shall be determined on the following:

Singles — 200 targets
Doubles — 50 pair
Handicap — 100 targets
All-Around — the sum of the above, 400 targets
Class championships — a minimum of 100 targets (not to be shot concurrently with the Singles Championship).

Zone tournament programs shall call for a minimum of 600 targets.

P. Grand American Qualification

No shooter shall shoot Handicap events at the Grand American Tournament (except Veteran, Sr. Veterans, Ladies, and Sub-Juniors) at less than 25.0 yards unless he has a minimum of 1500 registered handicap targets recorded for that year and/or the previous 2 years, of which at least 500 handicap targets have been shot since October 1 of the previous year and not later than the Friday preceding the first regular day of the Grand American of the current year.

Veterans, Ladies, Sub-juniors who have not met the minimum target requirements above may shoot in any Grand American Handicap event from their assigned yardage provided they forfeit all rights to trophies, options and purses.

No shooter shall shoot 16 yard events at the Grand American Tournament in less than Class A unless he has a minimum of 1500 registered 16 yard targets recorded for that year and/or the previous two years of which at least 500 have been shot since October 1 of the previous year and not later than the Friday preceding the first regular day of the Grand American of the current year.

No shooter shall shoot doubles events at the Grand American Tournament in doubles classification less than Class A unless he has a minimum of 1000 registered doubles targets recorded for that year and/or the previous two years, of which 500 have been shot since October 1 of the previous year and not later than the Friday preceding the first regular day of the Grand American of the current year.

It shall be the shooter's responsibility to inform the Handicap Committee as to his or her target eligibility.

Yardage earned for high score and all ties in any Grand American handicap event shot in the regular program (does not include preliminary events) may not be removed in part or whole by any committee action prior to the end of the Grand American tournament the following year.

Q. Special Rules For Members Of Other Shooting Organizations

If a shooter is a member of any other trapshooting association or was a member of such association the preceding year *and* shot targets in such association in the current or preceding ATA target year, he or she will shoot from the handicap yardage of whichever association shows the greater yardage.

A member who, at any time has previously been a member of another trapshooting association must shoot their last assigned yardage in that association (if it is greater) unless they have received an ATA 1000 target review and receive a yardage reduction and have not shot that associations targets for the period of time prescribed in the above paragraph.

It will be the responsibility of the shooter to notify the shoot handicap committee if he or she holds or has held a card of another trapshooting association. Failure to notify the shoot handicap committee of another trapshooting association card may be cause for penalty action resulting in forfeiture of entry fees and all monies and possible suspension from all ATA shoots for one year.

R. Options And Money Divisions

1. Added Money. No tournament promoter shall be in any advertisement or program mention any purse or money in excess of the money actually added or guaranteed. Examples of money divisions may be included provided it is clearly stated that the amounts listed are examples and not guaranteed amounts. The word "example" must be included. Failure to observe the above provisions shall be grounds for disciplinary action by the state association and/or by the Executive Committee.

The ATA does not guarantee and is not responsible for actual payment of added money, guaranteed money and prizes advertised or offered at any shoot except the money, prizes and trophies directly supplied by ATA.

2. At every registered tournament the cashier or other official in charge, shall be required to post on the outside bulletin board the names of the contestants who have entered the purse, options and other monies. Optional purses, etc., may be played only by and for the contestant himself. Any club or cashier may deduct up to ½ of 1% of the gross amount of purse and options to help defray cost of computations. Breakage accumulated by rounding off, is to be considered part of the ½%.

The cashier shall have posted on the bulletin board the amount to be paid each purse or option winner. In the event payment is made by check after the shoot is over and the contestants have left the ground, a payoff sheet for unposted events must accompany each check showing the amount paid for each individual event or option included in the payment.

Any reasonable request to inspect the cashier sheets must be honored by the shoot management. A shooter or a gun club must file a written complaint or contest any payoff or trophy award within 60 days after the competition.

3. Calcuttas

The ATA does not condone or encourage calcuttas at any registered ATA Trapshoot.

S. Payment And Overpayments

Anyone who presents a check at any shoot for fees and targets that is returned for insufficient funds or for other causes, may not compete in any registered shoot until full payment has been made to individuals or club to which it was presented. Clubs receiving such a check shall report the name and address of the shooter issuing the check to the ATA along with a copy of the check and a statement that the check was for registered targets and/or fees. After having been reimbursed the club *must* immediately inform the ATA so that reinstatement proceedings may be initiated.

Any ATA member who has been suspended for presenting a check that is returned for insufficient funds or other causes and thereafter becomes eligible for reinstatement shall be required to pay $25 to the ATA as a reinstatement fee.

Any club which conducts a registered tournament should make payment of all added money, purses, optionals, and other moneys to the shooters as promptly as possible. Failure to do so within 15 days may result in the cancellation of registration privileges of that club for the remainder of the year, and no further registration shall be granted to that club until all moneys due to shooters, the ATA and state organizations have been paid. The persons responsible, and/or officers of such delinquent clubs, shall be barred from shooting registered targets until such payments have been made.

Any competitor at a registered shoot, who, through error, has been overpaid on any purse, added money, optional, or other awards, and who is notified of the overpayment by registered mail, must return the overpayment within 15 days. Failure to do so shall result in disbarment from all registered shoots until payment is made.

T. Challenge And Protest

Any contestant may challenge the load of any other contestant. On receipt of a challenge the management shall obtain a shell or shells from the challenged party, and if after examination, the management finds the contestant violated the ATA rule, he may be disqualified.

A protest concerning a score or scores must be made before or immediately after the close of the competition to which such scores relate. A protest may only be made by a contestant.

U. Disqualification

1. A shooter may be disqualified for an event or for a whole tounament by the management

   a. if in the opinion of the management he is disrupting the harmony of the shoot;
   b. if he shoots at any place other than the firing line;
   c. if he fails to shoot at the yardage assigned to him;
   d. if he has failed to have his card punched for earned yardage at a prior shoot;

   e. if he behaves in an ungentlemanly or disorderly manner;
   f. if he interferes with the management's procedures in conducting the shoot;
   g. if he does not respond and report to the firing line when his squad is called to shoot;
   h. if he does not abide by the rules of the ATA and by the rules set out by the management and/or in the official program

2. It is the required duty of any registered shoot management to immediately remove and disqualify any contestant who consumes alcholic beverages while participating in any event or who is under the obvious influence of alcohol or drugs before starting any event, or who handles a gun dangerously on or off the firing line by deliberately or carelessly violating gun safety precautions thereby endangering contestants, spectators, or gun club personnel.

3. Disqualification for a single event does not prevent a contestant from participating in other events in the same tournament, and scores shot in other events are not affected.

4. If the infraction is severe the management may disqualify the contestant for the entire tournament and require him to leave the grounds.

5. Disqualification for a tournament does not prevent a shooter from participating in other tournaments.

6. All entrance monies in events not competed in as a result of disqualification are to be returned in full. Events which have been started do not qualify for refunds due to disqualification.

7. Scores shot in an event or a tournament for which a shooter is disqualified will not be registered, and any trophies or monies which the contestant has received for an event for which he is disqualified MUST be returned.

V. Suspensions, Expulsions, And Reinstatement

1. The Executive Committee may suspend any shooter or discipline shoot management who:

   a. presents a check at any shoot for fees and targets that is returned for insufficient funds or other causes;
   b. falsifies his scores;
   c. fails to have his handicap card properly punched for earned yardage;
   d. fails to return any overpayment after proper notification;
   e. is convicted of any gun or firearms violation;
   f. willfully, deliberately, or repeatedly violates the rules of the ATA as contained in the Official Rules Book;
   g. whose behavior constitutes cause for suspension in the opinion of the Executive Committee.

2. A shooter who is suspended is barred from shooting ATA targets or otherwise participating in ATA activities for the period of his suspension.

3. If the Executive Committee feels the violations warrant suspension for longer than 1 year, or expulsion, the member shall have the right of appeal if he complies with the terms and provisions of the By-Laws.

4. The procedure for suspension or disciplinary action is as follows:

   a. All complaints of violations of ATA rules by individuals and/or gun clubs, whether made to the ATA headquarters or to any ATA official, shall be immediately called to the attention of the ATA state or provincial delegate representing the state in which the alleged violation occurred.
   b. The delegate will then proceed to obtain such complaint in writing, specifying the exact rule(s) violated along with full details. The delegate shall make an immediate investigation and confirm, to the best of his ability, the details of the incident in question.
   c. Within ten (10) days of the first notice of the complaint,

and after complying with paragraph (b), above, the delegate shall serve written notice of the complaint upon the alleged violator, by certified mail, receipt requested, and require a written reply within ten (10) days of receipt. A copy of such notice of complaint shall at the same time be sent to the zone vice-president, along with a copy of the supporting file.

d. Upon receipt of any answer from the alleged violator, or if no such answer is received within the ten days, the delegate shall confer with such state officers as he deems necessary, and recommend appropriate action to the zone vice-president within seven (7) days.

e. The zone vice-president, upon receipt of the delegate's recommendation(s) shall review the entire file and write his own recommendations, with supporting facts, to all members of the Executive Committee within ten (10) days.

f. All other members of the Executive Committee will, within seven (7) days, advise the ATA president of their agreement or disagreement with the recommendations of the zone vice-president.

g. The ATA president will then immediately cause appropriate action to be taken in accordance with the majority vote of the Executive Committee Suspensions and/or expulsions made under this section shall conform to the applicable provisions pertaining thereto as fully set forth in the Amateur Trapshooting Association of America.

5. Reinstatement

Any ATA shooter who has been suspended for any cause must pay a $25 reinstatement fee when his period of suspension is completed or when, in the case of returned checks, he has reimbursed the club where the check was written.

W. Industry Personnel

Any person who (a) receives compensation for shooting or for the display or sale of the products or merchandise of any firm, company, corporation, or individual engaged in the manufacture, fabrications, importation, distribution, sale or servicing of arms, parts, ammunition, components, clay targets, or other products or services related to trapshooting or (b) received any allowance, remuneration (whether partial or total), or other consideration for attending, shooting at, or otherwise participating in trapshooting events, shall be deemed an Industry Representative upon receipt by the ATA of his or her written declaration setting forth such relationship and expressing the intention to be designated an Industry Representative. No Industry Representative shall compete for money or trophies in registered tournaments, except those events especially provided for Industry Representatives. An exception to this rule is tournaments sponsored by Indian, fraternal or similar organization and those events clearly designated as open to both Amateurs and Industry Representatives.

An Industry Representative may regain amateur standing after termination of the relationship which qualified him for designation as an Industry Representative by furnishing written certification thereof to the ATA via Registered or Certified Mail post-paid to the Manager, Vandalia, Ohio 45377. When he receives his new amateur card from ATA, he will then be classified as an amateur.

X. Amateurs

Unless a shooter qualifies as an "industry personnel," that shooter is considered an amateur and shall be entitled to all rights as set forth in these rules.

Y. All-America Team Requirements

	16's	Hd	Dbls
Men	3000	2000	1000
Women, Juniors	2500	1500	750
Sub-Juniors, Veterans	2000	1000	500
Sr. Veterans, Industry	2000	1000	500

1. Men must have competed in at least three different states; other categories in at least two states.

2. A person's age on Monday of the Grand American determines category.

3. The proper form for team consideration may be submitted to the ATA office before October 31st. This form is available at the Grand or by request from the ATA office or Trap & Field.

IV
The ATA Handicap System

The ATA Handicap system is the method whereby shooters whose ability to win has been demonstrated and shooters whose ability is unknown are handicapped by shooting a greater distance from the trap house. The minimum handicap is 17.0 yards and the maximum is 27.0 yards. A shooter's yardage is determined by rules governing new shooters, by yardage earned, or by his established handicap yardage which is based on known ability and 1000 target reviews.

At each State or Provincial shoot the handicapping and classifying shall be the responsibility of a committee appointed by the state association with the ATA delegate as chairman.

A. Central Handicap Committee

1. The Central Handicap Committee, made up of a chairman and 5 or more members, is appointed by the Executive Committee.

2. It is the responsibility of the Central Handicap Committee to control yardage of all members of the ATA. Any Central Handicap Committee member may increase a shooter's yardage at his discretion when applying the known ability rule. The only others authorized to increase a shooter's yardage are members of the Executive Committee.

B. Known Ability

Handicap and 16 yard averages and/or scores in both registered and non-registered shoots may be used as the basis for determining known ability. Scores abnormally low in relation to the remainder of the scores shot may be disregarded at the discretion of the handicap committee.

C. Earned Yardage

1. Yardage will be automatically earned by shooters of high scores in all ATA registered events, according to the table following. This additional yardage is indicated by punches on the shooter's handicap card.

Earned Yardage Table
High Scores (and all ties)

Number of Shooters	1st	2nd	3rd	4th	5th
15-24	½ yd.				
25-49	1 yd.	½ yd.			
50-124	1 yd.	½ yd.	½ yd.		
125-249	1 yd.	1 yd.	½ yd.		
250-499	1½ yds.	1 yd.	½ yd.	½ yd.	
500-1499	2 yds.	1½ yds.	1 yd.	½ yd.	
1500-and-up	2½ yds.	2 yd.	1½ yds.	1 yd.	½ yd.

2. Any score of 96 will automatically earn ½ yard provided it does not earn at least that much under the earned yardage table. Any score of 50 x 50 or 75 x 75 in events of that length will automatically earn ½ yard provided it does not earn at least that much under the earned yardage table.

3. The State Handicap Champion will automatically earn 1 yard.

4. Any score of 97, 98 and 99 will automatically earn 1 yard, a score of 100 will autommtically earn 1½ yard provided these scores do not earn at least that much under the earned yardage table.

5. The earned yardage table applies to events of 50, 75, or 100 handicap targets.

6. In case of handicap events of more than 100 targets, each 100 targets (or remaining part of 100 targets) shall constitute a separate event for earned yardage purposes and shall be reported as a separate event on the shoot report forms.

7. A shooter's card will be punched from the yardage actually shot. *It is the shooter's responsibility to see that this handicap card is properly punched before shooting another handicap event. Failure to do so will make him subject to disqualification or suspension.*

8. Industry shooters shall not be counted in determining the number of shooters in an event for earned yardage purposes. The number of amateurs starting the event will be the number used for the earned yardage table.

9. Any industry shooter whose score equals or exceeds that of an amateur earning yardage under the earned yardage table shall earn a like increase in yardage.

D. Penalty Yardage

The management of registered shoots may establish penalty yardage, if said conditions are printed in the program. In no event shall any shooter be assigned a handicap of less than the minimum yardage appearing on his handicap card.

E. Special Handicap Rules

1. A shooter must continue to shoot from the last yardage assigned or earned until he receives a target review, regardless of the length of time that has elapsed since that yardage was assigned or earned.

2. A shooter's handicap yardage may be reduced only as a result of a 1000 target review or a special review. No reduction may be made in the field.

3. A shooter's handicap yardage may be increased at any time during the year including immediately before and during the Grand American Tournament.
   a. because of earned yardage or
   b. as a result of a review or
   c. at the discretion of a member of the Central Handicap or Executive Committee.

4. A shooter at all times shall have the right to appeal any committee action to the Executive Committee.

5. Yardage earned for high score and ties in any Grand American handicap event in the regular program (does not include preliminary events) may not be removed in part or whole by any committee action prior to the end of the Grand American Tournament the following year.

6. If a shooter earns increased yardage while a reduction is in process the reduction shall automatically be void.

7. When multiple 100 target handicap events (marathon) are shot in the same day, only two 100 targets events may be considered as a maximum per day towards reduction. The two events considered out of the marathon must be those two in which the two highest scores are registered.

F. Reviews
1. —1000 Target Review

The shooting record of each member will be automatically reviewed for possible yardage changes after each 1000 registered handicap targets shot in the current and previous year if no yardage was earned.

   a. A shooter with a low purified handicap average accompanied by a relative 16 yard average will, with the approval of his state delegate, receive a one yard reduction, *except*

*(1)*No shooter will be reduced more than 2 yards in any target year.
*(2)*The known ability rule will be used in assessing a shooter's record.

   b. A shooter with a high purified handicap average will receive a "Special Review" for possible yardage increase.
   c. If a yardage change is made, the shooter will receive by mail a new membership card with the assigned yardage.

2. —Special Review

A "Special Review" is an evaluation by the Central Handicap Committee generated by a high purified average on a 1000 target review or initiated by a shooter through his state delegate or the Central Handicap Committeeman. The results of a Special Review shall be agreed upon by the Central Handicap Committee and the shooter's state delegate. If after a reasonable communication, a disagreement in yardage assignment exists between the state delegate and the Central Handicap Committee, the matter may be directed to the Executive Committee. A special Review may be used:
   a. To determine possible yardage increases for shooters showing high purified handicap averages on a 1000 target review.
   b. To determine possible yardage reduction for a shooter because of advancing age or physical disability. The review may be initiated by a shooter through his state delegate.

3. —Assigned Yardage Increase
   a. To consider appeals from increased yardage by assignment, a member may appeal an assigned yardage increase by writing to the ATA office after having shot 500 targets at the assigned yardage. However, for any further reduction, 1000 additional handicap targets must be shot.
   b. There will be no yardage increase by shooter request.
   c. *The only persons authorized to decrease or increase a member's handicap yardage are the members of the central handicap committee and the executive committee.*

V
Requirements And Recommendations For Conducting A Registered Shoot
A. Application

Proper blanks, obtained from the ATA (or local state secretaries) should be filled out and mailed to the state secretary for approval. If there are club dues or other obligations in your state, these must be enclosed with applications.

If application is in order, your state secretary will approve and forward it to ATA for certification registration.

Upon receipt of the approved application blank, the ATA will issue the registration certificate, provided all conditions of application have been met and that the date requested will not conflict with the dates of a tournament granted to another club or association in close proximity. The question of close proximity is left to the judgment of the officials of the state. A record of the issuance of this certificate of registration will be kept on file in the office of the ATA, prior to the holding of the tournament, necessary office supplies for the proper recording of scores will be sent to the club or association. Each gun club that throws ATA registered targets must have on file in the ATA office a signed affidavit that the traps used meet the specifications. The state ATA Delegate is responsible for the enforcement of this rule.

B. Preparation And Programs

1. Programs should be sent to an up-to-date list of shooters. It is recommended that the total amounts of money spent on trophies be included in the program.

It is required that ATA Shoot programs indicate the specific amount collected on behalf of the ATA and it is further required that such fees be set apart as a separate fee from all other fees and charges made by shoot management. No tournament promoter shall in any advertisement or program mention any purse or money in excess of the money actually added or guaranteed. Examples of money divisions may be included provided it is clearly stated that the amounts listed are examples and not guaranteed amounts. The word "example" must be included. Failure to observe the above provisions shall be grounds for disciplinary action by the state association and/or by the Executive Committee.

The ATA does not guarantee and is not responsible for actual payments of added money, guaranteed money and prizes advertised or offered at any shoot except the money, prizes and trophies directly supplied by ATA.

2. The management should ascertain that the gun club facilities are in good condition prior to the shoot and that an adequate supply of such things as shells, targets, bulletin sheets, squad sheet, scoring crayons, thumb tacks, average books, change, and spare trap parts is on hand. Adequate toilet facilities should be provided for, as well as drinking water and lunch.

C. Checklist For The Shoot

1. The management should arrange for:

a. Capable classifying and handicapping committee

b. Competent cashiers who will figure purses and options correctly and pay off as many events as possible before the close of the shoot.

c. Squadding personnel

(Note—At small shoots, all three of the above may be done by the same person or persons.)

d. Sufficient and trained trappers who are provided with a safety flag or other warning device to indicate when they are exiting the trap house.

e. Referees who know the ATA rules and whose decision on whether a target is dead or lost is final, subject to review only by the shoot committee or other governing body.

f. Scorers who have been adequately trained to call all targets, or only the lost targets as directed, and to record the scores correctly on the sheets provided.

g. Pullers who must be provided with an unobstructed view of shooters. It is illegal at an ATA shoot for shooters to supply their own pullers.

(Note—One person may serve as puller, scorer, and referee. If the person or persons serving in these capacities is negligent or inefficient, the management shall remove him or them.)

h. Any additional help needed to conduct the tournament efficiently, such as squad hustler, score board recorder, score sheet runners, and enough personnel to properly operate a shooting facility.

2. The management of any registered tournament, at its discretion, may reject any entry, or refund any entry. In all cases except as otherwise provided in these rules, the authority of the management of a registered shoot is supreme and all contestants must abide by its rulings.

3. The management shall appoint a judge or judges to be called upon for ruling on various matters when the occasion arises. If a judge has not been appointed, the president of the club, or in his absence, the secretary shall act as judge. The scorer must call upon a judge to settle any controversy regarding a score or when he has made an error by being ahead or behind in his scoring.

The officials of the ATA will not change the decisions of these persons made in accordance with these rules, or change the report of any shoot held in accordance with these rules.

4. At every registered tournament all targets on the official program shall be registered. Registered scores which have been made by any contestant as a result of duplicating any portion of the regularly advertised program will not be recorded. Special events may be held and the scores registered provided that shooters have been notified of such special events by shoot management, that the special event is announced and posted, and that at least five entries shoot and complete the special event.

5. The sponsors of registered tournaments are responsible for the payment of all added money, guaranteed money, purses, and/or prizes advertised or offered in their shoot programs. If the management of a registered shoot does not meet the above obligations, the ATA is not responsible for such payments and will not be liable.

6. The management shall see that the cards of any shooters earning yardage are punched. If for any reason a card is not punched at the shoot, the gun club should immediately inform the ATA, the shooter, and the shooter's State ATA Delegate in writing.

D. Follow Up Duties

Following the conclusion of a tournament the management is responsible or should delegate the responsibility for

1. Completing and sending to the ATA office:

a. The ATA report form with complete names, addresses, ATA card numbers, and accurate scores of all shooters

b. The earned yardage report.

c. Names and addresses of those paying ATA dues at the shoot.

d. A check for ATA daily fees collected at the shoot

e. One copy of the official shoot program

This must be done within 15 days following the last day of the registered shoot to avoid a $25 late shoot report fine which will be deducted from the rebate to the State in which the shoot is held.

2. Sending State fees collected to the State Association.

3. Sending a copy of the shoot report to *Trap & Field*

4. Reporting shoot results to the local radio and TV stations and the local newspapers

5. Making sure that scores are reported on any sub-events of 25 targets which is completed. In case the shooter is prevented by reasons beyond his control from completing a 25 target sub-event, the scores for that partial sub-event shall not be reported. Example, a shooter has shot 61 targets of a 100 target event when a storm permanently stops shooting. The mangement should report his scores for the first 50 targets only.

E. Keeping Shoot Records

The tournament management is responsible for keeping the records from all registered shoots for at least one year.

F. Gun Club Liability Insurance

Under a member group liability insurance program adopted by the ATA in August, 1979, gun clubs are eligible for special liability insurance provided they qualify as ATA Gun Clubs by holding a minimum of two (2) ATA registered tournaments each target year, with proper application and payment of premiums.

Insurance rate information and claims requests should be made directly to the ATA Insurance Administrator, Albert H. Wohlers & Co., 1500 Higgins Road, Park Ridge, IL 60068, or call toll-free 800-323-2106.

National Skeet Shooting Association Official Rules

SECTION I—EQUIPMENT

A. Targets

Standard targets of good quality measuring no more than four and five-sixteenth (4⁵⁄₁₆) inches in diameter nor more than one and one-eight (1⅛) inches in height shall be used.

B. Ammunition

1. Gauge Specifications—Lead shot only.

Shells commercially manufactured by reputable companies, which are clearly labeled and guaranteed as to lead shot sizes and weight are recommended for use in registered Skeet shoots. However, the National Skeet Shooting Association will accept results of shoots and register scores where reloads have been sanctioned by member clubs subject to state or regional association approval. Any shooter who will use reloads in a registered event must signify his intention to do so at time of entry. The National Skeet Shooting Association assumes no responsibility in connection with the use of reloads.

2. Checking Reloads

a. It shall be permissible for the shoot management to appoint a person, usually the chief referee, to pick a shell at random any time during each shooting event from each contestant using reloads. This shell is to be tagged with the shooter's name, witnessed by the shooter, and the shot load is to be weighed by management. If the load exceeds the maximum load permissible, as described below, the shooter's score will be disqualified. This table makes ample allowance for manufacturing purposes, but the use of a proper shot bar is cautioned (a 12-gauge bar designed for 7½ shot will weigh approximately 11 grains heavy when No. 9 shot is used). Shooters are to replace shells at their own cost. No refunds will be made when a score is disqualified.

Gauge	Ounce Lead	Grains Standard	Grains Maximum
12	1⅛	492.2	507
20	⅞	382.8	394
28	¾	328.1	338
410	½	218.8	229

To minimize interference with a squad, shooters should be asked to display their shells by a handful from each pocket. Further the shell selection should be made as the entire squad progresses from any station to the next station.

b. Any shooter may elect to have his shells weighed by management before entering an event. The shooter must submit all shells to be used in said event. After one shell is selected, weighed and approved by these standards, the balance of the shells shall be stamped, approved and sealed by some suitable method and not be opened until on the field where the event is to be shot in the presence of the field referee. Failure to have the field referee witness the breaking of the sealed boxes of containers on their respective fields shall necessitate the shooter using factory ammunition or having his score disqualified. Any shooter using approved and sealed ammunition shall be immune from further checking.

3. Checking factory loads

Any shooter found to be deliberately using commercial loads heavier than the maximum grains permissible as listed in 1-B-2-a shall have his score disqualified for that event.

4. Challenge rule

At shoots where shells have not been checked any contestant may, upon formal challenge presented to the shoot management, have the chief referee, who shall use timely discretion, select a shell from another contestant and have said shell checked as per Sect.1-B-2 or 1-B-3. To prevent abuse of a shooter with this rule, shoot management shall make known the challenger and the individual challenged. Entire groups or squads cannot be challenged for purposes of anonymity.

5. Shooters using reloads shall be required to furnish their own spares for defective ammunition.

C. Field Layout

A Skeet field shall consist of eight shooting stations arranged on a segment of a circle of twenty-one (21) yards radius, with a base chord exactly one hundred twenty (120) feet, nine (9) inches long, drawn six (6) yards from the center of the circle. The center of the circle is known as the target-crossing point and is marked by a stake. Station 1 is located at the left end of the base while standing on the periphery of the segment. Stations 2 to 6, inclusive, are relocated on the periphery at points equidistant from each other. The exact distance between Stations 1 and 2, 2 and 3, etc., is twenty-six (26) feet, eight and three-eights (8⅜) inches. Station 8 is located at the center of the base chord.

Shooting Station 1 and 7, each a square area, three feet on a side, shall have two sides parallel to the base chord. Shooting stations 2 to 6, inclusive, each a square area, three feet on a side, shall have two sides parallel to the base chord.

Shooting stations 2 to 6, inclusive, each a square area, three feet on a side, shall have two sides parallel to a radius of the circle drawn through the station marker. Shooting Station 8 is rectangular area 3 feet wide by 6 feet long, with the long sides parallel to the base chord. The marker for shooting station 8 is on the center point of the base chord.

The location of each shooting station shall be accurately designated. The marker for shooting stations 1-7, inclusive is on the center of the side nearest the target crossing point. At Station 8 the shooter will stand on the most distant half of the 3-foot rectangular pad from the respective high or low house.

A shield should be installed at the target opening of each Skeethouse so that the Skeet operator is not visible to the shooter when he is firing at Station 8. This precaution is desirable as a safety factor for the protection of the Skeet boy from possible injury from direct or ricocheting shot. As a safety precaution there shall be a barrier (wire, chain or rope) located between the shooting stations and the spectators. No spectators shall be allowed within this barrier and the referee shall be responsible for the enforcement of this rule. This barrier shall be mandatory at all state, regional and world championship shoots.

One target should emerge from a Skeethouse (called high house) at a point three (3) feet beyond Station Marker 1 (measured along the base chord extended), and ten (10) feet above the ground level. The other should emerge from a Skeethouse (called low house) at a point three (3) feet beyond Station Marker 7 (measured along the base chord extended), and two and one-half (2½) feet from the base chord extended (measure on side of target-crossing point), and three and one-half (3½) feet above the ground.

Suitable markers shall be placed at points forty-four (44) yards and sixty (60) yards from both the high house and the low house to indicate the shooting boundary limit (44 yards). These distances shall be measured along a line and the flight of a regular target (60 yards) from the opening (where target emerges) in Skeethouse through the target-crossing point. It is recommended that the 60-yard distance markers be suitably marked to indicate Station 8 ground level where possible.

The target-crossing point must be marked in a visible manner where physically possible. It is recommended to remove posts or box stands tangent to the front of the stations interfering with the shooter.

Each Skeet mount at world championship sites must be approved by the Skeet manufacturers and by a NSSA appointed representative. Unusual or undesirable field variations must be corrected before contract negotiations are completed.

It is recommended and desirable that the side of the Skeet house, from the bottom of the chute to the top of the house, be very light color or painted white where feasible.

Mandatory Positions for Referees

For shooting Station 1 (1R), stand six feet to the right and three feet back of the front of Station 1 where possible.

For shooting Station 2 (2R), stand six feet back and three feet to the right of Station 2.

For shooting Station 3, 4, 5 and 6 (3-4-5-6R), stand six feet back and three feet to the left of the respective station.

For shooting Station 7 (7R), stand six feet to the left and three feet back of the front of Station 7 where possible.

For shooting Station 8 (8R) stand on center line of the field, not less than 6 feet from shooter (and not more than 10 feet).

During "Doubles" shooting, as shooters are coming back around the circle, referees should stand six feet back and three feet to the right of station 5, 4, and 3.

Exception: A shooter may request the referee to move behind the station at station 3 or 5.

Recommended Positions for Shooters

It is recommended for courtesy to team members that shooters do not advance more than one-third of the way to the next shooting station until all shooters on the squad have completed the station. Furthermore, shooters should stand a minimum of six feet outside the shooting circle while waiting to shoot.

Recommended Procedure for Setting Distance on Targets

It is recommended to adjust the Skeet machine spring to a tension that will just reach the 60-yard stake, passing near dead center on the target setting hoop, under a "no wind" condition. Once this setting is made, it is unnecessary to change the spring tension during a tournament unless the spring becomes defective. The prevailing wind during a shoot may cause the targets to fall far short or long, but they are legal targets providing they pass through the setting hoop.

Clubs encountering too much target breakage may set the target as short as 55 yards under "no wind" conditions and they are still legal. Weakened springs should be replaced because over-tightening can result in spring and housing breakage.

SECTION II — REGISTERED SHOOTS

A. General

1. Identification of eligible shooters

Members shall receive a new classification card as soon as possible after October 31.

a. This card will be of high quality paper and is to be used throughout the shooting year. Classification cards will be a different color each year for ease of identification. Replacement cards can be obtained from NSSA home office if lost or accidentally destroyed.

b. Presentation of a classification card, indicating a member's shooting record and paid-up membership status, and plastic NSSA membership card is required for entry in a registered shoot.

c. Classification for the beginning of the year shall be indi-

cated in the appropriate place on each classification-shoot record card.

d. These cards also shall contain columns in which the holders are to keep their up-to-date running averages posted for each gun.

2. Qualifications and Responsibilites

a. Club

(1) Only clubs affiliated with the NSSA with affiliation fees currently paid up for the year concerned shall be eligible to conduct registered shoots. Evidence of club's status in this regard must be displayed in the form of official NSSA membership certificate for the appropriate year. Only clubs also affiliated and in good standing with their state or territorial association will be permitted to hold registered shoots in areas where such associations are active.

(2) Where state territorial associations exist, application for a registered shoot must be made through those bodies, which in turn, after giving approval, will submit application to the NSSA, which will issue proper certification and supplies on which to report scores, winners and make financial report. Where an area association does not exist, clubs will make application directly to the NSSA. The application form furnished by the NSSA shall include the number of targets in each event and may not be altered without 10 days notice. Shoot applications, properly sanctioned, must be postmarked or received by NSSA at least 10 days prior to the shoot date. Open shoots should be advertised to a majority of local contestants, and closed club shoots posted a minimum of seven days prior to the shoot date. Failure to so advertise may result in a disqualification of shoot scores. Exception may, however, be granted by the Executive Director on merit.

(3) It shall be the responsibility of the management of the club, association or other organization granted a certificate of registration, to see that each shoot is conducted in accordance with the official rules of the NSSA.

(4) The group or club sponsoring the shoot shall check the NSSA membership of each shooter before accepting his entry and shall be responsible for the annual dues if they allow a participant to shoot when said participant's membership in NSSA has expired.

All individual shooters in all registered shoots must be members in good standing of the NSSA. *It shall be the responsibility of the club holding registered shoot to check cards of all participants and enforce this rule rigidly.*

Management will be billed by NSSA in all cases where expired members are allowed to shoot. Management may seek reimbursement from said shooters.

(5) Management shall check the shooter's classification card to ascertain the proper classifications in which he should compete and enter on the shooter's classification card the classification in which it is entering him in each gun.

(6) Class winners must be reported if they are to be reported in the magazine.

(7) Scores shot in shoots on which complete records are not made by shoot management will not be recorded and the national association shall not be liable to refund fees received in such cases.

(8) It is the shoot management's responsibility to appoint a chief referee.

(9) Registered shooting at night is permissible. Applications for night registered shoots by clubs must designate on the face of application that it will be night shoot and all promotion by club shall clearly indicate that it is a night shoot. All scores recorded for night registered shoots will receive the same treatment as any other registered shoot. Participants in night registered shoots must accept the con-

ditions at the club where the shoot is held and no protest concerning shooting conditions, i.e. light conditions, natural or artificial, etc., will be allowed. At night registered shoots, white targets must be used.

(10) In the interest of safety, interference and time, only the club management's personnel shall be permitted to pick up empty shells from the grounds during a registered shoot, and extreme care must be exercised to prevent interference with other squads shooting.

(11) Shoot management shall determine the number of targets to be shot on a field. When shooting background is fairly uniform, it saves time to shoot 50 or 100 on the same field.

(12) Shoot management has the right to determine the rotation and shooting sequence of events, in their program, as well as shooting mixed guns in squads, unless their state association rules otherwise.

(13) All two-man and five-man events must be limited to club teams *unless* management exercises their prerogative of holding open or state team events duly announced in the program, or posted prior to acceptance of the first entry.

b. Individuals

(1) Residents of a state or territory must be members in good standing of their own state or territorial association before they can register targets shot in that state.

(2) It shall be the sole responsibility of the shooters to see that they are entered into all the events desired. The official cashier sheet/entry form must be used. Once entered, clerical errors are the responsibility of shoot management.

(3) Each shooter must verify his score and initial the official score sheet before leaving each field or accept it as the record. It shall be the responsibility of every shooter to enter in his proper class or classes at each shoot, including advancing himself in class when required by the rules based on averages at the completion of the regular string.

(4) A shooter who fails to keep all of his correct scores posted on his card and shoots in a lower class than the one in which his record places him shall forfeit any winnings earned while shooting in the wrong class for the first offense, and for the second offense shall forfeit all winnings and also be disbarred from registered competition for one year.

A shooter winning trophies or money by shooting in a lower class than the one in which he was entitled to shoot must return his winnings within 15 days after notification by NSSA headquarters that said winnings must be returned. Failure to comply within this 15-day period shall subject the shooter to suspension as an NSSA member and permanent disbarment from registered competition.

A shooter who enters, or allows himself to be entered in an event in a class lower than the class in which he was entitled to shoot forfeits all rights to any trophies or purses he would have earned shooting in his proper class unless the mistake is corrected prior to the distribution of such trophies or purse money.

(5) It is the responsibility of the shooter to see that his safety is off and his gun is properly loaded with unfired shells of proper size and load before calling for a target (for safety purposes).

3. Shooting order

The management shall determine the shooting order of the individuals in each squad at the beginning of the round, and the shooters shall adhere to this order.

If the order is changed during any succeeding round of the same event, each squad member shall be responsible that his name be in the proper order on the respective score sheet, and that the change be plainly indicated for the attention of the final recorder.

Each squad shall report to the field at its appointed time. Upon failure of a shooter to appear at the appointed time, where a regular schedule has been posted in advance, or after proper call, the squad shall proceed without the absent shooter and the offender be dropped to the first vacancy in the schedule, or if there is no vacancy, to the bottom of the list. Weather conditions shall not be deemed sufficient excuse for delay in taking the field or proceeding with the round, unless all shooting has been officially suspended at the discretion of the management.

4. Squadding restrictions

The squadding or practice shooting in a registered event shall not be allowed. Violations of this rule shall be sufficient cause for non-registration of all scores in the squad.

Exception: *If there should be a single entry in the last squad of any event, shoot management may allow no more than two additional shooters to shoot for practice, but only if requested to do so by the lone entry and said last squad.* Pacer for lone participant on a field in shootoff shall not be permitted.

5. Checks—payments, over-payments

Anyone who presents a check at any shoot that is returned for insufficient funds or other causes, may not compete in any registered shoot until full payment has been made to the individual or club to which it was presented. Any club receiving such a check shall report name and address of the shooter issuing the check to the NSSA and to its own state, territorial or district association.

Any competitor at a registered shoot who, through error, has been overpaid on any purse, added money, optional or other prize money and who is notified of the over-payment by registered mail, must return the over-payment within fifteen days. Failure to do so shall result in disbarment from all registered shoots until repayment is made.

B. Standard Event Specification

For the purpose of uniformity in records, averages, etc., the following provisions shall apply to all shoots registered or sanctioned by the NSSA.

1. Gauge specifications

12 gauge events shall be open to all guns of 12 gauge or smaller, using shot loads not exceeding one and one-eighth (1⅛) ounces. Twenty gauge events shall be open to all guns of 20 gauge or smaller, using shot loads not exceeding seven-eighths (⅞) of an ounce. Twenty-eight gauge events shall be open to all guns of 28 gauge or smaller, using shot loads not exceeding three-quarters (¾) of an ounce and .410 gauge guns using shot loads not exceeding one-half (½) ounce. A gun of larger gauge, which has been converted to take a smaller gauge shell may be used in an event for which it has been converted providing that the shell itself complies with the rules requirements for that event. No shot smaller than No. 9 (2mm) shall be used in any load.

2. Concurrent events

a. Events designated for veterans, seniors, sub-seniors, sub-sub seniors, women, juniors, sub-juniors, military service, two-man team or five-man team, may be shot concurrently with the corresponding event on the regular program, or separately, at the discretion of the management.

b. *No junior, sub-junior or collegiate shall be required to pay any part of entry fee that is to be returned to the shooters in the form of money, including open purses and concurrent purses, but not to include team events if the involved junior, sub-junior or collegiate is shooting as part of an open team.*

3. All-around titles

All-around titles must be an aggregate of all gauges offered in that registered tournament (special events such as preliminary events, Champion of Champions, etc., not to be included) and will officially be recognized by the NSSA only when they include championships or title events in at least three of the four standard gauges and load divisions defined in paragraph No. 1 above and a total of at least 200 targets. Provided that the foregoing shall not be deemed to forbid local awards of special prizes for events of combinations not recognized.

4. Minimum number of targets

No event of less than fifty (50) targets shall be designated as a championship or title event.

5. Open shoot registration

The term "open," as it may appear in any application for registration or sanction, or in the shoot program, if any, shall be deemed to mean "open to NSSA members without regard to residence."

6. Method of Breaking Ties

In all registered NSSA tournaments, ties shall be decided in a uniform manner as prescribed in the following paragraph unless the shoot management gives due notice of any deviation in its published shoot programs, or unless in the absence of a shoot program the shoot management post conspicuous notice of deviation at the place of registration, thus informing all shooters of deviation, before accepting entry fees.

a. All ties for championship titles, such as event champion, two-man and five-man teams, veterans, seniors, sub-seniors, women, juniors, sub-juniors, junior women, military, or any other concurrent title designated by the management, must be shot off by "miss-and-out" (sudden death). *Where the same individuals are tied for concurrent titles, such as event champion and senior champion, only one shootoff will be held to determine both titles, unless the shoot management announced in advance of the first shootoff that separate shootoffs will be held.* Management may combine other shootoffs only by approval of all the individuals involved in same.

b. After determining the position of all persons involved in shootoffs, all other awards shall be decided on the basis of the longest run in the event, forward beginning with the first target shot at or backward beginning with the last target shot at *(whichever is longest)*. If long runs are tied, the long run from the opposite end shall be used to break the tie. If long runs are still tied, "miss-and-out" shootoffs must decide.

c. Long runs for team scores shall be the total of targets broken by the members of the team combined up to the first miss by any member of the team; or the total number of targets broken by all members of the team after the last miss by any member of the team, whichever run is longest.

d. All ties for all-around championship must be decided by a miss-and-out shootoff commencing with the smallest gauge gun of which the all-around score is comprised. If a tie remains after this round, then the next larger gauge shall be employed for the next round. If a tie remains after all gauges have been employed, the shootoff shall revert back to the smallest gauge.

e. All other tied scores for all around awards shall be decided on the basis of the longest run from front or rear *(whichever is longest) in the smallest gauge event.* If this also results in a tie, the same method shall be applied to the next larger gauge until the tie is broken.

f. Shootoffs take precedence over long runs, so all persons competing in a shootoff must continue to shoot off for all places beneath the event championship for which they may be tied.

7. NSSA rules of procedure for shootoffs

NSSA rules shall apply subject to the following:

a. Shoot management may elect to use regular Skeet or a doubles event and shall follow NSSA rules for whichever event elected.

b. In employing doubles for shootoffs a (50) target event is not required. Further, shoot management may elect "miss-and-out" or full round total score for doubles shootoffs.

c. In shooting using total score of a complete round, the shooter with the highest score shall be determined the winner. Tied high scores must continue to shoot complete rounds until the tie is broken and the winners determined. Lesser place winners shall be decided by the highest scores and if a tie exists, long run from the front shall determine these winners, if still ties, continue to shoot until the tie is broken.

d. In "miss-and-out" shootoffs, long run from the front shall determine the winners. Ties shall continue to shoot the round until the tie is broken.

e. For Two and Five-Man Team Shootoff management may combine or separate teams for shootoffs; and

(1) If "miss-and-out," team winners shall be determined by the full team shooting until the first miss and comparing this long run with other squads involved. Any squads tied with long runs shall continue to shoot their rounds until the tie is broken.

(2) If "total score," the total of the team scores shall determine the winner.

f. Shoot management shall post notice of time of shootoff as soon as possible during each event and shall also announce same by the public address system if possible.

g. Contestants involved in shootoffs forfeit all rights to the shootoff if absent or if they do not report within five minutes of the time the shootoff is called. However, any such person shall be entitled to any award he would have won by finishing last in the shootoff. It shall be the shooter's sole responsibility to determine the time of the shootoff before leaving the grounds. Shootoffs may not be held prior to the completion of an event (registration for the event has closed and no possible ties or winners left on the field) or of events of that day *unless all parties involved agree.*

h. If completion of shootoff is prevented by darkness, as defined in Sect. IV-C, the management and the contestants concerned shall determine the champion by a mutually agreeable method, but if no mutually agreeable method can be decided upon, then the shoot management shall determine in what manner the ties shall be decided. Management should make every effort to schedule the last squad of the day early enough to permit normal shootoffs.

i. If shooters involved in a shootoff offer management a mutually agreed upon method of determining the places, management may accept. If management does not accept, shootoffs must continue and any shooter or shooters who refuse to continue forfeit as in paragraph "g" above.

Declaring of event co-champions at the world championship shall not be permitted. Contestants must continue to shoot or forfeit.

j. The shooting order for shootoffs shall be the sequence of finishing the event, where possible, and each lead-off man shall be dropped to last position on subsequent rounds.

k. Where shootoffs are held under lights it shall be compulsory to use white targets.

l. A shooter involved in a shoot-off with a broken gun shall be allowed a ten minute time limit to repair or replace a broken gun, and then must continue in the shoot-off.

8. Concurrent event awards

Any shooter charged an entry fee for a regular event and an additional entry fee for a concurrent event shall be eligible to win in both events unless clearly stipulated in the written program.

9. High gun system

In explanation of the high gun system: If, for example, in a class three should tie for high score and two tie for a second high score, the top three scorers would divide evenly the monies for first, second and third places, and the two tieing for second high score would divide evenly the monies for fourth and fifth places.

C. Eligibility
1. Individuals

a. Before participating in any events for money prizes, all shooters are warned of the following official rulings:

The United States Olympic Association and the Amateur Athletic Union both consider everyone who shoots for any money a professional and ineligible for all forms of athletic competition under their jurisdiction. The National Athletic Association has ruled that shooting for money does not impair eligibility of the shooter to participate in other sports conducted under its jurisdiction. Under the rules of the National Federation of State High School Associations, the problem is left up to the individual member state associations, some of which will permit shooting for money. (Parents of prep school students are urged to ascertain the position of their own state association.) Entries of minors in money events will be accepted only with the written consent of their parents or guardians. This written consent must be given to the NSSA and the scoreboard must carry the signatures of compliance.

b. No junior, sub-junior or collegiate shall be required to pay any part of any entry fee that is to be returned to the shooter in the form of money.

c. All competitors must be members of NSSA in good standing, with current dues paid up.

d. A sub-junior is any boy or girl who has not reached his or her fourteenth birthday.

e. A junior is any boy or girl who has not reached his or her eighteenth birthday.

f. A collegiate shooter shall be defined as a fulltime undergraduate student in an accredited degree oriented learning institution up to a maximum of four (4) years eligibility. A shooter is eligible to compete as a collegiate shooter prior to his freshman year as long as he produces a letter of acceptance from a degree oriented learning institution for one time only.

g. A sub-sub-senior is any man or woman who has reached his or her fortieth birthday.

h. A sub-senior is any man or woman who has reached his or her fiftieth birthday.

i. A senior is any man or woman who has reached his or her sixtieth birthday.

j. A veteran is any man or woman who has reached his or her seventieth birthday.

k. Any employee of an arms, target, and/or ammunition company who services registered shoots in his assigned area at the direction of his superiors and whose job is to further the sales of his company's products and who is compensated for his shooting, traveling and entertaining expenses by his company, shall be considered a professional and not eligible for amateur competition. Questionable cases shall be decided by the management of the company involved.

Ex-professionals are eligible to enter registered competition as amateurs 90 days after applying to NSSA with proof of job separation, provided such application is approved by the Executive Committee.

l. No contestant shall be eligible for more than one concurrent event based on age.

m. Where shoot programs offer special concurrent events based upon age, shooters entering such special events must shoot in the one for which they are qualified by age, if such a class is available. Example: Seniors cannot enter as sub-seniors if a senior event is offered. A shooter's age at the start of a program shall determine his eligibility to enter events based on age for the entire program.

n. In parent and child events, unless specifically stated otherwise in the shoot program, the child must be of junior or sub-junior eligibility age.

o. Neither state champions nor provincial champions will be recognized by NSSA unless sanctioned by a state organization, or provincial organization, recognized with proper by-laws on record at NSSA.

p. An individual must be a bonafide resident (permanent abode) of a state to be eligible for state championships or to shoot as a state team member. Persons with residence in more than one state must declare their eligibility by writing their state and club affiliation on the face of their current year membership card. Servicemen, by the same act, may choose their home state or the state in which they are permanently assigned for duty.

Persons who change their official abode shall become immediately eligible to shoot as individuals in the state shoot. They should contact NSSA for new membership cards reflecting change of address and present same before entering shoot.

q. No person shall be eligible for state competition in more than one state in the current year (from November of one year through October 31 of the following year.)

r. Shooters entering AAA class at the world championship must have earned that distinction by average, and are not permitted to declare into the class.

2. Five-man and two-man club teams (definition)

a. A five-man club team shall consist of five (5) individuals.

b. Team members must have been fully paid members of the club they represent for a period of at least 90 days prior to the date of the shoot (honorary, inactive, non-resident members, or members whose dues or assessments are in arrears are not eligible).

Such team members shall be accredited by the NSSA to the state in which they reside, but irrespective of residence, they may shoot as a five-man team for one club and one club only. They shall not be eligible to shoot for any state championships except in the state in which they reside. Such team members must be certified by the management of such club as having been active shooters at the club for a minimum period of 90 days before they are eligible to shoot for that club. A shooter who shoots on one club team, either two-man or five-man, shall by that act elect that club as the only club he shall represent in club team events during the current year. No person shall reside more than 100 miles from the club he represents unless he resides in the same state in which the club he represents is located.

Exception: Privately operated clubs, which require no paid membership, may with the approval of the NSSA be represented by either two-man or five-man teams if the members of such teams meet all of the other requirements except those applying to club dues and club membership. This rule shall apply to two-man competition.

c. Team members must not have represented any other club in a team event in any NSSA registered shoot at any time during the current year.

Exception: Service personnel who have, within this period, shot on teams sponsored by military organizations, such as division teams or teams representing specific departments of the same branch of service, and have been required to do so as a duty assignment, may immediately shoot on teams representing individual military clubs, providing that said former teams have been definitely disbanded and also providing that they have been members in good standing of the clubs they are about to represent for a period of at least 90 days prior to the shoot.

d. Be members in good standing of the NSSA with current dues paid up.

e. The club represented must be affiliated and in good standing with the NSSA with dues currently paid up.

f. State Championship Team Events. Any out of state team whose membership complies with state residence requirements and Rule II-C-2b, may enter club team events but may be subject to a surcharge at the discretion of the state association.

3. State five-man and two-man teams (definition)

a. A state team shall consist of five (5) individuals, each of whom is a member in good standing of the NSSA. Each member of a state team must be domiciled in the same state for at least three (3) months immediately prior to the date of the shoot.

b. State teams may shoot in national competition, or in state shoots if approved by the state organization.

4. Open five-man and two-man teams (definition)

An open team is one which is composed of members with no restriction as to club or domicile. Records established by open teams shall not be accepted to establish official records.

5. Team representation

a. No individual may shoot on more than one team representing the same or any other club in any one event. The members of a team must be designated before the team begins the event.

b. Each five-man club team and state team shall designate a team captain who shall be the team representative.

c. At the completion of each round, the shooters shall view their respective scores and initial them. However, in the case of team shooting, the captain of the team may assume the responsibility for the shooters and sign for his entire squad.

6. Two-man teams (definition)

a. All the foregoing eligibility provisions of individual, five-man club teams, state teams and open team representative shall govern in two-man competition.

b. No individual may shoot on or be a member of more than one team in any two-man event, except in re-entry events, where the program states that it is permissible.

7. NSSA World Championship five-man teams

a. In the NSSA World Championships all members of a five-man team will shoot in the same squad through that particular event. If any team member fails to finish with his proper squad for any reason whatsoever, the team shall be disqualified as such but not the members as individual contestants.

b. Under no circumstances, however will the provisions on broken gun and shooting up affect the requirement of shooting shoulder to shoulder throughout five-man team competition at the NSSA World Championships.

c. *In shoots other than the NSSA Championships, the management may deviate from this rule if they deem it to be advisable to conduct five-man teams in more than one squad. For convenience in tabulating team scores, it is more desirable to keep a five-man team in one squad.*

8. Exceptions to domicile and club membership team requirements.

The provisions of domicile and club membership of individuals on two-man teams and five-man (club) teams do not apply to:

a. Shooters who have affected a bonafide change in place of domicile with resultant change in club membership affiliation.

b. Clubs organized within less than 90 days prior to the date of the shoot, provided that members representing such clubs comply with Sect. II-C-2c.

c. New members of any club who have never previously fired in a team event in an NSSA registered shoot.

d. Former members of college teams and school teams who have become members of senior clubs after their graduation.

9. Armed forces team representation

For team representation the domicile of members on active duty with the Army, Navy, Air Force and other military establishments shall be defined as the place at which they are stationed by reason of proper orders. Retired, reserve, or National Guard personnel are not eligible for service team membership unless on active duty for a period in excess of 90 days.

10. Two-man and five-man team squadding

Two-man teams may shoot in separate squads, but five-man club teams and five-man state teams must shoot shoulder-to-shoulder, unless management published otherwise in their program or same is posted prior to accepting the first entry.

11. The spirit and intent of these rules shall be taken to be, to include all bonafide teams properly organized in pursuance of club and/or domicile requirements, and to exclude all teams of makeshift or pick-up character, organized on the grounds and seeking to take advantage of technicalities either herein or in program stipulations or omissions.

D. Protests

1. A shooter may protest:

a. If in his opinion the rules as herein stated have been improperly applied.

b. The conditions under which another shooter has been permitted to shoot.

c. Where he feels an error has been made in the compilation of a score.

2. How to protest.

A protest shall be initiated immediately when it is possible to do so upon the occurrence of the protested incident. No protest may be initiated by the shooter involved after thirty (30) minutes shall have elapsed after the occurrence of the incident for which a protest is desired to be made. Failure to comply with the following procedure will automatically void the protest.

A protest involving the scoring of a target, if filed immediately on the station, second shot, or shots will be fired and the results recorded and noted as a protest. The protest shall proceed in the prescribed manner.

a. State the complaint verbally to the chief referee. If not satisfied with his decision, then:

b. File with the shoot management a protest in writing, stating all the facts in the case. Such protest must be filed within 12 hours after the occurrence of the protested incident. If not satisfied with the decision of the shoot management, then:

c. File with the NSSA a written appeal, stating all the facts. Such appeal must be filed within 12 hours after the decision of the shoot management has been made known to the shooter. Protests in team events must be made by the team captain. Team members who believe they have reason to protest will state the facts to their team captain, who will make the protest if he feels such action justified by the facts. The shoot management may appoint a shoot judge to handle protests referred to it which have been handled in the manner stated above.

E. Disqualification and Expulsion

The shoot management shall upon proper evidence:

1. Disqualify any shooter for the remainder of the shoot program for willful or repeated violation of gun safety precautions which endanger the safety of shooters, field personnel and/or spectators.

2. Elect to refuse the entry or cause the withdrawal of any contestant whose conduct in the opinion of the shoot management is unsportsmanlike or whose participation is in any way detrimental to the best interests of the shoot.

3. Any shooter may be disqualifed from a shoot for misrepresentation of his status under the eligibility rules.

4. Expel any shooter physically assaulting a referee or any shooter using extreme, abusive language to a referee upon adequate evidence presented by the chief referee.

5. The shoot management shall report to the NSSA all cases of disqualification and expulsion and the reasons for same. Subsequent action by the Executive Committee could result in being expelled and barred from further membership in the NSSA.

F. Official Scores

1. All scores of records, to be recognized as official, must be shot under the official NSSA rules.

2. All scores shall be recorded as having been shot with the gun in which event they are shot, i.e., scores shot with a 20 gauge gun in a 12 gauge event must be recorded as 12 gauge scores. Such scores may not be included as part of a 20 gauge long run or average.

3. Only the scores shot on scheduled dates, approved by NSSA, shall be registered. Scores made in shootoffs shall not be registered, however, all NSSA rules shall apply in shootoffs.

4. No shooter will be permitted to enter an event more than once, even though his score has been disqualified.

5. The scores of any shooter who takes part in a registered shoot shall be considered official, and shall be registered with the NSSA even though the shooter had given notice that it was not his intention to have his score recorded.

6. While the management may refund the entry fees and permit withdrawal of shooters who would be required to compete under drastically changed and clearly intolerable weather conditions or darkness not confronted by a majority of participants in an event, scores of all shooters who do participate must be recorded. In the event of extreme weather conditions, power failure, trap failure, or unusually early darkness, the shoot management may elect to continue the event some other time (i.e., the next morning or the following weekend) but must immediately notify NSSA, with a full explanation, who will sanction the change, provided it is deemed in the best interest of Skeet.

7. When a contestant stops or withdraws without finishing an event in which he has started, his partial scores shall be reported to the NSSA along with the other scores of the event.

8. If a contestant stops or withdraws voluntarily, or after disqualification by the management, his partial score for the round in which he is shooting shall be entered as his score of targets broken for that full round of twenty-five targets. He shall not be penalized, however, for any of the remaining full rounds of that particular event. Where such withdrawal is the result of sickness or injury, the shooter withdrawing shall be charged only with the targets actually fired upon in compiling and reporting his score.

9. Reporting Requirements:

   a. It is the duty of each club or association holding a registered shoot to promptly:

   (1) Make payments of all money, purses and optionals to the shooters; and

   (2) Submit fees and reports due to its state association;

   (3) Send all required reports and fees, along with membership applications and dues, to the NSSA.

   b. The above reports must be postmarked no later than 15 days following the last day of the shoot. Failure to fulfill these obligations shall carry the following penalties.

   (1) Cancellation of all subsequent shoot dates for the of-

fending club or association.

(2) Denial of right to apply or reapply for any further registered shoot dates for a period of thirty (30) days in case of first offense, or ninety (90) days in case of second or subsequent offense or until obligations have been met.

(3) Officers of any delinquent club or association shall be barred from shooting registered targets until all required obligations of said club or association are met to the shooters, to the state association and NSSA.

10. Shoot/Financial Reports

All shoot reports must be made on standard forms furnished by NSSA. Financial report must include:

   a. NSSA daily fees collected at two (2) cents per target shot, and

   b. NSSA dues collected. Duplicate copies of all membership receipts of all types sold must be attached to financial report and must be completely and legibly filled out, including full name and complete accurate mailing address of purchaser. (Shooter buying membership receives original receipt.)

11. Official entry form/cashier sheet must contain legible full names or initials corresponding to their NSSA membership cards, the city and state of their residence and their complete scores. NSSA membership numbers of all participants must be given. This is all included on membership card. All trophy winners with full names, towns and scores must be listed in appropriate spaces on individual form.

12. The shoot management is responsible to see that each squad's scores are posted on the score board, preferably by the referee, when feasible, or by an official score man, within 30 minutes of the time the squad finishes shooting.

G. High Average Leaders

1. Minimum requirements

   a. For the purpose of determining yearly champions on the basis of average alone, leaders will be recognized if they have shot the following minimum requirements of registered targets:

	.410	28	20	12
	700	700	800	1200
Sub-junior	400	400	500	700

   b. Candidates for All-American selection must have shot the above minimum targets.

2. Long runs

   a. Long runs in an event shall be figured forward beginning with the first target *shot at,* or backwards beginning with the last target *shot at,* whichever is longest, and the optional shot be counted in the proper sequence where it was fired.

   b. Only scores shot in registered events shall be included in official long runs. Scores shot with a smaller gun than the one for which the event is scheduled shall not be accredited as part of a long run with the smaller gun.

   c. Shootoff targets and other non-registered targets shall not be counted as part of a long run.

   d. All long runs shall be compiled in the order in which the scoring appears on the official score sheets except the optional shot shall be counted in the proper sequence where it was fired. The sequence in which the official score sheets are posted must coincide with the sequence in which the scores were broken.

3. High all-around averages

For purposes of determining yearly all-around averages, the following formula should be used:

$$.410 \text{ gauge average} \times 25\% = \underline{\qquad}\%$$
$$28 \text{ gauge average} \times 25\% = \underline{\qquad}\%$$
$$20 \text{ gauge average} \times 25\% = \underline{\qquad}\%$$
$$12 \text{ gauge average} \times 25\% = \underline{\qquad}\%$$

4. Average for age groups

A shooter's age on May 1 (halfway mark of the 12-month Skeet year) shall determine his eligibility for high average consideration on all targets shot that season in any category based on age. Example: If a shooter is still a junior on May 1, his whole average for that season shall be considered his average as a junior. However, the day he is age 18, he loses his eligibility to compete in junior events. Likewise, a shooter become eligible for sub-sub-senior competition on the date he attains 40; a sub-senior, 50; a senior, 60; a veteran, 70.

H. Registered Shoot Reports

Two reports must be made on all registered shoots. Use forms provided by NSSA.

1. Financial report

List number of targets shot each day of shoot and remit to NSSA a daily registration fee of .02 per target.

Remittance and copies of receipts of all types of NSSA memberships sold must be attached.

2. Registered target official report

An individual entry form score sheet must be submitted on every shooter. This report must include number of targets shot at, broke, and class shot in or declared in. Complete information on N/C shooters must be included.

Regardless of what method was used in making awards, winners must be determined and reported under NSSA classification system. This applies even if no awards are made. Do not list winners above class champions unless such awards were made.

3. Clubs are required to deliver or mail a copy of official shoot reports to the shooter. They are however, required to retain copies of scoreboard and/or field score sheets on file for 90 days after the end of the applicable shooting year.

SECTION III - SHOOTING PROCEDURE

A. Definitions

1. Shooting position

Standing with any part of both feet within the boundries of the shooting station.

2. Gun position

Any position which is safe and comfortable to the shooter.

3. No bird

Any target thrown for which no score is recorded, or failure of a target to be thrown with the prescribed time limit of one second. This permits the throwing of instant targets, but gives a short time period in order to prevent a contestant from refusing a target which does not appear immediately after his call. If a shooter fires upon a target which appears after one second has elapsed his call and the emergence of the target, and also before the referee calls "no bird" provided he, in his sole judgment, decides that they delay exceeded the one second time allowance. The pull is not required to be instantaneous.

4. Interference

a. Any circumstance beyond the shooter's control which unduly affects opportunity to break any particular target.

b. The sun shall not be considered as interference. It must be accepted as a normal hazard.

5. Regular target

A regular target is one that appears after the shooter's call and within a period not to exceed one (1) second and which passes within a three-foot circle centered at a point fifteen (15) feet above the target crossing point. The target crossing point shall be measured from the level of Station 8. (This target, in still air, must carry to a distance equivalent, on level ground, to fifty-five (55) yards, from the Skeet house, but must not exceed sixty-five (65) yards.)

6. Irregular target

a. An unbroken target that has not conformed to the defi-

nition of a regular target.

b. Two targets thrown simultaneously in singles.

c. Target thrown broken. Under no circumstances shall the result of firing upon a broken target be scored.

7. Regular double

A regular target thrown from each Skeet house simultaneously.

8. Irregular double

Either of both targets of a thrown double as irregular targets or only one target is thrown.

9. Proof double

A repeat of a double

10. Shooting bounds

For Stations 1 to 7, inclusive, an area of forty-four (44) yards in front of the Skeet house from which the target is thrown. For station 8, the distance from the Skeet house to a point directly over a line with Station 4, 8, and the target crossing point.

11. Balk

Failure to shoot at a regular target or double

12. Malfunction of gun

Failure of gun to operate or function through no fault of the shooter.

13. Defective ammunition

Failure of ammunition to fire or function properly, i.e., failure to fire, provided firing pin indentation is clearly noticeable or firing of the primer only, where power charge has been omitted or not ignited, which is characterized by a very weak report and absence of any noticeable recoil. Components of the load remaining in barrel shall be considered as evidence of but not a requirement. Wrong size shells, empty shells and bloopers shall not be considered defective ammunition.

14. Blooper

Term used to describe an unusual burning of powder when a shell is fired, and is distinguished by a louder than normal booming report. Usually occurs in reloads and caused by tilting of the over-powder wad, incorrect pressures, or overload of powder. This cannot be considered defective ammunition.

15. Dead target

A target from which in the sole judgment of the referee a visible piece is broken as a result of having been fired upon.

16. Lost target

A target from which in the sole judgment of the referee no visible piece is broken as a result of having been fired upon.

17. Optional shot

The shot fired after the first 24 targets have been scored dead in any one round (Station 8 low house only); or fired following the shooter's first lost target. In the latter instance it must be fired from the same station and at the same house as the one first missed.

18. Skeet squad

a. A normal Skeet squad is composed of five shooters.

b. Any five (5) shooters may designate themselves as a squad. All other shooters shall be formed into squads of five (5) shooters each, as nearly as possible. Less than five (5) is permissible for expediency, but more than six (6) should not be squadded for safety reasons.

19. Round of Skeet

A round of Skeet for one person consists of twenty-five (25) shots, the object being to score the greatest number of dead targets. Twenty four shots are fired as described in III-B-1. The first shot scored lost in any round will be repeated immediately and the result scored as the twenty-fifth shot. Should the first shot "lost" occur in a double, the lost target shall be repeated as a single with the result of this shot scored as the twenty-fifth (25) shot.

If the first shot "lost" should be the first target of an irregular double, then a proof regular double shall be fired upon to determine the result of the second shot, and then the first target scored "lost" shall be repeated as a single and scored as the twenty-fifth (25) target.

Should the first twenty-four (24) targets of a round be scored "dead," the shooter shall take his optional shot at low house eight only.

20. Shooting up

The procedure of a late shooter shooting out of turn to catch up with his squad. (III-B-6)

B. General

1. Squad shooting procedure for a round of Skeet.

A squad shall start shooting as Station 1 in the order in which the names appear on the score sheet. The first shooter shall start shooting singles at Station 1, shooting the high house target first and the low house target second. The first shot scored lost in the round shall be repeated immediately as his optional shot. Then, loading two shells, he shall proceed to shoot doubles (shooting the first shot at the target from the nearest Skeet house and the second shot at the target from the farthest Skeet house before leaving the station. The second shooter shall then proceed likewise followed by the other members of the squad in their turn. Then the squad shall proceed to Station 2 and repeat the same sequence as on Station 1. The squad shall then proceed to Station 3 where each shooter will shoot as a high house single target first and low house single target before leaving the shooting station. The same procedure shall be followed at Stations 4 and 5.

Upon advancing to Station 6 the leadoff shooter will shoot singles in the same sequence as at the previous stations. Then, loading two shells he shall shoot doubles by shooting at the low house target first and the high house target second before leaving the station. The other shooters will follow in their turn.

The same procedure will be followed on Station 7.

The squad will then advance to Station 8 where each shooter shall shoot at a target from the high house before any member of the squad shoots at a target from the low house. The squad shall then turn to Station 8 low house and the leadoff shooter will shoot at the low house target. The shooter shall repeat the low house target for his optional shot before leaving the station, provided he is still straight (no lost targets in the round). the other shooters will follow in turn. At this time the shooter should verify his own score.

2. Rules and Procedures for Doubles Events

a. No less than a fifty (50) target event.

b. Shooting commences at Station 1 and continues through 7 backwards from 6 through 5, 4, 3 and 2. Rounds two and 4 will end with doubles on station 1 using the 25th shell from rounds 1 and 3. That is, rounds 1 and 3 will consist of 24 shots ending with doubles at Station 1.

c. When shooting doubles at Station 4 the shooter must shoot first at the high house target going around the stations from 1 through 7 and shoot at the low house 4 target first when coming back around the stations from 7 through 2 (or 1).

d. "No bird" shall be declared unless a regular pair of targets is thrown.

3. Shooters right to observe targets

At the beginning of each round the squad shall be entitled to observe two (2) regular targets from each Skeet house and shall have the option of observing one regular target after each irregular target.

Shoot management, State Association, State Chief Referee and/or Zone Chief referee shall have the right, where topographically possible, to make it mandatory to use a hoop or other suitable devices whenever a target adjustment is necessary.

4. Progress from station to station

a. No member of a squad shall advance to the shooting station until it is his turn to shoot, and until the previous shooter has left the shooting station. No shooter shall order any target or shoot at any target except when it is his turn. The penalty for shooting out of turn without permission of the referee shall be to score all targets so fired upon as "lost."

b. No member of a squad, having shot from one station, shall proceed toward the next station in such a way as to interfere with another shooter. The penalty for willful interference in this manner shall be disqualification from the event.

c. No shooter shall unduly delay a squad without good and sufficient reason in the judgment of the referee in charge of his squad. A shooter who persists in deliberately causing inexcusable delays after receiving a first warning from the referee shall be subject to disqualification from the event.

5. Broken gun

When a gun breaks in such a manner so as to render it unusable, the shooter has the option of using another gun if such gun can be secured without delay, or dropping out of the squad until the gun is repaired and finishing the event at a later time when a vacancy occurs or after all other contestants have finished the event. Nothing shall prohibit the shooter from missing one round because of a broken gun, having the gun repaired and then rejoining the squad for all later rounds that the squad has not started. In that case the shooter will finish any or all rounds, starting with the shot where the breakdown occurred, that were not shot because of a broken gun, on the proper fields and in the first vacancy that may occur, or after the event has been finished by all other contestants.

6. Shooting up

a. Where a shooter has registered in but does not show up to start an event with his squad, he will not be permitted to shoot up after the first man in the squad has fired a shot at Station 2. He may join the squad for all later rounds, but the round missed because of lateness must be shot on the proper field in the first vacancy, or after all other contestants have finished.

b. In the interest of conserving time the shoot management may modify this rule to meet special conditions, if it so desires.

7. Slow squads

It is suggested that shoot management use substitute fields when breakdowns or unusually slow-shooting squads are disrupting the normal sequence of squads. Under normal conditions, a squad should complete a round in 20 minutes. Squads desiring more time should not object to being transferred to a substitute field.

C. Scoring

1. The score in any one round shall be the total number of dead targets.

2. Targets declared "no bird" shall not be scored.

3. One "lost" target shall be scored on:

a. A balk or failure of gun to fire due to fault of shooter. Should this include both targets of a regular double, it shall be scored as first target lost, and a proof double shall be thrown to determine the result of the second shot only.

If a balk should occur, or his gun fail to fire because of the shooter's fault, when a proof double is thrown and the result of the first shot has already been scored, the second target shall be scored as "lost."

b. Each excessive malfunction or malfunctions of gun.

c. Doubles fired upon in reverse order.

d. Target broken after it is outside the shooting bounds.

e. Each target fired at when shooter fires out of turn without permission of referee.

f. Each target fired upon and allegedly missed because the shooter's gun had a bent barrel, or a bent compensator, or any other bent tube or accessory.

g. Each successive foot position violation

h. Each successive time balk. It shall be considered a time balk if a shooter deliberately delays more than 15 seconds for each shot on a station and the referee shall warn him once each round without penalty.

4. A shot shall be repeated for each instance of defective ammunition. If a shell having once misfired is used again, and fails to fire, the result shall be considered a fault on the part of the shooter and scored "lost."

5. No claim of irregularity shall be allowed, either on singles or doubles, where the target or targets were actually fired upon and alleged irregularity consists of deviation from the prescribed line of flight, or because of an alleged "quick pull," unless the referee has distinctly called "no bird" prior to the firing of the shot in the event of the "quick pull," or prior to the emergency of the target from the Skeet house in event of a "slow pull." Otherwise, if the shooter fires, the result shall be scored. The referee shall have final say as to whether he called "no bird" before the shooter fired.

6. If the brass pulls off a hull between shots on doubles, score as defective ammunition but do not score it as a gun malfunction.

7. If the brass pulls off a hull, or if defective ammunition occurs between shots on doubles, the referee shall rule that if the first target was a "dead bird," nothing is established, and a proof double shall be fired upon to determine the result of both birds. However, if the first target was "lost," it shall be so established and a proof double shot to establish the second shot result.

D. Malfunctions

1. A target shall be repeated for each allowable malfunction.

2. Only two malfunctions of any one gun in the same round shall be allowable. The third and all subsequent malfunctions of the same gun shall be excessive. However, when more than one person is using the same gun in the same round, this rule shall apply to each of said persons separately.

3. During the shooting of single targets, a shooter may load two shells except at Station 8 high house, or unless forbidden by club rules, and if the gun jams or malfunctions between shots, it shall be scored as a malfunction and the shooter permitted to shoot the target over. However, the shooter is still restricted to two allowable malfunctions with one gun in one round.

4. Malfunction on singles or first shot doubles

a. If the gun is handed to the referee in the same condition as at the time the shooter attempted to fire it, referee will exercise caution not to jiggle or attempt to further close the action, and will apply normal pressure to the trigger and the result will be declared a lost bird if the gun fires or a "malfunction" if it doesn't fire.

b. If however, the shooter is holding the trigger pulled and doesn't want to give the gun to the referee, the referee will place his finger over the shooter's and apply pressure as above after seeing the gun is pointed in a safe direction. The result shall be scored a "lost bird," if the gun fires, or a "malfunction" if it does not fire.

c. Afer exercising "a" or "b" above, the referee shall examine the gun for ammunition, etc. (Shooter's responsibility).

5. Malfunction between shots on doubles

If an apparent malfunction occurs between the first and second shot on doubles:

a. The referee shall apply the same procedures as listed under malfunction on singles (a, b and c, above) to determine if an allowable malfunction has occurred.

b. If an allowable malfunction has occurred, the referee shall rule that if the first target was a "dead bird," nothing is established, and a proof double shall be fired upon to determine the result of both birds. However, if the first target was "lost" then both birds shall be scored "lost."

6. If a gun "doubles" or "fan-fires" while shooting singles or doubles the referee shall rule a malfunction, and if the first target was a "dead bird," nothing established, and a proof single or double shall be fired upon to determine the results. However, if first target was "lost," it shall be established and a proof double shot to establish the second shot result.

E. Doubles or Proof Doubles

1. If the first target of a double is thrown irregular as to deviate from the prescribed line of flight and is not shot at, a proof double shall determine the score for both shots, whether the second target is fired upon or not. The referee shall be the sole judge of irregularity.

2. If the first target emerges broken, the double shall, in all cases, be declared "no bird" and a proof double shall be thrown to determine the result of both shots.

3. If the first target of a double is thrown irregular as to deviation from the prescribed line of flight, and is shot at, the result shall be scored for the first shot in accordance with III-C-5 and the following rules pertaining to the second shot shall apply: In shooting doubles, if the shooter is deprived of a normal second shot because:

a. The second target is thrown broken, or

b. The second target is thrown irregular as to deviation from the prescribed line of flight and is not shot at, or

c. The second target is not thrown at all, or

d. The second target is not thrown simultaneously, the result of the first shot shall be scored, and the second target only shall be declared "no bird" and a proof double shall be fired to determine the result of the second shot. If the shooter fires at the irregular target described (in b) above the result shall be scored unless the referee calls "no bird."

4. If a double is thrown but the targets collide, before the result of the first bird is determined, it shall be declared "no bird," and the result of a proof double shall determine the score of both shots.

5. If a double be thrown but the shooter is deprived of a normal second shot for any of the following reasons, the result of the first shot shall be scored, and the second target only shall be declared "no bird" and a proof double shall be fired to determine the result of the second shot only.

a. Both targets are broken with the first shot.

b. The wrong target is broken with first shot. (For proof double ruling see paragraph 8 below.)

c. The first shot is lost and a collision occurs before the result of the second shot is determined.

d. The second target collides with fragments of the first target, properly broken, before the result of the second target is determined.

e. The result of the first shot is determined, and interference occurs before the second shot is fired.

6. If a double is thrown and an allowable malfunction occurs on the first shot, it shall be declared "no bird," and the result of a proof double shall determine the score of both shots. If such malfunction is excessive, (not allowable), the proof double shall be thrown to determine the result of the second shot only.

7. There shall be no penalty for withholding the first shot when either target of a double is irregular. A proof double shall determine the score of both shots thereafter.

8. In shooting a proof double after the first target (of a double) is "lost," if the shooter fires at, or breaks the wrong target first, said proof double shall be scored as both targets "lost." If, in such a proof double after the first target (of a double) is "dead," the shooter fires at, or breaks, the wrong target first, it shall be scored as first target "dead" and second target "lost."

F. Interference

1. Any circumstance beyond the shooter's control which unduly affects his opportunity to break any particular target is interference.

   a. If a shooter fires his shot, the appearance of a target, or a piece of target, from an adjoining field shall not be ruled as interference, unless such target, or piece of target strikes or threatens to strike the shooter or his gun. It shall be the final judgment of the referee to consider the evidence and determine whether a target or piece of target strikes or threatens to strike shooter or his gun.

   b. If a shooter withholds his shot due to what he considers to be an interference, and if the cause is observed and ruled interference by the referee, the interference may be allowed.

   c. If a shooter still holds a shot for safety purposes, the referee may give the shooter the benefit of the doubt and rule interference, providing he agrees safety was involved.

2. If the shooter shoots at a target, he accepts it. He must abide by the result unless the referee considers that there was legal interference. Following are a few illustrations of what may be considered legal interference.

   a. A target box being thrown out the door in the shooter's line of vision between the time of the shooter's call and the firing of his shot.

   b. Opening the Skeet house door unexpectedly or suddenly under the same circumstances.

   c. Any sudden disturbance or exceptionally loud noise, except an announcement over the loud speaker.

   d. A bird flying directly across the target's line of flight just before it is fired upon.

   e. A child or any other person or animal running out on the field suddenly in the shooter's line of vision.

   f. A thrown object, or wind-blown object, blown through the air so as to cause a conflict (a piece of paper being merely blown along the ground shall not qualify in this category).

   g. All of these, and of course, a number of other occurrences can be allowed as interference if the referee, in his own judgment, feels there was sufficient interference to justify such a thing.

   h. The sun shall not be considered as interference. It must be accepted as a normal hazard.

G. Safety Precautions

The safety of competitors, field personnel and spectators requires continuous attention by all to the careful handling of guns, and caution in moving about the field and club grounds. Self-discipline is necessary on the part of the shooters, field personnel and spectators.

Where such self-discipline is lacking it is the duty of the field personnel to enforce discipline and the duty of competitors to assist in such enforcement. Team captains shall be held strictly to account for discipline within their respective teams.

1. No gun shall be loaded until the shooter is on the shooting station. Loading is considered as putting any part of a loaded shell in any part of the gun.

2. The loaded gun shall be kept pointed in a direction that will not endanger the lives of shooters, field personnel or spectators.

3. When not on the shooting station, the gun shall be carried with breech open. Pumps and automatics will have the bolt open. Fixed breech (double barrels including over and unders and side-by-sides) will be broken open.

4. When the shooter is on the shooting station and ready to shoot and a delay occurs, such as equipment breakdown, the gun shall be opened and all shells extracted.

5. During the shooting of single targets, the management may permit the loading of two shells at all stations except Station 8 high house. However, the management cannot compel the loading of two shells in the shooting of singles.

6. The loading of more than two shells in the gun shall not be allowed at any time.

7. Shooter will not be permitted to use a gun with a "release-type" trigger unless the referee and the other members of the squad are notified. Extra caution must be exercised if the gun is given to a referee who is unfamiliar with its operation.

8. Any shooter whose gun accidentally discharges twice within one round for mechanical reasons shall be required to change guns or, if time permits, have his gun repaired, before continuing to shoot the round or subsequent rounds.

9. When a shooter intentionally fires a second time at a missed target, he shall be warned by the field referee. The second time the shooter intentionally fires a second shot at a missed target in any round, the penalty shall be automatic disqualification from the event.

SECTION IV — REFEREES

A. Licensed Referee

1. NSSA-licensed referees shall pass prescribed written examinations with the aid of a rule book given by their state associations or NSSA affiliated clubs, and also eye examinations, using glasses if necessary. A visual card system will suffice and save cost of a professional eye examination. Applications for official NSSA referee cards and emblems shall be approved by the applicant's state association, where one exists, or by NSSA affiliated club where there is no state or district association. It is recommended that all state organizations adopt the policy of using only NSSA licensed referees as chief referees. All world championship shoot referees must be so licensed. All applicants for referee licenses must be paid up regular members of the NSSA.

2. Plan of approval of referees for NSSA World Championship shoots

   a. All applicants must be registered NSSA referees for current year.

   b. Each applicant must be recommended in writing by two presiding officers of his state association or by one NSSA director from his state or zone.

B. Associate Referee

1. NSSA Associate Referees must meet all eligibility requirements specified for NSSA licensed referees (IV-A-1), with the exception of paid up membership in the NSSA.

   a. An Associate Referee is eligible for an associate referee patch.

   b. Application for an Associate Referee status must be approved by applicant's state and/or Zone Chief Referee.

   c. An Associate Referee is not eligible to referee the World Championships.

   d. In no event can this designation be conferred upon an individual for more than five years.

C. Chief Referee

The shoot management shall designate a qualified chief referee, approved by the NSSA, who shall have general supervision over all other referees and who shall be present throughout the shooting. It is recommended that chief referees also have the responsibility of instructing all other referees and being certain they are acquainted with the rules and approved interpretations.

It shall be the chief referee and/or shoot management's responsibility to stop a shoot or shootoff when darkness or other conditions prevents a fair chance to shoot. This action must be carried out simultaneously on all fields. Example: Use of public address system or the shutting off of power; or a suitable signal, the significance of which is known to all referees. Use of the referee's eye test card — 5/16″ dot at 21 yards — is mandatory.

It is mandatory that each state association appoint a chief referee for its state where practical. It is suggested that this chief referee be placed in charge of all referees in the state and that he conduct training courses to develop better referees, and that he represents his state association at all registered shoots within the state. His scale of pay should be established by the state association and the cost should be borne by the state association and/or by the club holding the registered shoot.

D. Field Referee

The field referee is responsible for the conduct of shooting on the field to which he has been assigned. He shall have jurisdiction on the field to which assigned and in the area in rear of the field used by other shooters and spectators. He shall be completely familiar with the shoot program and with the NSSA rules. He must be constantly alert, impartial, and courteous though firm in the handling of shooters.

Upon protest, the referee shall rule upon the occurrence, and then proceed with the round, without delay, as if nothing had happened. At the completion of the round, he shall notify the chief referee.

It is better for a referee to continue to officiate at the same field.

The referee shall:

1. Announce distinctly "lost" or "no bird," as the case may be.

2. See that each shooter has a fair opportunity to shoot in his turn, and if in his sole opinion a shooter has been unduly interfered with while shooting, he shall declare "no bird" and allow the shooter another shot. Claims of interference may be allowed when a target or a piece of target, from an adjoining field strikes or threatens to strike a shooter or his gun, provided that such interference occurs after the shooter has called for his target and before he fires upon it.

3. Declare "no bird" as soon as possible when:

   a. The shooter's position is not according to rule. The shooter shall be warned by the referee of his illegal shooter's position, but if he continues to violate the position, he shall be penalized by the loss of one target for each subsequent violation in that round.

   b. Target does not emerge within the allowed time after the shooter's call.

   c. Target emerges before shooter's call.

   d. An irregular target is thrown in singles, doubles or proof doubles.

   It shall be the referee's first duty after releasing the target to declare "no bird" as quickly as possible when he determines that an irregular target has been thrown.

   (1) If the shooter fires before the "no bird" call, the result of the shot shall be scored.

   (2) In the case of doubles or proof doubles, if the referee's call of "no bird" occurs after the firing of the first shot (and said first shot was fired at a regular target) the result of the first shot shall be scored and a proof double shall be thrown to determine the result of the second shot only.

No Result of Firing On A Broken Target Shall Be Scored.

4. In any instance the result of shooting at a target after it has been declared "no bird" shall not be scored and the shot will be repeated.

5. Declare as "lost" dusted targets or perforated targets that are retrieved after landing.

6. Declare as "lost target" the third shot fired when gun has been loaded with more than two shells.

7. Suspend shooting when the targets thrown from any machine are repeatedly irregular, and order the machine adjusted or repaired. (He may, at any time allow a shooter making such request, to see a target, providing the request is reasonable and not excessive.)

8. Grant a shooter permission to shoot out of his regular turn where it is justified.

9. Disqualify, for the event, a shooter who in his opinion has willfully interfered with another shooter while the latter is shooting.

10. Disqualify, for the event, a shooter for repeated violation of any of the safety precautions listed in Section III or for any act that in the referee's opinion endangers the safety of shooters, field personnel or spectators.

11. It shall also be his responsibility to supervise the keeping of correct scores and to see that all scores are verified by the respective shooters before the score sheet is taken from the field. The referee's responsibility in seeing that shooters verify their scores is to announce after each round "Please check your scores." If an error in score-keeping is discovered on the field, the field referee shall remedy it promptly at the time of discovery. In the event there is any question as to the correctness of any score after the score sheet leaves the field, the chief referee or shoot committee chairman shall order the score corrected after checking with the field referee and the score sheet.

12. The referee shall be the SOLE judge of decision of fact. For example, his decision as to whether target is dead or lost shall be irrevocable, regardless of the opinion of spectators or other members of the squad.

13. Relief referees shall not take over the fields until the shooters have completed the round, except in cases of emergency, such as illness, etc.

14. No NSSA licensed referee may be disqualified in the middle of a round but he may choose to disqualify himself.

15. No member of a shooting squad may score or referee for other members of that squad.

E. Referee's Digest

(A summarization of suggestions and interpretations for the purpose of improving and standardizing Skeet officiating universally.)

Referees shall at all times be courteous and impartial. Your alertness and fairness in decision are prime factors in the success of any shoot. Your conduct will reflect on the NSSA and you should always bear in mind that the shooters make the association possible. Whenever possible, the referees should meet before the shoot and discuss any problems which might arise and familiarize themselves with the schedule for the shoot.

There should be a chief referee appointed by the shoot management before the shoot and he shall be in complete charge of and responsible for all other referees. It shall be the responsibility of the chief referee to appoint the necessary assistant chief referees and all other referees must meet with his approval. The chief referee shall designate and assign the referees to the fields and shall be held responsible for their conduct at all times during the shoot.

At all world championship shoots there shall be not less than one relief referee for each four shooting fields.

When assistant chief referees are used, they shall be held responsible for their assigned referees and any misconduct or irregularities shall be reported to the chief referee immediately.

Each referee shall be in charge of his field and shall see that all safety rules and field rules are complied with. He shall have jurisdiction over the spectator area of his field and allow none but authorized personnel on the shooting field during the shooting. The field referee shall notify the chief or assistant chief referee as soon as possible of any protest, irregularity or violation. Before the start of shooting, the referee shall be supplied with a squad sheet showing the shooting line-up and shall assemble the shooters at Station 1. He shall ascertain that each shooter is aware of his or her squad position and shall not change any squad's shooting order until approved by the chief or assistant chief referee after notification that the change or changes have been made in the office.

The referee should ascertain that the shooter is shooting a proper gauge gun for the event in which he has entered. *(Shooter's Responsibility)*

In cases where the management rules on the loading of one or two shells during the shooting of singles (NO EXCEPTION to be made at Station 8 high house, where it is NEVER permissible to load more than one shell) the referee should inform the shooters of the ruling.

The referee should, as a courtesy, inquire of the squad if there are any questions of rules or regulations not clear before starting to shoot. He may request that they check their guns to make certain that their safeties are off.

The referee shall inform the squad that they are entitled to view two regular birds from the high house and two regular birds from the low house prior to the starting of the squad, and the first shooter shall decide which one he wishes to see first.

The referee shall, at the command of the shooter to pull or mark the bird, respond to the call within one second, and if delayed or in doubt as to the call, shall declare "no bird" immediately.

When a call is given by the shooter and the bird emerges from the Skeet house and is fired upon, the referee shall declare, in a distinct and audible voice, "lost" or "no bird," if applicable.

The referee, at all times, shall see that the shooter is given a fair opportunity to shoot and if in the opinion of the referee, the shooter has been interfered with or caused by some condition beyond the shooter's control to interrupt the shooter, he, the referee, may declare "no bird." Be uniform, it is up to the referee to use good judgment in calling interference.

Every target declared "no bird" shall be repeated. Every regular bird scored on shall be shown on the score pad and the marking "X" shall signify "dead" and the marking "O" shall signify "lost." In the case of a malfunction of the shooter's gun, a small "m" shall be marked in the scoring book showing the station at which the malfunction occurred, thus assisting the referee in complying with the rule governing malfunction (Sec. III-D-2).

The position of the referees during the shoot is of vital importance both to the shooter and the referee. For required position, see field layout.

If the referee observes a shooter violating any of the rules on his field, he should, as a courtesy, inform him of the violation personally, but not as a reprimand before the squad. If the shooter fails or refuses to heed the referee's request, the chief or assistant chief should be summoned and the problem taken up with higher authority. Any call for the bird to be "pulled" or "marked" shall be executed only when given by the shooter on the station.

If a shooter should advance to the next station and call for a bird prior to completion of shooting by the entire squad at the previous station, the referee shall not pull the bird, if operating the traps, or if the birds are released from a pull house, the referee shall declare "no bird." If, in the referee's opinion, there is a reasonable doubt as to his correct decision, the ruling should be in favor of the shooter.

The referee shall see that no shell is loaded or dropped into any part of any gun until the shooter is on the shooting station.

F. Interpretations

Any regular bird thrown after the shooter calls shall be scored as follows: If any visible piece of the bird is observed by the official referee broken as a result of the shooter having shot, it will be scored "dead bird." Any bird thrown that emerges from the traphouse broken shall be declared "no bird" and shall be repeated. If the referee knows that a chip is broken off a target, it should be called "no bird" even if the shooter hits it before the referee calls "no bird." If the shooter misses it, it also must be called "no bird." In singles, if the bird emerges from the wrong house, it shall be declared "no bird" and another bird shall be thrown from the proper house. However, in the shooting of singles, if by error or for mechanical reasons doubles are shown, and the shooter shoots and breaks or misses the correct bird, it shall be scored as in singles, it shall be the shooter's prerogative to elect to shoot or withhold his shot when doubles are thrown in the calling of singles. If, however, the referee declared "no bird" prior to the shot, the bird shall be repeated. If, in the shooting of doubles, only one regular bird emerges and the shooter elects to shoot it, it shall be scored "dead" or "lost" and a proof double shall be thrown. If, however, the referee calls "no bird" prior to the firing of the shot, it shall be repeated.

When a shooter misses his first bird, he shall immediately, when shooting singles, repeat the shot, this being his "optional." If in the shooting of doubles, the shooter misses the first bird and a proof double is required the shooter shall complete the shooting of the doubles at that station and then take his "optional." If the shooter completes the round without a miss, he shall shoot his "optional" at Station 8 low house.

If more than one second elapses between the time the shooter calls for his bird and its release, "no bird" should be called and the shooter should not be penalized, PROVIDED HE HAS NOT FIRED ON THE TARGET BEFORE THE REFEREE'S CALL OF 'NO BIRD'.

There is a concrete block of designated shooting platform at each station of the Skeet field. The shooter must stand with any part of both feet within the boundaries of this platform. Any shooter with one or both feet definitely off the shooting station should first be made to shoot over and, if he persists in standing off the station, he shall be penalized by loss of the target for each subsequent violation in that round.

However, if the shooter missed the target while committing the first violation of shooting position, the result shall be scored "lost."

The shooter must not be considered at fault if he has complied with the manufacturer's operating instructions for loading the gun, and the gun does not fire. In the case of a gun going into battery (locking closed) for the first shot on doubles or any shot on singles, if the shooter has closed the action in accordance with the manufacturer's instructions, and if the bolt appears visually to be closed, the failure of a gun to fire shall be scored as malfunction.

Automatics

1. On an automatic the shooter is not required to push forward or strike the breech bolt retraction lever to insure locking the gun. This is a normal gun function.

2. The shooter must load the shell or shells into the gun and see that the action appears closed. If he loads 2 shells on singles or doubles, and if the second shell fails to go into the chamber or is thrown out of the gun, it shall be scored a malfunction.

Pump guns

1. The shooter is required to pump the gun, as recommended by the manufacturer, on doubles and to close the action completely forward (visually) on singles.

2. If the shooter "short-shucks" the gun, the hammer will not be cocked, a fault of the shooter.

3. If the lifter throws the second shell out of the gun it shall be a malfunction.

4. It shall be a malfunction if between shots on singles or doubles the gun returns the empty shell to the chamber provided the hammer is cocked.

5. The referee shall check for a malfunction as instructed under that title and shall then apply forward pressure on the forearm to see if the shell is lodged (a malfunction). However, if the gun closes smoothly, without jiggling, it is not a malfunction.

Double-barreled guns

1. The shooter is responsible for loading a shell in the proper barrel, or two shells for doubles.

2. The shooter must close the action in accordance with manufacturer's recommendations.

Shell catching devices

Where any device is attached to a shotgun which must be adjusted or removed to permit shooting doubles, it shall be the shooter's responsibility to perform such adjustment or removal. Failure to fire a second shot on doubles, due to such device, shall not be an allowable malfunction, and the bird shall be scored lost.

SECTION V— NSSA CLASSIFICATION

A. Definitions

1. NSSA Shooting Year

The NSSA shooting year shall be any twelve month period running from November 1 through the following October 31.

2. Current Year

The twelve month period November 1 through October 31 of the year for which classification is being determined.

3. Previous Year

The twelve month period immediately preceding the current shooting year, i.e. November 1 - October 31.

4. Initial String

The required minimum number of registered targets in each gauge necessary for an Initial Classification is 200.

5. Regular String

The required minimum number of registered targets in each gauge necessary for RECLASSIFICATION of a classified shooter is 300.

6. Initial Classification

The first classification of a newly classified shooter based on his INITIAL STRING of registered targets shot during the CURRENT year, or during the PREVIOUS year and the CURRENT year combined.

7. Regular Classification

a. The classification of a classified shooter at the beginning of the CURRENT year in each gauge will be based on all registered targets shot during the previous year, providing at least 200 targets were shot.

b. The reclassification of a classified shooter based on his average for totals of all REGULAR STRINGS of registered targets shot during the CURRENT YEAR.

8. Class Attained

The class in which a shooter would be required to shoot were he to compete in a subsequent shoot during the CURRENT year, whether or not he has ever shot in that class.

9. Classification/Shoot Record Cards

a. As soon as possible after October 31 of each year, each PAID UP member will receive from NSSA a classification/shoot record card.

b. This classification/shoot record card shall include provisions for club designation, targets shot, targets broke, running average in each gauge and shall be imprinted with:

(1) Member's name, address, membership expiration date and membership number.

(2) Shooter's class for the start of the current year in each gauge in which he is a classified shooter, or NC if he is a non-classified shooter.

(3) The number of targets shot at and broken in each gauge during previous year, if any.

(4) The highest class in which shooter shot during the *previous* year.

c. Any errors on shooter's new classification card, including those caused by failure of shoot reports to be received at NSSA headquarters in time to be included on new card, should be promptly reported to NSSA by the shooter so that a corrected card can be supplied to insure proper inclusion in permanent record.

10. Classified Shooter

a. One who has fired at least the required INITIAL STRING of registered targets, or more, during the PREVIOUS year, or

b. One who has fired at least the required *initial string* of registered targets, or more, during the *current* year, or

c. One who has fired at least the required *initial string* of registered targets, or more, during the *previous* year and the CURRENT year combined.

11. Non-Classified Shooter

A new shooter, or one whose record does not conform with any of the preceeding requirements for classified shooters.

a. NC must be offered in all registered events and will not be combined with any other class.

b. Awards and/or purses for the NC shooters may be optional with shoot management, BUT NOT MANDATORY.

c. NC shooters will not be eligible for awards other than NC category except for teams and other concurrent events. For classifying NC shooters on concurrent events see Sect. V-D-1.

d. For classification procedures see below.

B. Procedures

1. Maintaining Shoot Record Card

a. Each shooter shall bear the responsibility of promptly and accurately entering his own score with the date, etc., in the proper gauge division at the conclusion of each registered *event* in which he participates. Where a single *event* extends more than one day he should enter the total, not the day-to-day scores.

b. Shooter shall have his classification changed in reclassification spaces on his classification/shoot record card promptly whenever they have changed by averages on regular strings or cumulative regular strings.

c. The shooter is required to carry his card to each registered shoot and present it at registration.

(1) A shooter failing to present his classification card, for any reason, *may be assigned class AA at the discretion of shoot management.*

(2) In the case of a lost card, or accidentally forgetting a card, the shooter may sign an affidavit attesting to his classification, subject to specified penalties. Such affidavit must be attached to the shoot report when it is forwarded to NSSA for tabulation.

Note: Replacement for a lost card (including reported scores to date) may be obtained from NSSA upon request. If the original card is later found, the shooter should carefully consolidate the record, then destroy the extra card.

d. In the space provided for club on his classification/shoot

record card, each member shall designate, not later than his first competition in such events, the club he has elected to represent in club two-man and five-man team competition.
e. A shooter falsifying any entries or improperly using more than one card shall be disqualified and reported to NSSA for action according to Section II-A-2-b(4).

2. Classification/Reclassification of Classified Shooter
a. Using the Universal Classification Tables, a classified shooter's class for the state of the *current* year shall be figured on the basis of his average on the total number of registered targets shot during the *previous* year, however, such class shall be no lower than one class below the *highest* class in which he shot during the *previous* year.
b. A shooter shall maintain throughout each shoot his classes and running averages as they were at the time of entry. A classified shooter shall not be subject to changes in classification *during a shoot* for any reason nor have his classification changed for a consolation event held after the regular shoot.
(1) The only exception to the above is: An NC shooter who completes an initial string of targets, even at the end of a preliminary event becomes classified for all remaining events of that gauge.
(2) The total number of targets scheduled for an event are to be used in determining strings for classification and reclassification.
Examples:
(a) A non-classified shooter has shot 150 registered 12 gauge targets and enters a 100 target, 12 gauge event. He shall be classified on the total of 250 targets and *not* after shooting the first 50 targets of the event, which would total 200 targets.
(b) A classified shooter has shot 550 registered 20 gauge targets and enters a 100 target 20 gauge event. He shall be reclassified on the total 650 targets and *not* after shooting the first 50 targets of the event, which would total 600.
(c) A shooter who is classified at the beginning of the year on totals of targets shot during previous year will *reclassify* at the end of his first *regular string* and at the end of all succeeding regular strings shot during the *current year.*
Example:

	Shot	Broke	Average	Class
Current year	100	xx		C
	100	xx		C
	100	xx		C
Reclassify at	300	xxx	.xxxx	A
	100	xx		A
	100	xx		A
	100	xx		A
Reclassify on and again on	600 900 etc.	xxx	.xxxx	A

(d) Shooters must, however, always reclassify at the end of each regular string even though the correct number of targets for reclassification comes between the preliminary and the main event. Reclassification is not effective until *after* the shoot, but must be accomplished on the correct number of targets.
Example:

	Shot	Broke	Average	Class
Current Year	100	xx		C
	100	xx		C
	100	xx		C
	300	xxx		A
	100	xx		A
	100	xx		A
Preliminary	100*	xx		A

	Shot	Broke	Average	Class
	600	xxx		AA
Main Event of Above Shoot	100*	xx		A
	100	xx		AA
	100	xx		AA
	900	xxx		AA

*Note that shooter must reclassify at end of regular string *even though* he does not *change class* until *after* shoot.
(e) A shooter who becomes a *classified shooter* on combination of targets shots during the *previous* year and *current* year shall be *reclassified* on each succeeding *regular string* of registered targets shot during the current year. (Also see "Reclassification Limitation.")

Example:

	Shot	Broke	Average	Class
Previous Year	100	xx		NC
Current Year	100	xx		NC
Classify On	200	xxx	.xxxx	D
	100	xx		D
	100	xx		D
	100	xx		D
Reclassify on 400 shot in current year	400	xxx	.xxxx	B
	100	xx		B
	100	xx		B
	100	xx		B
Reclassify on 700 shot in current year	700	xxx	.xxxx	B

NOTE: After Initial Classification, targets shot in *previous year* are not used in calculating averages.
(f) A classified shooter who wishes to voluntarily declare himself up in class may do so. When he so elects, he must (at a registered shoot) have his card marked before competing in the event in the class for which he is declaring himself. His card shall be marked with the new classification by self-declaration in the class where he declared himself, and be entered on the Official Entry Form with notation "self-declared."

3. Classification of a Non-Classified Shooter
A new shooter or one who has not attained a classification during the previous year will be entered as *non-classified (NC)* in each individual gauge until he has shot an Initial String of 200 targets in each gauge.
a. Upon completing an Initial String, in each individual gauge, the shooter will be given a *classification* based on average.
Note: A NC shooter who completes an *initial string* of targets, even at the end of a preliminary event becomes classified for all remaining events of the gauge.
b. After this *initial classification,* a shooter will reclassify after each succeeding *regular string,* using the total number of targets shot during the current year and will follow procedures as outlined in items b. through f. of Classification/Reclassification of Classified Shooters.
c. A Non-Classified shooter who voluntarily wishes to declare himself classified may do so provided he declares himself in Class AA.
When he so elects, he must have his card marked (at a registered shoot) in AA before competing in the event for which he is declaring himself and Class AA must be entered on the Official Entry Form with notation "self declared."

C. Universal Classification Tables

1. Use of the Universal Classification Tables shall be required for all registered shoots and shall be in accordance with the following tables of averages:

For Open Individual

Class	12 Gauge	20 Gauge
*AAA	98.5% and over	
AA	97.5% to 98.49%	96% and over
A	95% to 97.49%	93% to 95.99%
B	93% to 94.99%	90% to 92.99%
C	90% to 92.99%	86% to 89.99%
D	86% to 89.99%	Under 86%
E	Under 86%	Only 5 Classes

*Class AAA attained only be average based on last re-classification.

Class	28 Gauge	.410 Gauge
AA	95% and over	93.5% and over
A	92% to 94.99%	89.5% to 93.49%
B	89% to 91.99%	84.5% to 89.49%
C	85% to 88.99%	81% to 84.49%
D	Under 85%	Under 81%

Class Double

Class	Doubles
*AAA	97% and over
AA	95% to 96.99%
A	91% to 94.99%
B	85% to 90.99%
C	80% to 84.99%
D	Under 80%

a. Shooter's correct class and average shall be posted on his shoot entry form.

b. Classification in each gauge gun is independent and shall be treated without regard to classification in any other gauge.

2. High Overall

Shoot management may establish the method of determining a shooter's class for high overall events in any manner they desire, i.e., 12 gauge classification, 4 gun average, or any other appropriate method. The method must be properly posted or published in the program.

3. Compulsory Classes

a. A class for Non-Classified shooters must be offered in all registered shoots for all events.

b. Only Classes AA, A, B, C, D and NC (also E in 12 gauge) shall be compulsory. Class AAA shall be optional and when AAA is not offered, Class AA shall include all shooters who would be in Class AAA if it were offered.

(1) It shall be the sole responsibility of shoot management to determine whether Class AAA shall be offered and its decision shall be published in the shoot program or posted before the shoot.

(2) Class AAA should be offered where the number of entries eligible for that class justifies doing so.

D. Team and Other Concurrent Events

1. The average for a *non-classified* shooter competing in a team or other concurrent event shall be considered the highest percentage in "B" class of the gauge entered.

2. Division of two-man team, five-man team, women and junior events into classes is *not mandatory*. In cases where shoot management should desire to establish classes in these events, they may do so.

When such classes are established, they should be designated by *number* rather than by letter, i.e. Class 1 (or I) XX — and over, Class 2 (or II) under XX—.

3. Classification for TEAM EVENTS shall be combined average of team member's scores, carried to the fourth decimal place at their initial or last reclassification. (i.e. .9525).

E. Limitations For Reclassification

1. *During the current year* a shooter is subject to reclassification *upward only*.

2. Each shooter classified at the beginning of the Skeet year will shoot in that class or a higher class as determined by average. Reclassification *down* will only be accomplished by NSSA headquarters at the beginning of the next Skeet year.

3. Any Skeet shooter who believes he is entitled to compete in a lower class due to illness, accident, age, etc., may appeal to the classification committee of NSSA after prior approval of his request by his state association. In the absence of a state association in the shooter's state, his appeal may be made directly to the classification committee.

4. Reclassification in all cases shall be subject to the restrictions and qualifications set out in this section and in the sections headed "Classifications."

SECTION VI — INTERNATIONAL CLASSIFICATION

The NRA and the National Skeet Shooting Association (NSSA) have common goals concerning the support and growth of International Skeet. The major goal, after joint compliance with UIT rules and procedures, is one of congruent classification rules and procedures. Achievement of that goal is reflected in joint application of the following classification procedures by the NRA and the NSSA. Paragraph numbers coincide with NRA rules.

19.1 Classified Competitors — Are all individuals who are officially classified by the NRA and NSSA for International Skeet competitions, or who have a record of scores fired over courses of fire used for classification (See Rule 19.4) which have been recorded in a Score Record Book or NSSA Classification Card.

19.2 Unclassified Competitor — is a competitor who does not have a current NRA or NSSA classification, either regular or temporary by Score Record Book (Rule 19.14). Such a competitor shall compete in the Master Class.

19.4 Scores Used for Individual Classification - Scores to be used for classification and reclassification will be as follows:

1) Those fired in individual and team matches in both NRA and NSSA competition (except Postal Matches).

2) Scores from Registered Leagues may be recorded during the league firing season in score record books but will only be used by the NRA Headquarters Office at the end of the league firing season for issue of Official Classification Cards.

19.7 Lack of Classification Evidence — It is the competitor's responsibility to have his NRA Official Classification Card, NSSA Classification Card, or Score Record Book with required scores for temporary classification (Rules 19.1 and 19.4) and to present classification evidence when required. Any competitor who cannot present such evidence will fire in the Master Class. A competitor's classification will not change during a tournament. A competitor will enter a tournament under his correct classification and fire the entire event in that class. Should it be discovered that a competitor has entered in a class lower than his current rating, the tournament records will be corrected to show the correct classification for the entire tournament.

19.8 Competing in a Higher Class — Any individual or team may elect, before firing, to compete in a higher classification than the one in which classified. Such individual or team must fire in such higher class throughout the tournament and not revert to earned classification for any event in that tournament.

When there are insufficient entries in any class to warrant an award in that class according to the match's program conditions, the individual or team concerned may be moved by the

Tournament Executive Officer (NSSA Shoot Management) to a higher class provided this change is made prior to the individual or team concerned having commenced firing in the tournament.

19.9 Obsolete Classifications and Scores — All classifications and scores (including temporary, Rule 19.14) except Master, shall become obsolete if the competitor does not fire in NRA or NSSA competition at least once during 3 successive calendar years. Master classifications and scores shall become obsolete if the competitor does not fire in NRA or NSSA competition at least once during 5 successive calendar years. NRA Lifetime Master classifications will not become obsolete.

19.10 Appeals—Any competitor having reason to believe he is improperly classified may file an appeal with the NRA or NSSA stating all essential facts. Such appeal will be reviewed by the NRA Protest Committee or NSSA Executive Director.

19.11 Protests—Any person who believes that another competitor has been improperly classified may file a protest with the NRA or NSSA stating all essential facts. Such protests will be reviewed by the NRA Protest Committee or NSSA Executive Director.

19.12 Team Classification—Teams are classified by computing the "Team Average" based on the classification of each firing member of the team. To compute the team average the key in Table No. 1 for the different classes will be used and the team total divided by the number of firing members of the team. Any fractional figure in the team average of one half or more will place the team in the next higher class. The "team average" will establish classification of team as a unit but will not affect in any way the individual classification of team members.

Table No. 1—Team

Class	Key
AA-Master	5
A	4
B	3
C	2
D	1

19.13 Reporting Scores—NSSA COMPETITIONS—Clubs registering shoots with NSSA will report scores and winners to NSSA on official shoot report forms as required by Rule II-f.

NRA COMPETITIONS—Sponsors of NRA registered shoots will report to the NRA all individual and fired team match scores fired over the courses stated in Rule 19.4. Scores will be reported as aggregate totals for all matches completed by a competitor. Scores will be reported to each NRA Registered League at the completion of the league schedule. NRA and NSSA will exchange all the reported scores above and utilize them in International classification.

19.14 Score Record Book (Temporary Classification)—At NRA registered matches a Score Record Book will be obtained by each unclassified competitor from the Official Referee, Supervisor, or tournament Statistical Office at the time competitor competes in his first tournament or from the Secretary of Registered League. He will record all scores fired by himself in all NRA or NSSA competition (except Postal Matches) until such time as he receives his Official NRA or NSSA Classification Card. Competitor will total all scores and divide that total by the number of registered targets shot. The average so obtained will determine the competitor's NRA or NSSA Classification at that time (see Rule 19.15 for average score for each classification).

Individual and team scores fired by the competitor during at least one tournament (Rule 1.13.1) or from the most recent league match (Rule 1.7) must be posted in the Score Record Book to establish a temporary classification. The Score Record Book will be presented by the holder at all NRA or NSSA competition entered until the competitor's Official NRA or NSSA Classification Card becomes effective.

Note: It is the competitor's responsibility to obtain the Score Record Book, enter scores and present it at each tournament until his official NRA or NSSA Classification Card becomes effective. When the NRA or NSSA Classification Card becomes effective the Score Record Book becomes obsolete.

19.15 Individual Class Averages—Competitors will be classified as follows and NRA Classification Cards issued accordingly:

International Skeet

AA Master	95.00 - 100.00
A	87.00 - 94.99
B	81.00 - 86.99
C	75.00 - 80.99
D	0 - 74.99

19.16 Establishing Classification—A competitor will be officially classified by the NRA or NSSA when the total score for a minimum of 200 targets has been reported. However, classification averages will be computed only after the total score for a tournament or league has been posted and, therefore, the average may be based on a greater number of targets, but will not be based on a lesser number. Total scores so reported to the NRA or NSSA will be posted to the Classification Record for the competitor concerned. When the scores for the stated minimum number of targets (or more if this minimum is reached during the scores of any tournament or league) have been so posted the average score will be computed. The competitor will be sent an Official NRA or NSSA Classification Card based on the average so computed and according to the table in Rule 19.15 which classification will become effective the date shown on the card issued by the NRA or NSSA.

19.17 Reclassification—A competitor who has been classified by the NRA or NSSA will be reclassified as follows:

a. A record of all completed (see Rule 19.9) NRA or NSSA Competition (except Postal Match) scores fired by a classified competitor will be maintained in the NRA Headquarters and/or NSSA Headquarters.

b. When additional scores of 300 targets have been posted, the competitor's average will be established by dividing the total score by the number of targets represented. This average will be computed as outlined in Rule 19.16 at the end of the tournament or league in which the minimum number of targets, or more have been posted.

When a competitor's new average places him in a higher class, he will be reclassified accordingly and notified by Headquarters. (Note: This paragraph applies to NRA only.)

c. A competitor who believes his classification is too high may file a request with the NRA Protest Committee or NSSA Executive Director that his classification be lowered. Such a competitor must remain in the class concerned until at least 600 targets have been posted to his classification record. When the average of such shots places the competitor in a lower class he will be reclassified accordingly. When a competitor has been so classified downward, and by scores fired in NRA or NSSA competition (except NRA Postal Matches) has again earned his former classification, such classification shall become final and the competitor shall retain the earned classification until reclassified into a higher class as outlined in paragraph (b).

d. A reclassified competitor shall be sent a new NRA classification card which will become effective on the date shown on the card issued by the NRA. NSSA members are responsible for keeping up-to-date records and moving to a higher class when required.

6933